BECOMING MEAD

BECOMING MEAD

The Social Process of
Academic Knowledge

DANIEL R. HUEBNER

THE UNIVERSITY OF CHICAGO PRESS

CHICAGO AND LONDON

DANIEL R. HUEBNER is assistant professor of sociology at the University of North Carolina at Greensboro.

The University of Chicago Press, Chicago 60637
The University of Chicago Press, Ltd., London
© 2014 by The University of Chicago
All rights reserved. Published 2014.
Printed in the United States of America

23 22 21 20 19 18 17 16 15 14   1 2 3 4 5

ISBN-13: 978-0-226-17137-1 (cloth)
ISBN-13: 978-0-226-17140-1 (paper)
ISBN-13: 978-0-226-17154-8 (e-book)
DOI: 10.7208/chicago/9780226171548.001.0001

Library of Congress Cataloging-in-Publication Data

Huebner, Daniel R., author.
  Becoming Mead : the social process of academic knowledge / Daniel R. Huebner.
    pages cm
  Includes bibliographical references and index.
  ISBN 978-0-226-17137-1 (cloth : alk. paper) — ISBN 978-0-226-17140-1 (pbk. : alk.
paper) — ISBN 978-0-226-17154-8 (e-book) 1. Mead, George Herbert, 1863–1931.
2. Sociology—Methodology. I. Title.
  B945.M464H94 2014
  301.092—dc23

                                                                      2014001189

♾ This paper meets the requirements of ANSI/NISO Z39.48-1992
(Permanence of Paper).

to Bob Wiley

CONTENTS

ILLUSTRATIONS

Figures

Text Boxes

ACKNOWLEDGMENTS

I wish to express my gratitude to those people who helped make this project possible. My interest in and knowledge of the topics addressed in this book was fostered by discussions at the University of Chicago with Andrew Abbott, Elizabeth Clemens, Andreas Glaeser, Hans Joas, Ryon Lancaster, Donald Levine, John Lucy, John Levi Martin, Moishe Postone, and Robert Schwartz. Without the inexhaustible encouragement and insightful guidance of Abbott, Glaeser, and Joas, this project could not have been accomplished.

My colleagues were an outstanding source of support and commiseration throughout the research and writing. In particular, I would like to thank Mary Akchurin, Emily Art, Julia Burdick-Will, Paola Castaño, Brian Cody, Michael Corey, Gordon Douglas, Suzy Smith, Michaela Soyer, and Bijan Warner for many discussions and for their camaraderie. In addition, I had the benefit of many other discussions with a large number of Chicago faculty members and students at different stages of this project from which the final product certainly improved.

In a consequential meeting, Andrew Abbott suggested I check out the manuscript collections at the University of Chicago Library, especially the notes of Ellsworth Faris from his courses with George Herbert Mead. The resulting investigation raised more questions than answers and provoked me to begin connecting the problems of interpretation of Mead and his students with my interest in the sociology of knowledge. I also had the good fortune to attend Abbott's practicum "Library Methods for the Social Sciences," which contributed substantially to my education in archival and primary document research.

Researchers could hardly ask for a better home base than the Special Collections Research Center at the University of Chicago. The outstanding staff, over and above their excellent holdings, makes it a thoroughly enjoyable and productive working environment. In particular, I would like to thank Barbara Gilbert, Julia Gardner, and the many student pages for all of their assistance and patience with my incessant questions and requests. I would like to thank the helpful staff and faculty at the University of Illinois–Chicago Special Collections, the American Baptist Historical Society, the Chicago History Museum, the Institute for American Thought, the University of Michigan Bentley Historical Library, the Minnesota Historical Society, the Northwestern University Special Collections, the Schlesinger Library on the History of Women in America, the Southern Illinois University Morris Library Special Collections, Richard Ford and the staff at the University of Chicago Office of the University Registrar, and the archivists and librarians across the globe who humored me by answering my odd questions and checking into collections for me. For a week in March 2010 I turned a set of desks at the Peirce Edition Project at the Institute for American Thought into a field headquarters, and had the outstanding benefit of the resources and feedback of David Pfeiffer, André De Tienne, and Cornelis de Waal.

Thanks also go to the many scholars (of Mead and otherwise) who have traded enthusiasm and information with me remotely or in person. I greatly appreciated discussions with chairs, co-presenters, commentators, and audiences at academic conferences, including the American Sociological Association, the Social Science History Association, the History of Science Society, and the International Sociological Association Research Committee on the History of Sociology. I would also like to thank the students in my courses for discussing issues related to my research in more detail than they likely expected. I consistently found that in preparing for class, in conducting class discussions, and in assessing student work, my own thinking was advanced by the participation of outstanding students.

I wish to express my gratitude to Doug Mitchell and Tim McGovern at the University of Chicago Press for their care and dedication in seeing this project through the editorial process, and to the manuscript reviewers for their thoughtful comments. A portion of this project was supported by an Andrew W. Mellon Foundation/University of Chicago Division of the Social Sciences Dissertation Fellowship. Sections of chapter 5 are reprinted from "The Construction of *Mind, Self, and Society*: The Social Process behind G. H. Mead's Social Psychology," *Journal of the History of the Behavioral Sciences* 48, no. 2 (2012): 134–53; and "Scholarly Publishing Projects in the Great Depression: The Works of G. H. Mead and the Payne

Fund Studies," in *Knowledge for Whom? Public Sociology in the Making*, ed. Christian Fleck and Andreas Hess (Farnham: Ashgate, 2014).

Finally, I would like to extend a special thank-you to my family for their unconditional love and support. It is to my mother and father, brother and sister, and my partner that I owe by far the largest debt of gratitude for continuing to shape who I am.

INTRODUCTION

O ne of the defining characteristics of academic scholarship in all disciplines, what makes it scholarship, is the concerted pursuit of knowledge in its many forms in collaboration with others. The knowledge produced in scholarship is not only of the objects of study but also of other scholars (scholarship as a social enterprise) and of oneself (scholarship as a self-reflexive enterprise). This is especially evident in the social sciences and humanities where the object of study is more or less immediately other humans who already create their own understandings of one another, of themselves, and of their social worlds. In the course of their practical work, scholars in the humanities and social sciences encounter questions regarding their knowledge. What and how do we know about another scholar, about others' works of scholarship, and about concepts or propositions attributed to others? How do those understandings arise, change, accumulate, or disappear? These are the kinds of questions the following study pursues, and it does so by the novel focus on tracing the large body of (often controversial) knowledges made about a particular well-known individual in the human sciences: George Herbert Mead. By identifying the complex social action processes through which knowledge is produced in this case, the study contributes to the expanding literature in the sociology of knowledge and the history of the social sciences and humanities.

The following sections of the introduction outline the motivations, background, tools, and materials of the study. I begin by identifying the problematic, but not entirely unique, position Mead occupies as an individual and conceptual resource in the human sciences, and especially in sociology. This case was selected for extended, monographic examination on the basis of its problematic status and because of the extensive documentation available for such analysis. By this combination, it serves to make visible the processes through which understandings of an intellectual are produced. Following this, I identify the set of conceptual tools utilized in the analyses by drawing from recent theoretical work in the social nature of knowledge and action. The key insight proves to be in understanding knowledge as action and, hence, subject to an examination of its production in social action processes.

This conceptual formulation provides the connecting link between the disparate parts of the study, integrating them into a single processual account. And it allows the case study simultaneously to develop a thoroughly inductive empirical inquiry and to be consonant with a productive theory of social action. Theory informs the modes of inquiry at the same time that the narrative displays the empirical features of the case. The implications of these issues are developed in the section on the practical considerations resulting from the theoretical discussion. The methods of data collection and examination are then detailed, beginning with a discussion of the ways in which historical documentation can contribute to understandings of social action. The major types of archival and primary document research utilized in the study are enumerated and some consideration is given to the conscientious examination of the data that come from such research. Finally, I outline the basic progression of the substantive chapters and conclusion as a way of cuing the reader in to the overall structure of the study and some of its key arguments.

MEAD AS A PROBLEM OF KNOWLEDGE

George Herbert Mead is problematic. It is in sociology, more than in any other discipline, that Mead is treated as an important theoretical resource and as a foundational figure, where he is known primarily for his theory of the social nature and genesis of the self, as the quintessential forerunner of the Symbolic Interactionist perspective, and as a central theoretical resource for the Chicago School of sociology. This is despite the fact that he was a philosopher who never taught a course primarily listed in sociology, and who taught and wrote about a wide variety of topics far outside of the concerns for which he is predominately remembered, including experimental and comparative psychology, the history of science, and relativity theory. Indeed, although his long-time colleague and friend John Dewey (1931, 310) memorialized Mead as "the most original mind in philosophy" of his generation, he has never had anywhere near as high a profile among philosophers as did other intellectuals of this generation, including

Dewey. Much of the following study is directed to these problems, but it is worth underscoring at the outset the seemingly enormous gap between a dominant foundational "myth" of Mead and the actual historical person who lived and acted day to day.

The work by which he is overwhelmingly known and for which he is cited is *Mind, Self, and Society: From the Standpoint of a Social Behaviorist* (1934). This book was one of several put together after his death, primarily from notes taken by stenographers and students in his courses and from unpublished manuscripts, as a way of preserving a published legacy to Mead and of systematizing his philosophy. As the former students and junior colleagues who compiled the materials noted at the time, there was no indication that Mead would have intended such materials for print, and he surely never sought the publication of such materials in life. These posthumous volumes have been controversial since they were published, and *Mind, Self, and Society* in particular has been subjected to a long history of criticism for the seemingly idiosyncratic view it gives of Mead's philosophy and the rather unclear authorial status of much of the text. Nevertheless, *Mind, Self, and Society* is a popular book that has served as the introduction of many to Mead. Put in admittedly oversimplified terms, Mead is known in a discipline in which he did not teach for a book he did not write.

There has been increased scrutiny of Mead in recent years as a philosopher and social theorist as part of the broader revival of interest in classical American pragmatism, and discussions of Mead have been incorporated into new discourses, including the growing literatures on animals and society, cognitive science, and science studies. As a result of the problematic nature of much of what constitutes our knowledge about Mead, a critical multidisciplinary dialogue about him has developed. Works in this critical scholarship have often sought to move beyond the dominant interpretations of Mead, especially those stemming from *Mind, Self, and Society*, to significant original research, combining a detailed attention to Mead's intellectual biography with a more nuanced explication of his developing philosophical positions. Recent work has also sought to recontextualize and reinterpret Mead through a better understanding of his own practical social action rather than through his largely posthumously produced legacy. In this environment, there have been serious, interrelated contentions about what Mead really meant, what should count as authoritative source material of his thought, which concepts or propositions are most characteristic of Mead's philosophy, who can claim to speak as an authority for and about Mead, and how ideas attributed to Mead are to be empirically understood and examined. What all of these concerns have in common, and what this study seeks to address, is Mead as a problem of knowledge, or rather as many problems of knowledge.

To anticipate the substantive analyses in the study, one might say that the problems get worse before they get better. My research demonstrates that for much of his career Mead was known primarily as a public intellectual who spoke at social reform events rather than as a professional writer, that much of what was published under his name was originally given in the form of public speeches, and that the body of his publications bears only a tenuous relationship to his own interests. Major portions of Mead's public life that have definite bearing on the development of his concepts and reorient the context of his thought have been completely unaddressed, even in the biographical literature on Mead.

Continuing along this line one might note that, far from being a font of knowledge soaked up by his students and deposited in their notes, Mead continued to design his classroom environments and interactions with students in such a way that they would be informative of his own thinking. That is, he worked to have his students teach him. Conversely, his students took assiduous notes not unequivocally to record Mead's philosophy, but for myriad reasons relating to their own intellectual interests. A huge amount of such documents from Mead's courses still exists in many different forms scattered far and wide, but they have not figured in interpretations of Mead and are, indeed, largely unknown. No one, not even the former students and colleagues who worked on it, intended *Mind, Self, and Society* in the form that it was eventually published, and its peculiarities can be understood only by tracing its construction as a process of solving practical problems involving responsibility for aspects of the project, available materials and their discovery, the use of these materials as documents of Mead, and Great Depression economic perceptions.

As demonstrated further in the following analyses, the often-controversial claims made of Mead by influential students depended fundamentally on their sense of participating with him in those claims, a sense that they received from their own interactions with him in life. The published references to Mead throughout his life, of which there were many, came primarily from people who knew him personally and who referred to their interaction with him rather than his published works as the sources of their knowledge. Even after his death, the dynamics of citation patterns and the development of dominant understandings of Mead were fundamentally determined by social connections to Mead and his students more than by the external discovery of Mead's works. Small shifts in local institutional arrangements had major consequences for the development of a particular interpretation or reception of Mead in sociology. In the course of each of these discoveries, some aspect of the presumed understanding of Mead—his social life, publications, influence, posthumous legacy—comes into question.

Mead is not the only author to be in such a predicament, although the problems in regard to Mead are of such an intensity, are so well documented, and are of such a size that analysis can be particularly illustrative. Mead is one of a prominent group of intellectuals, treated as foundational authors in the humanities and social sciences, whose legacy is obviously the result, at least in part, of major posthumous interventions by other scholars. One need only think of theorists who are known in large part through the compilation and publication of manuscripts or other materials after their deaths, including Karl Marx, Charles S. Peirce, Max Weber, R. G. Collingwood, and Alfred Schütz. Or an even more direct comparison would be to those who are known in large part through the materials of students or followers documenting their teachings, including Aristotle, G. W. F. Hegel, Ferdinand de Saussure, and Harry Stack Sullivan. Indeed, none of the major problems of knowledge involved with the study of Mead are unique to this case, although their acuteness is perhaps peculiar.

At every point one is confronted with problems of knowledge, but merely formulating the topic this way does not solve those problems. Instead, this treatment, the implications of which are elaborated below, is intended to bring together in a productive direction a variety of inquiries often treated separately. In particular, in considering the work of other scholars, it is too easy to assume a meaningful distinction between those who study how an intellectual like Mead worked and thought in context (the typical domain of contemporary intellectual biography); scholars who work to understand concepts or propositions attributed to an author like Mead in their own work, but do not investigate the production of those concepts themselves (the vast majority of authors who refer to Mead); and those who study the production of "founders, classics, and canons," to borrow Baehr's (2002) phrasing (the domain of disciplinary histories, sometimes shading over into history and sociology of knowledge). Put in a common register, we have Mead's knowledge of himself, his work, and his social context; our knowledge (or interpretation, understanding) of Mead; and the knowledge of how our knowledge of Mead is selective or eccentric.

The separation of these problems collapses entirely when one notes that the knowledge in each case is held and made by people, predominately academics, about whom knowledge and interpretation may also be made. Indeed, having a knowledge made about oneself is one of the goals of scholarship to the extent that individuals wish to have their work referred to and serve to motivate further productive work by others. Scholarship as an ongoing social enterprise—a "community of inquiry" in the formulation of classical American pragmatism—is necessarily one in which scholars work with knowledge of one another. What and how scholars know about themselves and about one another is central to the ways in which scholarship develops and builds upon itself. Each of the problems outlined above revolves in some way around the knowledge produced by one scholar or group about another scholar or group (including self-knowledge, the case when that other scholar is oneself) in the course of their intellectual endeavors. This intrinsically social production of knowledge is the central conceptual topic of this study. In order to develop the analytical tools through which to investigate the production of knowledge, I turn to recent work in the social sciences.

SOCIOLOGY OF KNOWLEDGE, ACTION, AND PROCESS

The sociology of knowledge (including the various formulations of a sociology of intellectuals, ideas, science, intellectual life, and so on) has a long history of self-reflexive study on the nature of knowledge in academic disciplines, including the social sciences and humanities. Indeed, perhaps one of the defining features of scholarship on the social nature of knowledge is the predilection to turn the same tools toward one's own thought. Even a cursory examination of the development of the sociology of knowledge as a field, although no doubt rewarding in certain respects, would lead us far afield from our immediate concerns, so I identify only a few particular moments of interest.

From the 1970s there were major shifts in the sociology of knowledge and the sociology of science (a productive offshoot, in part, of the former) that have been characterized in various ways (cf. Collins 1983; Swidler and Arditi 1994; McCarthy 1996; Camic and Gross 2001). In the sociology of science, a variety of new schools of thought effectively shifted the focus of the field from one that studied the social organization of scientists with emphasis on institutionalized norms and values and systems of meting out reward and sanction (esp. Merton 1973) to the study of the production of scientific "knowledge" through social practices. This group of perspectives has been exceedingly productive in empirical inquiry, as it opens up a wide field of inquiry into the processes through which knowledge is constructed in the social practices of scientists. Indeed, the sociology of knowledge as a whole has shifted toward the study of the production and communication of knowledge through the organization of social practices, and (to the extent that any semblance of coherent focus existed in the disparate previous efforts) away from the structural social determination of knowledge. That is, instead of studying formal systems of ideas and imputing them to sociohistorical actors, empirical inquiry is directed to how knowledge is constitutive of social action processes, including the contentious action of intellectuals in their attempts to establish legitimate claims to knowledge in their local institutional contexts. This move has proved productive in reinvigorating work in the sociology of knowledge— sometimes now designated the "new" sociology of knowledge—and has offered new directions for studying the nature of knowledge in scholarship itself.

Building on and synthesizing previous scholarship in this direction, which they review in detail, Camic, Gross, and Lamont (2011) have recently edited a volume of work on "knowledge making practices" in the social sciences and humanities that indicates the convergence of interest in this kind of critical inquiry. This volume has set the tone for the "new" sociology of ideas and its reflexive application to the social sciences. The editors' emphasis in introducing the volume and the research agenda is on the empirical inquiry of "social knowledge" in a broad sense, one that treats norms and technologies along with facts as topics of investigation in "knowledge making"; that encompasses all phases of knowledge production, evaluation, and application; and that is sought in a variety of sites and temporalities. Knowledge is thus understood not in the sense of something that is always and everywhere true, but as an empirical feature of the ways in which practice is accomplished. That is, one can study "making" or "producing" knowledge in this empirical sense without having to adjudicate whether it is "real" knowledge, or exempting some kinds of knowledge from analysis. "Practices" they define as "the ensembles of patterned activities" or "modes of working and doing" by which "human beings confront and structure the situated tasks with which they are engaged" (Camic, Gross, and Lamont 2011, 7), and the editors stress the "forms," "branches," "types," or "repertoires" of social knowledge in order to leave open to empirical analysis the "multiplicity" of such practices. Ultimately, the differences between the phases or modes of knowledge are not held as categorical distinctions but rather serve as an invitation to undertake rigorous work on the particularities of the relationships between knowledge and action in empirical contexts.

As the terminology indicates, work in the sociology of knowledge in recent decades has been in dialogue with developments in the theory of social action and process, especially the so-called practice turn or practice theory in the social sciences. Undoubtedly the single most well known author associated with this perspective is Pierre Bourdieu, but this orientation to practice draws from a broad range of authors and works. Indeed, as has been sometimes pointed out (e.g., McCarthy 1996), the traditions of phenomenology and pragmatism likewise contribute to a sociology of knowledge that examines knowledge as constitutive of embodied social practices. In particular, a phenomenological or hermeneutic focus may enrich the notion of practice with its emphasis on tacit, experiential knowledge and the complex processes of interpretation or understanding, while a pragmatist focus contributes to the emphasis on the social and prospective nature of action. It should, of course, be noted that these are little more than one-sided characterizations, and that these "traditions" are not essentially closed off from one another.

For much of the analysis that follows, it is sufficient to emphasize this synthetic statement. A variety of recent and classical authors agree in broad strokes on the orientation of the study of knowledge around the nature of social practices of knowledge production. This perspective may be asserted to be productive here, but it can only fully be justified in the course of the study by the ways in which it is shown to orient the empirical analysis. To this extent, and for much of the analysis of the study, it makes no practical difference to say that practice theory, phenomenology, or pragmatism prompts the analysis, only that it draws from a general orientation to social action. I draw most explicitly upon pragmatist social theory because it forms an object of study for this project and because I have found its specific formulations to orient work in productive directions. In particular, several recent authors have argued that the encompassing and empirically sensitive conception of social action originally formulated by the early American pragmatists avoids the potentially problematic reductions in the conceptions of action implied by more conceptually parsimonious, global theories of intellectuals and knowledge (cf. Gross 2009; Aboulafia 2010).

We can go further in this regard by noting that one of the accomplishments of pragmatic philosophy has been to provide a coherent statement of how knowledge takes part in social action processes. John Dewey, in an early statement, argued that the "problem of knowledge" does not have "its origin, its value, or its destiny within itself," but is instead one that "social life, the organized practice of mankind, has had to face." Thus, "the problem of the possibility of knowledge is but an aspect of the question of the relation of knowing to acting, of theory to practice." Instead of being a "self-sufficing purveyor of reality," knowledge should be conceived of as "a statement of action, that statement being necessary, moreover, to the successful ongoing of action" (1897, 4). In this conception, then, knowledge is not to be understood as the correspondence of mind with the world, or even as the accompaniment of action, but as itself a necessary phase within action.

Hans Joas (1996), in his work to develop the implications of the pragmatist theory of action and to contrast it with other conceptions, indicates that its defining features are its "situational" notion of intentionality, its essentially "corporeal" understanding of action, and its emphasis on the primacy of "sociality" in the genesis and development of action. These features give a pragmatic theory of action, in Joas's view, the capacity to understand the diversity of human actions and to account for its creativity without recourse to residual categories or outside explanations. Indeed, those features that might otherwise be counterposed against intentional action—for example, situation, body, society—are made intrinsic to the nature and understanding of action itself. As an integral part of the pragmatic theory of action, human action is understood to be self-recursive in the sense that human actors have the socio-corporeal capacity to take the problematic course of action itself as the occasion for reflection and reconstruction. In this sense, knowledge is understood to be something that for human beings extends beyond given situations—as the possibilities of action presented to the actors in those situations—and hence as a project that entails consequences for oneself and others to come.

If, following the implications of recent scholarship, action is the category through which to understand knowledge, and if action in this encompassing sense is seen as participant in its own trajectory or ordering, then a central concern in understanding knowledge is the nature of the dynamics or mechanisms that structure that process. In this vein Gross (2009) recently proposed a "pragmatist theory of social mechanisms" as "composed of chains or aggregations of actors confronting problem situations and mobilizing more or less habitual responses." For much of the recent literature on mechanism (which has been one of the leading concepts by which the enactment and course of social action processes has been explained) the concept is used to identify general cause-effect transactions that are effectively waiting to be set off in essentially the same way across time and place. The typical understandings of mechanism shift the locus of explanation such that they presuppose assumptions about the rational or responsive nature of individuals as actors. But understood from an encompassing, pragmatic view of action, mechanism is the coming together and interlocking of such transactions in the empirical social organization of action itself, such that mechanisms are not eternal forms waiting to be activated, but come together and are structured by the particular situational contexts of social action and, hence, are subject to transformation with the action itself.[1] For authors in this tradition, the transformational quality of social process, especially the development of understandings on the part of social actors in the course of action, is one of its key features. As a consequence of this understanding of social process, the analyst must also attend seriously to the investigative and narrative strategies by which process is examined and represented in social research.

PRACTICAL CONSEQUENCES FOR EMPIRICAL INQUIRY

On the basis of this understanding of action, problems of knowledge may become the occasion for the study of the production of knowledge in social action processes, a study that investigates its conditions, modalities, dynamics, and cumulations. I derive two fundamental commitments from the emphases of this pragmatist theory of action that help structure the inquiry that follows. The first is to treat the production of knowledge as prospective. This means addressing the possibilities of social action as they emerge in the course of action itself, and as they are understood by the actors involved. This does not mean literally remaining within the perceptual limits of any particular historical social actor. Instead, it means that historical action may not be explained merely by its understood result from the perspective of present presumptions or understandings. The goal is to link or articulate actions in a way that shows how knowledges have developed over multiple temporalities ranging from immediate situations to century-long discourses. This preference for prospective analysis may be stated as a principle, but it can only be fully justified in the course of the analysis. That is, it is an appropriate analytical orientation precisely because it works to illuminate things that would not otherwise be visible.

The second commitment, necessarily related to the first, is not to employ labels as analytical shortcuts to the explication of social processes. Chief among these is the notion of "social construction." As it was developed by Berger and Luckmann (1966), the notion entails a detailed, empirically verifiable process of creating or "constructing" reality in the process of everyday social life by a continual dialectic of institutionalization and internalization of socially produced reality. But as the phrase is sometimes casually used, it serves more as a label to avoid or dismiss the need to detail empirical processes. To say that Mead is "socially constructed" is not to show it (not to mention that one of the rhetorical implications of this phrasing is that others have done this "to Mead," who was consequently somehow passive in his own construction). Instead, the narrative I develop is committed to detailing action at the level of actual empirical actors and situations; such a commitment results in a fundamentally different quality of understanding from a presumptive label.[2]

One of the key innovations of the case study that follows is to combine a study of intellectual reputation or canonization and a study of a particular individual's biography and works in a single monographic account. It is the theory of knowledge production outlined above, which treats both aspects as action processes with empirical interconnections with one another, which provides the essential conjunction between these domains. As mentioned above, the study of disciplinary histories tends to be fairly distinct from individual works on intellectual biography. As a whole, the extensive literature on intellectual reputations and canonization processes has lacked a principled way of connecting the work scholars do to secure their own reputations with the work done by others in "mythologizing" them. In practical terms, this means that it is easy to treat reputation or canonization as a process that happens to a person or work by others separated in time and place from that person or the production of that work (typically after the person in question is deceased), and that it is similarly easy to treat intellectual biography as an account that attaches unproblematically to the bounds of a particular individual's life.[3]

The present study offers a way to overcome such problems in the literature. I demonstrate in the analyses that follow that it is possible to subject an intellectual and those who interpret him to the same analyses as contextually situated social actors who create knowledge through and about their social actions, actors whose knowledge production practices are necessarily implicated in one another's intellectual projects. To explain the construction of Mead's reputation without examining the determinate ways he produced the possibilities of that legacy in the interaction he had with his students and colleagues, or to explain Mead's biography without identifying the ways it was essentially indebted to his students and colleagues, would be wholly inadequate. As the following analyses demonstrate, the social action of Mead in producing understandings of himself, others, and his social contexts is necessarily participant in the intellectual projects of his students and other interpreters. In this sense, the book is doubly about "becoming" Mead. It details both Mead's own self-creation through his social action and the creation of Mead in the representations made of him by others, while also bringing into question the separation of these two phenomena. "Becoming" has a productive double meaning, then, which stresses both Mead's intellectual development and the formation of Mead as an icon for a set of concepts influential in social science. In the course of the study, and in the conclusion, I identify particular contemporary works that examine the social production and distribution of ideas where relevant, and in several places I further outline the advantages of the approach taken in this study.

By focusing on the social processes of knowing about Mead over time, this study does not have to begin either with the premise that there is a single "true" Mead waiting to be distilled or that Mead is merely an invention of others. Either premise is more a conviction than an empirical question, and would pose the analyses in a narrow or leading way: is the later institutionalization of particular understandings of Mead in certain academic disciplines a recognition of his founding act, or is there an identifiable individual or set of individuals who "found" Mead? Instead, the analysis in this study places these problems in a more satisfying framework and provides a new way to examine them productively. That is, if the analysis is posed in such a way that it studies in detail the process or sequence of knowledges produced and how those knowledges are interrelated with one another, then there is no need for such oversimplifying premises. And the study of knowledge production has the benefit of treating the ongoing debates about foundational figures as so much more fodder for analysis. Any claim about Mead or other author does not actually result in any essential rhetorical closure. The problems remain empirically open for anyone who wishes to proffer another claim or comment on the claims made. From the standpoint developed in this study, such debates are themselves evidence of how we make and use knowledge, and by locating these problems within the broader social practices of knowing this work serves to open an avenue for the examination of our own ongoing practical accomplishment of scholarship.

It is worth emphasizing that the analyses that follow have two simultaneous purposes. On the one hand, they constitute a contribution to the literature on George Herbert Mead. Those interested in Mead or the interpretations made of him will be supplied with ample material. On the other hand, the analyses are an attempt to make an extended analysis of knowledge production in academia as a concrete process of social actions. I will have failed in my purpose if the reader comes away only with some esoteric facts about Mead or only with a few speculations on knowledge.

The two tasks are intimately connected in that the specific details—the real people, places, situations—are the tools by which I explicate the social process of knowledge production. As detailed below, I employ strategies of presentation that attempt to use the specific details to locate the reader in the experiences described and to present an immanent level of analysis alongside the more explicit and abstracted conceptual analysis.

In these analyses, I must undoubtedly presuppose a variety of educational, economic, and political institutional structures and modes of practice that I cannot investigate within the practical bounds of the study. In particular, I rely on the preexistence of modern university organizations and attendant modes of scholarly communication and commerce such as book and scholarly journal publishing, which make up much of the backdrop or staging of the action. Where relevant I give additional information by reference to primary or secondary literature on educational, economic, and political conditions. The institutions concerned and the knowledges produced are primarily limited to the field or domain of modern academia, although broader public concerns are conscientiously juxtaposed with this more delimited concern in chapter 1. In addition, part of the analysis serves to contrast the actual functioning of these social institutions in the practices of the particular historical persons under examination with the presumed understanding of their workings from our present-day knowledge and experience with universities, publishers, and the like. Especially noteworthy, the knowledge production practices outlined in the following chapters are local in a more fundamental sense that we are likely to presume in that scholarly meetings, publications, and long-distance travel are directly linked to significant social relations between those involved.

A couple of other terminological caveats are in order as well. I have tended to treat the terms "scholar," "academic," and "intellectual" as more or less interchangeable in the analyses that follow, using them as generic terms for individuals in their capacity as producers of knowledge (especially those employed in educational institutions). In addition, I use the term "understanding" sometimes in exchange for "knowledge" where it fits better semantically, and of course I use both terms to describe empirical phenomena, not normative judgments. In both cases I can no doubt be charged with conflating distinctions other analyses might find salient.

CONSIDERATIONS OF METHOD AND DATA

Although it may seem counterintuitive at first, the study of social action has quite often been accomplished by means of historical documents. Indeed, any attempt to develop a comprehensive understanding of social action must develop a way of examining action that has already occurred or that occurs outside of one's immediate observable presence. For example, W. I. Thomas, one of the earliest to develop a "situational" analysis of social action, was also the person who demonstrated the use of "human documents" (especially "life histories") in sociological analysis (Thomas 1966; Thomas and Znaniecki 1918–20). And Max Weber's "interpretive" sociology was developed in part out of concerns with understanding the historical social action through which social institutions like bureaucracies were established and transformed (Weber 1978 [1922], 2001 [1904–5]).[4] If the social analyst were merely a participant in the action, or could directly ask the participants about their meanings and intentions and observe the action unfold, notions like "ideal type" and "definition of the situation" would add little to the sociological explanation beyond what was directly accessible to the experience of the analyst. Instead, Weber and Thomas use Benjamin Franklin's aphorisms and the letters of Polish peasants, for example, as indicators of meaningful social action outside their own (and their readers') immediate experience. Note also that in both examples one of the major reasons for the kinds of historical documentation used was to have a concrete, practical way of addressing large-scale and long-term social transformations, processes that eluded both participation in and observation of the whole.

Documents do not merely have to serve, however, as "records" in the sense that they leave a durable account or depiction of action that they accompanied. This certainly captures one of the primary purposes of newspaper reports or the minutes of a meeting in most historical or social scientific research. And it is often sufficient for the purposes of analysis to utilize documents in such a way, but it is not the only way documents may be treated. Instead, they can also be understood as meaningful actions themselves on the part of those social actors who produce and handle them. This allows the investigator to ask questions like: how and why were they produced, by whom, under what circumstances, in response to what, in order to accomplish what? This treats documents, in Bakhtin's (1981) terms, as utterances in social dialogues. Written words and pictures—indeed whole novels or monographs—are no less social in this sense than spoken words; they are saturated by intentions and accents of meanings of social actors, oriented in environments of utterances already made and toward anticipated answers, and permeated with the inflections of social tensions and worldviews.

Moreover, documents can contribute to the self-structuring of action by mediating and coordinating action sequences (Smith 2006). This is especially true of an enterprise like scholarship, where the reading, writing, discovery, and handling of documents are supposed precisely to be consequential for trajectories of subsequent action. And, because of their relative durability over time and mobility across space, textual documents can articulate the connections and bridge the gaps between local settings of immediate social practice. In this way also, documents are central to the possibilities of historical research as itself a set of social actions. This understanding makes documents consequential in a much more fundamental sense, as structuring and participating in social actions rather than merely accompanying and recording them. In the analyses that follow this introduction, I treat the available documents in each of these ways in order to make the most of their ability to serve as indicators of social action.[5]

Turning now to the empirical data, it should be noted that perhaps the major reason Mead is a particularly illustrative case for a study of the production of knowledge is because of the huge amount and excellent quality of documentation available to the researcher. This is certainly one of the primary reasons why I chose to focus on this case to the exclusion of others. As the chapters that follow demonstrate, these materials detail a wide variety of documents indicative of practices by social actors in their attempts to understand themselves, each other, and their social contexts. And these documents can be productively analyzed and organized in such a way so as to trace prospectively and in detail the complex articulation of social practices by which understandings of George Herbert Mead have come about. In directing my research I have sought documents that can contribute to the examination of social action processes, that is, documents with a sequential or cumulative character and those that can be interpreted by reference to the meaningful social actions in which they were implicated. It is also important to note, in the selection of Mead as a case study, that while the documentation is extensive, it has proved to be of a manageable size for the accomplishment of a monographic examination. This might not be said about authors for whom documentation by and about them is too voluminous (consider attempting the same for Marx or Freud) or for whom there is not a sufficient variety of different forms of documentation available. In that regard, studying Mead has the benefit of being practically possible and can serve to suggest directions for other examinations of knowledge production.

The center of my research for four years was the examination of documents in archival collections. I have inspected materials from ninety different archival collections at ten institutions, with especial focus on the extensive collections at the University of Chicago Special Collections Research Center. I have also received substantial materials remotely from fifteen additional archival collections, and I have corresponded with librarians, archivists, and researchers at a variety of other institutions in search of materials. By far the single most important collection of relevant documents is the George Herbert Mead Papers, but this study would not have been possible, by a wide margin, on the basis of those documents alone. The archival collections that ultimately contributed substantively to the analyses are listed in the bibliography. Collectively, they contain many thousands of pages of personal correspondence, organizational records, manuscripts, notes, pamphlets and offprints, and other such materials.

Of particular note, my research has documented the existence of seventy-nine sets of classroom notes, some only fragments, taken in Mead's courses. This body of notes is every set I have been able to discover in archival collections available to public research and is by far the most comprehensive body of such data brought together for examination. By way of comparison, *Mind, Self, and Society* is primarily composed of materials from two sets of notes (with small fragments from several others, discussed in chapter 5). The complete listing of these materials forms an appendix to this study. Another set of documents particularly important to the analyses that follow is a restricted-access collection of instructors' reports that records the complete student registration for all of Mead's (and all other instructors') courses taught at the University of Chicago from 1894 to 1931. While I am not permitted to report this listing as such, I am able to make extensive use of it in characterizing Mead's classes and in placing particular individuals in those classes.

In addition to archival collections, I have utilized a variety of published and quasi-published documents as primary materials, gathered by the physical perusal of journals and books and by full-text searches in several different types of electronic database. One set of such documents that I have physically examined is the dissertations and theses of all students in selected disciplines at the University of Chicago from 1894 to 1935, amounting to approximately 1,000 volumes. These documents, along with published and unpublished accounts from students, are used to trace the influence and representation of Mead's courses in the work of his students. Another set of data consists of approximately 300 newspaper reports that detail the public life of George H. Mead, especially his speeches, reform efforts, and travels. These materials have been compiled primarily from several searchable newspaper digitization databases with supplemental research in paper and microform newspaper collections. I relied heavily on digital tools that have become available in recent years that make large-scale comparative bodies of data available in ways not practically possible before, although I am certainly aware of the shortcomings of many of these resources. In addition to newspaper digitization projects, these include professional citation databases, biographical information databases, digitized book repositories, full-text journal article databases, and online search tools for archival collection inventories.

Several of these resources have provided the raw data for the construction of datasets of (1) all references to Mead in major published journal articles and reviews from 1894 to 1955, including all informal references in addition to formal citations, and (2) all citations to works by Mead recorded in the Web of Science database from 1956 to 2010. These unique datasets of approximately 1,150 entries and 8,000 entries, respectively, contribute substantially to the ability to trace the development of the patterns of published reference to Mead over time, especially when combined with author biographical information from a variety of sources. My examination of these sources and my archival research has also contributed several new entries to the comprehensive bibliography of Mead's known published works, as reported at the end of this study in an appendix and discussed in a few instances in the text.

No single kind of source used in this study is without limitations, qualifications, or problems. Archives, when well processed and maintained, are outstanding sources of information, but even the most outstanding facilities depend essentially on the materials they receive and the questions researchers pose to those materials. In my research I have tried to address the selective and somewhat capricious nature of documents in archives by two main checks. The first is to attempt to triangulate or cross-check information with other archival collections and published sources. The second is to remain suspicious of the records that do exist: to pose counterfactual explanations to them, for example, and not to assume that some fact is not true merely because a certain piece of information does not exist in a particular collection. This same suspicion is important to electronic databases of published materials as well. In several places in the following analyses, I report information on the basis of a fairly comprehensive examination of certain bodies of data gathered from these sources. These analyses are accomplished only after a variety of checks and the use of multiple data sources, but are still reported as suggestive or comparative findings not to be taken as facts in their own right. Indeed, it would be naïve if, after having discovered several significant groups of documents previously unutilized in such analyses, I were to propose that no further discoveries

could be made by similar research. In the conclusion I return conscientiously to a discussion of "discovery" in historical research. Where each of
the various forms of archival and primary documentation is treated in the
study, additional description of the methods of its discovery and examination is given.

THE ANALYSES THAT FOLLOW

Seven substantive chapters make up the empirical analyses of this study.
Each chapter is intended to focus first and foremost on the detailed examination of a particular aspect of the case and only secondarily on the more
formal social theory of knowledge production. It should be kept in mind in
reading the following chapters that the kind of argument being undertaken
in these analyses, based on the identification and examination of particular sequences of social practices, requires this level of empirical emphasis
and detail. As indicated above, the twin red threads that the reader may
follow are the production of knowledge in social action processes, on the
conceptual level, and the historical details of understandings by and about
G. H. Mead, on the empirical level. This study examines aspects of Mead's
intellectual biography along novel lines and in greater detail than has previously been done, but these analyses are also done with a definite intent
to make them relevant to a larger argument about the nature of knowledge
production. Indeed, part of the argument being made is precisely that it is
in working through a particular set of empirical problems that we are en-
abled to understand knowledge production in a novel way. The case study
as a whole returns in the conclusion to address the theoretical implications, and consequently those looking for the formal conceptual discussion are directed to each of the chapter conclusions and to the concluding
chapter.

The chapters are organized so that the analysis in each builds on previous analyses chronologically and in terms of abstraction. That is, they
trace the production of knowledge by beginning in Mead's own social action and following the transformations over the course of time. The analyses benefit from being read in order because they are structured so as to
contribute to the overall account of a knowledge production process. Put
one way, the analysis follows a path from Mead's immediate social environment and experience into his classes, from there into his students'
notes and plans, from there into their continued interpretations and in-
scriptions of him, and from there into the academic discourses at-large. In
each case, the analysis works against presuppositions of Mead in the very

process of showing their development as forms of knowledge. Different narrative strategies have been employed conscientiously in sections of the analysis, in the service of putting together a coherent and readable study that answers to the conceptual tools outlined above.

Following this introduction, the study turns first to the social experience of George Herbert Mead himself. Chapter 1 uses the critical literature on the intellectual history of Mead and his social context in order to locate peculiar aspects of Mead's own knowledge-making practices. Examining Mead's public speaking provides the opportunity to identify how his own understandings of himself and his immediate environments were related to his intimate personal relationships and belie our taken-for-granted understanding of Mead as a self-standing figure. By identifying this set of situations and contexts, the analysis in the first chapter establishes a way of finding Mead's own interests and social actions historically and provides an entry point to begin tracing the production of knowledge.

Chapters 2 and 3 represent attempts to reconstruct peculiar phases of Mead's social life. The first of these chapters takes as its focus the investigation of Mead's physiological and comparative psychology. The analysis demonstrates the emphatic participation of Mead in these studies, despite their relative neglect in the scholarship on Mead. I argue that an examination of such topics both challenges the typical teleological view of the development of Mead's philosophy and points out novel and suggestive points of connection around the practice of science. Chapter 3 examines Mead's extended personal engagement with the social transformations in Hawaii and their fundamental importance for the development of his social philosophy. The chapters of this first section set the stage for the later examinations both by bringing into question the received knowledge about Mead and by locating analysis in the course of Mead's social experience.

In the chapters that follow these, the center of the analyses moves away from Mead, in a sense, although he figures continually and actively in the processes by which others have produced understandings of him. Chapter 4 examines Mead's classroom instruction, including the demographic structure of his classes, the variety and uses of classroom notes, the engagement of his students with his teaching, and the influence his students had on him. The chapter takes up the acknowledgment of Mead's self-production through speaking and writing and demonstrates its implication in the various intellectual endeavors of his students. And the chapter serves to contrast the understanding of student notes as records of speech with one in which they are understood as practical pedagogical tools in a broader sense.

Chapter 5 investigates the construction of the posthumous volumes by which Mead has predominately come to be known, with special focus on *Mind, Self, and Society*. The investigation demonstrates that the problematic status of these volumes can be fully understood only by examining the practical accomplishment of putting the volumes together as a social process over time. In this process the editor, Charles Morris, was important, but the result also depended essentially on the particular sequences of documents examined, the way documents had been put together by students and stenographers in Mead's classes, and perceptions of cost and sales made in the depth of the Great Depression.

The final section details the transformational processes whereby Mead went from an individual personally encountered by his students and colleagues to an objective set of theoretical concepts and propositions. Chapter 6 examines the "intellectual projects" of two of Mead's most influential former students, Charles Morris and Herbert Blumer. The chapter investigates each separately in detail, identifying the particular ways in which each referred to and mobilized claims about Mead, how they claimed authority for their positions, and how their representations of Mead appeared plausible to them. The analysis demonstrates that a key to understanding each aspect of these cases is in the development of a sense by both individuals of participating emphatically in collective intellectual projects with Mead. They gained this sense in their interactions with him in their early academic careers.

Chapter 7 assesses the large-scale dynamics of references to Mead as they have developed over the last century, with a focus on the crucial shifts in early patterns. The analyses identify the central and continuing importance of personal relationships in patterns of reference to Mead, especially in the considerable body of informal references that do not refer formally to any of his works and in the importance of the ways Mead was incorporated and reincorporated into the academic institutions at the University of Chicago. Only after his death, with the profusion of posthumous volumes and memorial statements, did more mediated relations develop between Mead and the authors of works that refer to him, but even then direct social relationships remain important. In addition, the chapter identifies how shifts in the academic institutions both locally and nationally had significant impacts on the way Mead was interpreted and received in different disciplines.

The conclusion takes the task of bringing together the various strands and themes of the study. First, I examine the analyses in the empirical chapters in order to identify the broader lessons of the study. Second, the contributions of the study regarding the production of knowledge in social action processes are discussed. Finally, this leads to reflections on the nature of sociological study into scholarship and knowledge with especial emphasis on the problems of historical research and self-reflexivity. The empirical study of knowledge participates in the very process that it investigates, and so provides the unique venue for discussions of the intrinsic problems or possibilities of scholarship.

No individual set of documents, concepts, individuals, or mechanisms provides the key to the ways Mead has been treated in scholarship; instead the study demonstrates that only a focus on empirical social action processes as they connect and change over time can adequately explain the production of knowledge about Mead. Only this focus can reconnect the present foundational myth and the historical man. In this way the study provides a novel analytical frame through which to reexamine the often problematic processes of knowledge making in academic scholarship.

PART I

Rethinking Mead

CHAPTER ONE

Public Participation

As with other high-profile social theorists and philosophers—the so-called founders of modern academic discourses—a critical literature has developed around George Herbert Mead. The Mead critical literature has developed especially in the last quarter century, fittingly late for someone who has been gaining recognition and becoming increasingly a part of institutionalized academic discourse over a long course.[1] The literature is "critical" in the sense that it takes as its object the dominant, received notions about Mead. Of course, this implies that one can identify a set of definite ideas by which Mead is primarily known, ideas that belie the particular contexts of their production and use, and against which such a critical literature would be motivated to develop. Tracing the production of these dominant ideas is a project of later chapters of the study, but it is worth emphasizing here that such a view of Mead as a conceptual resource for the social sciences—as a brand name for a distinctive set of general propositions and concepts about social life—has invited a particular kind of criticism. The critical works have, by many paths, sought to rediscover evidence of the actual social activities of the historical George Mead as a way of understanding his ideas.

For the purposes of this chapter, I point out only a few of the outstanding features of the broader literature and only address individual pieces separately when relevant to particular claims made. In recent synthetic summaries of Mead's contribution to the sociological canon it has become fairly standard to point out that the process of his canonization was highly problematic (e.g., Shalin 2011a; Silva 2006, 2007). A special focus of many works has been reclaiming or reassessing Mead's local social-reform efforts, including his work supporting and promoting the social settlement houses, publicly mediating labor disputes, advocating for universal public education and vocational training, advancing women's suffrage, and ensuring the rights of immigrants and racial minorities, among other concerns (Barry 1968; Diner 1972; Deegan and Burger 1978; Joas 1997 [1985], chap. 2; Shalin 1988, 2011b; Cook 1993, chap. 7). These critical works almost invariably point out the importance of the local social institutions in Mead's long-time home city of Chicago, a center of rapid growth and change, and especially the unique congeries of reformers and intellectuals at the new University of Chicago (esp. Rucker 1969; Diner 1972; Deegan 1988; Campbell 1992; Feffer 1993). There has also been an expanding recent literature that reexamines Mead's writings in light of the social transformational events of his lifetime, especially World War I (e.g., Joas 2003; Silva 2008; Deegan 2008). Just so, this literature as a whole locates Mead in historical time and place, and in connection with his actual social relations.

It is easy to view this literature largely as intellectual biography, and so of note primarily to those with a pre-existing interest in Mead as an individual, or in some aspect of the time and place of his thought. Indeed, several of the works are self-identified as recording Mead's intellectual biography, or the biographies of the institutions or other people connected with Mead. Even at their most targeted, however, these works are not written only for the amusement of a few initiates. They contain various claims, sometimes implicit but often quite prominent, that we gain something beyond the facts themselves through such work. By knowing about the time and place of Mead's works we gain in some way a better understanding of the concepts or ideas attributed to him (indeed, this goes almost without saying, in as much as such literature is oriented toward correcting or amending the received view of Mead). Dmitri N. Shalin in particular has recently identified this contrast as one between a (false) initial understanding that is overcome by discovering a further knowledge of Mead as an intentioned actor:

> The image of Mead many sociology students form in the years of their apprenticeship is that of an armchair philosopher, dispassionately discoursing on the nature of mind, self, and society and largely removed from the practical concerns of the day. It is usually later that they learn that Mead was at the forefront of the contemporary movement for social reform and at some point seriously contemplated a career as professional reformer. (Shalin 2011b, 37)

Throughout the study, I use the critical insights of the existing literature to push even further. Especially in light of recent calls to utilize the history of the social sciences and humanities as evidence in a renewed sociology of knowledge (e.g., Camic, Gross, and Lamont 2011), I think one can treat the growing body of literature on Mead as very productive in posing broader critical questions for knowledge in modern academic disciplines. Put simply, the way evidence has been presented and claims mobilized with regard to Mead open much broader fields of examination about what constitutes evidence and what such claims presuppose.

In this chapter, I take up two sets of such analyses. First, in reaction to the dominant understandings of Mead, much of the critical literature has brought new sources of evidence, or alternative readings of existing evidence, to bear in order to reassess Mead. In this way, there is already a movement that implicitly brings into question the authority of particular forms of documentation—that is, what should count as an authentic source of evidence and how? By relying on evidence drawn from letters, manuscripts, notes, reports, and so on, "publication" becomes a problematic category. Second, by emphasizing context this literature raises questions about how ideas are dependent on definite times, places, and persons, especially for their genesis. I think this calls into question what constitutes "context" more fundamentally than it does "ideas," because the former bears the explanatory burden. In the following sections, I take these problems together as invitations to return to the case of Mead for further insights, and in the chapter's conclusion I begin to work out some of the ways such analysis takes us far beyond Mead, himself, and into the features of knowledge production.

PUBLIC SPEAKING

The emphasis on Mead's actual participation in social life among newer critical works is instructive in redirecting inquiry with regard to his publications. At its most basic, the question becomes one of how we are to understand the connection between Mead's life (especially his activism) and his scholarship. In this endeavor, as the analysis serves to demonstrate, a productive starting point is the acknowledgment of Mead as a public speaker. My research, which is surely not exhaustive on this point, has documented nearly 200 public speeches given by Mead over the course of his professional life.[2] In many cases the evidence I am able to gather only lists the fact that Mead gave such a speech or gives some indication of the general topic. But for nearly half of these talks there is some additional information, either from summaries in newspaper articles or other periodicals, or because the talks can be plausibly matched to known works or manuscripts of Mead that still exist.

It becomes clear in working through these materials that Mead was almost assuredly known in his own lifetime more widely for his public reform efforts than for his contributions to professional philosophy or social thought. An announcement for an address he was to give at the University of Kansas in 1911, for example, noted, "Mr. Mead is an excellent talker and comes with a national reputation as a speaker" (quoted in Mead 2000, 47). While this "national reputation" was likely an exaggeration of Mead's renown, it stresses the kind of perceptions of him at the time. Mead's immediate audiences for his talks on social settlements, vocational education, and labor strikes often numbered in the hundreds and, on at least a few occasions, well into the thousands.[3] In comparison, the participants in professional meetings who heard him give papers and the audiences of students who heard him lecture were typically much smaller. Indeed, one might note that despite teaching for thirty-six years at the University of Chicago almost without break in over 200 classes, Mead had lectured to a total of only about 3,000 students (due in part to the small size of many classes and the large number of repeat students), a topic discussed further in chapter 4.[4] On a few single occasions Mead spoke publicly to more individuals than he would ever teach in his entire academic career, although I readily note that the comparison between students of quarter-long academic lecture courses and the participants in a few contentious public meetings at which Mead briefly spoke is rather facetious.

More significantly, many of these public speeches were written up in newspapers and other periodicals, which, it goes perhaps without saying, reached a far larger readership than professional academic journals. In the evidence I have been able to gather, Mead was mentioned by the largest number of different newspapers in connection with the following events: the opening of the Chicago Physiological School in 1899 (reportedly the first experimental school dedicated to the study of children with learning disabilities) of which he was a trustee, the Chicago garment workers' strike of 1910–11 that he worked to arbitrate, the protests over a Board of Education rule change making it easier to fire public school teachers without cause in 1916 against which Mead was one of the vocal critics, his views on wartime "conscientious objectors" in 1918, and his resignation from the University of Chicago in 1931.[5] Likewise, Mead's own published writings in newspapers, reformist journals, and philanthropic bulletins reached wide audiences.[6]

It is not necessary to be dogmatic on this point. Indeed, as I demonstrate in other chapters, Mead had a considerable influence through his lectures and professional contacts in his own lifetime, which proved to be central to establishing and promoting a lasting legacy of ideas attributed to him. However, I think it important to emphasize here, in returning to questions of Mead's actual social practices in his lifetime, that things may have looked quite different from the perspective of the public at the time. It is, of course, symptomatic of his time and place, and of his political stance, that Mead spoke in public so frequently. The late nineteenth and early twentieth centuries are times in the United States, especially its growing industrial cities, of traveling lecture bureaus, university extension lectures, "Open Forums," "curtain speeches" at popular entertainment shows, "speakers' tables" on the issues of the day, labor rallies, campaign whistle-stops, and other forms of public speech, not to mention growing newspaper and periodical circulation and the explosion of radio broadcasting.

In this environment, those intellectuals and reformers identified with the Progressive movement were apparently among the leaders in the promotion and use of such public speech platforms, both in exposing social ills and in widely disseminating the latest intellectual discoveries. As Abbott (2010) has demonstrated by reference to sociologist and minister Charles R. Henderson, the public of the Progressive era in Chicago was actually more akin to an "archipelago of publics" in which loose connections were woven between groups of Protestant and Jewish reformers, Catholic charities, the universities, the elite's "clubs," professional associations, and governmental organizations, among others.[7] It is in this environment that Mead's close friend John Dewey (1927) worked to understand the nature and precariousness of the public sphere that was in evidence around them, and especially the constitution of such publics around the social problems of modern life. Mead was strongly involved in several of these movements to bring contentious issues into the public for discussion (such as his promotion of an elected rather than appointed school board) and to foster the broader distribution of general knowledge (such as his university extension lectures and talks on philosophy and science at local community centers).[8] Joas (1997 [1985]) and others have dubbed Mead in this light a "radically democratic intellectual."

SPEAKING AND PUBLISHING

There is a danger in the way I have posed the analysis: in emphasizing Mead's practical social reform work one may, in effect, reinforce rather than question the distinction between his practical engagement and his scholarship. That is, to the extent that one attempts to make a clear shift from his academic papers to his reform work, one retains the boundary as a salient one. No doubt Mead recognized distinctions between various aspects of his life, but such a clear-cut division between one body of professional academic work and one or more delineated reform projects is problematic to maintain and does not do justice to the complex connections across Mead's activity. In order to point out some of these lines of connection, the practical contexts of Mead's "major" academic publications are key. Treating, for the moment, the twenty-five papers published together under the title *Selected Writings* (Mead 1964c) as an indicator of those considered Mead's "major" academic contributions, one finds that at least sixteen of them were substantially based on papers presented publicly, many at meetings freely open to the public-at-large, but some at more circumscribed professional meetings. (The bibliography of Mead's works at the end of this study indicates the talks connected with specific published papers, where I have found reasonable evidence to that effect.) This assessment, based on my own historical research, almost certainly underestimates the actual number of such direct connections, and for the moment it excludes all the less direct connections between the concepts or ideas in published articles and Mead's engagement in public and private discussions.

In several cases, this acknowledgment that Mead's articles were publicly presented helps reorient the reading of these texts by locating them as parts of particular ongoing dialogues and in reference to specific issues of concern. For example, "The Philosophical Basis of Ethics" (Mead 1908e) was originally given at the Chicago Ethical Society Congress on December 30, 1907. The article title was originally the name of the session at which Mead presented, not of the individual paper, and the session also included contributions by University of Chicago divinity professor George Burman Foster, Ethical Culture movement founder Felix Adler, Chicago philosopher Addison W. Moore, and American historian D. S. Muzzey, with leading Chicago figure of the Ethical Culture movement William M. Salter (William James's brother-in-law) presiding over the discussion. The Congress was held in conjunction with the Chicago national convention of Ethical Culture societies, and the Congress was reportedly intended to bring in other viewpoints from outside the formalized Ethical Culture movement.[9] The Congress program was organized by Jane Addams and Charles E. Zueblin, and the discussions included James H. Tufts, Emil G. Hirsch, and Shailer Mathews, among Mead's other colleagues.

Mead's particular take on ethics in his paper was to examine it from the "evolutionary point of view" in which moral consciousness and the moral environment were codeveloped in situations of practical social action. In explicating this understanding of ethics in front of the participants of the Ethical Culture movement he argued that the standpoints of the "publicist and the reformer" and of the "pulpit" were inadequate to the extent that they maintained a fixed view of the moral society (either previously existing or coming into being) that did not permit the codetermination of the practical realities of a situation and the moral necessity of action. Hence, when Mead argued that this evolutionary view permitted social scientific investigation to guide ethical action by directing analysis to the conditions of particular situations, it would have been apparent to his audience that he was also attempting to make a case for the kind of pragmatic social scientific work championed at the University of Chicago over the exhortative stance of many involved in the Ethical Culture movement.

Likewise, "The Nature of Aesthetic Experience" (Mead 1926a) was originally given as a talk at the National Motion Picture Conference in Chicago on February 10, 1926.[10] The conference was the fourth such gathering organized by a group of Protestant clergymen and social reformers to consider the moral influence of motion pictures. The Chicago conference talks were solicited and organized by Hilda Merriam, the wife of political science professor and Chicago city alderman Charles E. Merriam. Mead's talk was in a session chaired by his colleague in philosophy T. V. Smith, with another paper on "Pictures and Imitative Behavior" read by his sociology colleague Ellsworth Faris. L. L. Thurstone, professor of psychology at the University of Chicago, was supposed to present on "Motives Prompting Movie Goers," and Herman Adler, head of the Institute for Juvenile Research connected with the university, was to have presented on "The Relation of the Motion Picture to Crime," but both had apparently fallen ill.[11] When read in the context of the conference, at which the focus of debate was movie censorship and the moral (i.e., presumably immoral) influence of the silver screen, the sessions held by Chicago philosophers, sociologists, and psychologists constituted a sustained argument for the need to subject media influence to scientific investigation and to specify how particular influences are accomplished, if at all.

Mead argued that in modern industrial society there was little satisfaction to be found in the typical social organization of work—"unaesthetic toil"—so satisfaction was sought increasingly in forms of "reverie." But visual images (movies were still almost all silent) do not actively foster thought in the same way the "imagery of words" does—he reminded the audience, "We do our thinking in the form of conversation"—and so visuals do not lend themselves to promoting participation in and expansion of shared social experience. But even so, just because they often satisfied little more than "very immediate, rather simple, and fairly primitive" impulses, did not necessarily mean, in Mead's view, that the movies promote the expression of repressed antisocial impulses—in his words, "catharsis" was not the same as "reversion" to impulse. Instead, analysis must consider the particular direction given to the impulses by the complex progression of images. In the heated political context of a conference focused on movie censorship, it is little wonder that no questions were directed to Mead in the subsequent discussion, and that those who spoke used the opportunity primarily to make stump speeches.[12]

T. V. Smith (1931, 369) later wrote in a memorial statement that "conversation was [Mead's] best medium; writing was a poor second best. When he wrote, 'something,'—as he says in one place of another matter—'something was going on—the rising anger of a titan or the adjustment of the earth's internal pressures.'" That is, Mead was motivated to write when "something was going on," when contemporary events or conditions stirred him to write out of "anger" or "adjustment." One could continue to provide similar points with regard to a wide variety of Mead's published papers, as the majority of article-length pieces that appear on bibliographies of Mead's work are more-or-less definitely traceable to public presentations. Even the set of articles that elaborates most directly the nature of social consciousness and the social self, published from 1909 to 1913, are versions of the arguments given in talks before being published.[13] Such an analysis, however, could easily become overly deterministic, finding in the particular occasion for the paper its sole cause or purpose. "The Philosophical Basis of Ethics" paper is not encompassed by its occasion or by its overall thrust, although they help us understand the kind of position Mead was taking, in part by indicating with whom he was in dialogue. And the same goes for "The Nature of Aesthetic Experience," which, for example, is also explicitly in dialogue with the aesthetic theories of Freud and Dewey, although they were not among his local audience. Indeed, it appears that one of the characteristics of Mead's public speeches was to treat the particular occasions as opportunities to elaborate arguments that fulfilled both more immediate and more farsighted intellectual goals simultaneously.

Moreover, the recognition that many of Mead's published works were first given as speeches helps us understand the seemingly peculiar mode of presentation used in these papers. Mead—whose father was a professor of homiletics; whose mother was a language tutor, instructor in English composition, and later college president; and whose schooling included formal instruction in rhetoric and oratory—was steeped in the modalities or rhetorics of public argumentation, so it is unlikely that the construction of his speeches was accidental. Authority, in Mead's argumentation, is mobilized by recourse to the common sense intelligence of the addressee, not by rigorous demonstration through tests: he typically used illustrations from common experience rather than formal analyses and marshaled allusive phrases as cues to his audience. Argument in Mead's papers is built up almost conversationally, rather than by a logic of hypothesis testing, as in the typical research paper. He seems to have structured his papers as a "reasoning through" by the posing of successive alternatives or considerations and by the working out of implications. When he cited other authors, which was fairly rare, especially compared to present-day citation conventions, it was almost always in the form of simple references incorporated into the text—for example, "the position taken by Dewey," "the *Social Psychology* by Professor Ross," "in the language of Theaetetus"— rather than by a bibliographical apparatus of formal footnotes (which were sometimes added later to his papers). Put simply, Mead's public speeches were argued and styled quite differently from the standard contemporary journal articles. In this mode of argumentation, of course, Mead was not alone, as published papers of his colleagues were often much closer to this model than to the apparatus of formal reports that dominates contemporary professional journals.

The fact that these pieces often preserved no explicit indications of having been previously presented when they were eventually published (e.g., many do not note the conference at which they were presented in footnotes or elsewhere) raises another set of questions. In many cases, as in the examples outlined above, the critical stance Mead took with regard to the occasions for some talks would have been good reasons not to make any special acknowledgment of those occasions. However, more important, it appears, is the recognition that the decision to publish these papers was not unequivocally made by Mead alone, a topic taken up in the following section. And it should be noted that from a work like *Selected Writings* are left out all of Mead's book reviews, paper abstracts, newspaper articles, editorial notes, committee reports, dictionary entries, memorial statements, and other disparate published writings.[14] It is in these pieces that one often sees Mead in context more emphatically, oriented directly to particular other individuals, ideas, and social institutions, and in which Mead is not merely talking about, but talking to, particular people for particular purposes.

Before turning to the connections between Mead's published works and his colleagues, one point in particular may be underlined. That Mead's participation in public debates was integral to his intellectual work is acknowledged in existing literature, but it can be further underscored by a focus on the way in which Mead's practices and speeches amplify one another—that he practiced what he preached, so to speak. In the instances highlighted above, and in a variety of other possible examples from Mead's life, he sought to present an argument for the public assessment of claims made on the basis of the study of empirical social reality. It is characteristic of Mead's self-reflexivity that he explicitly acknowledged and advocated this exemplification of content by the form of speech. When he addressed the "Chicago School Situation" at Hull House in the wake of Mayor Fred A. Busse's summary dismissal of his school board in 1907, for example, Mead (1907b) argued that the larger issue at stake was the understanding of the school system as a "great social institution," rather than a "technical institution." That it was treated as a "technical" institution under "the absolute authority of an expert" (on Busse's replacement school board this meant an empowered superintendent and a board composed of corporate executives) was one of its "gravest defects." Instead, the "community as a whole" should be represented in the administration of schools, and the schools should be progressively reorganized so as to "adapt" the schools to the "demands of the community about us." First and foremost,

> we need on our school board those who represent intelligently the social interests of the largest groups of children . . . those whom we know to be exercised about the social conditions of the children, who go into and come out of their homes, who can conceive life from their point of view. The school board should represent the community, because the next generation of the community must get its interpretation of life in some part from the schools, and because only through such intelligent representation can the social pressure be brought fairly to bear upon the conscience of the community. (1907b, 284–85)[15]

Hence, he sought to move discourse from the halls of power into the public in the service of securing the best representation of the community as a whole in those halls, and to move discourse from opinion and manipulation to informed discussion and collective action. And by focusing on these claims made in public rather than by "experts" in closed professional settings, the real impact of this argument becomes much clearer: he was doing precisely what he advocated. Mead was, after all, a person not in any official capacity who was giving his informed examination of the public schools to public audiences for public discussion. The form of Mead's talk as well as its content was directed toward promoting democratic public debate.[16]

PUBLISHING AND SOCIAL RELATIONSHIPS

Mead's closest colleagues were often quite directly involved in the publication of his papers. Perhaps most influential among these was his long-time colleague James H. Tufts (whose daughter married Mead's son). As editor of the *School Review*, the *International Journal of Ethics* (from 1914), and the annual "Social Psychology" issue of the *Psychological Bulletin* (until taken over by Mead in 1911), Tufts oversaw the publication of at least seventeen of Mead's articles and reviews, including works often identified as major interventions: "Social Psychology as Counterpart to Physiological Psychology" (1909e), "Social Consciousness and the Consciousness of Meaning" (1910d), and "The Genesis of the Self and Social Control" (1925). If one expands out to other journals edited by his close friends on the University of Chicago faculty, one has to acknowledge Mead's nearly forty articles, reviews, and editorials that appear in the *Psychological Review*, the *American Journal of Sociology*, the *American Journal of Theology*, the *American Historical Review*, the *Journal of Political Economy*, and the *Elementary School Teacher* (not to mention the *University of Chicago Record*, the *University of Chicago Magazine*, or the *Decennial Publications of the University of Chicago*). One can point to instances where Mead likely felt obliged to publish papers at the request of his colleagues, as in his yearly contributions to Tufts's issue of the *Psychological Bulletin*, or his seminal chapter "Scientific Method and Individual Thinker" in the volume *Creative Intelligence* edited by John Dewey.[17] One could push this argument further by pointing out the clear connections Mead bore to the organizations that published many of his other works (like the *City Club Bulletin*, where he was an active participant and president for a period) and to the individuals with input into the publication decisions at certain institutions (like Louis F. Post, editor of *The Public*, whom Mead knew through the Chicago City Club and the Chicago Literary Club). And one can acknowledge the rather intimate personal connections in the early years of the emerging professional associations at which Mead presented papers and in whose journals one finds many of Mead's articles.[18]

None of this means, of course, that Mead's overbearing colleagues sweated work from him, but rather that these published works were inscribed in significant social relationships. It bears emphasis that behind

the names of the journals in which Mead most often published stood
not mere acquaintances but long-time colleagues with whom Mead had
personal relationships, including James H. Tufts, John Dewey, Shailer
Mathews, Harry Pratt Judson, Charles R. Henderson, and others.[19] The
early University of Chicago faculty formed a relatively homogenous generational cohort that participated together in the same educational and civic
organizations for decades, and hence formed a rather close-knit group.
That Dewey, in particular, was a constant and important companion in
Mead's early intellectual career is well acknowledged (e.g., Dykhuizen
1973; Coughlan 1975; Cook 1993), and is only further supported by recent
publications of Dewey's correspondence and notes from his early lectures
(Dewey 2010).[20] The importance of this small group of close colleagues for
the promotion of Mead's ideas is discussed further in chapter 7.

There is another set of papers, abstracts, and reports that appear primarily in conference proceedings volumes or in the proceedings of conferences reported in regular academic journals; it is often unclear whether
Mead had much of any input into the publication of these talks. Some of
Mead's earliest works, for example, are known only as abstracts that appear in the *University Record* of the University of Michigan (1894b), the
University of Chicago Record (1896a, 1896b), and the *Psychological Review* (1895b). Other publications appear as reports of Mead's talks at conferences, including those of the Illinois Society for Child-Study (1897b),
the National Conference of Charities and Corrections and its successor
National Conference of Social Work (1909d, 1918h), the Western Drawing
and Manual Training Association (1911a), the Conference on Charities and
Corrections for the State of Illinois (1913b), the National Conference on
Vocational Guidance (1914b), the Illinois State Bar Association (1917e), and
the Vocational Supervision League (1918–24).[21] Some of these—the Western
Drawing association and the Illinois Bar, for instance—simply recorded
the proceedings of the spoken conferences as they happened (typically by
employing a stenographer); they are "captured" speech in this sense. What
they lose in the deliberateness and reflection of later revision they arguably gain back in recording the spontaneous discussions that accompanied
the talks. Absent some definite supporting documents one way or another,
however, they leave insoluble the question of whether Mead or any of the
other authors recorded in these proceedings intended them to be published
or considered them part of their oeuvres.

The issue of publication is further complicated in Mead's case by the
fact that, as Dewey (1931, 311) put it, "he was always dissatisfied with what
he had done; always outgrowing his former expressions" and "reluctant

to fix his ideas in the printed word." Mead even dismissed an attempt made during his life to bring together a definitive set of essays (Orbach 1998). And his correspondence indicates that he was quite aware of the often loose connections between what he wanted to write and what he published—otherwise we might have had articles by Mead on the evolutionary "Appearance of the Mammals," "the economic status of woman," or the "tragic condition" in Greek and Shakespearean drama.[22] Miller (1973, xxxiv) reported that Mead was known to type out statements meant only for himself and his close confidantes (especially his daughter-in-law Irene Tufts Mead) in order to help him think through some topic, and to set them aside just as quickly. Mead, then, was a person who discarded some ideas he worked out, disliked at least some of his written work, and dismissed attempts to gather a definite body of works. But at the same time, he was someone who Dewey (1931) thought was always turning over the same central problems in different ways, and in a few of his published works drew connections to his own previous contributions.

As T. V. Smith (1931, 369) noted, Mead's published writing "does not reflect him transparently." The fact that there is an uneasy relationship between the published papers and Mead's interests or intentions should make us skeptical of relying too heavily on one strict category of works—his professional journal articles, for example—as the privileged source of what should count as Mead. This fact might also give us courage to search farther afield for evidence of him. But perhaps most fundamentally, it should push us to examine the various texts written by Mead and others about him as documents of something beyond themselves: as indicators of Mead as a person emphatically engaged in the concerns of his social contexts and as meaningful utterances in ongoing social dialogues with other people about actual places and things. This chapter does not propose to solve the problem of what should count as Mead's work. Instead the analysis is intended precisely to open this question up more conscientiously than it has been previously and to begin working through issues of importance to the rest of the study.

CONCLUSION

Following the lead of existing critical literature, the chapter has tried to catch some glimpses of Mead's social experience. As were others among his close colleagues, Mead was a public figure who spoke to large audiences much more frequently than he published, and spoke as an authority on a much broader slate of issues than general social theory. More of his written work stems from his public speaking than is immediately apparent, and this work was originally in dialogue with the problems of Mead's practical concerns more directly than is typically assumed. The rhetorical conventions of public speaking pervade Mead's work, and indeed there is a play back and forth between the form and content of his work that only becomes apparent when seen as public speech. His existing publication record is evidence at least in part of intimate and meaningful social relationships among colleagues and does not serve as a clear indication of an accumulating set of definite propositions or concepts Mead felt were his own. In this sense, studying the content of Mead's published works also means examining their location in a process of social actions.

This examination helps us understand the way in which public participation may be related to the formation of concepts, by seeing public speeches and public documents as moments in complex social dialogues. For Mead, papers and speeches were neither the autochthonous, singular origin of concepts nor the final statements, the punctuation marks, that closed debate. This would be enough to seriously bring into question much that is taken for granted about Mead, but it also underscores more fundamentally the incongruence of our attempts to understand and use Mead, on the one hand, and his own social experience on the other.

In addition, this analysis highlights the peculiar workings of intellectual life in the late nineteenth and early twentieth centuries in the United States. Mead was both a scholar who wrote papers for professional academic journals and a public intellectual making value-laden claims about the nature of society and politics. These cannot be easily segregated into two distinct projects, especially in light of the practical and rhetorical nature of his public speaking traced in this chapter. Likewise, the formal institutional structures of scholarship familiar to contemporary academics—such as large conventions organized by discipline with many concurrent panels, blinded or anonymous peer review of manuscripts, publication benchmarks for promotion—were not institutionalized in the same way during this earlier period. Although academics of Mead's generation no doubt wished to excel or progress professionally, the normative structures of professional rewards and academic career paths were not those of contemporary academia. Indeed, the institutionalization and professionalization of certain academic disciplines in the United States affected Mead's students, especially his students after World War I, in ways quite different from his own generation (a topic traced in later chapters).

The analysis in the following chapters serves to further provoke this sense of incongruity by placing Mead in still more remote contexts. What if it could be shown, for example, that Mead designed and carried out psychophysical experiments, conducted animal behavior studies, prepared human brain specimens, and speculated publicly on the mechanisms by which hypnotism could be proven effective as an anesthetic in dentistry? Such a finding would suggest that Mead's philosophy was the product, at least in part, of concerted laboratory hypothesis testing rather than mere participation in everyday social life, and meandering experimentalism rather than rationally accumulated knowledge. And what if it could be further demonstrated that during his lifetime Mead was considered (and considered himself) a serious participant and interpreter of the social problems of a tropical island culture subjected to colonization? This would seem to imply that our grasp of how Mead understood his own context and the breadth of his own experience of social conditions is rather tenuous. In both cases, these findings would pose serious problems to the typical understandings or narratives surrounding Mead.

Chapters 2 and 3 present Mead in his own emphatic processes of knowledge production by the use of extended examinations around particular issues. Together these first three chapters attempt to give a more complex and multifaceted understanding of the ways in which Mead produced knowledge in his own social life. This analysis is undertaken not for the purposes of displacing one definitive interpretation of Mead or his context in favor of another. Instead, by identifying in very concrete ways how Mead engaged in processes of knowledge production far outside the typical understandings of his work, we are in a better position to analyze the ways in which Mead's scholarly practices are related to the ways others have produced understandings of him. Later chapters then use these insights to examine the production of dominant understandings of Mead's work in American academia as a way of understanding the social processes of scholarly knowledge production more generally.

CHAPTER TWO

Laboratory Science

Where did Mead look for his evidence? What did he do in order to try out ideas or check facts? Where do we find what we might call Mead's own process of discovery? If we are interested in knowledge production as an active, practical endeavor experienced emphatically by the knowledge producers, and not merely the abstract movement of ideas, then these questions are crucial.

With regard to Mead, the obvious first answer to this set of questions is that he made reference to immediate social experience. His is a common-sense social theory in that it makes extensive recourse to evidence and problems available to every competent person in the course of his or her own experience. This naturalistic way of orienting thought was clearly important to Mead and is the source of his ubiquitous everyday examples drawn from sports games, children's play, popular literature, fights, conversations, and the like. These quotidian examples appear throughout *Mind, Self, and Society* (1934) and in his many published papers, and they have become favorite turns of phrase in the dominant interpretations of Mead. As pointed out in the previous chapter, these illustrations are part of the rhetoric of Mead's spoken and published work. And as an exemplification of his objective, social view of social psychology, these examples come from shared, rather than private, experience.

Mead's didactic use of such everyday examples should not, however, lead us to conclude that his philosophy is merely anecdotal and therefore lacks rigor. That is, there is a difference between his use of these examples in his social psychological lectures and public speeches and their definitive place in generating and validating his problems and concepts. A first step away from this assumption is in the recognition made in the critical literature of Mead's active participation in and consequent conceptualization of the social movements of his time. I give some additional indication of this in discussing the importance of the social problems of Chicago and Hawaii to Mead's thought.

Mead was an active organizer on behalf of coordinating systematic data on relevant social conditions, and he personally participated with others in the preparation of major reports on the Chicago school system, the public library system, and the living and working conditions around the University of Chicago Settlement House. Mead was also an advocate for dedicated clearinghouses or bureaus for the processing and comparison of such social data.[1] One could also note that Mead participated in the creation of the University of Chicago Laboratory School, the Chicago Physiological School, and the Juvenile Psychopathic Institute (later the Institute for Juvenile Research) designed to provide for the systematic test and observation of child development and pedagogy, and he toured kindergartens and vocational education programs. In these various endeavors Mead was an active participant in the production of knowledge through investigation.

This chapter takes such inquiries into domains of investigation that have typically been ignored or underestimated in Mead's life, especially his work as a practicing laboratory scientist. In these examinations we gain a sense of some of the domains that Mead considered to be continually generative, of the kinds of questions and problems that he posed, and of his own practices of scientific discovery. When combined with Mead's work exploring the logic of everyday social experience and his work to institutionalize the collection of systematic social data, these inquiries demonstrate at a practical level the connections between Meadian philosophy and science.

Mead was emphatically engaged in processes of investigation. His endeavors along these lines, discussed below, are not only difficult to explain on the basis of an image of Mead as an armchair philosopher (to borrow a characterization from Shalin 2011b, quoted in chapter 1). Mead's laboratory practices and idiosyncratic research topics are difficult to reconcile with his well-known theory of the social nature of the self and his supposed reliance on natural, commonplace experience, central to the Symbolic Interactionist tradition in the social sciences. And his scientific investigations are also outside of the typical compass of critical scholarship on Mead. As the first chapter pointed out, much critical examination has focused on Mead's participation in the social events of his day—Mead as a citizen-philosopher. However, Mead was also at various times in his career engaged in serious original research in laboratories—Mead as a scientist-philosopher. It is one thing to acknowledge that Mead's philosophy was

well informed by contemporary research and another entirely to say that
his philosophy was informed by his own practical research endeavors. In
the following chapter, I demonstrate that the latter position is thoroughly
supportable by available documentation and significantly changes the way
we understand the formation of the ideas for which Mead is known.

LEARNING THE PRACTICES OF SCIENTIFIC DISCOVERY

Prior to Mead's graduate studies in Germany he had been exposed to much
recent scientific research on physiology and psychology and to the practical production of scientific knowledge.[2] At Oberlin College, where he received his bachelor's degree from the Department of Philosophy and the
Arts in 1883, he had classes in a variety of scientific pursuits that included
hands-on demonstrations and experiments in physics, botany, astronomy,
chemistry, zoology, engineering, and mineralogy.[3] Despite Oberlin's emphasis on religious education (Mead's father was professor of sacred rhetoric
and pastoral theology there from 1869 until his death in 1881), the college's
science teachers, Charles H. Churchill (physics, astronomy, engineering),
A. A. Wright (botany, geology, zoology), and Frank F. Jewett (chemistry,
mineralogy, physiology), were all active practitioners of scientific research,
apparently kept up with contemporary research in their fields, and were
early promoters of participatory science learning. Jewett, in particular,
who had come to Oberlin in autumn 1880 to teach chemistry and mineralogy, encouraged students to experiment in the newly completed microscope and chemical laboratories at the college (Jewett and Jewett 1922).

Although it may seem counterintuitive, Mead was fortunate to have
the chemist Jewett for his only physiology class in the last quarter of his
senior year despite the fact that Jewett professed no special knowledge of
the topic and had never taught it before coming to Oberlin in 1880 (Jewett
and Jewett 1922, 7). In effect this meant that Jewett chose one of the new-
est, highly regarded, and capacious textbooks, H. Newell Martin's *The Human Body* (1881), to introduce his students to the field, and to learn the
latest work himself, by teaching. Through this work Mead was exposed
to the findings of contemporary experimental physiology, including the
connections between physiology and psychology, which are treated substantially in no fewer than ten chapters of Newell's text. The book reports
the results of experiments from the recent German and English scientific
literature alongside many of Martin's own devising, especially on frogs.
Although the kinds of experiments and demonstrations done by students

in Oberlin's science classes were not intended to push the boundaries of scientific knowledge,[4] they would have been quite an education into research practices and results for eager students like Mead, and these exercises would have provided students with alternative models for the mobilization of knowledge and authority from those learned in their Evidences of Christianity or Rhetoric classes.

Mead was a voracious reader who made attempts to keep up with philosophy and science in his years after college, according to his correspondence with college friend Henry Castle. And no doubt, Mead participated in consequential exchanges on the relations between the sciences and philosophy in courses with Josiah Royce and George Herbert Palmer and in conversations with William James while attending Harvard (cf. Cook 1993, 14–18). The same goes for his first semester in Germany, at the University of Leizpig in 1888, where he heard lectures on metaphysics from leading experimental psychologist Wilhelm Wundt, among others (Joas 1997 [1985], 18). But there is little evidence that in his reading, or at Harvard or Leipzig, he had any real exposure to ongoing psychological (or other) laboratory experiments, outside of lectures and whatever conversation he may have had. Indeed, Mead apparently did not take any psychology courses with James at Harvard or with Wundt at Leipzig. This changed when Mead made the consequential choice to study at the University of Berlin (Friedrich-Wilhelms-Universität) after his first and only semester at Leipzig. In early 1889 he had the unexpected boon of consulting with G. Stanley Hall, "the most eminent physiological psychologist in America," who recommended Mead study with prominent psychiatrist and criminologist Enrico Morselli at the University of Turin.[5] Mead also exchanged letters with his erstwhile mentor William James, who apparently argued against Turin and for Berlin.

On the basis of new evidence, it is clear that one of the particularly significant factors in James's view was the presence of Hermann Ebbinghaus, a professor of experimental psychology in the Prussian capital. Just over a month after advising against study in Turin, James wrote a letter—part introduction, part recommendation—on Mead's behalf to Ebbinghaus. In that letter James asked Ebbinghaus to advise Mead on how best to pursue study leading to a doctorate at Berlin, adding, "I know [Mead] intimately and have the highest opinion of his moral as well as his intellectual character. . . . I should not think of so encroaching on your time, were I not assured of Mr. Mead's exceptional des[s]erts."[6]

James definitely recommended Mead to Ebbinghaus, and it seems quite likely he also recommended Ebbinghaus to Mead. In his published work, James was very enthusiastic about Ebbinghaus's (1913 [1885]) pathbreaking experimental study of memory, which he reviewed in the journal *Science* (James 1885), highlighting the ingenuity that went into the study and calling it an "original addition to heroic psychological literature" on the basis of the immense number of repetitive tests Ebbinghaus performed on himself. He discussed substantially several of the German experimentalist's works in his two-volume *Principles of Psychology* and other publications. He wrote in the *Principles* (James 1890, 1:548–49) that Ebbinghaus's recent critical examinations of the anomalies of "psychophysics" elaborated "probably the most 'real' hypothesis" to date to explain the postulated relationships between physical stimulus and perceived sensation.[7] This was an exceptional claim for him to make in light of the massive literature that had developed on the topic. Ebbinghaus reciprocated by discussing James's *Principles* in depth in his advanced seminars from the early 1890s.[8]

By his second semester at Berlin, Mead was a participant in Ebbinghaus's experimental psychology laboratory.[9] Indeed, the only class for which he registered that semester was Ebbinghaus's advanced course on "Psychology with Consideration of Experimental and Physiological Psychology." In Ebbinghaus's laboratory, Mead worked with a small group of other research assistants: Emil Böse, Paul Nikalaus Cossmann, Max Dessoir, Franz Eulenburg, Carl (or Karl) Pappenheim, K. A. Oskar Relander, Charles A. Strong, and Arthur Wreschner. The laboratory at the time was reportedly relatively small and only moderately equipped despite the university's premier status (Krohn 1892). Only a few of the students conducted independent experiments; most apparently worked with Ebbinghaus or other more advanced students on their projects, likely helping to devise experimental procedures and apparatuses and perhaps serving as experimental subjects on occasion.

The experiments being conducted at the time when Mead was a laboratory assistant included studies of color perception, with examination of after-images and partial color-blindness, by Ebbinghaus (1890, 1893); studies of the sensations in the skin, including touch, pressure, proprioception or "muscle-sense," and temperature, by Dessoir, with aid from Hermann Munk's veterinary institute (discussed below) and help administering experiments from Wreschner (Dessoir 1892; Krohn 1892); and perhaps additional experiments on the perception of lifted weights conducted over several years by Wreschner (1898). Charles A. Strong wrote to his former teacher William James on January 5, 1890, specifically identifying one of the ways in which Mead spent his time in the laboratory:

I am taking [Ebbinghaus's] *Übungen* [laboratory exercises] this term, and find him overflowing with ideas and good humor, a man of superb vigor. I am working with Mead, a man who took his [bachelor's] degree at Harvard not long ago, over the Hipp Chronoscope, just to get an idea of the instrument; a Finlander [i.e., Relander] is the third member of the party. (James 1999, 4)

The chronoscope (discussed further below) was the standard device for the measurement of reaction times in psycho-physiological experiments. According to Strong, these experiments seem to have been primarily didactic (at least for him) in the sense that he undertook them to gain practice at using such devices effectively. Strong's correspondence does not mention whether these chronoscope experiments conducted by Mead, Relander, and himself were intended to contribute to any of the substantive ongoing studies in Ebbinghaus's laboratory.

All of these sets of experiments have in common a huge number of repetitions and variations of tests, ingenious mechanical apparatuses devised to precisely measure the desired phenomena under controlled conditions and rule out alternatives, and a focus on the relationships between physiological and psychological events. If Ebbinghaus's published works are any indication of his laboratory supervision and instruction, Mead would have been exposed to a rigorous but not dogmatic scientific methodology: a method that did not rule out possibilities prior to test, did not ignore the messiness of scientific practice but attempted to address it with conscientious precautions and checks, employed systematic measures (including statistical measures of standard error) for the determination of relative confidence in results, and sought to craft explanations based on parsimonious principles consistent with the latest findings of other scientific disciplines (cf. Boring 1950, 386–92).

In 1890, at the very time Mead was working in the psychology laboratory, Ebbinghaus and Arthur König cofounded the *Zeitschrift für Physiologie und Psychologie der Sinnesorgane* (Journal of Physiology and Psychology of the Sense-Organs), a periodical for which the specificity of the name belies the general range of its topics. In the first issues of the journal, Mead's lab mate Charles A. Strong wrote reviews of English-language works on the anatomy of the brain and sense organs and Ebbinghaus wrote reviews and original contributions on the controversies of psychophysics. In addition to these, there was a remarkable range of other works reporting the latest experiments and theories on perception, physiology, plant biology, the history of psychology, and broadly related topics. Ebbinghaus's journal immediately became the premier independent psychology journal in the German language; its rival, Wundt's *Philosophische Studien*, primarily published the results and views of the Leipzig laboratory (Boring 1950, 389). Because Mead was closely associated with Ebbinghaus at the time, it seems quite likely that he read at least portions of the *Zeitschrift* during or shortly after his time at Berlin.

From Ebbinghaus's journal or through his lab mate Dessoir, or both, Mead was almost certainly exposed to the controversies then beginning to boil over in German academia regarding the possibility of subjecting paranormal phenomena to psychological experiments along the lines pursued by London's Society for Psychical Research and the psychiatric clinics in France. Dessoir had cofounded the Gesellschaft für Experimental-Psychologie zu Berlin (Society for Experimental Psychology in Berlin) in late 1888 to investigate such phenomena as hypnotism, telekinesis, clairvoyance, hallucination, somnambulism, and other forms of "parapsychology"—a term Dessoir coined (Wolffram 2009). In its first years the Berlin group reportedly conducted hundreds of different research experiments on parapsychological phenomena, some almost definitely involving students at the university, where several of the core members of the society worked.[10] And in 1889 Dessoir gave a talk to his society on the hypnotic experiments in the study of "double consciousness"—*das Doppel-Ich* (Dessoir 1890). Mead's lab mate, Charles Strong, even reported to their shared former teacher William James that he had attended a meeting of the society during which Dessoir read "a brilliant paper on the different disciplines of psychology and the relation of each to hypnotism," and that as a result Dessoir invited him to apply for formal admission to the society (James 1999, 2–3). In Ebbinghaus's *Zeitschrift* and Wundt's *Philosophische Studien* in Leipzig there were also major contentious discussions about parapsychology in the early 1890s.

From his lectures with Wilhelm Waldeyer in General Anatomy and Hermann Munk in Physiology, Mead gained a thorough understanding of the workings of the central nervous system that built on his previous physiology course at Oberlin. Both professors were already well known for their scientific discoveries, and were in the process of new discoveries while Mead was at Berlin. Waldeyer was at work on a synthesis of recent neuroanatomy, which led to the first articulation of the coherent "neuron theory," that identified the "neuron"—a term Waldeyer coined—as the fundamental functional unit of the central nervous system, which was in turn built up by the connections between these units (Waldeyer 1891). Waldeyer also made comparative study of the brains of various apes and was director of the anatomical theater at the University of Berlin, where he held lectures. He was known to illustrate his anatomical lectures, which naturally focused on the nervous system, with demonstration dissections of brains and displays of hardened brain preparations, by means of which he led students methodically through the "regions of the brain and cord; the finer anatomy, nuclei of the cranial nerves, and especially the course of fibres" (Taylor 1893).

Hermann Munk was in charge of the veterinary institute associated with the university and was known for his detailed work on the functions of the cerebral cortex (Munk 1890). James (1890, 1:41–42) credited Munk's experiments with demonstrating the distinction between "sensorial" blindness (insensitivity to light) and "psychic" blindness (inability to distinguish meaningful objects from visual impressions) and demonstrating the "hemiopic" nature of vision (that the hemispheres of the brain control different sides of the eyes)—although James also derided Munk's "absolute tone" and "theoretic arrogance."[11] On the basis of his experiments in which he observed the behavioral changes resulting from ablating or removing different portions of the brains of dogs, monkeys, rabbits, and birds, Munk was a major proponent of the localization of mental functions, especially of the occipital cortex as a center for vision. Dessoir (1947, 223) recalled later that after Munk's lectures he would discuss the controversial or difficult issues with groups of interested students, and that his experimental work, which students could observe in the veterinary institute, was far more extensive and rigorous than his slim publication record suggested. Again, Charles Strong described the experimentation that went on in Munk's laboratory in his January 5, 1890, letter to William James:

> I spoke up one day and asked Munk if I might n't have a chance to experiment a little on frogs, and Dessoir at once said he would like to participate. Munk assented, and since then we have had a table to ourselves in one corner of the laboratory, and while Munk in his old coat is applying the electrodes to dog's brains at the other side of the room, Dessoir & I dissect out nerve-muscle-preparations, stimulate beheaded frogs & study their reflex motions, prepare dead ones for the Bell experiment [i.e., stimulation of certain nerves resulting in twitching of the specimen's muscles], etc. (James 1999, 2–3)

Among Mead's instructors at Berlin, Waldeyer, Munk, Ebbinghaus, Wilhelm Dilthey, and Gustav Schmoller were active members of the Royal Prussian Academy of Sciences during his study there. Indeed, although

it is easy to make a supposed distinction between philosophers and scientists, it is important to recall that these boundaries were not located
along the lines that we might suppose. For example, Ebbinghaus was officially listed in the philosophical faculty of Berlin, while Waldeyer and
Munk were on the medical faculty. During the time Mead was at Berlin,
Dilthey (2010 [1890]) published what he called a "psychological analysis"
of the "origin of our belief in the reality of the external world," which
engaged with the recent work of physiologists, neurologists, experimental
psychologists, and others in attempting to solve one of the ultimate problems of critical philosophy.[12] And the philosopher Friedrich Paulsen, with
whom Mead took the most philosophy classes, was himself a student of
psychophysical psychology and a leading figure in contemporary debates
about pedagogical psychology.[13]

The research and teaching of the individuals placed them as partisans
in making claims about the relations between empirical science and philosophy, on the nature of cause and explanation in mental phenomena, on
the relation between the physiological features of the body and the experience of the psyche, on the nature of measurements and tests, and on the
social or moral consequences of science. Indeed, as Joas (1997 [1985], 18)
has pointed out, Mead's time at Berlin was in the years immediately prior
to the major contention between Ebbinghaus and Dilthey (two of Mead's
primary professors) regarding whether the fundamental nature of psychology was explanatory-natural scientific or descriptive-interpretive. The fact
that Mead moved out of Ebbinghaus's laboratory and proposed a thesis under Dilthey, along with his later criticisms of psychophysical psychology
(discussed below), seem to indicate that this incipient controversy (however experienced in the years leading up to it) was not without an impact
on Mead. It was in Berlin, more than in his previous education, that Mead
encountered contemporary scientific controversies firsthand, embodied in
his own participation in experiments, lectures, and reading.

One might even add before leaving the topic that Mead's dentist in Berlin was also a scientific innovator: Willoughby Dayton Miller, professor
of operative dentistry at the University of Berlin, was the first dentist to
publicly champion the revolutionary consolidated "germ theory" of Ber-

lin medical professor Robert Koch, in whose laboratory Miller worked.
And right at the time that Mead was seeing him (repeatedly) for a painful
tooth abscess, in March 1889, Miller was first preparing to publish his argument that bacterial microorganisms could be shown to be the cause of
large classes of oral disease, a proposition that would become the basis of
later dental pathology (Miller 1890, 1891).[14] Miller, of course, developed the

practical consequences of his theory in his dental practice, especially in his use of antiseptics in surgery.

PRACTICING EXPERIMENTAL PSYCHOLOGY

Mead did not complete his degree at the University of Berlin, having been offered a position as instructor in the philosophy department at the University of Michigan beginning in autumn 1891, with special focus on physiological psychology and the history of philosophy. Over the course of the next three years in Ann Arbor, Mead began to deploy the knowledge and skills he had developed in designing experiments of his own and in teaching experimental physiological psychology. Mead's attempts to develop studies of psychical phenomena were far more extensive than is typically acknowledged, and ranged into examinations of neurology, animal behavior, and parapsychology as well as psychophysical experiments.

In his first year at Michigan he began to formulate a philosophy, notably in collaboration with department chairman John Dewey, that understood the human mind to be part of functional organic processes of action, and identified those individual actions as phases of a larger social process (Cook 1993, 28–31). He wrote to his wife's parents at the end of that first year of this new synthesis of "abstract philosophy and daily life," and identified his particular task in this endeavor:

> For me in Physiological Psychology the especial problem is to recognize that our psychical life can be read in the functions of our bodies— that it is not the brain that thinks but the [sic] our organs in so far as they act together in processes of life. This is quite a new standpoint for the science and has a good many important consequences—especially does it offer new methods of experiment which must be worked out.[15]

This also echoes Dewey's view at the time, that physiological psychology was "on present methods" merely "experimenting without any universal or principle," but that he, Alfred H. Lloyd, and Mead were at work on a "hypothesis for unifying mental phenomena which can be tested in the laboratory" beginning with the functional "reflex arc" process or circuit, in order to give meaning to "studies of time reactions, r[h]ythm, time perception, & attention." Dewey noted that in spring 1892 they were "just getting into shape for some laboratory experimenting."[16] Thus, although Mead worked hard (in between his six new courses that year) to develop a standpoint from which to design meaningful experiments, he apparently did not do much actual experimenting on this new basis in his first year at Michigan.

By the end of the 1892–93 year Mead had definitely designed and carried out experiments along the lines he had been planning. Dewey wrote in May 1893 that Mead was at work on the "biological side" of sensation: "He is trying to see if one could get back of the present qualities and show the sensation as a condensation or precipitation of past organic activities, so that everything which is aesthetic now was once practical or teleological."[17] Dewey and Mead were also planning experiments on "mental images" in order to assess attention and rhythm. They were beginning to test propositions that would be central to the "functional psychology" that they developed in the following years, which argued in part that the action of biological organisms in accomplishing practical ends was the fundamental process that generated what we treat in our more complex personal experience as sensation, representation, and other "mental" or "psychical" phenomena. After two years together Dewey and Mead were only beginning to be able to subject their hypotheses about the nature of mental life to meaningful experimentation, no doubt in part because of the untilled soil they sought to work. Likely many of these experiments were conducted on themselves (as Ebbinghaus had done to such "heroic" effect), but there are reasons to believe that they were also conducted on, and with the help of, Mead's students in psychology, a topic discussed further in the text.

At least part of the difficulty in carrying out experiments lay not in the conceptual difficulties, but in practical limitations. Mead wrote to his father-in-law in 1893:

> I am getting my laboratory into greater activity all the time. This week I shall have electricity as a motor-power and then can start my measuring apparatus. It is very hard to get a time-measuring apparatus that can be depended upon for small intervals of time for all of these chronometers require some electromagnet, and the lag which these always involve can not be calculated accurately.[18]

Until their last year at Michigan, Mead and Dewey relied on mechanical apparatuses with magnetic mechanisms for recording reaction time intervals (almost surely a Hipp chronoscope, the standard equipment for such work, an apparatus with which Mead had previous practice, and one in use at the time in the physiological laboratory at Michigan). Chronoscopes and other such devices were a major topic of discussion and frustration in late nineteenth-century psychophysical experiments, where much time and effort was spent ensuring the proper calibration of equipment and attempting to correct errors in measurement (Canales 2009; Daston and Galison 2007).

A description of the experimental psychology laboratory from February 1893 detailed the substantial additions to the "meager supply of apparatus" made over the last year in order to assess very fine differences in reaction: a kymograph with recording drums to finely measure muscle reactions, a "reochord" to measure electrical resistance, a variety of precise time-marking devices, apparatuses for testing perceptions of sound tone (including a specially tempered harmonium) and stereoscopic vision, and other "instruments for anthropometric study" along the lines of Francis Galton's studies, all in addition to the "ingenious though simple" custom apparatus designed and built by Henry S. Carhart, professor of physics at Michigan and specialist on electrodynamic mechanisms, to replace the existing chronoscope.[19] With these new devices, Mead wrote to his father-in-law, he hoped to study attention, "trying to get some simpler expression for it than is given now," and to assess the "connection between the senses of temperature and that of pressure."

Further, these apparatuses apparently led Mead to reflect on the problems of measurement as such, and in particular to articulate a critique of the view that small measurement differences in physics and psychology—the so-called personal equation in experiments—were evidence of a "psychical" field or substance that existed in addition to (i.e., had a separate existence from) physiological processes of measurement that could be measured as a psychical quantum (Mead 1894a). Instead, he argued to the gathered scholars at the American Psychological Association in December 1893 that the "psychical" existed through means-ends action in the accomplishment of practical life processes and hence was not a separate "something" that could be measured apart from physiological processes.[20] Of course the converse of this proposition is that, in Mead's argument, the space and time measured are also ultimately constructions of the organism in interaction with its environment, such that it makes no sense to talk about a separate objective environment apart from the organisms that co-constitute it. In this presentation and in his reviews in the first volume of the *Psychological Review* (Mead 1894c, 1894d), Mead posited that his standpoint provided a key to making psychology consistent with the other sciences—as something within rather than merely accompanying biological and physical phenomena. It is perhaps fitting that just as he gained access to higher-precision measuring devices, Mead concluded that these devices could not do away with the practical accomplishment of measurement. This conclusion was not based on ignorance, but on serious attempts to work through the minutiae of experimental study with some of the latest technologies designed precisely for that purpose over the course of four years.

Little known is that during his time at Michigan Mead also made studies of human nervous tissues. In the same letter to his father-in-law in which he wrote of getting electric power for his apparatuses, Mead also remarked that his "study of the nervous system [was] going on as well." And the February 1893 description of the laboratory noted that the experimental psychology courses that year were going to examine "the nervous system studied from the standpoint of its function in the organism, the results of efforts to localize functions in the brain, and the light which pathological cases throw upon this subject. The use of brain models and slides and undissected brains from the medical department is granted [to the psychology] department." In fact, Mead was even preparing his own brain specimens as part of his work. According to Henry Castle, who was staying with the Meads at the time, Mead had a bit of a "sad affair" one morning in December 1893 when he destroyed equipment and nearly burned down his laboratory in an effort to prepare a brain specimen by curing it overnight under a gas lamp.[21] Among the equipment destroyed was a "valuable microscope," indicating that Mead was likely making his own histological studies of the neurological tissues he prepared. And he was using facilities from the biology department to investigate "some of the lowest forms of the metazoa" in order to determine "to what extent the nutritive functions of the animal influence the development of the sense organs."[22] A former student of Mead's psychology classes also reportedly recalled that his laboratory instruction included the "tedious routine" of dissecting frogs (Raphelson 1968, 9).

During this time, Mead was conducting behavioral studies of live animals as well. This much is directly intimated by the university calendar, which for 1892–93 described Mead's advanced psychological seminar as including "investigations into psychical phenomena of living organisms" with "laboratory work and lectures" and his Experimental Psychology class as giving a "statement of psychological problems in terms of the organism" with "lectures, demonstrations, and experiments."[23] An announcement for the psychology department in June 1893 announced a "line" of investigation and coursework on "Comparative Psychology so-called; a study, that is, of the psychology of lower animal forms" that would be developed with students suitably prepared in biology into "a study of the method of the evolution of animal intelligence."[24] Conducting behavioral studies of living organisms made perfect sense from the standpoint of functional psychology precisely because they would demonstrate "psychical phenomena" through the actual responsive behavior of the organism. Although detailed evidence into the particular studies made is lacking, it appears that functional psychological study of animal behavior predates the move of Dewey and Mead to Chicago and the later development there of rigorous animal behavior experiments in a specially designed laboratory by John B. Watson, Harvey Carr, and others.

In June 1894, just as his last school year teaching at the University of Michigan ended, Mead gave a talk on the possibility of using hypnotism as an anesthetic in dentistry to a well-attended meeting of the Michigan Dental Association; the paper was later published in extenso as Mead's first full-length professional journal article (Mead 1895a).[25] In the talk he reviewed the long history of hypnotic suggestion and its therapeutic effects from ancient Greece and Egypt through medieval Europe to the present, and then listed at length the scientific research into hypnotism that had been done over the previous century (including that of Dessoir and several other Berliners). Drawing from this review of the professional literature, he argued that "suggestion" is the fundamental psychological process involved in hypnotism, and that it is not a pathological condition but rather a normal one: every object of our attention tends to call out immediate reactions that "hypnotize" us in that sense. Hypnotic states, then, are in psychological terms merely heightened suggestive conditions in which there is an absence of multiple stimuli to check immediate reactions (Mead 1895a, 9, 33). After detailing and criticizing Wundt's theory of hypnotism, which relied on a hypothesized (but not fully substantiated) parallelism between psychological and physiological conditions in explaining the phenomena, Mead outlined case studies of the therapeutic applications of hypnotism culled from recent German-language literature on the topic and concluded by advocating caution in light of potential dangers to prevent the indiscriminate use of hypnotism.

Oral comments were made on Mead's talk by two Michigan dentists, who added further testimony of the usefulness of hypnotic suggestion as a dental anesthetic from their employment of such techniques in their own practices.[26] Although there is no indication from the paper that Mead made any independent examinations of hypnotism, it does indicate his wide reading on the topic, and notes that, at one point in his research, he did ask people about their experiences being hypnotized (Mead 1895a, 37).[27] Moreover, the paper indicates Mead's self-conscious reflection on his own experience of interpersonal suggestion, for example, "if, in the twilight, a friend should point out to me some dark object and call it a dog, out of the dim outlines my eye would construct through the memory images which I have of these animals, the picture of a dog" (33–34). Indeed, this is the first published work by Mead that strongly attests to his early thinking about the complex influences of interpersonal relationships.

Much of Mead's previous learning, apprenticeship, and experiment came together in the 1893–94 two-semester course on "Special Topics in Psychology," which according to the University of Michigan's announcement of courses covered "some of the chief points of psychology (sense-perception, attention, instinct, psycho-physical law, hypnotism, etc.), from the standpoint of modern experimental methods" accompanied by readings in James's *Principles of Psychology* and G. T. Ladd's *Elements of Physiological Psychology.*[28] This was the final advanced seminar on experimental psychology given by Mead at Michigan. But in this case we do not have to rely on the course description because a set of notes exists for this class, taken down by student Robert Clair Campbell.[29] According to the notes, the course began with a detailed exposition of the basic distinctions made in the field between the physical and psychical, and their relations. While the physical is always experienced through consciousness, the physical is also a continuous and necessary condition of the psychical. Psychological or mental experience is accomplished through the physiological processes of the nervous system—what Mead called the "simple nervous arc" at one point. Indeed, memory, recognition, judgment, association, and attention are all explained in terms of normal processes of action, in Mead's course. The nature of the act of which they are a part becomes the determinant of how and when ideas or objects are associated, recalled, separated, or attended to. In Mead's quasi-Hegelian terms used throughout, the action project was the "identical element," the "whole" present in and "governing" each of the "parts." Each act is connected with other acts in more complex action projects, and ultimately in the "general life process" as the largest "whole." In order to make this theory relatable, Mead repeatedly used illustrations drawn from everyday life, especially a scenario of a person who has to walk to the post office in order to pay bills by mail, which he used to help explain the nature of habitual action, the conditions of recognition of objects, conscious deliberation as the problem-solving of inhibited action, and the location of acts as phases within larger acts.[30]

In this course Mead reported quite extensively on his experimental work on the nervous system and sense organs, animal behavior studies, and psychophysical experiments. Mead gave detailed descriptions of both the gross and microscopic structure of the nervous system and of the eyes, ears, and skin. For example, on the basis of his experiments on the skin, he apparently proposed to the class that sensations of smoothness, hardness, and wetness were second-order constructions built from combinations of the primary perceptions of pressure and temperature (136–37). Regarding the brain, Mead argued that there are a variety of ways of experimentally assessing the localization of mental functions—"vivisection in animals," "dissection of peculiar specimens of humanity," "watch [the] actions of ind[ividual who is] diseased & dissect brain after death"—still, the brain does not appear to have any ultimate "center," but rather complex networks for the coordination of tendencies to act (145–46). His examinations of microorganisms apparently led him to conclusions about the evolution of the sense organs from an original "tactile" sense, and the development of sensitivity and motility as ultimately related to processes of gaining nutrition (89–90). Indeed, the "food process" was a central guiding thread in the course, apparently because in Mead's view it connected the functional psychology of action with evolutionary biology.

From observational study of the behavior of cats, Mead began to raise questions about the nature of "mental images" in the process of action. According to Campbell, Mead noted that a "cat's movements follow one another in such a way as to show that they are being used as means to an end" (51–52). But Mead was led to question whether this observation must necessarily be "explained by mental images," whereby a cat supposedly pursued definite ends-in-view like those identifiable in human conscious experience. According to the notes, Mead proposed that a solution could be found in a biological statement in terms of the "environment as determining the actions of life" rather than an (introspective) psychological statement in terms of will and mental image. Campbell's notes even seemingly report the data and results of a demonstration conducted in class on the time taken to make associations between pairs of words. Mead apparently argued that one could not, on the basis of such experiments, successfully distinguish a "psychical time," as some psychologists had posited, by subtracting the "reaction time" from the "total comprehension time" (119–21). Indeed, "there is nothing to show that it is not phys[iological] time," the "time required for the processes in the brain to take place." The notes also record many other specific points that were reported later in Mead's published works or his later lectures, including his physiological theory of emotion (1895b), his theory of hypnotic suggestion (1895a), and his proposal that the organism constructs the nature of its environment through its physiological sensitivity to particular stimuli (1932, 1934).

COMPARATIVE PSYCHOLOGY

By the time of the move to Chicago in autumn 1894, Mead's specialty was, according to Dewey's correspondence with President William Rainey Harper, primarily "comparative" rather than "experimental" psychology.[31] Mead had become quite critical of psychophysical tests, which by their very nature required elaborate technical apparatuses for the assessment of minute differences (typically of time), and most often established artificial conditions for the isolation of stimulus and response from normal, complex action processes. Whether Mead took up new independent neurological or behavioral studies at Chicago is not clear, but he definitely remained strongly interested in the activities of the psychological laboratory for many years.[32] Through reports of psychology students including John B. Watson, Jessie B. Allen (later Charters), and Wallace Craig (discussed in additional detail in chapter 4), it becomes clear that Mead spent many hours observing and offering suggestions on comparative psychological studies of rats, monkeys, guinea pigs, and pigeons until at least 1908.[33]

No doubt informed by his own studies and his observations of his students' laboratory studies, he wrote quite a few contributions to comparative psychology, including discussions of the nature of animal perception, cognition, instinct, and emotion, and a review of the early literature on the topic (Mead 1895b, 1904b, 1907d, 2001). Mead actively participated in the local "North Central" Psychological Association (also intermittently called the "Northwestern" or "Western" branch of the American Psychological Association), which alternated meetings between the University of Chicago and Northwestern University (cf. Campbell 2006). This is where he first publicly discussed the "Image or Sensation?" question in animal perception with former student W. C. Gore (Mead 1904b), heard Watson's "Imitation in Monkeys" (1908), and introduced his work on "social consciousness" and the "social self" (Mead 1910d, 1913a).[34]

In his first academic quarter at Chicago Mead began teaching a semi-regular course on comparative psychology, which was apparently the first course offered explicitly on that topic in any major American college.[35] For half a decade, his were the only courses on comparative psychology in the United States, and he continued to teach some version of the course a total of fifteen times through 1911. His first class was a two-quarter seminar in 1894–95 with sociologist W. I. Thomas, among others, as his first students (further discussed in chapter 4). Other subsequently well-known intellectuals who took Mead's early comparative psychology courses included psychologist Helen Bradford Thompson (later Woolley), social reformer

Frances Alice Kellor, and economist Wesley Clair Mitchell. After the split between the psychology and philosophy departments in 1904–5, he continued to teach the course with the qualification that it was "theoretical" comparative psychology; John B. Watson and later Harvey Carr (both of whom had taken courses from Mead) taught the corresponding "experimental" comparative psychology.

Among students who left records of the course are sociologist Charles A. Ellwood (1909, 1912) for 1899, philosopher and psychologist H. Heath Bawden (1901) for 1900, psychologist Walter Van Dyke Bingham for 1905, and social worker Juliet Hammond for 1911.[36] Bawden's existing notes from the 1900 course, in particular, offer a remarkable picture of the ways Mead's early engagement with comparative psychology set the conditions for his examination of reflective intelligence. For Mead, according to Bawden, intelligence was defined biologically in terms of functional control of the environment by an organism, and hence digestion, circulation, and breathing are all part of intelligence in this comparative organic sense. This dissolves the absolute distinction between an objective environment and a self-enclosed organism by positing that there is an environment only to the extent that particular sensitivities exist for different organic forms. And Mead thought that this perspective could offer a clear evolutionary principle for the co-constitution of particular environments and organic capacities, especially in the increased control over nutritive processes. Complexity of control comes in two forms of increasing mediation, through social organization and through the sophistication of manipulatory capacities in the organism. Complexity of mediation was thus the organic basis for the distinction of different levels of intelligent activity. Mead considered in detail the manipulatory capacities of organisms like spiders, and the "social" differentiation of species like ants and bees, before concluding that one could find the particular conditions for the development of human intelligence in the combination of the human hand and vocal communication. Indeed, by 1900, as indicated by Bawden's notes, Mead apparently had developed the basic outline of his theory of the emergence of significant symbols through the organization of vocal gestures in the social-communicative act.

Mead is, of course, most well remembered for his theory of the social nature and genesis of the self. But to focus only on the published articles that explicitly elaborate that perspective beginning in about 1910 is to make problematic distinctions in Mead's work. After all, he was in his late forties by then, and had been teaching, researching, and writing for two decades. More to the point, without understanding some of the previ-

ous work Mead had undertaken one is liable to make one-sided or erroneous assessments of his arguments. In particular, Mead's "behaviorism,"
his discussion of gesture, his criticisms of the parallelism of Wundt and
the "expression of emotions" of Darwin, his critiques of the notions of
instinct and imitation, and his distinction between animal and human
intelligence, all fundamentally depend on his experimentation and observation of animal behavior. That is, they are not merely abstract, theoretical points made on the basis of anecdote and intuition, although *Mind,
Self, and Society* and other works may make them appear so. The kind of
argument Mead made in his later social psychology lectures becomes understandable as a project on the basis of his previous work. Otherwise, the
criteria Mead set for such inquiry into the emergence of human reflective
intelligence—for example, that an explanation should not presuppose the
existence of any particular innate self-indicative or representational faculties because they are not demonstrable from the intelligent behavior of
animals—could appear as mere thought experiments from unnecessarily
restrictive, arbitrary premises. On the contrary, Mead's work on the problems of animal learning and intelligence in his comparative psychology
led him to push as far as possible the logic of a nonreflective intelligence,
and to look for indicators of intelligence in organic behavior rather than
by analogy with one's own introspective experience, both of which in turn
informed the conditions of his examination of how the peculiar capacities
of humans developed and were manifested.[37]

When Mead referred in his social psychological lectures and essays to
the features of human physiology, it was not an idle or conciliatory gesture. One might instead note that Mead took seriously, and wrote explicitly into his social psychology, the whole functioning of human bodies—
what Joas (1997 [1985]) has aptly termed and examined in detail as Mead's
"practical intersubjectivity." It is essential to the theory that the humans
who interact have not only central nervous systems for the coordination
and selection of actions, but also bones articulated in a particular manner so as to manipulate (and hence, to construct) objects and produce particular gestures, muscles for the accomplishment of actual movement in
space and time, particularly configured senses (especially hearing, sight,
and touch) for the attuning of humans physiologically to the actions of one
another, alimentary tracts for the basic processing and emergence of an environment that attracts and continually stimulates the organism in a way
that also rejuvenates it, a cardiopulmonary apparatus for the accomplishment of tension and rhythm in action (and hence of emotion). All these
features are explicitly treated—in their specificity—as intrinsic to the

accomplishment of human social life. In contrast, Mead (e.g., 1930, 1934) thought that even the work of his peers, including Charles H. Cooley, was marred by an understanding of human interaction in which bodies were treated primarily as the occasion for symbols, representations, or images of one another. To imply, as certain passages of James's and Cooley's work seemed to do according to Mead (1934, 173), that the human self is primarily an affective-cognitive phenomenon based around a "feeling" of self in the individual's experience, is to make distinctions that, from Mead's perspective, depend on the social-physiological process of human action having already accomplished the possibility of reflective intelligence.

Mead was a person who got his hands dirty quite literally in calibrating mechanical apparatuses, handling animals, and dissecting and preparing neurological specimens. As a result, when he spoke and wrote about psychological measurement, the nature of animal perception, or the physiology of emotion, his opinions and claims were based on his own actual tests and engagement with contemporary work by others. These were topics in which he was trained and in which he conducted independent investigations. Mead was engaged firsthand in the processes of scientific discovery in these endeavors, although his own published works often belie that personal experience.[38] Indeed, Mead's frequent references to the nature of problem solving of the research scientist in experiment and laboratory are not mere metaphors for him but express Mead's own experiences with the ways in which science is practically accomplished as any other problem solving activity.

CONCLUSION

John Dewey, seemingly ever an attentive observer of his friend, wrote of Mead shortly after his death:

> His interest in the concept of emergence is, for example, a reflex of that factor of his own intellectual experience by which new insights were constantly budding and having then to be joined to what he had thought previously, instead of merely displacing old ideas. He *felt* within himself both the emergence of the new and the inevitable continuity of the new with the old." (Dewey 1932, 33–34, emphasis in original)

These remarks were made in Dewey's preface to the posthumously published Carus Lectures in which Mead treated the actual social process of investigation as a key to the problems of the philosophy of process, time, and relativity (Mead 1932, 7–10). In his remarks Dewey concisely encapsulated the way in which Mead's work continued to be a reflective response to his own experiences of discovery.

Mead's philosophy bears the imprint over and over of having been in contact with rigorous scientific investigation. He had a detailed, hands-on training in a variety of forms of scientific research in both his undergraduate and graduate work. In the latter, he was even one of a few advanced students who worked as laboratory assistants in the experimental psychology laboratory at Berlin. When he took up his first professional position at Michigan, he began designing experiments that could inform his emerging theoretical perspective, including experiments on higher mental functions, preparation of neurological specimens, and study of animal behavior. This work also informed his criticisms of the implications of psychophysical measurements, the nature of animal perception and cognition, and the mechanisms for the accomplishment of human reflective intelligence.

Through these endeavors, Mead worked to submit his own speculations to a rigorous sense of the conditions as they presented themselves to the experience of other people or nonhuman organisms. A sufficient explanation, then, requires one to work out the developments from those conditions. In this sense the task is considerably more challenging than projecting oneself into the place of another person or organism, because it requires a thorough disciplining at precisely those points where recourse to one's own experience would presolve the problems of the examination. Instead of being satisfied with an explanation of animal intelligence on the basis of mental representations, for example, Mead sought to attend to the biological nature of the organism in its functional sensitivities to the environment. Mead's philosophy is thus doubly structured around the actual process of inquiry in that it both explicates that process and exemplifies the process in its explication.

Mead's various assays into scientific hypothesis testing and examination were not mere passing phases of his interest. It is tempting to treat his philosophical oeuvre by glossing over the practical development of his conceptions over the course of his investigations. But this denies both the more emphatically particular aspects of Mead's various works and their no-less-emphatic dependence upon one another. In regard to the former, Mead worked in earnest on what may well seem to us as peculiar (and even misguided) investigations in laboratories and elsewhere over the first years of his professional career. His efforts at psychophysical experiments, curing brain specimens, or investigating the anesthetic benefits of hypnotism, are difficult to merely assimilate to Mead's later work. There is no indication that these endeavors were "in the service of" developing what we might consider Mead's "mature" social psychological work in the sense that he had this course in his mind from the start. That is, when one recognizes the serious investigations Mead made into these and other phenomena over the course of many years, one cannot adequately conceptualize them as mere way-stations on the route to a definite or presupposed endpoint.

Mead's later work is nevertheless dependent upon his earlier work. His examinations of the social nature of the self never eschewed his earlier physiological or neurological studies, but instead made them intrinsic to his later perspective. When Mead attempted to account for the formation of symbolic capacities, he sought to tie their formation to definite physiological "mechanisms." In this sense, we might say that the "symbolic" is continually and necessarily dependent on the "presymbolic" in Mead's work, even as symbolic communication fundamentally transforms the nature of physiological capacity by locating it in a more encompassing position capable of self-reflection and progressive change. As a result, an examination of his processes of discovery helps us gain a better understanding of a dynamic unity of Mead's work and expose Mead at his most self-reflective regarding the nature and progress of knowledge.

This examination, along with the others in this part, helps motivate the analysis of later chapters by allowing us to pose an important question more pointedly: how have these and other aspects of Mead's own production of knowledge been written out of the ways in which Mead was understood? What combination or emphasis placed elsewhere, practical limitations of time and attention, and opportunities opened or closed by the structure of academia help us account for the knowledge we have and the knowledge we do not?

CHAPTER THREE

Hawaiian Sojourns

In much of the critical literature, as discussed in the first chapter, the implicit context for G. H. Mead's ideas is Chicago: its social institutions, public problems, and faculty connections. And as my analysis has demonstrated, there are very good reasons for linking Mead to Chicago, where Mead lived for most of his adult life, and to underscore the importance of his social life and relationships in that city for his academic work. It is not necessary to deny the importance for Mead of Chicago (as well as Ann Arbor, Berlin, Leipzig, Oberlin, and South Hadley) to bring into question the use of Chicago as the essential index for the "context" of Mead's thought and writing. Indeed, such a view threatens to conflate context with place-of-residence in the analysis. Context becomes, in this view, an anchor or pushpin in our explanation that tethers connections of people and institutions to something that appears more-or-less definitely fixed or delimited. In order to raise questions about this view, I utilize the following extended examination to take Mead far away from his Chicago residence while remaining quite within his own immediate experience. This means pushing back against the notion of a single geographical context and delimited set of local social connections in understanding Mead's ideas.

The following sections identify the complex and influential impact of Hawaii on Mead by tracing the course of his experiences with those islands. Mead's engagement with Hawaii constitutes a whole domain of his social experience that is fundamentally underemphasized and has not previously been thoroughly examined, but which has an impact on the way we understand him as an intellectual and a historical person. As I demonstrate, the shift to Hawaii is not a displacement of Chicago but a way of showing how both geographical places take on their significance in relation to an individual's own course of social experiences—experiences that, at least sometimes, place locales in dialogue with one another. Hence, this analysis builds on and emphasizes rather than negates previous work on the importance of Mead's intellectual biography, and allows us to reflect more generally on the nature of context.

IMAGINING HAWAII

Mead was intrigued by the Hawaiian Islands long before he first visited them in the summer of 1897. His closest college friend, Henry Northrup Castle, and his friend's older sister and Mead's future wife, Helen Kingsbury Castle, were the children of one of the most prominent American settler families on the Islands. Their parents, Samuel Northrup and Mary Tenney Castle, had arrived with early missionaries to the Islands but were not ordained missionaries themselves (Castle 2004, 14ff.).[1] Samuel Castle, who arrived in 1837 with his first wife Angeline Tenney (Mary's sister, who died in 1841), helped handle the financial matters of the missionaries and eventually set up a private business with a partner, Amos Starr Cooke. By investing in the rapidly expanding sugar production industry, Castle & Cooke became one of the "Big Five" companies that dominated commerce in the Kingdom of Hawaii, the brief Republic of Hawaii, and the subsequent US Territory of Hawaii. As a college student, Mead heard stories about the Islands from Henry, and he saw scenic pictures sent to Henry by his sister Helen.[2] Mead (1902, 809) later wrote of his time at Oberlin that Henry "could see beauty in the skies and trees of Oberlin, because he had seen so much greater beauty in Hawaii. His descriptions of the Islands seemed to me then somewhat mythical." George Mead and Henry Castle also lived together in Cambridge, Massachusetts, and in Leipzig and Berlin, Germany, as they continued their education, and they kept up a correspondence when they were apart that contained many mentions of the Islands.

The grief shared by George Mead and Helen Castle over the death of Henry's first wife in a carriage accident in Honolulu in 1890 made Hawaii all the more real to Mead. Frida (Steckner) Castle was a German woman whom they had all gotten to know well while studying in Germany. Mead wrote to Helen and Henry's sister, Harriet Castle Coleman: "You will understand how I have followed Henry with aching heart, and how I have constructed from Henry's and Helen's descriptions from the letters Helen has so kindly let me see and the photographs an almost visible picture of the beautiful home [in Honolulu] in which he has been so tenderly lifted up and supported."[3] The engagement and marriage of Helen Castle and

George Mead in Berlin was also likely fostered by their consolation of one another over this loss so close to them both (Cook 1993, 22).

After dabbling in legal practice in his brother William's law office following college, Henry Castle took up responsibilities as editor of the newspaper *The Pacific Commercial Advertiser* in Honolulu.[4] In spring 1892 Helen traveled back to the Islands (with Alice Chipman Dewey), and for several months in 1893 Henry stayed with the Meads in Ann Arbor, taking intermittent classes at the University of Michigan and participating in the discussions with the Deweys and Meads (Dewey 1997, no. 14129). In January 1893, when the hereditary ruler, Queen Liliuokalani, was overthrown by a group of settlers in favor of constitutional democracy and annexation to the United States, the Castles were vocal supporters of the revolution. The letters the Meads received from the Castles and discussions George had with his wife, his college friend, and others must have proved a unique education for him into the revolutionary republican politics of the settlers, and into the nature of society more generally.[5] He wrote in April 1894 to Helen and Henry's parents, "I have a tendency to envy Henry occasionally for the part which he has in such very moving events. To be experimenting in governments and social conditions on such a large scale is a laboratory practice which goes beyond my facilities."[6]

The Hawaiian Revolution was in many ways a major watershed event in American national identity. Having been only marginal to American policy until then—apart from figuring in debates about trade reciprocity and tariffs—Hawaii became one of the major contentious issues of American foreign policy in 1893. Republican President Benjamin Harrison agreed to a treaty of annexation with the revolutionary Provisional Government in his last weeks as president, but this action was immediately withdrawn by Democrat and anti-expansionist Grover Cleveland when inaugurated in March 1893. Cleveland briefly pushed to reseat the queen, but his administration became mired in debates with Congress and in two separate government investigations into the possible collusion of agents of the US government in the revolution (which would have made it an illegal military action against a sitting government instead of an internal revolution). These proceedings drew on without definite moves by the Cleveland administration either to forcibly reseat the queen or to annex the Islands. After Republican expansionist William McKinley was elected in 1896, the issue again arose in prominence, and renewed efforts were made by the government of the newly proclaimed Republic of Hawaii to promote annexation. But the decisive opportunity occurred after the United States became involved in the Spanish-American War in April 1898.

Among the issues discussed in heated congressional debates during this short war were Hawaii's strategic importance as an outpost in the Pacific, the risks of outside influence (especially from Japan) if annexation was further delayed, the economic opportunities that might result from annexation, and how to address the issue of the Islands' nonwhite majority population and labor force.[7] A special joint congressional resolution was signed into law on July 7, 1898, making Hawaii a US territory. It was the first US territory outside the North American continent, the first in the tropics, and the first acquisition in a rapid succession of outlying US possessions including the Philippines, Guam, Puerto Rico, and (as an independent protectorate) Cuba at the turn of the twentieth century. Indeed, Hawaii's annexation marked a turning point where American continental "Manifest Destiny" became American hemispheric "Imperialism"—a claim made explicitly and publicly in newspaper editorials and reports of congressional debates. In an address Mead attended, historian Frederick Jackson Turner (1911), famous for his "Significance of the Frontier in American History," argued that the United States had become an "imperial republic" as a result of its new overseas "dependencies and protectorates" in Hawaii and the Philippines and, thus, also a "new world-power, with a voice potential in the problems of Europe, Asia, and Africa."

Sociologist Robert E. Park, who in 1893 was a newspaper correspondent in Michigan, interviewed Helen Mead for a report on the revolution, and a letter she had received from one of her relatives was circulated on the Associated Press wire service across the country in December 1893.[8] Helen's brother William R. Castle, in addition to being a drafter of the original annexation treaty and special commissioner on behalf of the Republic of Hawaii to the United States, was on the "Committee of Public Safety" that instigated the revolution, and in the Provisional Government established after the coup he was president of the Board of Education. Her brother James B. Castle was Collector-General of Customs in the Finance Department of the Provisional Government and member of the Board of Immigration, and her brother-in-law Edward G. Hitchcock was retained as marshal, the highest law-enforcement officer in the Republic.

Henry Castle had in the meantime taken a new wife, Mabel Wing, a teacher in Honolulu, who was pregnant with their daughter, Elinor, when Henry left for Germany in autumn 1894 with his daughter from his first marriage, Dorothy. He wanted Dorothy to meet her German relatives and learn a bit of the language of her departed mother while he took up his philosophical studies again. While they were in Germany, there was an attempted counterrevolution in Hawaii in January 1895, and Henry made

preparations to hurry back. The steamship he and Dorothy took was struck
by another boat en route to the United States and they were both killed.
This tragedy, even more devastating than the first, happened at the beginning of Mead's second quarter teaching at Chicago. Jane Addams recalled
the effect of the tragedy in connecting the Meads firmly with Hawaii in
the minds of the other intellectuals and social reformers of the city:

> My first relationship with Helen Mead was during those early years of
> her husband's connection with the University, when their lives were
> suddenly overshadowed by a great tragedy. The loss of her brother and
> his little daughter by sea, as they are returning from Europe to the Ha-
> waiian Islands, seemed to set apart these young people so lately come
> to Chicago, not only in the shadow of the sorrow but to place them into
> the background of the mountains and waters of the Pacific.[9]

FIRST IMPRESSIONS

All this happened before George Mead ever stepped foot in Hawaii, which
he first did on July 1, 1897.[10] He was accompanied on his voyage by his wife
and toddler son, Henry Castle Albert Mead; his sister and her husband,
Alice E. Mead and Rev. Albert T. Swing, professor of church history at
Oberlin College; and his mother's twin sister, Harriet Storrs Billings. They
were met en route by several of Helen's relatives, who escorted them on
the long ocean voyage from San Francisco. The party was also soon met
in Honolulu by George's mother, Elizabeth Storrs Mead, who was president of Mount Holyoke College, and her traveling companion, Louise F.
Cowles, professor of geology and former acting president at Mount Holyoke. Indeed, several reports in Hawaiian newspapers heralded a genuine
"educational revival" happening in Honolulu that summer as a result of
such a large number of educators converging on the city (many of whom
were from this single party). The "revival" also included the future US
Commissioner of Education, Elmer E. Brown, who was then professor of
pedagogy at the University of California–Berkeley.[11]

Mead gave a lecture to the "Summer School," a special program of continuing education for Hawaii's teachers, on "The Relation between Play
and Education."[12] Brown was the featured lecturer over the summer, but
Mead and others gave special lectures. In his talk on the "Educational
Value of Play," Mead pointed out that in the kindergartens the spontaneous
play activity of the child was being increasingly made use of in education.
He argued that this was "following Nature's plan" in that animals also

learn by means of play. Instruction, he thus proposed, should be further structured so as to utilize the child's spontaneous interest at all levels of schooling. While this "cannot suddenly change our entire school system," Mead argued, it can tap the "great reservoir of energy" in the child and lead to better treatment and more productive study of children. In addition to this speech, the Meads likely participated in a variety of other discussions and observations of educational reforms in Honolulu that summer in connection with the Summer School, but I am unable to discover much documentation on this point.

While they were in Hawaii, the Meads had their share of society gatherings and extended family commitments. But these were often at the same time introductions into the politics of the Islands. For example, they were present at the formal gala and reception held by the newly arrived US minister to Hawaii, Harold M. Sewall, and his wife as part of the Independence Day celebrations at the American Legation.[13] Their social obligations also were the occasion for their travels outside metropolitan Honolulu, to Kaneohe Bay and the Koko Head Peninsula on Oahu, to Hilo on the island of Hawaii (the "Big Island"), and to Haleakala Volcano on Maui. At Kaneohe Bay they were treated to a native Hawaiian luau at the estate of Francis M. and Julie J. Swanzy, close friends of the Castles. On Maui, George Mead and several others hiked into the Haleakala crater while staying with Horatio B. Bailey, the son of a missionary who came over on the same voyage as Samuel Castle.[14] Perhaps most notably, the Meads toured the conditions of the native and immigrant populations on the island of Hawaii, likely in connection with the large sugar plantations owned by the Castles on that island. Upon returning to Honolulu, Mead reported his impressions to a meeting of the Hawaiian Mission Children's Society held at Helen's mother's home. According to a newspaper report of the meeting, Mead was "much impressed" by the scarcity of native Hawaiians and noted that the race relations on the island raised "many interesting social questions."[15]

This sentiment presages the considerable interest Hawaii would come to have as a "sociological laboratory" of race relations (e.g., Adams 1924), especially from the 1920s, with the development of the University of Hawaii's Department of Sociology and its Social Research Laboratory, and independent institutes like the Pan-Pacific Union and its Research Institution.[16] Speeches by Mead's brother-in-law Reverend Swing, his mother, and others also demonstrated a strong interest in Hawaii's intricate race relations and immigration issues. Of particular interest, there was a quickly growing population of Japanese and Chinese migrants, enticed by offers of employment on the labor-intensive sugarcane and fruit plantations, who had come to outnumber both the native Hawaiian population and the white settlers by large margins by the turn of the century.

Although in Chicago the Meads were close to many prominent social reformers and intellectuals, in Honolulu they were close to those in power, who were often members of their immediate family or their close personal associates. At one dinner and discussion of educational issues on August 8, 1907, for example, George Mead was in a small company consisting of the US Secretary of Commerce and Labor, a US Representative and future Speaker of the House, all of the first three territorial governors of Hawaii, and leading private citizens including a newspaper editor, a school superintendent, a top banker, several prominent lawyers, and the manager of a large plantation.[17] Helen's brother William R. Castle organized the dinner, and these prominent guests included two other Castle brothers and several of their business partners among the only twenty guests. And at their seasonally adopted home, Mary Tenney Castle's house in Honolulu, they had much the same caliber of interlocutors. As one account of the Castles' residence put it:

> Here was [a] genuine open house. All were welcome, but the fiber of the informal organization that tacitly understood the Castle home to be headquarters had in it the individualities that build states. Religious, literary, musical and aid and auxiliary societies here had their birth and were forwarded and given permanent place in the great field of usefulness which had its hot house or nursery within the walls of the old homestead's inviting parlor. Many movements of the greatest moment and most lasting and beneficial effect to the church, to society at large, to the various nationalities assembled in the Islands were launched from the Castle place. On the occasions of extraordinary gatherings in Honolulu the house was well understood to be a haven of rest and entertainment for friends from out of town till the last inch of space was in use. (Towse 1900, 135)

The Meads stayed in Hawaii for seventy-eight days during that 1897 trip, beginning their return journey just in time for the start of autumn classes at the University of Chicago. This is a journey that George and Helen made at least twelve subsequent times, always for extended stays, over the next three decades, and they also arranged travel to the Islands for several prominent friends, including Jane Addams, John and Alice Dewey, and Harriet Park Thomas.[18] This first voyage set the tone of many later sojourns by its combination of social gatherings, nature hikes, and public speeches.

When he returned to Chicago in September 1897, George Mead was involved in several public debates about Hawaiian annexation to the United States, which became the occasion for penetrating work on the nature of democratic social institutions. In addition to organizing talks on annexation at the University of Chicago's Sociology Club and participating in the discussions on the issue at the Commercial Club of Chicago, Mead wrote a long article for the *Chicago Tribune* that was published January 22, 1898.[19] In that piece, he argued that there was an aspect of the situation that had been almost completely ignored in public discussion, but that fundamentally changed the stakes: annexation did not negate, but rather depended on, the self-ruling capacity of the population of Hawaii.[20] Just as American municipalities must have self-supporting local institutions, so must any territory to be annexed, he wrote. But at the same time, annexation could ensure that, by incorporating them in a larger set of social institutions, local political rivalries would not threaten the stability of the territory as a whole. This transformed the question of annexation, in Mead's view, into one of whether the Republic of Hawaii had sufficient democratic customs and traditions to perform the tasks of self-governance if annexed and whether annexation could help protect and foster those institutions.

The bulk of the article, then, turns to examining the institutions of Hawaii, including its government, schools, churches, public works, and especially its industry. Mead detailed the massive scale of plantation production in the republic and its pervasive influence on the class and race structures. A few wealthy firms dominated industrial production, headed by a small group of owners. Unlike British "crown colonies," however, these owners were not primarily absentees, and so had personal and financial interests in addressing the "problems of government and social organization that have to be met." There was a "mechanic class" of mostly white settlers who enjoy "political privileges" but did not have the same influence in business matters. The "laboring class" was primarily made up of Chinese and Japanese immigrants, who had not entered into the "social life of the community" because they did not have a "common heritage of political power, civilization, or race to protect them against the pressure of money-getting as represented in Occidental employers."[21] The dwindling population of native Hawaiians, Mead thought, was completely marginalized in this industrial economic structure except as fishers or sailors for interisland trade. He worried that the native Hawaiians were likely to die out, a consequence of "the deadly gift of civilization," despite the prevailing protective attitude of "their white friends."

The racially stratified economic system, and especially the conditions of the laboring class, were problematic for the growth of American democratic institutions, he acknowledged, but he thought that at the same time labor conditions were improving and could be further improved by the regularization of trade reciprocity with the United States and by furthering the practical work of building institutions that had been started by missionaries. It was, after all, Mead wrote, the missionary "element" that rebelled against the perceived authoritarianism of the monarchy, that reformed property rights to protect and promote individual property ownership by natives, and that introduced vocational education, which gave the natives a "living chance in the new world into which they have been so rapidly ushered." That the "white community" has been able to maintain "the essentials of good government" under these "exigencies," Mead wrote, demonstrated that when such institutions were "assured by annexation" the Hawaiians would be capable of self-government.

Especially noteworthy about this article is that it is Mead's first published examination of a complex social group as a whole. While his formative experiences witnessing the social reform movements in Germany and especially his exposure to the complex problems of metropolitan Chicago should not be underestimated, it is in reference to Hawaii that Mead first attempted to grasp the essential structuring principles of a society rather than to focus on a particular problem or institution. One need not agree with all aspects of his analysis—the paternalistic stance of the argument with regard to the native and East Asian immigrant populations, for example—in order to recognize a sober attempt to comprehend the workings of a dynamic social whole and to reframe a contentious public debate. And the article attempts to accomplish these goals not in an abstract or idealistic way by mere appeals to the consciousness of community or ethical duty, but by means of an examination of the specific interlocking of social, economic, and political institutions. Not only that, it reports on the complex problems of Hawaii to a Chicago readership. And although as a newspaper article it is necessarily brief, it could be read as a novel contribution to the kind of institutionalist political economics in development at the University of Chicago (especially by Thorstein Veblen and Wesley C. Mitchell) through its institutional analysis of race and political influence in a rapidly changing society.

When Hawaii was formally annexed in July 1898 the Meads were back in the Islands, and participated firsthand in the events. For example,

George Mead led a small group up the slopes of the volcanic cone outside of Honolulu, Diamond Head, and planted the American flag at the peak, taking "formal possession in the name of the United States" on July 16.[22] That summer, by arrangement of the Castles and others interested in education, the teachers' Summer School was headed by Col. Francis W. Parker, the head of Cook County Normal School (the premier teachers' college in the Chicago area), and the person John Dewey (1930) once called the "father of the progressive educational movement." His wife, Frances (or Frank) Stuart Parker, and her colleague Annie E. Allen, also gave public lectures; both were instructors at Cook County Normal School, in oratory and kindergarten training, respectively. The Parkers stayed with Helen's relatives and held discussions with the Meads while in Hawaii (Parker 1909).[23] The newspapers also recognized Helen Mead's pioneering efforts that year to establish "university extension" programs in Hawaii—a move to democratize higher education by providing broader access to university lectures for those unable to attend regular classes.[24] The following summer, though the Meads did not travel to Hawaii, they likely helped arrange to have John Dewey head the Summer School lectures. That year, Dewey furthered the work to establish a permanent system of university extension lectures and assayed the growing immigrant slums of Honolulu in person.[25]

The Castle family had a long-standing commitment to the promotion of education through their positions in the government and local schools and through their extensive philanthropy. For example, Samuel Castle had been trustee and treasurer of Oahu College (later known as Punahou School), an independent school system founded initially for missionaries' children and later expanded to public enrollment. All of the Castle children had attended the school, and Helen, her sisters Caroline and Harriet, and Henry Castle's second wife Mabel all taught there for periods of time.[26] In 1894, with the death of Samuel, the family devoted a large portion of their substantial personal assets to a permanent charitable trust in his name. And with the death of Henry Castle and his daughter Dorothy, they used monies from the trust to create the Henry and Dorothy Castle Memorial Kindergarten. The trust also contributed a large sum to the founding of the Free Kindergarten and Children's Aid Association in 1895, and continued to support it over the years (Castle 2004).

The family's increasing connections to the luminaries of the progressive education movement through Helen and George Mead, especially to John Dewey, led them to invest significant funds in experimental education projects, including Dewey's Laboratory School in Chicago, and to extended research and educational stays for Harriet Castle Coleman in Chicago (Castle 1989, 2004). In particular, the Castles donated money for the furnishing of Dewey's Laboratory School facilities and an initial fund for teachers' salaries, both through their trust and as individuals. Teachers trained at the University of Chicago Laboratory School were brought to Hawaii to staff the new institutions like the Castle Kindergarten (Castle 2004, 39ff.). Because of the influence of the Castles and others interested in progressive education in Hawaii, it became something of an early center for such experimental efforts (Castle 2004, 42; Towse 1900, 134), while similar reforms promoted in American cities, it appears, often encountered more substantial resistance from existing educational interests. Many of the educational institutions established by the Samuel N. Castle Benevolent Trust (later incorporated as the Samuel N. and Mary T. Castle Foundation, partly on Mead's advice) are still in operation in Hawaii, and the foundation continues to be active in educational philanthropy.

HAWAII IN MEAD'S WORK

From Mead's early experiences of Hawaii, he had apparently become enough of an authority on the topic to be asked to review the latest literature on the social and political history of Hawaii for the *American Historical Review*.[27] In that work, he argued there was a growing fascination in the United States for Hawaii that must be attributed to a combination of causes: (1) the territory's "political situation" as "(virtually) our one real colony," (2) the "dramatic events" of Grover Cleveland's attempt to reinstate Queen Liliuokalani after the revolution led by American settlers deposed her, (3) the "religious interest" in the Islands as the "scene of the most rapid work of evangelization that has ever attended our modern missionary work," and (4) the "anthropological interest in the islanders and their primitive society and its institutions" (Mead 1900b, 786–87). In the course of his review of Edmund J. Carpenter's *America in Hawaii* and Lucien Young's *The Real Hawaii*, Mead drew from his own personal knowledge of the recent events to confirm, emphasize, and correct aspects of their accounts of the political history leading to annexation of the territory. In particular, he underscored the lengths to which President Cleveland was apparently willing to go in a "situation with which he was too little conversant," by authorizing the use of American naval force to reseat the queen, and he deemphasized the role of British intrigues in the process (789–90).

Perhaps more noteworthy in regard to the work for which Mead is primarily known, however, is that this set of reviews is the earliest in which he took seriously comparative ethnological evidence in understanding the nature of social structure and development. In reference to William F. Blackman's *The Making of Hawaii: A Study in Social Evolution* Mead pointed out that the examination of native Hawaiian culture calls into question academic assumptions about primitive peoples. For example, despite the lack of industrial economic organization, there was a highly organized political structure, which Blackman argued had its origins in the development of religion. That is, political power among the natives was at its core priestly power organized along lines of magic, fetish, and idol, and was not constituted primarily by economic power (Mead 1900b, 787). The review is also Mead's first mention of the idea of "double" selves, as part of Hawaiian religious experience. The recognition that many different cultures have some notion of a *Doppelgänger* was a key support, Mead (1934, 140) later argued, for the claim that responding to one's self as a social object is universal in human experience. In addition, Blackman questioned notions of an undifferentiated primitive communalism, which he argued was assumed in much anthropological work, by demonstrating the complex social arrangements, such as monogamous marriages, of native Hawaiians (Mead 1900b, 787). To Mead, Blackman's work demonstrated that the lack of industrial development (from restrictions like a natural lack of metals) had not likewise involved a "restriction of social advance" on native Hawaiian society.

Mead also addressed Blackman's multifaceted handling of the impacts of Western settlement on native society, including acknowledgment of the devastation of disease, the strain of industrial production, the change of food and clothing customs, the introduction of alcohol, the "removal of most of the motives for effort and activity which had given them stimuli for life and continuous interest in it," and the detrimental effects of missionaries' "rigid conceptions of morality that were too far distant from the social organization they attempted to reform." Those missionaries brought institutions such as schools and trades that promoted the "social and political education" of "characteristics of independence, self-reliance, social and political intelligence and fundamental righteousness," but at the same time these institutions paved the way for the "crowding out" of native life by large-scale whaling and sugar production performed by East Asian immigrants, and resulted in the virtual "extinction" of the native population (Mead 1900b, 788).

Over the course of regular travels to Hawaii, Mead continued to make efforts to study the social conditions of Hawaii and to give public talks, much as he did in Chicago. In 1905 Mead gave talks on "The Relation of

School and Home" to the Mothers and Teachers Club of the Honolulu
Young Women's Christian Association, on "A Philosopher's Diagnosis of
the Times" to the Research Club of Honolulu, and on "Moral Consciousness" as a lay sermon to the Central Union Church.[28] During that same
stay, Mead traveled with his son, his brother-in-law William R. Castle,
and Castle's law firm partner D. L. Withington, to the Kona District on
the island of Hawaii. They were there to promote Castle's plan to encour-
age sugarcane growth in the district, especially among small independent
planters, and to assess plans to build a cooperative mill to grind the cane
of small planters.[29] This and other like excursions gave Mead closer access
to the problems and practical realities of everyday life for a wide variety of
social strata on the Islands—something much closer to an ethnographic
sensibility than to an armchair philosopher.[30]

Mead's public talks in the territory were, thus, not merely the occasion for him to address the problems of Chicago to Hawaiian audiences.
For example, despite his considerable knowledge of municipal reform in
Chicago, his talk on "Recent Municipal Movements" to the Research
Club of Honolulu on September 18, 1907, took as its topic "the new charter
of the city and county of Honolulu and the work of the recent [Territo-
rial] Legislature" as well as "immigration matters" in the Islands. A report of the talk described Mead as "thoroughly at home with his subject"
and the talk as having "created quite an interest among the listeners."[31]
Mead spoke as "a strong believer in the rights of the people in the matter
of public utilities" and contrasted the progress that European municipalities had made in public ownership of utilities with the failures of such efforts in the United States. From this point of view, he criticized the new
municipal charter of Honolulu for failing to limit the "franchise giving
powers of the [Municipal] Board of Supervisors," noting that all franchises
granted by a city "should be adequately safeguarded by law from possible
corrupt officials and a just proportion of profit from them made returnable
to the city."[32]

In several cases, he seems to have explicitly connected his social reform
work in the two cities, Chicago and Honolulu. On November 13, 1899, he
spoke at Hull House on the "Hawaiian Islands"; his talk was accompanied
by stereopticon slides, which presented his audience with vivid images of
the territory.[33] Later, on September 14, 1909, Mead gave a keynote address
about social settlement work at the opening ceremonies of a new gymnasium building at the Palama Settlement, Honolulu's settlement house
modeled after Chicago's Hull House.[34] And in his major address on the
"basis and function" of the social settlement movement to the students

of the University of Chicago, he used anecdotes from his discussions with scientists studying leprosy in Hawaii in order to illustrate the new "moral consciousness" at the base of the settlements and other ameliorative work: increasingly, social betterment was not treated as "an obligation to undertake a disagreeable duty" but rather a "growing interest in an intellectually interesting problem" through the application of scientific methods to human problems (Mead 1908a, 109–10).[35] When Mead talked about "strikes and the general sociological problems arising from them" to the University Club in Honolulu on September 15, 1911, he relied upon his recent experiences of the meat packers' and garment workers' strikes in Chicago as illustrations to discuss the problems facing any industrializing city.[36] The local parallels were clear enough to Hawaiians, who had witnessed their largest strike to date from May to August 1909; at its peak over 7,000 Japanese workers were on strike for higher wages equal to those of other plantation workers (Kotani 1985, 30ff.). Mead had been in the Islands in the aftermath of the strike in 1909, which had included workers on the plantations owned by the Castles, and during that summer he toured the conditions of agricultural workers alongside Territorial Governor Walter F. Frear.[37] When Mead lectured on "vocational training in public schools" to the teachers' Summer School in 1913 he was addressing a topic of practical concern for both Hawaii's and Chicago's massive labor classes.[38] Although the cities—Chicago and Honolulu—were of different orders of magnitude at the turn of the twentieth century, they were experiencing many of the same social problems connected with rapid expansion and industrialization, including assimilation of immigrants, contentious race relations, disease epidemics, overtaxed education systems and other public services, and labor unrest.

HAWAII AS OFFICIAL DUTY AND AS SPORT

Mead not only spoke as an authority in Hawaii, but also spoke on behalf of Hawaii in an official capacity on at least one occasion. A National Farm Land Congress was called to discuss the various issues of agriculture in the United States and suggest new national agricultural policy in November 1909 in Chicago, and delegates were appointed from the various states and territories of the country to attend. Governor Walter F. Frear officially named Mead the head delegate for Hawaii and his personal representative to that convention.[39] He was reportedly appointed because of "his familiarity with the people, conditions and public lands of Hawaii, having on several of his visits there accompanied Governor Frear on trips of investigation."[40] Mead's primary obligation for the Congress was to speak on the conditions and opportunities of agriculture in the territory, which he did on the morning of November 18 to a large assembly in the grand ballroom of the newly finished luxury La Salle Hotel in downtown Chicago. In his speech he gave detailed figures regarding the production of sugarcane, pineapple, banana, avocado, coconut, cassava, rubber, matting sedge, sisal, castor, and hemp, and assessed the possibilities of increasing the production of coffee, cotton, soybeans, and tobacco.[41] He identified the practical considerations intrinsic to the production of different crops, including the scale at which they had to be grown to be profitable, the number of years before a mature yield could be expected, the availability of public and private lands, the efforts needed to clear vegetation for planting, the amount of labor and initial capital needed to have a reasonable chance of success, and the needs of interior and oversea transportation of crops. This level of detail, he hoped, would be

> sufficient to indicate the kind of an undertaking which the American farmer will shoulder in going to the Hawaiian Islands. . . . His task will be to understand a new type of agriculture under new conditions. He will be trying an experiment of his own fortunes and perhaps of the fortunes of the Islands themselves. The prospect is one to appeal to the imagination of the man with energy and intelligence.[42]

This analysis was also couched in an appeal for Americans to take possession of the Islands "more completely" through residence and cultivation in the wake of the "tide of oriental population which has threatened to take possession of the gateway to our Western Coast!" The constitutional government, commercial and agricultural production, American schools, and churches developed by missionaries had created a community of American "sentiment and institution" that was unified, at least externally, by annexation. But industrial production, especially the sugar industry, imposed the necessity of a massive labor force such that out of 170,000 people living in the territory at the time, only 13,000 were "in all essentials Americans," 35,000 were native Hawaiians, and the rest were immigrants from Japan, China, Korea, Portugal, Spain, Puerto Rico, and elsewhere. Mead even warned that "the power that holds Hawaii commands the western coast of the continent and has the only base of supply for over 2000 miles." That is, the speech appealed to nationalist concerns as well as economic ones in promoting American opportunities for settlement in the territory. Precisely because Mead was acting in an official capacity it

is difficult to assess how committed he was to the call outlined in the
paper. However, it appears not to be inconsistent with Mead's later view,
articulated especially in relation to World War I, that American national
security was implicated in the integrity and expansion of its democratic
institutions. And this speech, along with his other discussions of the social institutions of territorial Hawaii, suggests that it was with reference
to Hawaii that Mead outlined this view early in his intellectual career. It
is worth noting that, despite his extensive reform work, Mead appears not
to have held a comparable official role on behalf of another government.

In addition to the occasions Hawaii afforded to examine social institutions, the landscape was also something to be experienced, for Mead,
through physical exertion. As has already been pointed out, Mead and others frequently toured rural agricultural conditions and, beginning with his
first stay in Hawaii, he hiked up and into volcanic craters on many occasions. Although these hikes were often leisurely excursions, there were
several times in which Mead was in real danger. On January 11–12, 1905,
for example, Mead became lost overnight among the unmarked trails in
the Manoa Valley outside Honolulu on his way back from a hike up Mount
Olympus in early afternoon.[43] He was reportedly discovered by Japanese
employees of the Castles in the middle of the night who had been looking
for him for several hours, but on the way back two of the men fell down a
steep embankment and one man suffered a head wound that was initially
thought fatal, although he reportedly recovered. Mead almost fell as well,
according to reports, and then rushed back up the trail to find help for the
injured man, which caused him to become lost again. He was discovered at
dawn suffering from exposure, cold and hungry, by mounted police officers
who had been summoned when the previous search party returned injured
and without him. The report of the rescue in the *Hawaiian Star* newspaper
called Mead "a very hardy mountain climber" who, if not for losing his
way, would have made the "severe" hike "without inconvenience," and
the *Honolulu Evening Bulletin* noted that when Mead got back to Chicago
"he will probably recall his visit to Honolulu more vividly by a reference
to getting lost in the wilds than by any native folk-lore that he may have
acquired while in Hawaii."

Mead's most thoroughly documented hike was apparently a tour of the
Na Pali region (now Na Pali Coast State Park) on the island of Kauai in
late August 1909. George Mead and his son Henry accompanied Governor
Frear and others on a tour of tropical flora, volcanic precipices, waterfalls,
and other natural features by foot, "sampan" boat, and horseback over at
least five days, camping each night.[44] During the trip, the party toured

coffee plantations worked by Korean laborers and were guided, educated, and entertained by groups of native Hawaiians (Frear 1911). The tour also served as an exploratory survey of hydrological conditions on the island, conducted by US Geological Survey experts Marshall O. Leighton and Walter C. Mendenhall, who had recently arrived in Hawaii for that purpose. The survey was the first of its kind, and newspaper accounts noted that it signaled "the beginning of Hawaii's participation in the national movement for the conservation of natural resources," a move strongly endorsed by the territorial governor.[45] In addition to newspaper reports, Frear prepared his own extensive account of the tour, accompanied by photographs taken by geologist Mendenhall and apparently written in the form of a guide and enticement to potential tourists (Frear 1911).[46] One of Mendenhall's seven published photographs captures George Mead, his face shaded by a cap, standing on a precipice in Honopu Canyon with Governor Frear and others (see fig. 3.1). In his article, Frear called Honopu "perhaps the most wildly picturesque, weird, wonder-inspiring valley in Hawaii" (25). No doubt this part leisure, part survey, part promotional tour was one of the major events that led to Mead's representation of Hawaii at the Farm Land Congress in Chicago three months later.

In another incident on September 4, 1911, Mead was part of an expedition of the recently formed "Trail and Mountain Club" led by Governor Frear attempting a record climb up the Palolo Valley on Oahu, along the Ka'au Crater ridge to the highest summit, and down into the Waimanalo coastal area.[47] During a grueling part of the climb down precipitous slopes in a dense fog the group used fastened ropes, and at one point a landslide reportedly carried Mead to the verge of a "pali," or volcanic cliff, where he lay unconscious until revived. He suffered a sprained wrist in the course of the climb as well, and after finishing the descent he elected to call a car for the return trip. Several other members of the twelve-man party reported almost falling to their deaths or suffering serious injuries, including the territorial governor, who "more than once balanced on the edge of eternity and a pali." Although that incident appears to have been the peak of Mead's experiences with strenuous mountain climbing, he was reportedly still hiking mountain trails during his 1928 summer vacation in New Hampshire, at the age of sixty-five.[48]

Although Mead has previously been acknowledged as an avid bicyclist and jogger (Miller 1973, xxxii–xxxiv), attention has not been paid to his participation in a wide variety of hiking and climbing activities. Moreover, these activities were not merely tests of physical exertion and exercise for Mead. His high-risk mountain hikes, especially, were apparently

Figure 3.1. G. H. Mead on precipice in Honopu Canyon, Kauai. *Source*:
"Descending from Honopu Canyon," photograph taken by W. C. Mendenhall
August 1909, published in *Mid-Pacific Magazine* 1, no. 1 (January 1911): 18.
The original caption identifies the individuals (from top) as "Senator E. A.
Knudsen, Prof. G. H. Mead, Artist J. A. Wilder, Governor W. F. Frear."

the occasion for Mead to reflect (after the fact) on the nature of spatial perception as dependent on the possibilities of action, and on the "construction" of new physical objects in the process of solving practical problems.
Mead used illustrations of this kind in which individuals were hypotheti-
cally confronted by a "chasm," "cliff," "ditch," or "precipice," for example,
over and over in his manuscripts and published works (e.g., Mead 1903a,
103; 1934, 122–23; 1936, 116–17; 1938, 11, 114, 131, 143, 179, 261, 369, 376;
2001, 51). He also used mountain vistas and hikes in his examples of the
ways in which humans take a social, rather than merely physical, attitude
toward nature (1926a, 386; 1934, 183–84). As with other experiences drawn
from practical life, he used examples of this kind in his lectures as illustrations to which students could relate.[49] It is in such instances that one
can see quite emphatically the physiological or "embodied" nature of the
processes of consciousness for Mead, and can perhaps witness his own autobiographical affirmations of this understanding. Dewey (1931, 312) even
noted that those who accompanied Mead on "his walks through mountains, where his physical energy and courage never flagged" told him "how
naturally and spontaneously any turn of the landscape evoked from [Mead]
a memory of English poetry that associated itself with what he saw and
deeply felt in nature."

CONCLUSION

Look back into the past for Mead, even when done critically, begins with
a construct of its object. The existing historical literature on Mead has, of
course, contributed to our understanding by recontextualizing Mead and
his ideas in relation to Chicago and elsewhere. To the extent that a concept like "context" has a real critical edge, however, it is in the ability
to remind us that our taken-for-granted view of an individual, no matter
how thorough, seeks to encompass or make finite for our own purposes
something that necessarily belongs to other times and places than our
own. In order to further substantiate this view in a more concrete way, the
chapter turned to investigating the wide-ranging significance of Hawaii
for Mead. He became strongly invested in Hawaii from his college days on,
as his closest personal relationships and some of his most affecting personal losses were directly tied to those islands. By the time he first visited,
Mead had been exposed to ardent talk and vivid images of the people and
places, especially in relation to revolution and annexation. Over his many
long sojourns on the Hawaiian Islands Mead was introduced firsthand to

its pressing social issues by leading citizens, and became a participant in its public debates. He served on an official behalf for the territory and explored its landscapes, all the while reflecting on the broader significance of the problems of the moment and placing them in dialogue with analogous issues from elsewhere in his experience.[50]

In a sense, we find that Mead's thoughts about society and action did not merely extend out from Chicago, as extrapolations from the peculiarities of its social politics. Nor did his thoughts merely come as if from nowhere, without the impress of actual social practices. They are ruminations that owe much to setting the practical problems of several concrete social experiences in dialogue with one another—as when the problems of Honolulu and Chicago were explicitly used to inform each other.[51] By putting them firmly in a different context, Hawaii brings together and helps specify the relations between various aspects of Mead's public life—social settlements, education (vocational, university, kindergarten), democratic governance, social consciousness, race relations. And in connection with Hawaii, perhaps even more than Chicago, one gets a sense of how Mead worked to understand social transformation as a process that is eminently problematic and complex, but at the same time is responsive to social action and constituted by definite social institutions. In this light, context comes to mean a focus on the course of social experience of a historical person outside our own, tracing the development of actions and ideas over an individual's changing configuration of immediate social situations.

Moreover, it is in Hawaii that we witness Mead in a rather peculiar role, as the dependent and beneficiary. We cannot readily retain the notion of a theorist who discovers knowledge on his own. Indeed, we cannot even reasonably retain the image of a person who gains social knowledge by merely electing to join in the various goings on—that is, one where the ends are social knowledge and betterment but where the means or occasions are individual will. In Hawaii, Mead was fundamentally dependent on personal guides and intermediaries for his participation in and understanding of social life—cicerones who pointed out the local features, not only of the geographical, but also of the social, economic, and political landscape. If Mead had any advantage in these situations it was in his thorough knowledge and practical experience of analogous social problems that he could bring to bear in understanding his peculiar Pacific surroundings. And it is in Hawaii that we get an especially vivid understanding of how George Mead was dependent, above all others, on his wife Helen—her connections, resources, and experience. This is a milieu into which she initiated him, and in which her family name, not his, served as the passkey.

If this is more than a mere muddying of the waters it should point the direction for subsequent analyses of this study, and ultimately toward a reconceptualization of aspects of the way knowledge is produced by and about an individual in modern academia. The charge from the above analyses is to follow these leads along the tracks of the actual social experiences of those who have attempted to understand Mead. It is easy enough, on the basis of the above analyses, to point to a difference between Mead as a historical person—the public intellectual, laboratory scientist, and traveler—and a set of received notions about Mead. The real challenge is not to jump from one to the other or dismiss one account or another but to follow the empirical trails leading from one to the other in identifiable sequences of social action. Accordingly, the following chapter turns toward an analysis of Mead's classroom instruction, a set of situations in which Mead's speaking and writing are implicated in the many projects and problems of his students, and in which we can ask more pointed questions about the nature and direction of social influence on the formation of ideas. From there we are able to follow in detail the ways Mead's own understandings are interrelated with those of his students and colleagues, which are central to the processes by which a certain set of documents and concepts become attributed to Mead.

PART II

Notes and Books

CHAPTER FOUR

Lectures, Classrooms, and Students

George Herbert Mead is well remembered as a profound lecturer whose classes had a major impact on his students. At his memorial service his long-time colleagues emphasized this point. Edward S. Ames, who spoke first, remarked:

> [Mead's] class room lectures were vigorous pulsations of out-reaching, exploring thought. Students might take the same course more than once and yet find it new and radiant. His lectures were the fruit of searching study but they were never confined to manuscript or even to the sketchiest notes. He simply sat behind his desk, and while his hands toyed with a piece of chalk, his mind unfolded fresh and profound interpretations of philosophy and life. (E. S. Ames 1931, 4–5)

And James H. Tufts, who closed the service, added:

> [Mead] was a stimulating teacher. An alumnus who had elected a somewhat advanced undergraduate course under him remarked to me some years later: "We sat there on the front seats while he poured out his wealth of learning, shot through with flashes of insight and interpretation. Some of it went over our heads, but we got a vision of something high and large to look up to and work toward." To advanced students he was an inspiration. At one time I had occasion to take account of the theses for the doctorate in preparation, and found that nearly or quite half had their inception in his lectures. The lecture was his medium, as the seminar was that of Addison Moore, and each was master of his chosen instrument. (Tufts 1931, 26)

Similar statements may be found in a variety of remembrances published later by former students, in manuscript interviews and questionnaires from former University of Chicago graduate students, in correspondence of Mead's former students to one another, and in reviews of the books based on materials from Mead's lectures.[1] In the written documents of Mead's students, it is not uncommon to find remarkable statements of admiration and devotion. Surely one of the most unabashed is that of George E. M. Shelburg in a letter to Charles Morris:

> In explanation of my attitude toward Mr. Mead, and hence toward his lectures, I may say that I felt as I attended his classes a reverence akin to worship, a respect and an inspiration such as no other lecturer or lecture at the University ever called forth. Here is some one who had a vision, a sight of a new land and came back to report on it simply and fearlessly. It was not a diluted version or a rehash of the report of some other pilgrim, for search the library as one would, one never found his tracks.[2]

Indeed, the prevailing understanding of Mead's work already depends predominately on material from Mead's lauded courses. As I detail more fully in chapter 7, over four-fifths of all journal article citations to Mead since the mid-twentieth century (over 6,000 citations) have been references to *Mind, Self, and Society: From the Standpoint of a Social Behaviorist* (1934), which was compiled posthumously from students' and stenographers' notes from a variety of Mead's courses. Likewise, *Movements of Thought in the Nineteenth Century* (1936), and portions of *The Philosophy of the Act* (1938) are constructed from materials that originated in classroom lectures, and *The Philosophy of the Present* (1932) in lectures to a professional association. The claims made in published scholarship over the last century about what Mead really meant have relied heavily on reference either to these written records of Mead's lectures or to his students' recollections of their courses with him. And in recent decades, a new wave of publications based on students' notes from Mead's courses has appeared, including *The Individual and the Social Self* (1982) edited by David L. Miller, *The Philosophy of Education* (2008a) edited by Gert Biesta and Daniel Tröhler, and "The Evolution of the Psychical Element" (2008b) edited by Kevin Decker. While critical scholarship has sometimes advocated restraint in the use of lectures to stand for Mead's philosophy (e.g., Joas 1997 [1985], 46), other recent works have called for the cautious reappraisal of materials from Mead's lectures (Decker 2008; Silva 2003).

In this chapter I attempt to demonstrate that in order to learn something new from Mead's lectures we have to approach them with different questions, and that by doing so we can also begin to identify process dynamics in the production of knowledge more generally. If we attempt to ask only what the lecture notes can or cannot definitively tell us about Mead's philosophy we risk missing the opportunity to examine them in the complex social contexts in which they were created, and thus cannot overcome the difficulties of the texts as records. By studying the social context of Mead's courses, this chapter also serves as a preface to subsequent analyses by establishing a distinction between how notes were used by students in this pedagogical situation and how some of them were later used in publications and public contentions about what Mead meant. This analysis highlights problems regarding the supposed "authorship" of statements, the purposes of lectures in knowledge, and the structure of knowledge production in pedagogical situations of teacher and students.

The data I have brought together for this chapter are as follows: (1) the complete records of every individual Mead taught in every course he taught at the University of Chicago, from a restricted-access archival collection of instructors' records.[3] (2) Seventy-nine sets of notes from students and stenographers taken in those classes with Mead that I have discovered over the course of my archival research. This body of notes is every set I have been able to discover in archives available to public research, and is the most comprehensive group of such data brought together for examination.[4] A complete listing of the student notes I found forms an appendix to this study. Through this archival research I have also gathered a wide variety of correspondence regarding Mead's courses from former students that is essential to the analysis. (3) I have documented all references to Mead in over 1,000 dissertations and theses at the University of Chicago in selected disciplines from 1894 through 1935, including 111 theses that make some mention of Mead.

LECTURES AS PROBLEMS

Before addressing the surviving materials that seem to offer a record of Mead's speech in the classroom, it is worth considering some of the problematics of the classroom itself. First, the decision of what should count as a proper lecture is more challenging than one might suspect. Mead taught not only lecture classes at the University of Chicago, but also various seminars and other collaborative courses. He also gave courses at Michigan (1891–94) and Berkeley (1929).[5] He gave lectures in the University

Extension division to nontraditional students and to audiences of social-workers-in-training at the Chicago School of Civics and Philanthropy and the Chicago Commons School of Social Economics. Indeed, Mead spoke in front of a wide variety of professional associations as well as civic organizations and private clubs. If we admit all of these as potential sources for a full accounting of Mead's public life, then we lose something of the specificity of the formal lecture. This solution ultimately substitutes a problem concerning the boundaries of the lecture for one concerning the boundaries of public speech. And we are still confronted with serious questions of authorship if, as demonstrated in chapter 1, many of Mead's publications originate in public speeches and most of his speeches were made in settings of dialogue with other individuals.

The problem cannot be avoided altogether by restricting the study only to Mead's regularly scheduled lecture courses as the University of Chicago. First, the relationship between courses and instructors was not always simple. For example, in John Dewey's 1899–1900 Theory of Logic, the course that in some ways formed the centerpiece of his teaching at Chicago, Mead and Tufts each gave introductory lectures while Dewey was delayed in returning from his summer travels to Hawaii.[6] Substituting for one another, it appears, was not uncommon practice among the instructors at Chicago, but little of this is acknowledged in the way courses are attributed to particular instructors. In fact, courses like the long-running "Movements of Thought" (begun at Michigan and brought by Dewey to Chicago) or the introductory courses in logic and ethics were taught at different times by virtually all the professors of philosophy at Chicago, as were more advanced courses on individual philosophers, including Kant and Hegel. As a result, they posed at least some limitations for their individual instructors. Sometimes multiquarter sequences of courses offered by different professors were designed to neatly dovetail with one another, further limiting the capriciousness of any one course.[7] And as academic departments split off from one another, courses by almost the same name—including several in social psychology—were offered concurrently in different departments (a topic I address in greater depth in chapter 7). In this environment it is difficult to establish an irrefutable claim that a particular course of lectures expresses only the intentions of its designated lecturer and not a host of other considerations.

In addition, even in the classroom Mead did not have the same relationship to his students across all his class offerings. Mead's courses at Chicago ranged in size from an audience of one (in the winter 1907 seminar on the Logic of Mathematics taken only by Arthur R. Schweitzer) to at least eighty-seven (in the spring 1916 Social Psychology course). Although Mead is known primarily as a lecturer, he gave twenty courses at the University of Chicago that were specifically identified as "seminars," and a total of seventy-nine courses with fewer than ten students. Over half of these small courses of under ten students took place in the first decade of Mead's thirty-six-year career at Chicago, and during this period virtually the only courses that were over ten students that Mead taught were the introductory lecture courses on logic, ethics, and the history of philosophy. Evidence suggests that Mead likely preferred the smaller courses with "advanced" students to the larger introductory lectures.[8]

Despite the connection implied between giving lectures and having large audiences, one can trace Mead's continued preference for small advanced courses, both in seminar and in lecture format. Figure 4.1 displays the fluctuations in total enrollment for Mead's social psychology classes by quarter. Note, first, that Mead offered the course more frequently (including twice in 1910 and 1912) as the attendance began to rise. When the numbers more than doubled after 1913, Mead instated a regular seminar in "Social Consciousness" in order to work through advanced issues in smaller groups—the seminar had sixteen attendees (including eight auditors) in 1913, its first year.[9]

The explosion of registrants for Mead's lectures came primarily from

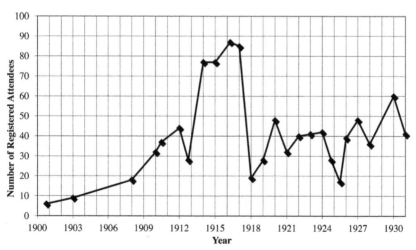

Figure 4.1. Registered students in Mead's social psychology courses by date. *Source*: Adapted from Examiners' and Instructors' Grade Reports, vols. 9–156.

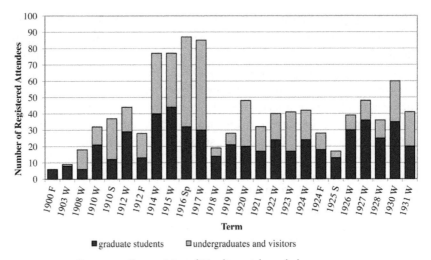

Figure 4.2. Composition of Mead's social psychology courses.
Source: Adapted from Examiners' and Instructors' Grade Reports, vols. 9–156.

undergraduates and interested nonstudents, not from graduate-student enrollment.[10] Figure 4.2 demonstrates that although the graduate enrollment
fluctuated, it does not account for the peak attendance, nor did it fluctuate
nearly as much as the enrollment of undergraduates. Indeed, in the largest
course he ever gave, the spring 1916 Social Psychology, Mead lectured to
forty-four undergraduates, thirty-two graduate students, and eleven registered visitors (and likely others not registered). After 1917 Mead's course
became reconfigured as "Advanced Social Psychology," open primarily
only to graduate students or those who had previously taken newly formulated introductory courses. While this alleviated the demographic pressures for the moment, Mead retained his Social Consciousness seminar as
well. In 1917, Mead also began offering credit to advanced students as research and grading assistants in his larger courses, which no doubt further
mitigated the workload.[11]

In the philosophy department at Chicago great stress was placed on
the proper structuring of classroom and research environments for advanced students, especially when the faculty's ability to do so was under
threat. Over the first three decades of the university's existence, according
to department chair James H. Tufts, the physical space of the philosophy
department was moved seven times, and was "virtually deprived of any
home."[12] Each time a move was proposed, the priorities of the department

were effectively the same: enough space for their departmental library to be freely accessible to their advanced students and dedicated seminar rooms close to (preferably opening onto) the departmental library. This departmental library and seminar arrangement was central to the mode of scholarly knowledge production they developed, and especially to the instruction and research of advanced students, where the books and journals apparently figured as frequent, integral participants in the discussions.[13] The importance of this access was only underscored as the size of the graduate student enrollment expanded rapidly after World War I; as Tufts put it, they did not question "the importance of undergraduate work," but put their stress on ensuring that "facilities for graduate work should not be so seriously impaired" in light of the fact that graduate enrollment was "considerably greater than it has ever been before."[14]

The registered visitors to Mead's classes were often also a considerable presence, as the 1916 Social Psychology numbers already demonstrate, although they are easily overlooked. Over his career at Chicago he had 140 different individuals register as visitors in his classes (many of whom also took classes from Mead for credit in other quarters), and at least twenty-eight of them registered as a visitor for more than one class. Although the records do not provide direct notations regarding why the students registered in this way, several different patterns are identifiable. A large portion, perhaps the largest, of the visitors were graduate students or fellows in neighboring departments, including divinity, psychology, education, sociology, and political science who audited Mead's classes—officially registering to attend the lectures without credit, and hence without the requirement to complete class assignments—in much the same way that students at the University of Chicago and elsewhere still do today. One would expect to find among these students individuals who were motivated by the content itself, rather than by fulfilling degree requirements, and indeed one finds quite a few of those who would become vocal advocates of aspects of Mead's perspective, such as Victor E. Helleberg, Maurice T. Price, Kimball Young, John K. Hart, Issei Misumi, Curt Rosenow, Ethel Kitch, and Jessie Taft. There were also a considerable number of exchange students from various parts of the world who audited these courses. One also finds quite a few nonstudents among the visitors, especially social workers and educational professionals in Chicago and elsewhere. This includes, for example, Caroline Hedger, physician in the meatpacking district of Chicago and consultant for the philanthropic Elizabeth McCormick Memorial Fund (see Eliot 1924); Ira I. Cammack, superintendent

of schools for Kansas City; and Mary E. McDowell, head resident of the
University of Chicago Settlement House.[15] The number of registered visitors peaked in the 1914–16 period and virtually disappeared from Mead's
registration sheets after 1917, likely a result of the restructuring of courses
and registration guidelines in this period. In addition, summer courses,
which Mead taught more often than not at Chicago, had a unique mix of
students, many of whom could not take courses during the regular year.
When William James gave lectures in Chicago in the summer of 1905
he sat in on Mead's courses; he described the audiences in a letter to his
wife as consisting of "great hulking teutonic ploughboys over 25, and fe-
male teachers, healthy looking, and dead in earnest, taking notes" (James
2003, 70).[16]

The overall population of attendees for Mead's courses continued to
expand after 1917 in all his classes, not only those in social psychology. By
the last years of his career the only courses that did not have more than
ten registrants were a few of his advanced courses on the history of philosophy. By 1918 the Social Consciousness seminar was already becoming
something of another lecture course, itself, with twenty-four registered
students. After 1920 he discontinued this seminar and replaced it with a
series of other experimental seminars entitled "Experience and the Self"
(winter 1921), "Relativity from the Standpoint of Pragmatism" (spring
1923), "The Problem of Consciousness" (spring 1924, 1926), and "Dewey's
Experience and Nature" (winter 1926), among others.

Despite the frequent claim—voiced perhaps most strongly by Tufts—
that the lecture was Mead's "medium," we find evidence that he repeatedly attempted to produce intimate environments where he could work
face to face with interested students. Undoubtedly Mead still "lectured"
in these smaller courses—existing records would seem to indicate this—
but the acknowledgment of this pattern reintroduces the importance of
his students into a consideration of his courses. Mead was not speaking in
front of a recording device for his own sake or in front of a merely anonymous audience, but in front of students as part of a pedagogical enterprise.
And Mead did not merely reiterate the same concerns in his lectures but
worked to keep them relevant and novel, especially in light of the wildly
fluctuating composition of his classes. In the remainder of the chapter, I
attempt to demonstrate that these facts have important implications that
have never been seriously considered both for what the lecture notes from
Mead's courses can tell us, for the understanding of Mead's intellectual development, and in establishing the conditions for the subsequent production of a knowledge of Mead as a social psychologist and social theorist.

LECTURE NOTES AS RECORDS

One of the possibilities seemingly offered by a large collection of notes and other materials is the comparison of multiple unique sets of notes from the same course. Indeed, in the notes I have discovered, there are fourteen courses in which more than one set of notes exists. And of the twenty-five times the famous Social Psychology or Advanced Social Psychology course was offered, I have discovered substantial student materials from thirteen. For example, there are three sets from different students taken in the winter 1921 Advanced Social Psychology course. These three sets represent the highest ratio of notes per registered student and per graduate student from any of Mead's classes (3 of 32 and 3 of 17, respectively).[17] None of these sets of notes were used in *Mind, Self, and Society*, nor were any others from the 1921 course. They are from sociology graduate student Ernest Bouldin Harper, philosophy graduate student Van Meter Ames, and sociology graduate student Martin Hayes Bickham.[18] I have selected a few passages from the notes on topics of some importance to debates on Mead, which I reproduce verbatim from their notes, although in typed form. The first is from the lecture on January 7, 1921, on the phases of the act in relation to emotion, pleasure, and pain. Text box 4.1 represents, as far as I am able to establish, the same moment in the exposition.

One could take up several different analyses of these notes. Bickham's appear more complete and may therefore be more accurate, but they may at the same time be more elaborated from the student's own concerns. Two of the three contain numbered points outlining the act's three stages, but they are not perfectly identical. All seem to contain the core idea that pleasure and pain are located at the end of the act while emotion appears at the beginning of checked action and interest is what carries through the act. Individual words and phrases recur in some or all of the notes—for example, "misnomer," "affective," "conflict"—but at that level of detail one loses the actual argument that is being made. Similar examples could be garnered from a number of other courses that have more than one existing source, but I will include only one other. From the same sets of notes, text box 4.2 reproduces a portion of their records from the lecture on February 1, 1921, when Mead was apparently discussing the relation between play and the emergence of the self.

Again we see some of the same issues as the previous example: not quite identical wording but the same general idea. One may note, however, that where these notes especially overlap is on the clear distinctions and turns of phrase: achievement versus endowment, taking the "role" of the

TEXT BOX 4.1. Comparison of students' notes from January 7, 1921

E. B. Harper's Notes, p. 6	V. M. Ames's Notes, pp. 6–7	M. H. Bickham's Notes, p. 10
Pleasures and pains belong to the end of action, emotion to the process of conflict itself. There are three stages: affective states (1) Conflict—Emotion. (2) The Process: adjustment Interest. Pleasant. (3) Culmination Pleasure or Pain.	Misnomer then to call emotion a series of pleasures and pains, for they belong only to the end of the act. In the action itself the affective content is what we call interest—is pleasant act is why different from the pleasure of satisfaction at the end of the act. Person who can get no interest in an act is the congenital tramp—are a certain number of persons of that sort.	A misnomer to call an emotion a series of pleasures and pains. Emotions enable us to estimate our ends. To see some person. Read some book. Different as you look back. Different type of affective in action itself. The affective cement is *interest*. This is a pleasurable affective state. Thus three stages in act. 1. Innovation—1 beginning of act. 2. Interest—2 process of act 3. Satisfaction—3 completion of act. Pleasure or pain Man who cannot get up Interest is "congenital tramp."

Source: George H. Mead Papers, Box 15, Folder 13; Box 14, Folder 1; Martin H. Bickham Papers, Box 1, Folder 14.

TEXT BOX 4.2. Comparison of students' notes from February 1, 1921

E. B. Harper's Notes, p. 25	V. M. Ames's Notes, p. 32	M. H. Bickham's Notes, p. 36
The "self" is developed through play in which the child is not himself but takes the role of another. The self is not an endowment but an achievement: process of thinking is one of putting one's self in the position of another.	A self is not an endowment, but an achievement. Conduct of person who has taken many parts is controlled by all those attitudes. Playtime of life is time in which the child gets the roles of others and incorporates them in himself.	A self is an achievement not an endowment with which we come into the world. Illustrated in play of child which takes roll of another. Control is approached in self-consciousness. Does not use this roll to control his own conduct. Perfectly mature. Doing what will help him later in life. Play-time of life is when child is making over into his own life these rolls of others.

Source: George H. Mead Papers, Box 15, Folder 13; Box 14, Folder 1; Martin H. Bickham Papers, Box 1, Folder 14.

other. More general questions arise: does a "fuller" set of notes mean that the student filled them with Mead's or with his or her own words? If we find, for example, that certain phrases appear together more often in one set than another for the same course, which set is right? I don't want to dwell on the problems of diagramming the exact relation of these notes to one another; instead, I want to point out that they are and remain ambiguous as direct records of Mead's lectures or as constructions by students.[19] While some confidence is gained about particular words or phrases, as well as the general argument being made, one cannot easily adjudicate between the records or reconstruct the lecture as delivered. Other points could be made from comparison of these sets of notes. For example, Harper's notes refer repeatedly to previous coursework with Ellsworth Faris with asides like "See Faris: 'Social Control' 1920" or "Cf. Faris 'Stimulus and response'" (14). That is, the notes are in a sense "multivocal," with the students posing other speakers into the text and thus making the result a product of the students' social history rather than the course as given. But these concerns already point to a different analysis, one that views them as practical pedagogical devices in an essentially social context rather than as deficient transcripts of monologues.

In chapter 5 I demonstrate that even the stenographic transcript made in Mead's 1928 Advanced Social Psychology class does not resolve this issue, for two reasons. First, even this transcript is not literally verbatim. There are portions of the transcript in which words or phrases are missing, or where there are clear indications that the stenographer did not understand the word or phrase spoken. The second, and more endemic, problem is that the stenographer had to interpret what series of utterances made by Mead constituted complete thoughts, with punctuation and line-returns after them. That is, the transcripts introduce the stenographer as an active participant in the production of the lecture text. As I show in that chapter, these decisions had definite impacts on the later interpretations and manipulation made of this transcript. This interpretive problem is intrinsic to the transcription of spoken language, which frequently does not fit formal grammatical rules. Beyond this, of course, is a whole host of other questions about what relation even the most accurate record of impromptu speech can have to an author's published works.

All accounts of Mead's lecture courses agree that he spoke without written notes. Mead would apparently often circle back to earlier points for further explication or leave off the comprehensive examination of some points in favor of other topics. In addition, not only was each successive lecture uniquely located in a nonlinear progression, but also the whole focus of courses nominally addressing the same topics (e.g., "social psychology") was subject to shifts in response to Mead's momentary interests and broader intellectual development—ranging from remarks about books he had read to excurses on major intellectual projects like his later examinations of relativity theory. Although students reportedly viewed questions to Mead as detracting from the flow of the exposition (e.g., Cottrell 1980), there is evidence for significant intervention on the part of students into the lectures. For example, the fullest stenographic transcript available from Mead's courses, that from Advanced Social Psychology winter 1928, records forty-six questions asked by students and answered by Mead over the course of the lectures, an average of about one question per lecture. It only makes sense that this complex, impromptu course of speech would be eminently difficult to record, and as chapter 5 demonstrates, likewise difficult to form into a coherent, systematic body of knowledge.

Ultimately, the most complete records left from Mead's courses cannot obviate the interpretive problems of using the written materials to reconstruct his speech. Of course this does not mean the notes cannot be used as a source of evidence about Mead—indeed, they already are so treated—but those claims remain contestable and can themselves be subjected to empirical analysis, a task of later chapters. Attempts to establish what Mead actually said and to distinguish it from students' editorial comments in a sense pose misleading questions, because they place the lecture notes in a frame that they were not originally intended to occupy: a framework of adjudicating the "real" versus "constructed" Mead, of establishing Mead the authentic font and founder of a discourse. But what if his students were not only or primarily interested in recording Mead's exact wording? Do we seriously believe this is what was required to pass the class, or that this is what interested students in Mead's lectures, or what they felt was necessary in order to carry Mead's philosophy out of the classroom? Indeed, students' accounts of Mead's classes would seem to indicate that in at least some cases they appreciated Mead's lectures despite his peculiar exposition.[20]

LECTURE NOTES IN PEDAGOGY

I propose to locate the students and their notes back in the original pedagogical situation and to investigate what they were actually doing. We get a start on this analysis by following up on the notes discussed above from the 1921 Advanced Social Psychology course. When Bickham received a mimeographed letter from Charles Morris in November 1931 asking former students of Mead whether they had any notes from courses with him, he responded:

> I have what I consider a very good and carefully taken set of notes from my course in social psychology under Professor Mead. . . . They are not altogether verbatim, but follow very closely Mr. Mead's own language, as I was always very careful to take his words and put them down in long hand in my notes. They cover the entire course and are invaluable to me. I used them last summer quite successfully and with great interest in my class in educational sociology at the University of Illinois. I will probably have to use them there again this coming summer so could not think of letting them out of my possession for any length of time. (GHMP, B 2, F 3)

In Bickham's papers archived at the University of Illinois–Chicago, one finds his lecture notes for this Educational Sociology course.[21] They indicate that Bickham spent two class periods on the topic "The Emergence of the Self: Discussion of Mead's Theory." Bickham's summary of Mead led into further lectures on the integration of the self, the techniques for the investigation of personality, and the importance of these concepts to students of education. The exams from his course also indicate that the students left with a working knowledge of Mead, along with C. H. Cooley, W. I. Thomas, and others. Although he referred the students to a few of Mead's published works, according to his notes, his exposition relied primarily on Mead's lectures. That is, Bickham continued to work with and on these notes long after the course was over. He read and reread them and used them as an aid in his own teaching. A similar case can be made for Van Meter Ames, who apparently reread his notes repeatedly and drew from them in writing professional papers on the philosophy of metaphysics and religion.[22]

We find further evidence that the notes served a number of different purposes as pedagogical tools from a more systematic examination of the letters Charles Morris solicited in preparation for *Mind, Self, and Society*. These records show that students exchanged notes from missed lectures, shared course papers with one another, and in some cases even seem to have been in possession of one another's entire sets of course notes. Students possessed a variety of note-taking styles. For example, shorthand or other abbreviation techniques were not uncommon skills in the early twentieth century, for educated women as well as men, and students recall taking stenographic notes or remember others doing so.[23] Existing notes

demonstrate that students used a variety of different strategies in organizing their notes, including making outlines, quoting aphorisms from Mead,
reorganizing them as a set of definitions, and preparing post-course summaries by lecture.[24] One even sometimes finds extensive, supporting bibliographical apparatuses including lists of works referenced, synopses or
summaries of topics or whole lectures, lists of exam questions, and annotations alongside the notes, which indicate the kind of practical work done
by the students upon the lectures. Many students turned in condensed,
typed notes from their classes as final papers.[25] The students Mead employed as graders took assiduous notes in attempting to ensure they could
adequately grade student work.[26]

   If we consider these courses as social situations in a broader sense, and
acknowledge that the boundaries of the classroom or the notebook do not
delimit the relationship between Mead and his students, we are better able
to understand the classes and notes in the context of the intentions and
actions of the students. That is, instead of looking at notes as a failure of
what we want them to be, we can understand them in terms of the functions they actually served in the students' experience. In particular it is
in this movement between speech and writing, and the reworking of writing in the light of further dialogue, that objectifications of a knowledge of
Mead appear in a systematic way—quite literally in the form of notebooks
and papers as "objects"—but these objects are not yet brought together for
the purpose of creating a single systematic edifice. Instead, these students
engaged in a disparate array of their own projects that intersected in their
coursework. This understanding is essential if we are to take seriously the
subsequent developments in the discourses about Mead.

THE MEADIANS OF THE 1910S

Such an analysis is most easily demonstrated by an extended illustration.
In the second half of the 1910s there was a group of graduate students in
philosophy and sociology whose records are sufficiently preserved to identify something of the complex relationship they had with one another and
with Mead's courses. Almost none of the individuals in this group are remembered as important interpreters of Mead or contributors to his reputation (with the notable exception of Ellsworth Faris, who appears on the
margins of this group). The students highlighted are, of course, not the
only group that could have been chosen for such an analysis. They are
illustrative in part because of the variety of records surviving for several

of these students and in part because this group is less well known than others, helping to emphasize the alternative this analysis presents to one that begins from present knowledge instead of historical context. While I make no claim that this group is representative of Mead's students, they do illustrate at least some of the ways students actually did engage with Mead, without subordinating this analysis to the immediate purposes of demonstrating Mead's construction.

The center of this group was in some ways Maurice T. Price, son of Ira Maurice Price, a professor of Semitic languages at Chicago. Price first took courses with Mead in 1909 when he was an undergraduate student in philosophy at the University of Chicago. After a period studying theology at Oberlin College and Rochester Theological Seminary he returned to Chicago to take up a graduate degree in sociology. During his time at Oberlin, Price met Ethel Kitch, who had also taken Mead's Social Psychology course and was then an instructor at Oberlin, and fellow student Winifred Raushenbush, the daughter of the well-known Social Gospel minister Walter Rauschenbusch.[27] According to his correspondence with Raushenbush, Price became quite a herald of Mead's social psychology when he took the course in winter 1915 and audited it again the following year. He shared the perspective he gained with Raushenbush, and the two of them managed to convince the Oberlin administration to allow Ethel Kitch to teach a seminar on social psychology there.[28] The way Raushenbush talked of the course it seems likely that they were literally using notes from Mead's course, but the documentation is not sufficient on this point. When the seminar began in the autumn, she remarked to Price, "What wouldn't it mean to be comparing notes with you. . . . Have I told you what we are going to work on with Miss Kitch when we finish Mead's Social Psy?," and more pointedly, "My enthusiasm is Social Psychology à la Mead per Buddy [i.e., Maurice] à la Miss Kitch."[29]

In addition to promoting Mead's social psychology to his friends, Price helped organize an informal weekly discussion group that ran the quarter after the winter 1915 Social Psychology course. The spring discussion group was apparently attended by, among others, Mead and Ellsworth Faris, and Raushenbush reportedly made pilgrimages up to Chicago from Oberlin to sit in on the proceedings. In that group they discussed issues of social conflict and the labor movement, pathological and neurological psychology, the work of Freud and Morton Prince, and the concepts of sublimation and catharsis.[30] This informal group was apparently organized on the model of Mead's regular seminars on Social Consciousness in which he worked with advanced students to push the boundaries of his social psychology by reference to contemporary issues. The 1913 Social Consciousness seminar had been attended by Ellsworth Faris and Ethel Kitch, among others.

Price and Raushenbush (who came to Chicago as a graduate student in 1917) became friends with other Mead enthusiasts in Chicago, including Armand Burke, Margaret Daniels, and Grover Clark, according to correspondence.[31] Armand Burke is the person who registered for the most courses with Mead of anyone—totaling fifteen, including eight independent research courses; Margaret Daniels took eight courses with Mead, and reportedly took down stenographic notes from some of Mead's courses; and Grover Clark also took notes from some of Mead's courses, typed them up, and apparently circulated them to other students.[32] Members of this group were also close with the Meads personally, spending time in their home and befriending the Meads' niece and ward, Elinor Castle.[33]

The members of the group discussed and explored the radical topics of the day, including socialism, women's rights, free love, Nietzsche, Freud, and Eastern religions, in their attempts to understand the contemporary world and their own identities. The correspondence of Winifred Raushenbush, in particular, indicates the importance that the social psychological perspective introduced by Mead had for her identity and generational independence. In response to her minister father's pointed concerns about the effect of her relationships with these fellow students on her reputation, she wrote:

> I don't intend to be guided by conventions. I am an experimenter it seems by nature and I have just one principle in life, that of concreteness. I want to make my outer social environment correspond to my inner mental makeup. I don't believe in an outer authority even in youth; that's what conventions are. The morale of the new age casts authority and fear overboard and steers its own course, conscious of its own strength. . . . What is reputation anyway? Merely the esteem of a certain group or certain groups. I have had social psychology and I know our dependence on other people for esteem and for the roles we play, like the good or poor response of an audience is that of one's social response. I am gradually learning to widen my audience, although, can't dispense with the "quality" of my smaller audience of friends. But I sincerely question whether the class of friends and acquaintances that ones parents have collected are not more of a hindrance than a help, for all their goodwill.[34]

All of the students from this group who wrote theses or dissertations explicitly acknowledged the influence of Mead on their work, and most made some direct reference to their own coursework with him. Grover Clark quoted from his notes from Social Psychology and Social Consciousness courses in his 1918 philosophy master's thesis *The Stages of the Social Self Compared with those of the Hegelian Dialectic*, and he added that "the material presented in these courses is not available in printed form, and hence it has been impossible to give references" (Clark 1918, 3). Armand Burke's 1923 philosophy dissertation *The Significance of Adjustment in Aesthetics* also quotes from Mead's "unpublished lectures in social psychology" (Burke 1923, pt. II, n. 11). And Maurice Price wrote a 1922 sociology dissertation, *The Analysis of Christian Propaganda in Race Contact*, under Robert Park in which he attempted to interpret the contact of Christian missionaries with indigenous peoples from the point of view of a Meadian social psychology. He wrote,

> The psychology of this process whereby others become the medium through which one arrives at self-consciousness and social consciousness, has for years been taken up elaborately in social psychology lectures by Professor George Mead of the University of Chicago—although he might not acknowledge our statement of it. A typewritten transcription has been made from a stenographic report of his lectures, it might be remarked. (Price 1924 [1922], 223b)

Throughout his thesis he quoted repeatedly from that "stenographic" transcript. This is the first definite mention of the transcript that would later be placed in circulation at the University of Chicago Library and then pulled from the shelves after Mead died to be used in the compilation of *Mind, Self, and Society*. At that time there was much speculation about who the original note-taker was for this stenographic transcript, including opinions that it was likely the work of Margaret Daniels.[35] While on file from 1924 to about 1931 this transcript was quoted directly in five other dissertations in sociology and philosophy. Indeed, in all, forty-four theses from philosophy, sociology, psychology, education, and divinity through 1935 refer to the author's coursework with Mead in one way or another.[36]

From this extended illustration it becomes clear that we cannot answer the question of what role Mead's courses played in the broader context of his students' lives by means of some facile assumption of students as mere "recorders" or "amanuenses." Notes were taken down, sometimes stenographically, not for the purpose of having the definitive answers, but as the basis for discussions on the issues of the day in seminars and informal settings.[37] Through their courses with Mead and their discussions with one another, these students did not get a series of facts but a shared perspective that they worked to understand, and at the same time they pushed the limits of this perspective in serving to define their own educational pursuits, social concerns, and personal identities.

One can grant all of this analysis and still argue that ultimately what the students were doing was merely trying their best under practical limitations to learn Mead's conceptual system and to use it for their own purposes. The above vignette does not give a particularly strong sense of the reciprocal influence that Mead's students had on him. Indeed, we would be remiss if we did not acknowledge that the pedagogical situation was also one of learning for Mead as well as his students. For example, surviving student papers from Mead's courses as well as students' notes indicate that one of Mead's perennial teaching strategies was to have students write succinct statements of the analysis on some central topic that had been developed in the course as class assignments. These Mead would apparently read over and give comments on. Mead also seems to have given days of review or classes set aside as question-answer sessions. It is quite plausible to see these not merely as work for his students, but also as possibilities for self-monitoring on the part of Mead; they would likely have given Mead a way of seeing the object his students made of his lectures. Charles Horton Cooley explicitly noted this phenomenon in his autobiographical *Life and the Student*: "A University teacher has one great advantage over more solitary scholars, as regards the building of a novel structure of thought, in the fact that he may count on an intelligent audience to welcome, confirm or correct his work during the process of production" (1927, 173).

MUTUAL INFLUENCE—W. I. THOMAS

Perhaps the most compelling way to demonstrate what Mead learned from his students is to examine the dynamism of his courses over time, to "put them in motion" so to speak. In order to do this, the following section examines the relationship between Mead and two of his former students who helped define the subsequent track of his studies, W. I. Thomas and John B. Watson.

William Isaac Thomas came to Chicago in 1894 to start a second professional career in sociology, leaving a position as professor of English at Oberlin College. As a graduate student and instructor in the department, he registered for three courses with Mead: a two-quarter sequence on Comparative Psychology in autumn 1894 and winter 1895, and a course on Methodology of Psychology also in winter 1895. These are courses from the first two quarters Mead taught at the university, and Mead's first opportunity to teach directly on these topics, instead of on the experimental physiological psychology and history of philosophy he had taught at Michigan. We have John Dewey's word that they had an impact on Thomas. In a letter to his wife, Alice Chipman Dewey, on December 12, 1894, he wrote:

> Speaking of Mr. Mead, I think his app[ointmen]t at Chicago much more than justified, he has got his bearings pedagogically. . . . His advanced class in comparative psychology was only taken by a few, but one of those was an instructor in sociology, who told me that it was the most wonderful thing in the way of method he had ever seen; he said he had been hunting for a scientific method in sociology, "& rationality had previously eluded him both in men & books," but now he got a method which opened up something systematically every time he used it. He is going to give courses in anthropology—really in the psychology of social development. As he has a mind, he will be a valuable ally; the first outpost for philosophy which isn't bad for [our first] 3 mos. [at the University of Chicago]. (Dewey 1997, no. 00246)

My research confirms that this "instructor" can be none other than W. I. Thomas, because the only other people who took this course were two education students and a divinity student.[38] Although I have discovered no notes from this course, let alone notes from Thomas's hand, Mead described the general accomplishment of his winter 1895 Comparative Psychology that Thomas took in a letter to John and Alice Dewey dated March 24, 1895:

> In Comp. Psy. I got the synthetic principle at the basis of development stated in Biological [???]—that every advance is the response of the organism to new or enlarged food supply i.e. a response to a stimulus not to an influence. That adaptation of the sensomotor system, at anyone prior—distinguished from the alimentary system can then take place only within the comparatively narrow limits set by advance made in the alimentary system in response to the new stimulus—I have in part worked this out with reference to the appearance of the mammals. (Dewey 1997, no. 00256)

Thomas apparently retained much from these courses because in 1917 he remarked, in apparent agreement with a portion of the above statement, that "it was Professor Mead, I believe, who defined the animal as a mechanism for utilizing a non-nutrient environment as means of reaching a nutrient environment" (Thomas 1917, 160). And in 1928, in response to L. L. Bernard's mimeographed questionnaire to sociologists about their own lives and accomplishments, Thomas noted Mead among his major intellectual influences (published as Baker 1973, 245; cf. Abbott and Egloff 2008).

On the other hand, by the time Thomas had come up for his degree, he had apparently made a major impression not only on the sociology department, but also on Dewey and Mead. In a glowing letter of recommendation to the president of Columbia University on July 16, 1898, Dewey wrote:

> Mr. Thomas, to my mind, is without any doubt opening up a distinct new field in Sociology. . . . In a general way, I may say that his work represents the attempt to discover concrete laws of social growth through the application of modern psychological methods to historical material. . . . I have been greatly struck with the surety and sanity of Dr. Thomas' insight into the psychological factors in social growth and with his capacity to marshall and interpret the facts of primitive society, especially, from this point of view. . . . His work is highly appreciated, not only by the students in the Department of Sociology, but also by all the members of the teaching force in Philosophy, as well as by students in Psychology and Social Ethics, many of whom elect his courses. Personally I should feel it a distinct loss to my own department if Dr. Thomas should not continue his work here. (Dewey 1997, no. 01886)

Thomas, of course, elected to stay at the University of Chicago, where he eventually became full professor. As a result, one can trace Thomas's influence on Mead as it worked back into Mead's classes over the early years of the twentieth century. While the existing notes and materials documenting Mead's psychology from the 1890s demonstrate that he focused primarily on the evolution of animal intelligence and its relation to reflective, human intelligence, by the second decade of the twentieth century he was considerably more focused on a comprehensive notion of comparative psychology, one that incorporated not only animals, but also social, child, pathological, and folk or race psychology.[39]

This shift is a complex one that must be properly attributed to a variety of factors, but it is not impossible to perceive the influence of W. I.

Thomas. For example, in the notes preserved by a student from one of Mead's courses in 1911, Thomas is the single most cited author, including references to his 1907 *Sex and Society* and his 1909 *Source Book for Social Origins* (Biesta and Tröhler 2008, 15). He is cited to make a series of propositions regarding how fundamental social attitudes (such as the parent-child relationship) are at the origin of social organization, and how the original orientation of man toward nature is as a social, rather than physical, object. Likewise, notes from the 1915 Social Psychology course indicate that Mead took one lecture to discuss Thomas's "The Mind of the Savage" section from the *Source Book* in which he apparently brought out many of the same points. Irene Tufts noted that, from this analysis, Mead proposed that the "mind has [the] texture of [the] group itself" and the organization of the group gives rise to abstract ideas and an understanding of nature.[40]

In turn, Thomas's *Source Book* cites Mead twice for his "important review" of Wundt's multivolume *Völkerpsychologie* (Thomas 1909, 326, 910). In his discussion, Thomas echoed Mead's assessment that Wundt's achievement in this work was the thoroughgoing application of the "psychological method" to the "interpretation of early society" (909–10; cf. Mead 1904c, 1906c). Indeed, one of Thomas's and Mead's common interests was apparently the engagement with Wundt's attempt to bridge the domains of the social and psychological, especially through his "folk psychology." It is noteworthy that Mead developed a new take on Wundt through this dialogue in the first decade of the twentieth century, having been primarily oriented toward his "physiological" psychology prior to this period and only from about 1904 on engaging with his "folk psychology." In this endeavor Mead had a colleague, if not a guide, in Thomas, who had been interested in ethnology and folk psychology at least from the days of his graduate study in Germany in the late 1880s.[41] In a later recollection of Thomas's courses in 1909–11, Emory S. Bogardus (1959, 367) noted that Thomas explicitly built on Mead's gestural theory of language, tracing "some of the origins of meaning that are found in behavior and in gestures which may be 'truncated acts' (Mead)."

From about 1905 to 1910 Thomas and Mead actually even lived together in a two-flat building at 6016 Jackson Park Avenue (now Stony Island Avenue), with the Thomas family living above the Meads. According to correspondence and other accounts they celebrated at least some holidays together and apparently discussed one another's work.[42] Thomas had two adolescent sons at the time who, one after the other, registered at the University of Chicago and took social psychology courses with Mead.[43]

The older, William Alexander ("Bill") Thomas, took the 1912 Social Psychology course and the 1913 Social Consciousness seminar. In the latter
course he was a particularly active participant and gave a class presentation on Freud's psychology in relation to Mead's.

W. I. Thomas was one of the first major American sociologists to take
Freud seriously (cf. Abbott and Egloff 2008), and in 1913 we find his son
explicitly examining the conceptual relations between Mead and Freud in
front of the former.[44] Indeed, the notes from this seminar, taken by Ellsworth Faris, are the first surviving materials from Mead's courses to mention Freud at all, although Mead had begun to discuss the dissociation of
personality and the importance of new work in pathological psychology
several years earlier.[45] According to Faris's notes, Thomas apparently interpreted Freud's psychology in terms of Mead's categories, an approach
that Mead himself had taken toward Freud and pathological psychology
earlier in the seminar. Freud's "complex," for Bill Thomas, was a "tendency seeking to free itself" akin to Mead's notion of "impulse." While
Freud emphasized the complex as an "idea" that attempts to "get past the
censor," Mead's emphasis was "on the conative side" in which impulses
seek expression through a variety of stimuli. Extending the argument
further, Thomas posited that there is dissociation in our normal lives as
well, as disparate impulses vie for expression. Ultimately, Thomas argued,
Freudian psychology relied on elements of an older Associationism which
did not recognize that ideas (or "complexes") are the result of the conflict
of actional impulses rather than the cause of their conflict.

As with Wundtian folk psychology, Mead's interest in Freud remained
throughout the rest of his career. In his later lectures he continued to refer
to Freud, especially to his notion of a psychological "censor," which Mead
apparently thought akin in some respects to his notion of the "me" that
set the conditions for expression of impulse (e.g., Mead 1934, 210–11, 255).[46]
It is not overstepping the available data to say that Mead's engagements
with Freud and with folk psychology were strongly tied with his relationship to Thomas, even if the direction of influence is sometimes difficult to
pinpoint. The complex relationship between Mead and Thomas continued
after Thomas left the university, and ultimately extended even beyond either of their lifetimes.[47]

When Thomas was fired in 1918, Ellsworth Faris was the person
brought in to teach his courses. And as I identify in chapter 7, Faris used
those later courses in part to introduce sociology students to Mead's philosophy alongside the work of Thomas, Dewey, and Cooley as part of a
unified sociological social psychology. Faris also tracked his sociology

students into Mead's classes. Mead's later "advanced" social psychology courses set aside much of his earlier work on traditional psychological topics and focused on the social nature of mind and the self, a topic that likely facilitated the interest and enthusiasm of sociology students more than his work on animal psychology or the physiology of emotions. Thus, not only was Mead influenced by Thomas over the years, but he was also reframed by another former student, Faris, in a way that led him to adapt his later social psychology courses to questions of common concern to Chicago sociologists, and especially to those of Thomas.

J. B. WATSON

John Broadus Watson serves as another illustrative example. He first took courses at the University of Chicago in autumn 1900 and in his first semester attended Mead's Social Psychology lectures. This was the first time the later-famous course was offered, and including Watson there were six registrants for the course, all graduate students in philosophy. Watson subsequently registered for Mead's summer 1901 Kant's Cosmogony course. In a later autobiographical statement Watson recalled that he did not get much out of his philosophy courses at Chicago with Dewey, Mead, James H. Tufts, and Addison W. Moore (Watson 1936, 274). Instead he found much more stimulation in his animal experiments supervised by James R. Angell and H. H. Donaldson. He took his PhD in 1903 with a thesis entitled "Animal Education," in which he studied the correlation between the psychological behavior and neurophysiological development of white rats. He stayed at Chicago as laboratory assistant and instructor of psychology (and reportedly designed the first laboratory for experiments on animal behavior [Warden and Warner 1927]) until 1908 at which time he left to take up the chairmanship of the psychology department at Johns Hopkins (Watson 1936, 275).

In writing of Mead in his autobiographical statement, Watson averred, "I didn't understand him in the classroom, but for years Mead took a great interest in my animal experimentation, and many a Sunday he and I spent in the laboratory watching my rats and monkeys. On these comradely exhibitions and at his home I understood him" (Watson 1936, 274).[48] What, in particular, Watson understood from Mead is not recorded, but some indication of Mead's thought on animal psychology in this period can be given. In 1903 Mead had published a major—if largely forgotten (cf. Joas 1997 [1985], 65)—statement of functional psychology in which he argued that consciousness was not constituted by a mental or psychical "substance" like older psychological theories argued but was to be defined in terms of its function in the "development of reality" for the organism (Mead 1903a; see also Mead 1904b). He extended this argument to "animal perception," finding that in order to solve the problem of not being able to delve into animal consciousness through introspection, psychologists instead had to admit that perception was a "process of mediation within the act" or "conduct" of the animal (Mead 1907d). From his first days at Chicago, Mead was also giving regular courses on comparative psychology in which he argued that intelligence was not a faculty located in a particular set of life forms or intellectual structures, but must instead be understood in terms of the action of the organism in its attempts to practically control its environment.[49]

Watson remembered that the first "tentative formulation" of his later "behaviorism" was given at Chicago "as early as 1904," but with "little encouragement" from his colleagues (Watson 1936, 276). This remark was intended, it appears, to refer primarily to Angell, who made his criticism of the behaviorist "creed" public: "part of the program seems to me rather Utopian and impracticable and other portions appear to disregard somewhat obvious distinctions and difficulties" (Angell 1913, 261). But it wasn't until moving to Johns Hopkins in 1908 that Watson says he "began to perfect" his "point of view about behaviorism," a process that he acknowledged was indebted in part to Knight Dunlap, among others (Watson 1936, 277–79). In 1913 he published his first paper proclaiming the new perspective, and the following year he expanded this statement into the monograph *Behavior: An Introduction to Comparative Psychology*. In both works Watson argued for a "unitary scheme of animal response" that "recognizes no dividing line between man and brute" and which makes "behavior, not consciousness, the objective point of attack" (Watson 1913, 1914).

A major advance of this new perspective, Watson thought, was the proposal that mental images could be understood in terms of kinaesthetic responses, an argument he credited to Mead's article "Concerning Animal Perception" along with work by Dunlap (Watson 1914, 18). In his 1911 Comparative Psychology lectures, Mead credited this same proposal—that animal imagery is essentially kinaesthetic—back to the work of Watson and Harvey Carr at the Chicago psychology laboratory.[50] This is likely the work reported by Watson in his 1907 *Kinaesthetic and Organic Sensations*, in which he acknowledges his indebtedness to Mead for "many valuable suggestions" (iii). Indeed, Mead's paper on "animal perception" was publicly presented for the first time at the same session of the American Psychological Association as Watson's "kinaesthetic sensations" research.[51]

By 1915 Mead was regularly assigning Watson's *Behavior,* and later his 1919 *Psychology: From the Standpoint of a Behaviorist,* in his social psychology classes.[52] From at least 1921 until the end of his life Mead explicitly identified his own position as "behaviorist" or "behavioristic" in his social psychology lectures and in his publications (e.g., Mead 1922).[53] But he often did so with the proviso that his perspective was more satisfactory than Watson's in that it took into account the broader social process in which behavior was implicated and because it used behaviorism as a methodological commitment in order to explain the emergence of human mind and self without having to presuppose a mental substance like the older psychology or exclude subjective phenomena like Watson (see e.g., Mead 1934, 2–3).[54] Of course the nonidentity of Watsonian (and later psychologists') behaviorism and Mead's notion of behaviorism is perhaps more profound even then Mead, not seeing subsequent developments, was able to articulate. As Joas (1997 [1985]) has convincingly argued, Mead's "behaviorism" was essentially a thoroughgoing theory of social action, and Mead's self-identity as "behavioristic" obscures much for contemporary readers for whom the term connotes Skinnerian or Watsonian psychology.

In preparing materials from Mead's late social psychology courses for publication after his death, Mead's former student Charles Morris employed the term "social behaviorism" to distinguish Mead's stance from Watson's (a subject discussed in greater depth in chapters 5 and 6). Morris's notes from Mead's courses indicate that he had heard his teacher assert that his own social psychology was a "behavioristic view and approach to the subject" but one that did not, like the "radical behaviorists," eliminate introspection.[55]

Mead was at least partly responsible for Watson's behaviorist perspective. He had outlined a quasi-behavioristic theory in the language of Deweyan functionalism, and had both spoken about it in lectures and published portions of it while Watson was at Chicago. Watson remembered the mutual understanding that he and Mead developed around his studies of animal psychology, a topic that was one of the central problematics of Mead's functionalist comparative psychology. This mutual understanding appears to be borne out in the references bandied back and forth between Watson and Mead. Even after he left Chicago, Watson continued to give at least a modicum of credit to Mead. But at the same time, Mead came to be defined—in large part through his own efforts at first—in relation to the perspective of his student. Mead defined his own social psychology in his later years in specific relation to Watsonian behaviorism, which no doubt pushed Mead to specify his own perspective more definitely. And after his death Mead became further defined in relation to Watson when another of his former students inscribed a definite relationship between Watson and Mead into the very title of his posthumous legacy, *Mind, Self, and Society: From the Standpoint of a Social Behaviorist.*

As these examples illustrate, the origin of ideas and the direction of influence is not easily located in one place or resolved in one direction. Instead, when we acknowledge the complex relationship of Mead and his students over time we find that some of them had continuing influences on him. And we see that in both cases addressed above, those relationships continued to be redefined by later student-teacher relationships: for a post–World War I generation of Chicago sociologists Ellsworth Faris helped define the relationship between Thomas and Mead through his own relationships to them (further addressed in chapter 7), and Charles Morris helped define the relationship between Watson and Mead through his own coursework with the latter (further discussed in chapter 6). Thomas and Watson are not the only possible illustrations; over and over Mead taught students who influenced his teaching in significant ways. One need only acknowledge that two of the three other long-term faculty members of the Chicago philosophy department while Mead was there, Edward S. Ames and Addison W. Moore, were former students of his, that he then cotaught or substituted in courses with them, and that he taught children from both of their families.[56] In this way one begins to get a sense of the complex relationships, especially as they develop over time, between Mead and his former students.

CONCLUSION

When located in their original contexts, we find that the various individuals who sat in Mead's classes were pursuing many different things: self-identity, understandings of religion, method, social problems, passing grades. If we are looking for a "logic of identity" among these various projects, I think it is productive to conclude that one of the things they have in common is a pursuit and production of knowledge, in a broad sense. In these endeavors Mead's lectures were not treated only or even primarily as the end or answer, but as a means. That is, to the extent that the lectures were deemed useful to students, it was because the concepts or perspectives outlined in them became points of orientation, one might say "tools," in their own projects. Even at their most discipular, Mead's students do not serve as his adoring but errant scribes. Consider the quotation early in the chapter from George Shelburg. Surely we can acknowledge that he felt a "reverence akin to worship," a "respect," an "inspiration," and at the same time note that Shelburg looked past this idol to the "new land" in which Mead was a pilgrim.

If we accept this view that Mead's students were engaged in a variety of what we may call "intellectual projects," we are actually better able to find a common ground in which Mead's words and actions do not have to be treated as ontologically different from those of his students and interpreters, but are instead identified as ways of knowing about himself and his social world that are continuously and necessarily interconnected with the projects of others. A notion of intellectual project has been more or less informally used in a wide variety of works on the history and sociology of ideas, but little work has been done to give this notion more substantive analytical value. I use the word "project" along the lines elaborated by Alfred Schütz (1967, 59–60), for whom it meant a "reflexive looking-forward-to" or ongoing "anticipation" intrinsic to action, and for whom the core of everyday reality was "intersubjective," or experienced and held in common with others. To speak of intellectual projects, then, is to direct attention to the collective undertakings of scholarship or other intellectual endeavor that bring individuals together around common plans or goals. Because they are intersubjective, these projects are likely to be experienced as particularly momentous and to influence an individual's self-understanding, and because they are projective, they can be multiple and overlapping.

This sense of a common ground between Mead and his students is more or less explicitly acknowledged in a memorial statement for Mead by student Van Meter Ames (Edward S. Ames's son), who wrote: "He was not lecturing to us, delivering what was old stuff to him. He was thinking out loud and we were overhearing his thoughts. We were sitting in his inner forum, which was merely the room in which we all were gathered. The distinction between inner and outer had disappeared" (V. M. Ames 1931). In this view it is not a matter of Mead versus his students, but rather Mead as a social actor among other social actors, all working to interpret something novel and that nevertheless (and without contradiction) centered on the words of one of them. The above analyses demonstrate, for example, that Mead did not "learn" things only once and then merely reiterate them. Instead, concepts and individuals important for his work—for example, "sociality," "behavior," Wundt—he relearned or learned in a different way as he taught them to students, as he considered them in light of other works, and as his students and colleagues taught him.

It is also clear from the examinations made in the chapter that Mead treated the practical problems of pedagogy in his classes seriously and conscientiously. There is strong evidence that Mead worked to construct classroom environments conducive to the exploration of complex issues with motivated students and that his classes were intended to advance his own understanding as well as that of his students, whenever possible. It should perhaps come as no surprise that someone who wrote so productively about teaching and education as a social enterprise should have worked to foster conducive social environments in his own classrooms.[57]

As with his students, knowledge was for Mead not a record but a project or projects pursued over time and in common with others. It is in the interactions and relationships that Mead developed with his students and colleagues, especially when the topics of discussion were related to Mead's philosophy, that the dynamics of the formation and articulation of ideas are especially visible. We can pinpoint some of the particular moments when these innumerable intellectual projects come together, as in the classes in which Mead and his students worked to interpret his philosophy in light of Freud, or when the laboratory assistants sought to make an experimental examination of his functional psychological perspective.

The two extended studies of Thomas and Watson were not chosen at random, and it should go without saying that not all of Mead's students affected him as profoundly (or that all of his students were affected as strongly by Mead). The major impact these two former students had on Mead's work appears to have occurred especially in the first decade of the twentieth century. This coincides with the period in which previous authors have identified a fundamental transformation in Mead's theory that resulted in his thoroughgoing analyses of the constitution of the human self in the dynamics of simultaneously practical and intersubjective action (see Joas 1997 [1985]; Cook 1993). This is the period in which the students of the Dewey years at Chicago, including Thomas and Watson, were developing their own work at Chicago and during which Dewey left for Columbia. The relationships between Mead, Thomas, and Watson are by no means the only relevant ones in the transformation of Mead's self-understanding but the analysis has attempted to demonstrate that in both cases the mutual and enduring influences were much more intensive than the trivial revisions to one's ideas that one might attribute in some form as a result of any intellectual exchange.

The analyses in this chapter of the actual pedagogical situations of

Mead's courses over time are important to the other analyses of the study. With a focus on the interconnected knowledge projects of Mead and his students, we can then get a sense of how particular former students, especially Herbert Blumer and Charles Morris, mobilized claims regarding the relation of their own work to Mead's. And it is in dialogue with his students that we begin to see Mead as an actual learner and knowledge producer, someone who worked through ideas in the course of social interaction, not in isolation—which helps add another aspect to the analyses in part I. But the immediate task is to examine how the intensive social and pedagogical contexts outlined in this chapter can help understand the posthumous legacy built around Mead. Key to this analysis are the extensive private collections of notes produced in Mead's classes and an analytical focus on the social action processes in which these documents are incorporated and transformed.

CHAPTER FIVE

The Construction of *Mind, Self, and Society*

*M*ind, Self, and Society: From the Standpoint of a Social Behaviorist,
a volume published by the University of Chicago Press in December
1934, poses an acute problem for anyone who attempts to use the text as a
transparent source of knowledge about the social theory of its attributed
author, George Herbert Mead, because it was constructed posthumously
from a collage of stenographers' and students' notes and unpublished manuscripts.[1] In terms of its impact on subsequent scholarship, *Mind, Self, and
Society* has been unquestionably the most influential text documenting
his distinctive social theory, far more so than any of the work published
in his own lifetime.[2] Put simply, what is known about Mead's influential
teachings derives predominantly from *Mind, Self, and Society*. I leave the
question of how this dominant interpretation of Mead, which relies on
Mind, Self, and Society, was built up and how it changed over the course
of the twentieth century until chapters 6 and 7, and will focus for the moment on the volume itself.

Behind the published text of *Mind, Self, and Society*, with its apparent claim to transparently present its attributed author's views, there lies
a process through which the writings were not merely made available
through publication, but were constructed. That is, Mead did not write
the vast majority of words of the volume, most being based on notes taken
by students and stenographers in his courses, nor did he intend materials
like those for publication. Further, the classroom notes of these students
and stenographers were themselves substantially transformed and reinter-
preted as they were incorporated in the text of the volume. It was a well-
acknowledged fact by the people involved in the process of constructing
this legacy that their "combined efforts have not been able to produce the
volume which we wish George H. Mead might have written," and yet "it

was the consensus of opinion among [Mead's] students and his colleagues that [this material] should be published. In this opinion his family and friends concurred" (Morris 1934b, vii; Moore 1936, vi, ix). That is, without guile or caprice, the project appeared entirely reasonable from the perspective of those involved, despite the admitted construction of the very material presented, and despite the contentious reactions to the subsequent published volumes.[3]

Current critical scholarship has sought to reassess Mead primarily by eschewing a focus on *Mind, Self, and Society*, because of the volume's problematic nature, and instead to reconstruct Mead's social thought by other means. As a whole, this scholarship has greatly improved our understanding of George Herbert Mead by examining his life and thought beyond the bounds of *Mind, Self, and Society*. However, very little has been done to consider what may be gained by analyzing the actual construction and publication of the posthumous volume by which Mead is primarily known, despite the implicit claim motivating much of this scholarship that *Mind, Self, and Society* cannot adequately represent Mead. Only very recently has this latter set of questions been tackled in a substantial way (cf. Silva and Vieira 2011; Cook 2013).

This chapter seeks to address *Mind, Self, and Society* from a radically different direction than has been previously attempted in order to demonstrate that taking seriously the book's "construction"—and hence understanding more clearly how such a problematic book came about—means explicating a novel interpretive process of relations between social actors and physical documents within situations constrained by practical circumstances over a course of time. The chapter examines the project of creating a posthumous legacy for Mead more generally, but with a particular focus on *Mind, Self, and Society*, for two reasons: there is significantly more surviving data about the construction of that volume than either of the other two published by the University of Chicago Press, and it is the most important of the volumes in terms of later influence.

The following analysis illustrates how adequately understanding *Mind, Self, and Society* as a text requires a thorough acknowledgment of the consequential, interpretive process by which it was created. First, no individual freely designed this book after his or her own wishes without considering other social actors, available documents, and practical constraints. Second, no social consensus to draft the definitive and approved "Mead" existed among interested parties, and while there was certainly deliberation about what should serve as Mead's thought, debate depended upon the particular documentary materials available to the actors. Third, what counted as an appropriate document of Mead's thought and how it compared in terms of authority with other possible texts were decisions made under practical situational constraints. And fourth, the final text was not the result of a single agglomeration of textual fragments. Rather, it was the result of particular events—meetings and deliberations, writing or discovery of documents—that must be understood in their temporal sequence and interconnection to account for the peculiar structure of the published book's content.

In order to accomplish this analysis, I draw upon archival research in the George Herbert Mead Papers and the University of Chicago Press Records in Chicago, the Charles Morris Collection in Indianapolis, and supplementary materials from several other collections. Through this research I have brought together a substantial and unique dataset of correspondence and notes from which to reconstruct the process of creating this text. As will be demonstrated, these materials preserve an extensive record of the unfolding social process from within, and therefore serve as particularly illustrative data for an analysis of the construction of the volume. This chapter is not, however, intended as a definitive and complete critique of the content of *Mind, Self, and Society* from the standpoint of a more "objective" understanding of Mead. Instead, I try to demonstrate through the explication of important episodes and examples how the published text is the result of a particular social process of construction.

POSTHUMOUS PROJECTS TO SECURE A LEGACY

When George Herbert Mead died on April 26, 1931, the publication of a volume like *Mind, Self, and Society* out of a patchwork of reconstructed classroom notes from his Social Psychology courses and various unpublished manuscripts was not a foregone conclusion. At that time there were already several incipient projects to bring Mead's work to greater attention. One Festschrift for Mead—along with James H. Tufts, Addison W. Moore, and Edward S. Ames—had already come into print (Smith and Wright 1929), and a second one dedicated to Mead and Tufts was being seriously considered.[4] Mead had just given a well-received series of Carus Lectures in December 1930 that was to have been reworked for publication.[5] Several stenographic transcripts and extensive student notes from a variety of Mead's lecture courses were already known to exist. As is discussed below, these notes were in private circulation among some of Mead's students and colleagues, and there had been periodic attempts to convince Mead to publish these materials in his lifetime. None of these documents, with the partial exception of the Carus Lectures, came to be published in a form closely resembling the initial intentions of their promoters. Their efforts, however, indicate a strong desire among a core group of Mead's colleagues and students to see him given greater recognition in print. And there was clear acknowledgment of the existence of various materials through which to achieve this goal.

Because the Carus Lectures were already under contract with Open Court Publishing Company, they became the organizing center of early proposals for Mead's legacy. Mead died before he could significantly re-edit the notes, so his son and daughter-in-law, Henry C. A. and Irene Tufts Mead, chose Arthur E. Murphy to work on the materials.[6] John Dewey hoped that Murphy would include "enough of mss [unpublished manuscripts] of Mead's own" as a companion volume, and Edward S. Ames, who was also a long-time colleague and had taken over as chairman of the Chicago philosophy department after Mead's resignation, wanted the Carus Lectures to include some of Mead's "more important [published] papers."[7] Both colleagues began to feel that such publications were more fitting than a Festschrift dedicated to Mead, and they continued to lend their considerable influence to proposals for publishing more of Mead's works. Although initially receptive to including additional materials along with the Carus Lectures, Open Court soon decided against publishing any companion volumes.[8] As it was, Murphy ultimately did manage to include three unpublished manuscripts and two previously published articles by Mead in the single volume (Murphy 1932, 8). However, any attempt to bring together a substantial corpus of additional materials as a legacy to Mead would have to go beyond the bounds of the Carus Lectures.

Indeed, the publication of the Carus Lectures as *The Philosophy of the Present* (Mead 1932) seems only to have whetted the interest of those who wanted to see Mead's teachings preserved. The recognition that the publication of these lectures was already likely to stand as a posthumous legacy to Mead, that they were edited not by Mead but by a former colleague, and that they included a variety of materials of different origins including lectures, manuscripts, and published articles, seems to have added legitimacy to the enterprise of further publication projects. Ames had suggested to Henry and Irene Mead that they consider Charles W. Morris, a former student of Mead, to work with Murphy on the supplementary materials for *The Philosophy of the Present*.[9] As it became clear that the volume of Carus Lectures would not allow enough of Mead's work to gain a wider audience, Ames continued to push the possibility of a volume of Mead's published works. He got the Meads' and Arthur Murphy's approval to have

Morris head up this project, which he envisioned as being fairly straight-forward, saying: "It is not our thought that these articles will need editing or interpreting for this publicati[o]n but it is more just the work of getting them together and seeing that they are arranged etc."[10] It was unclear to Morris at this point, however, whether this was to be considered a separate project from the Carus Lectures, whether a selection of Mead's writings or all of them should be included, and whether the volume should include only reprinted journal articles or a selection from Mead's whole oeuvre.[11]

Within days, the scope of the nascent project expanded rapidly. Ames reported that Irene Mead was in possession of materials from a couple of Mead's courses, Movements of Thought in the Nineteenth Century and Social Psychology, and that she had consulted W. W. Norton and Com-pany, who would consider publishing either one or both of them.[12] Arthur Murphy, before leaving Chicago to take up a position at Brown University, apparently suggested to the Meads that they invite Merritt H. Moore to edit the transcript of Mead's introductory Movements of Thought lectures (Moore 1936).[13] And Morris was seen by Murphy, Ames, and the Meads as the appropriate person to look over the notes from Mead's Social Psychol-ogy course.

By the end of May 1931, only a month after Mead's death, there were already four active publishing projects in his name, consisting of his 1930 Carus Lectures, his compiled published works, a stenographic transcript of his Movements of Thought lectures, and student notes from his Social Psychology course. In subsequent weeks, several other projects were pro-posed as additional materials began to pile up. Mead's son and daughter-in-law provided Morris with several substantial unpublished manuscripts written by George Mead that were not included in the Carus Lectures vol-ume, and these were increasingly considered another potential project for publication. And as Morris began to gather materials for his projects, he noted the large amount of student and stenographic lecture notes extant from Mead's courses on the history of thought. He proposed to the Meads and to the University of Chicago Press at various times a volume to bring together those "historical lectures."[14]

From a few nascent ideas of making Mead's thought better known there developed a constellation of overlapping and indefinite potential projects, each with its advocates and its materials from which to draw. Early de-cisions proceeded primarily on tentative mutual agreement; Mead's fam-ily consulted with his former colleagues, students, and publishing houses on the appropriate moves to take. In the correspondence, there is strong evidence of a dense network of mutually felt personal obligations among those involved, not only toward Mead and his family members, but also to his former colleagues in light of their authority and to the young prospective editors of the materials in light of their devotion. Still, for all the desire of these individuals, the various projects were only plausible on the basis of the discovery of various sets of materials. And as will be developed below, the projects came increasingly to incorporate additional masses of material including hundreds of pages of unpublished manuscripts by Mead, dozens of students' and stenographers' notes from Mead's lectures, and reprints of dozens of Mead's published articles. These texts were not for the most part pregiven at the start, but were discovered or reconstructed in the process itself.

Thus, the claim that the three volumes ultimately published by the University of Chicago Press, *Mind, Self, and Society* (1934), *Movements of Thought in the Nineteenth Century* (1936), and *The Philosophy of the Act* (1938), "represent the three main fields of Mead's work" (Morris 1934b, v) only legitimates the result of the process rather than illuminates its organizing principle. At the beginning it was not clear what materials would end up in publication, and, indeed, several of the projects did not come to fruition and many thousands of pages of manuscript materials still remain unavailable in published form. There was no consensus or even any clearly defined guidelines by which publishing decisions were to be made. But where deliberation alone could not determine the proper course, the available materials presented problems that proved consequential.

THE "SOCIAL PSYCHOLOGY MATERIAL"

When Charles Morris came to Chicago in late summer 1931 to take up his new post in the philosophy department, he had waiting for his examination several copies of typescript notes apparently taken down from one of Mead's relatively early lecture courses in Social Psychology by a student, possibly Stuart A. Queen in autumn 1912.[15] In looking over his apparent charge from Henry and Irene Mead, Morris "came to feel that there was no clear understanding of what [he] was supposed to do."[16] Was he to bring together a volume of all Mead's previously published writings on social psychology, or edit this copy of social psychology lecture notes for publication? Should references be made to other sets of notes? Should previously unpublished manuscripts be included? What sort of "authority" should the notes be considered as having?

In responding to his concerns Irene Mead also admitted that she "was disappointed when [she] came to read over the Social Psychology material," expecting it to be a "verbatim transcript" like the manuscript from "Movements of Thought in the Nineteenth Century."[17] She agreed with Morris's suggestion that if it was to be published the material would have to be expanded by reference to other sets of notes and published alongside some of the more "important published papers dealing with the self and social thought" as Murphy had done with the Carus Lectures. Irene Mead gave Morris access to some manuscripts that "seemed to [her] to deal with the Social Psychology material" and continued to search for others. Morris, after "rather carefully" reading over the social psychology notes, indicated his ambivalence even more strongly: "There is much that is fine there, but also much that Mr. Mead would not like to have seen in print. The editing will have to be very extensive."[18] He suggested that they "write to the best students of the last few years in Mr. Mead's course" to get other sets of notes, which they could either use in place of the "fairly old ones" they currently had or at least "supplement the material" and confirm the validity of the content of those notes. It is important to indicate that, at this point, the project was still an exploratory one about which there was considerable question and hesitation, and no definite plans to print this material had been made. As late as April 1932, Morris's (and formerly Mead's) colleague T. V. Smith (1932, 208) could publicly assert that Morris was editing a volume that would contain Mead's published "articles upon social-psychological problems" in addition to records from his "justly famous course at the University of Chicago on 'Social Psychology,'" despite the fact that no volume consisting primarily of his published articles appeared for another three decades.

Morris prepared a circular letter to some of Mead's former students that was sent out October 31, 1931, asking whether the recipients had any suitable lecture notes on Mead's Social Psychology courses or knew of anyone else's notes that could be considered for possible publication. In particular, he indicated that he was looking for especially full notes from the last few years of Mead's life. T. V. Smith (1931, 368) published a memorial article in the *American Journal of Sociology* at the beginning of November 1931, lamenting the lack of "visible work" that would give "more than a mere semblance of the impression of substantiality received by [Mead's] friends from the impact of his expansive and seminal mind" and mentioning the possibility of "forthcoming posthumous volumes." These two appeals, which arrived in the mail of many of Mead's former students within days of one another, had a definite effect.[19] Over the following two months Morris received dozens of responses from Mead's former students, of which at least some are preserved in the George Herbert Mead Papers. These letters report a wide variety of responses from students. Over two dozen sets of notes from Mead's Social Psychology courses are specifically mentioned by the preserved letters, several other sets from courses that bear on Mead's social psychological thought are reported, and there is also a great deal of speculation about the existence of note-sets from other students. The accounts in these letters had a substantial impact on the subsequent course of the publishing project, not least because the sheer volume of materials they represented proffered a considerable credibility and the apparent possibility of systematicity to the project.

STUDENT LECTURE NOTES, FOUND AND MADE

As a former student of Mead, Morris was already aware of the veritable marketplace of lecture notes that existed from Mead's courses, a topic discussed in chapter 4. Some students had valued their notes so highly that they had them bound or used them as the basis for their own classes. Students had exchanged or handled one another's notes and class papers. Many students were aware of full sets of notes from other students enrolled in the courses or from persons paid to record the lectures. A note-set for one of Mead's social psychology courses had at one time been in circulation at the University of Chicago library and was cited in several Chicago dissertations.[20] Indeed, several enterprising students had even attempted to record as completely as possible Mead's lectures for some later publication.[21] And some of Mead's friends and colleagues, including psychiatrist Adolf Meyer, had pleaded with him to publish notes made by his students.[22] There was, thus, a large body of material of variable quality, but always highly valued, in private hands at the time of Mead's death.

Based on the students' descriptions of their notes, Morris graded their potential quality directly on the letters he received. He marked them "good," "fair," "poor," or "none." He then began following up on a select few of the responses. In several cases, Morris's notes to himself indicate that he asked students to transcribe their notes or otherwise rewrite them into a more complete form.[23] That is, not only were the contents of the potential volumes constructed in the sense of selected from among the possible notes, but there was also a literal construction of the materials themselves for the volumes. As Morris received sets of notes, he read through them and annotated them on separate sheets of paper that he saved among his preparatory materials for *Mind, Self, and Society.* That he annotated them separately indicates he was conscious of the need to preserve the original materials either for deposit in the Department of Philosophy

(Morris 1934b, vi) or for return to the original owners.[24] These annotations demonstrate that by early 1932 Morris had read through at least fourteen sets of notes in preparation for the volume, including notes from his own courses with Mead and notes from courses far removed from social psychology, strictly defined—courses such as "Aristotle's Metaphysics" and "Relativity from the Standpoint of Pragmatism."

Several interpretive processes involving these texts began to overlap in this phase of the project. First, Morris and Irene Mead, in deciding to write only to select former students from later courses, overlooked several very full sets of notes that have since come to light.[25] In looking specifically for later courses, they in effect asserted that Mead's latest lectures were to represent the whole of his intellectual development and thought, and disabled any possibility of using the volumes to be published to explicate the intellectual development of Mead's social psychology or the breadth of topics discussed primarily in earlier iterations of the course. Second, the former students' responses were already interpretations of the relative quality of their own notes without the benefit of any large body of materials to which to compare them. Morris's grading scheme further builds on this interpretation by using the students' responses, and not the materials themselves, as the basis for his decisions. Moreover, in asking students to rewrite their notes he in effect asked them to build a whole new layer of interpretation into the materials he would then receive, a layer that would be indistinguishable to Morris from the notes as written in the classroom. It of course goes without saying that the classroom notes were themselves works of interpretation by the students.[26] Finally, in annotating the sets he received, Morris further interpreted the content of the notes; throughout, he summarized and paraphrased material and determined what was an important point worthy of attributing to Mead.

In each layer of interpretation, the decisions are entirely reasonable given the considerable practical constraints on time, money, and effort that structured the possibilities open to all those involved. This was, after all, at a time when copying manuscripts, for example, most often meant literally retyping them with the use of carbon paper or preparing mimeograph stencils page by page, not to mention the physical transportation time and cost of the materials. Morris could not reasonably ask dozens of students to ship him their various notes for his assessment, nor could he be expected to have every possible set of notes reproduced. Instead, he asked students to assess their own notes' relative worth and, if promising, write them up in a form that would be more useful to the project. From Morris's and Irene Mead's perspective, the most recent students of Mead would be the ones easiest to track down, most likely to still have relevant materials, and to have materials that recorded Mead's most developed thought. The further implications of these decisions will be considered below in the discussion of the making of the final volume. But an account of the final compilation of *Mind, Self, and Society* cannot adequately build the volume out of these materials alone and must instead acknowledge the fundamental shifts that occurred in response to the discovery and interpretation of the text that would contribute the bulk of the published book.

THE "VERBATIM" TRANSCRIPT OF 1928

Little did anyone involved know at the time that all of these student notes would ultimately only contribute supplementary content to *Mind, Self, and Society*. Morris became aware at some point of the existence of the collection of stenographic notes solicited by George Anagnos, a former student who apparently wanted to publicize Mead's teachings, and financially sponsored by Alwin C. Carus.[27] Carus had collected a dozen particularly full sets of notes, some of which were simply purchased from students who had already written them up, and others of which were made by professional stenographers hired by Carus. Morris arranged for the Meads to buy the complete collection for $300 in June 1932, but this arrangement was made only after some contention over the legal ownership of the notes was resolved.[28] Hence, it was not until summer of 1932 that Morris had free access to the stenographic transcript that would ultimately form the bulk of *Mind, Self, and Society*, long after he had begun to compile, annotate, and arrange students notes, and long after he had invented the title—and with it the basic structure—of the volume.[29]

Through this purchase Morris came into possession of a 320-page typed transcript of almost 150,000 words made from Mead's winter 1928 Advanced Social Psychology course, which then displaced all the other materials Morris had previously collected and became "basic" to *Mind, Self, and Society* (Morris 1934b, vi).[30] This is the only transcript for Mead's social psychology courses in Morris's possession that could claim to be a nearly verbatim record, and it was from one of the last years of the course, so it is understandable why Morris, the Meads, and the University of Chicago Press would prefer this text. With this transcript, Morris finally had gathered all the material that would be considered for inclusion in the final product, including also the several sets of students' reconstructed notes, stenographic transcripts from other courses, and an unspecified number of Mead's unpublished manuscripts dealing with social psychological themes.

Given Morris's practical selection criteria it is clear that the 1928 stenographic transcript was the best material from which to construct the final volume, but this fact did not also make it merely a transparent medium, or the definitive source, of Mead's thought as such. First, the text is not entirely verbatim. There are several places in the transcript where missing words or phrases are indicated, and places where clear errors of transcription appear in the text. In both cases, Morris most often simply edited out the sentences in which these omissions or errors occur.[31] Morris also deleted passages in which the stenographer failed to accurately capture the reference Mead was making. For example, when in the discussion of the dissociation of personalities Mead referred to some "psychological novel dealing with the disassociation of the pathological processes," the stenographer did not catch the title or the pseudonym of the study's patient, later tentatively identified in writing on the transcript, I think correctly, as Morton Prince's study of "Miss Beauchamp," *The Dissociation of a Personality* (1905). Prince's work is not otherwise referred to in any of Mead's published writings, but other sets of notes indicate Mead was quite familiar with this work. It is difficult to know exactly what impact this and other omissions may have had on understandings of Mead's thought, and when taken as individual examples most are probably of more interest to a select few historians of social psychology than to the average reader of *Mind, Self, and Society*.

In other cases, however, there are words or phrases that are questionable given what is otherwise known about Mead's published work. For example, this transcript includes the phrase "universal discourse" five times where it can be argued that "universe of discourse" is more likely what Mead spoke. The former phrase does not appear in any of Mead's published writings, unlike the latter.[32] "Universe of discourse" was a concept used extensively in philosophical logic in the nineteenth and early twentieth centuries, including in the works of Charles S. Peirce, William James, Josiah Royce, and Mead. Yet, this substitution of phrase may have been plausible to a person not well versed in philosophical terminology who was reconstructing the transcript from pen strokes representing abbreviated phonetic elements. Despite the phonetic similarity, the semantic difference between the two phrases is nontrivial, and has likely contributed to idealistic interpretations of Mead's theory of language universals.[33] Similar stenographer errors likely arising from ignorance of philosophic terminology and history were pointed out in the transcript that made up *Movements of Thought in the Nineteenth Century* (e.g., Tsanoff 1937; Randall 1937).[34] Such examples begin to bring out the strongly interpretive aspects of stenography behind the appearance of transparency (Wellman 1937).

In typing a transcript, the stenographer had to interpret what series of phrases spoken by Mead constituted complete thoughts, a challenging endeavor itself given the nongrammatical structure of much spoken language. Each constructed sentence was entered on a separate line on the original stenographic transcript, making each one appear as a self-contained aphorism. The transcript has no other breaks by paragraph or topic, excepting the breaks between each new lecture. Thus, what appears as virgin material is already the result of interpretation, and treating the transcript as a neutral medium disguises the way this form of presentation made plausible a naturalization of certain phrases as individual aphorisms without necessary relation to the topical progression. Indeed, analysis of Morris's annotations on the transcript indicates that he often extracted individual sentences or groups of sentences, deleted others, and sometimes reorganized the sequence of sentences with regard to one another. That is, the interpretive maneuvers of the stenographer, presented in the homogeny of the typed transcript, became the basis upon which Morris made further determinations in the text.

To give but one example of this line-by-line editing, I quote a paragraph from the famous section of *Mind, Self, and Society* on the "'I' and the 'me'" and compare it to the transcript from which it is drawn. The published paragraph reads:

> There is neither "I" nor "me" in the conversation of gestures; the whole act is not carried out, but the preparation takes place in this field of gesture. Now, in so far as the individual arouses in himself the attitudes of the others, there arises an organized group of responses. And it is due to the individual's ability to take the attitudes of these others in so far as they can be organized that he gets self-consciousness. The taking of all of those organized sets of attitudes gives him his "me"; that is the self he is aware of. He can throw the ball to some other member because of the demand made upon him from other members of the team. That is the self that immediately exists for him in his consciousness. He has their attitudes, knows what they want and what the consequence of any act of his will be, and he has assumed responsibility for the situation. Now, it is the presence of those organized sets of

attitudes that constitutes that "me" to which he as an "I" is responding. But what that response will be he does not know and nobody else
knows. Perhaps he will make a brilliant play or an error. The response
to that situation as it appears in his immediate experience is uncertain, and it is that which constitutes the "I." (Mead 1934, 175)

The corresponding passage in the 1928 lecture transcript, retaining the
line breaks and wording as originally transcribed while indicating the
lines cut out in italics, reads as follows:

There is neither "I" nor "me" in that at all.

The whole act is not yet carried out.

The preparation takes place in this field of gesture.

Now, in so far as the individual arouses in himself the attitude of the
other this is organized, it is an organized group of responses.

You have one response from one and another response from another.

*If all of these responses have an organized value for him, as in the il-
lustration I gave of the baseball nine, now his own attitude, so far as
he is self-conscious is dependent upon his ability to take the attitude
of the second baseman and the other members of the team so far as
they are involved in the play.*

*There is an organized sort of an attitude on the part of all which be-
longs to him as a member of the team in any such play.*

And it is due to his ability to take the attitude of these in so far as they
can be so organized that he gets what we term self-consciousness.

Now, taking all of those organized sets of attitudes gives him
his "me."

That is the self he is aware of.

He can throw the ball to some other member because of the demand
made upon him from other members of the team.

That is the self that immediately exists for him.

And it exists not simply as that of a being that is attacked or approved but exists in his consciousness.

He has their attitude and knows what they want and what the consequences of any act of his will be, and has responsibility for the situation.

Now, it is the presence of those organized sets of attitudes coming back upon himself that constitutes that "me" and to which he is responding.

Ques. by Std [question by student]. *Can an individual be conscious of an object without responding to it?*

[Answer:] *That brings up the question of just what we mean by consciousness.*

He assumes the attitude of the beginning of the response whenever he is conscious of it.

We don't carry the response out.

A tree might excite the attitude of climbing in the individual but we don't actually climb the tree.

There are responses of that sort which are present in what we term attitudes, those beginnings of reactions, responses to an object that is involved in all of our experience.

So in that sense we certainly would be conscious of them.

As I have said the term "conscious" is ambiguous, we use it sometimes when we simply mean the presence of the object in our experience and also where we have a definite conscious relation.

Going back to our discussion.

Such a group of attitudes in the individual which represents those of all the members of the team.

Those go to make up the "me" of the individual, that is, these ges-
tures, all of them, calling out a certain response in him in relationship
to them.

They are what constitutes a responsible individual under the cir-
cumstances.

Because he has the attitude of every member of the team involved in
the play calling out for response.

But what that response will be he doesn't know and nobody else
knows.

It may be that it is very definitely indicated but perhaps he wouldn't
make it.

Perhaps he will make a brilliant play or an error.

The response to that situation as it appears in his experience immediately is uncertain and it is that phase of it that constitutes the "I."[35]

In addition to the minute editing of phrases throughout, whole sets of lines
are simply excised—not least the student's question and Mead's answer
regarding the relation between consciousness and response. However, in
reading the transcription one can also appreciate the eminently problematic nature of the task set for Morris: making a concise, systematic, and
nonrepetitive monograph out of this particular transcript of impromptu
speech. Discovering the basic guidelines or organizing principles with
which Morris worked to prepare this material requires an understanding
of the social expectations of what the final volume would look like, nego-
tiated by Morris and the University of Chicago Press, and his own understanding of what the texts contained.

MAKING *MIND, SELF, AND SOCIETY*

The project to bring into press something of a synthesis of G. H. Mead's
social psychological thoughts was, from very early on, organized around
the working title "Mind, Self, and Society," first proposed by Charles Morris on August 21, 1931, before he had any of the solicited student lecture
notes, which he received in November and December 1931, and before he

had the 1928 stenographic transcript, which he apparently first saw in February 1932 and began editing in July of that year. For the employees of the University of Chicago Press, the title was useful to differentiate that project from the other volumes being considered in a Mead series. It became so naturalized that some employees advocated for its use as the final main title on the basis of their understanding that it was the "name of the essays used by [G. H.] Mead," instead of recognizing it as Morris's invention.[36]

It was in one of his letters to Irene Mead, mentioned above, a letter primarily discussing his impressions of the early (1912?) Social Psychology notes he had been given upon arriving in Chicago, that Morris first suggested the eventual title of the text. These notes were the only substantial materials, besides Morris's notes from the courses he had personally taken with Mead and perhaps a few unpublished manuscripts, to which he had access at the time that he suggested it. Indeed, "Mind, Self, and Society" is quite a succinct description of the progression of topics presented in that set of notes. According to the surviving transcripts of those notes in the George Herbert Mead Papers, the social psychology course began that year with a discussion of the nature of perception, consciousness, and other traditional psychological concepts that were largely absent from later sets of notes. These topics could be plausibly considered an examination of "mind." Then, after explicating the genesis and development of the "self," which formed the nearly exclusive focus of the later social psychology courses, the early set of notes indicate that Mead explicitly addressed the structure of "society," including the nature of institutions, abstract social relations, classes and castes, and the impact of democratization on social organization (Mead 1982).[37]

The frequent complaint in later scholarship that Mead's view of society lacks a recognition of social structure is largely correct for the "Society" section of *Mind, Self, and Society*. This is because Morris took material from the 1928 lecture transcript, which Mead intended as an attempt to utilize the "view of the self as a means of interpreting society," and labeled them in a way that implied that this was Mead's view of society as such.[38] This quoted phrase does not appear anywhere in the published text of *Mind, Self, and Society*. Throughout the 1928 transcript there are indications that Mead was concerned with examining the way in which the emergence of selves transformed the organization of society. He was thus focused on society as perceived and acted upon from the standpoint of the emergent self, and not with any structural or topographical analysis of "society" in a strict sense in that course.

Despite ultimately basing the text primarily upon other materials

and utilizing text from the early (1912?) notes only in footnotes, Morris
retained the working title as the organizing principle for the contents. In
order to make the materials fit this organization Morris was compelled to
reorganize the presentation of topics and to fill out the exposition in the
1928 transcript with materials from other lecture notes and manuscripts.
Contrary to Morris's published claim that "the volume is based upon (i.e.,
organized around) a stenographic set of notes taken in 1927 [sic], and the
order of the material in the volume is the order in which Mead presented
the material of the course" (Morris 1937c, 560), a perusal of Morris's notes
on that transcript indicates that the reorganization was very extensive—as
the above quotations from the published volume and manuscript illustrate.
In order to keep with the organization implied by the entrenched working title, Morris fabricated the material to conform to the topic instead of
the topics to fit the material.[39] He added or emended transitional phrases
throughout the work in order to fit together materials that were not con-
tiguous in Mead's exposition, but which Morris felt were topically related.

In addition, only after Morris received and read over the 1928 stenographic materials did he begin to emphasize Mead's "behaviorist" perspective with regard to the potential social psychology volume in meetings with the University of Chicago Press. In July 1933 Morris began to
describe the Social Psychology lectures as containing "the kernel of [G. H.]
Mead's Social Behaviorism," which even prompted some discussion at the
press of using the title "The Philosophy of Social Behaviorism" for the
volume.[40] Morris's emphasis on Mead's "behaviorism" was at least in part
a response to the strong engagement Mead is recorded as having with psychological theories of conduct, especially that of John B. Watson, in the
first six lectures of the 1928 course. Of course, as chapter 4 already pointed
out, Morris had heard Mead talk about Watson and behaviorism in his
own courses, so the 1928 transcript likely activated his own recollections
about the emphasis Mead placed on a critical examination of Watson. The
suggestion of the subtitle, "From the Standpoint of a Social Behaviorist,"
was first made in a meeting between Charles Morris and Chicago Press
general editor Gordon J. Laing on July 26, 1933. Morris reportedly proposed
in that meeting that the form of the title should directly parallel the title of Watson's *Psychology: From the Standpoint of a Behaviorist* (1919)
because Mead's book would prove to be "the second great document in
the literature of behaviorism."[41] In terms of the content of the text, this
reading resulted in the incorporation of a substantial amount of those six
early lectures into an introductory section on "The Point of View of Social
Behaviorism." Mead never used the phrases "social behaviorist" or "so-

cial behaviorism" in any extant lecture manuscripts or published writings although he did describe his position as "behavioristic" (Cook 1993, 70–71; Joas 1997 [1985], viii–ix), but Morris apparently found the phrase illustrative in indicating precisely how Mead's behaviorism would be more adequate than Watson's. The passages in which those phrases appear in the published text of *Mind, Self, and Society* were added by Charles Morris, by his own admission (Morris 1934b, xvi).

The way in which the other previously gathered materials were incorporated back into the text of the volume also resulted in several of the published text's peculiarities. First, approximately a third of the volume comes from a set of reconstructed notes from the 1930 Advanced Social Psychology course, consisting of 184 typewritten pages authored by Robert R. Page. This former honors undergraduate philosophy student rewrote his notes apparently over the course of a year and a half, while he pursued graduate study at Cambridge University.[42] It is unclear why Morris chose to rely so heavily on these materials, given the numerous other sources to which he had access, apart from his own assertion that they were "faithful and full notes of another devoted student" which "greatly enriched" the stenographic transcript (Morris 1934b, vi) and his apparently friendly relationship with the Page family.[43] At any rate, the places where these notes go to make up the text are not indicated, despite having completely different authorial provenance and despite having come from a different year of the course than that of the stenographic transcript. These notes also contribute to forty-one of the eighty-five footnotes in the volume. The Page notes contribute some distinctive analyses found in none of the other sets of notes, including the "triadic" or "three-fold" relation of meaning, and unique phrases including "social process of experience" and "conversation of significant gestures." The word "social" appears far more frequently in those notes than in others, as do plurals like "attitudes," "gestures," and "mechanisms."[44]

Ten other sets of notes from Morris's previously gathered corpus contribute to footnotes, and are indicated by year, although not by author or course.[45] The fact that Morris used his annotations on these materials as the source for contributions to the final text, instead of the sets of notes themselves, resulted in several cases in paraphrases or summations serving as direct quotations from the notes. As with the 1928 transcript, Morris in effect changed even the content that he included in the volume, in addition to the selection and rearrangement of the material. Morris also added in passages from at least eight manuscripts written by Mead, many of which were also reused in the composition of *The Philosophy of the Act*

(Mead 1938). In all of this, however, there is no evidence of any capriciousness or deliberate misinterpretation. The indications, rather, are that Morris tried to bring coherence and topical progression to a widely disparate
corpus using the practical techniques and materials he had available. As
he put it, the volume "aims to do this task of systematization" that Mead
did not do, "partly by the arrangement of the material" (Morris 1934b,
v–vi). Still it was a heavily interpretive process, one in which other scholars have noted that Morris "engaged in creative editing" (Cook 1993, 71)
and "took such liberties in supplementation and emendation that one can
never be sure whether a sentence is Mead's or Morris's" (Joas 1997 [1985],
xii).[46] In his reassessment of the universe of materials available for the
study of Mead, Stevens (1967, 557) concluded succinctly that the posthumous volumes are "ideologically comprehensive and reliable, historically
and genetically deficient, and have had too predominant an influence to
date in the understanding of Mead."

PUBLISHING IN THE GREAT DEPRESSION

The fact that *Mind, Self, and Society* was coming up for publication in the
1933–34 publishing year, in the depths of the Great Depression, did not
go unnoticed by the employees of the University of Chicago Press, who
in 1932 had suffered their first significant loss of sales volume in over a
decade and were already anticipating further declines.[47] On June 12, 1933,
Donald Bean, manager of the University of Chicago Press, and Charles
Morris met and drew up a plan to publish the various projects as a single series of memorial volumes, four months after the social psychology
material had been individually approved for publication under the title of
"Mind, Self, and Society" by the Board of University Publications.[48] The
program of publication as subsequently proposed to the board was for a
"Philosophic Works of George H. Mead" including projected volumes in
"Mind, Self, and Society," "Movements of Thought in the Nineteenth
Century," and "The Philosophy of the Act." This combined plan was particularly appealing to Charles Morris, who had assumed something of a
de facto leadership role in the projects as a whole, because he sought to
model the Mead projects into a "complete works" along the lines of the
six volume (later eight volume) *Collected Papers of Charles S. Peirce* co-
edited by his colleague Charles Hartshorne.[49] A series format had the benefit, they thought, of allowing the volumes to be marketed together at a
reduced price for the set, which more people could afford "even in these
times."[50] Given the economic conditions and the fact that they could not

presuppose a market for books by G. H. Mead—who had never published a book in his life—they proposed a scheme of advanced subscription to gauge interest and ensure sales.

This system of financing was intended as a way to minimize the amount of money Henry and Irene Mead would have to pay out of pocket while maximizing the amount published. In the proposed arrangement, Henry Mead would pay the entire cost of the first volume not made up through subscriptions in the hope that the volume's subsequent sales would finance the publication of later volumes.[51] Because the series was approved by the press "provided satisfactory financial arrangements can be made"—their phrase for the requirement of outside funding to under-write publication—Henry Mead would have been expected to pay the total amount of all the volumes (estimated at over $9,000 at the time) absent some self-financing scheme.[52] The rolling financial scheme that was de-vised by which the sales from each published volume would finance later publications had definite effects on the whole enterprise. For one, it served to determine the order in which the volumes would appear. "Mind, Self, and Society" was seen as having the largest sales potential and the pos-sibility of some textbook sales, so it was published first; "Movements of Thought" was the second most likely to have healthy sales and so was published next, leaving "The Philosophy of the Act" as the third volume.[53] Various proposals that had been voiced for a "published works" volume or one on the "history of thought" did not get published because of the ex-haustion of financial resources.[54]

The financial dependence of the volumes upon one another also sig-nificantly delayed the publication of the second and third in the series. The correspondence indicates that all three of the projects subsequently published were at least roughed out by the end of 1933. Yet *Mind, Self, and Society* was not published until December 1934, *Movements of Thought in the Nineteenth Century* until April 1936, and *The Philosophy of the Act* until May 1938. That is, between the invitation to begin the projects and their culmination in publication lies an interval of seven years, the trough of the Great Depression. The preparation of the first volume for publica-tion did not begin until after the solicitation of advanced subscription had yielded its apparent saturation point of 200 subscribers.[55] The sales from the first volume were modest and, in order to make possible the pub-lication of the second volume, the press agreed to pay about half of the production costs as long as Henry Mead agreed that the sales therefrom would go to recouping that investment before production of the third was considered.[56] And the third volume, which was thereby put in jeopardy, was only possible because a second change in the contract with Henry Mead was made such that he agreed to forego all royalties in perpetuity in exchange for the university agreeing to cover any deficit incurred by its publication.[57] In each case, decisions were delayed to enable sales receipts from previous volumes to minimize further outlays from Mead's family or the press. These delays came as an irritation to individual and library subscribers of the volumes, who inquired in correspondence about their status. It is difficult to measure the extent of the negative effect this had on sales of the volumes, however, something of the precariousness of the whole enterprise is exposed through the ad hoc solutions found to the recurrent problems of financing the volumes.

The economic limitations did not only shape factors external to the actual content of the volumes. The early discussions regarding *Mind, Self, and Society*, for example, proposed including a large manuscript to have been entitled "Mind and Body from the Standpoint of a Pragmatist," which was not ultimately included in the volume, although it did later reappear as the 100-page-long chapter xxi in *The Philosophy of the Act* (Morris 1938).[58] Instead, a shorter (forty-two page) untitled manuscript was substituted, and it consequently comprised the first three "Supplementary Essays" in the published work (Morris 1934b, vi). Later correspondence on *Mind, Self, and Society* indicates that there was additional consideration of including some material amounting to 212 pages, but cost estimates showed it to be infeasible.[59] This material was unidentified in the correspondence in terms of its content, but Morris was in possession of thousands of pages of stenographic transcripts and unpublished manuscripts from which this material could have been drawn. Indeed, the fourth of the "Supplementary Essays," a ten-page essay entitled "Fragment on Ethics" that appeared at the end of the published *Mind, Self, and Society*, came from this collection. It was severely edited down from its original form: a 243-page stenographic transcript from Mead's 1927 course in "Elementary Ethics" (Morris 1934b, vii). Taken together, these decisions show both the acute restriction and nonfixity of the content of these volumes. That is, not only did financial considerations result in the determination of content negatively, by preventing much of it from publication, but it also influenced content positively, by promoting the inclusion of shorter thoroughly abridged materials.

Much the same is true of the other two volumes. In response to being told that his edited manuscript for *Movements of Thought* was likely too long for publication, Merritt Moore admitted to doing "something by way of cutting down the appendix on French thought."[60] This appendix was originally a 148-page set of notes from Mead's 1928 course in "French Philosophy of the Nineteenth Century," which was cut to 92 pages in the published version.[61] And when the press was working to secure funding from the university for the publication of *The Philosophy of the Act,* Morris was informed that the administration probably would not agree to the deal "unless the number of pages is cut down or [Henry] Mead underwrites the project in some way."[62] Morris did cut down a section entitled "Categorical Fragments" from 103 to fewer than 50 pages and placed them as an appendix at the end of the volume.[63] In addition, he decided against including some of Mead's previously published material in the volume in the hope that it would appear in a subsequent "published works" volume. The "categorical fragments" had already been heavily edited down. According to Morris, they were "taken in the main, from student notes on courses on Aristotle, Bergson, Dewey, Hegel, Hume, Leibniz, 'Philosophies of Eminent Scientists,' and 'The Problem of Consciousness'" (Mead 1938, 626) and were primarily the responsibility of the associate editor Albert M. Dunham. If the materials referred to in this note are indeed the transcripts preserved in the Mead Papers, then as mentioned above they amount to thousands of pages of unpublished material. This last case illustrates particularly well how the uncertainty about subsequent publications led in a number of cases to the inclusion of materials in severely fragmented form, and the inclusion of materials that were not otherwise appropriate for the themes covered in the volume. As the publication enterprise continued to shift and its financial stability progressively faltered, any clear delineation of material was forfeited to the desire to see any of it in print.

None of the three volumes published in the series was significantly re-edited, again because the costs resulting from new typesetting and manufacture would have made such a measure financially "impossible."[64] Only the most significant typographical errors were fixed in subsequent impressions, and in no case did these changes amount to the alteration of more than a few single phrases. This means that all of the determinations made in the physical appearance and content of the volumes made under the pressures of the Depression are retained to the present.[65]

CONCLUSION

Mind, Self, and Society as published is already the product of an intensive social process that has interpreted and given peculiar form to Mead's thought. This chapter has sought to reveal the hitherto-understudied "construction" of the book by which Mead is most well known as an empirically identifiable process, and to illustrate how a few of the particular turns the process of creating the book had taken have likely conditioned what is generally known about Mead. For example, the analysis has attempted to demonstrate that the contextually specific interpretations made by various individuals on particular texts have made possible notions of "universal discourse," "social behaviorism," and the supposedly astructural presentation of social structure that have presented problems for Mead scholarship. And in this process of systematizing a single Meadian theory across a disparate array of texts the creation of *Mind, Self, and Society* disguised the contextual nature of Mead's lectures and manuscripts and has prevented easy access to an understanding of Mead's intellectual development. This is particularly important to point out in light of the fact, as illustrated in the first section, that Mead cannot be adequately understood as having one set of definite fixed ideas across his intellectual development and coursework, and the various notes from his courses are not merely records of his thought as such, but evidence of a variety of complex social projects.

The immediate task of the chapter has been to indicate how a more adequate understanding of the peculiarities of the structure and content of *Mind, Self, and Society* is possible by focusing analysis on the social process through which the volume was created. Despite the attribution of the book to George Herbert Mead, it should be evident from the explication above that the text did not merely begin as some singular conceptual insight in the head of an individual. In *Mind, Self, and Society*, the work of different individuals who created physical materials for disparate purposes within their own social situations is literally subsumed into a single-authored volume. In his capacity as editor, Charles Morris was clearly consequential in the result, but his position was neither entirely stationary nor authoritative throughout the process, which also directly involved other former students and family members of Mead, professional stenographers, and the employees of the University of Chicago Press and other scholarly presses. Indeed, it is no exaggeration to say that no single person intended this volume.

In addition, the endeavor of engaging with texts was an ongoing practical accomplishment for the social actors involved. The course of constructing the volume was not guided by a set of insights present from the beginning or a consensus of opinion about the way Mead's teachings should be presented, or even what Mead's teachings were. Those involved tended to focus on how to best accomplish particular tasks on the given textual materials within perceived practical constraints rather than question the entire process or its end product. Indeed, while one can say that Morris and others have a strong authorial presence in the text, one may also notice that many of his seemingly eccentric decisions were actually attempts to make readable the texts he had available to him. Where and when a particular text was discovered or interpreted in relation to the trajectory and current possibilities of the overall process entailed consequences for the final outcome. The published text of *Mind, Self, and Society*, then, cannot be fully explained as simply the agglomeration of several disparate materials that were spliced together, but must be understood rather as the result of a particular temporal sequence of actions that were given direction (or changed direction) at identifiable moments because someone found or read particular texts. For example, because work was begun to edit the 1928 stenographic transcript after over a year of work on numerous other documents meant that, although it could contribute the bulk of the words in the published text, it would have to be rearranged and supplemented in ways that fitted it to the topical structure already in place for the book. Likewise, the problems of the older, nonverbatim notes to which Morris originally had access led him to suggest soliciting students for other materials in the first place.

By tracing in detail the process through which this systematic representation of Mead's thought was constructed I have attempted to identify the particular situations, actors, and texts that help explain the result. From the above analyses, and from the previous analyses in part 1, the single, systematic edifice of Mead's social thought as represented in these posthumous volumes (and especially in a few key passages) begins to be more understandable as an accomplishment at the same time that is givenness comes into question. We are able to identify at least some of the ways in which individual textual documents are related to particular contexts and individuals, in which Mead and his students influenced one another in particular ways, and in which Mead's actual social practices are related to his philosophical notions. From this perspective the dominant understanding of Mead has become, itself, a problem for analysis, rather than a presumed starting point. How is it that a few texts, passages, concepts, or propositions come to stand for a person's thought and in what sense can they be said to do so? One aspect of this already appears in the examination above of how certain books were constructed and attributed to Mead. But these are the questions that the next two chapters aim to address in earnest by reference to the actual interpretations made of Mead's significance by two of his most influential former students and the larger patterns of reference to Mead in published literature over time. In these endeavors, we are able to see how the particular form of this published legacy to George Herbert Mead was appropriated and selected in scholarship.

PART III

Influence and Interpretation

CHAPTER SIX

Intellectual Projects

The previous chapter detailed how the practical social enterprise of publishing a posthumous legacy for Mead under the given circumstances, and as circumstances changed, resulted in a rather idiosyncratic result. However, the resulting documents are only one aspect of the development of particular dominant understandings of George Herbert Mead. Their existence cannot itself explain how Mead was incorporated into particular academic discourses and into the work of particular individuals, except insofar as we are willing to ascribe the appropriation of a work or author to some nebulous sense of "content fit" (cf. Camic 1992). Such an explanation would be difficult to sustain because of the existence of Mead's various published papers and the existence in other scholars' work of at least some comparable ideas to Mead's. Instead, this chapter attempts to fill the gap in between the presence of published documentary materials and their employment by examining the actual processes of interpretation and mobilization of claims regarding Mead by other authors.

In much of the sociological literature on intellectual "reputations" and "origin myths" they are implicitly treated as something produced in a different space and time, and by different means, from the author's work itself—where the interpretation or knowledge of an author is separate from the author's production of knowledge. But as chapter 4 already showed in part, Mead's philosophy was permeated by interpretations made of it by his students that were constitutive of his own philosophical work. In this chapter, the converse argument is proposed, that the intellectual projects of Mead's students are permeated by his philosophy. In both cases interpretation is inherent to the knowledge-making process. Indeed, as the analysis below demonstrates, a key to understanding the interpretations and claims made by Mead's students is to be found in the peculiar social relationships they formed with him in life, which created a sense that they participated with him in a larger intellectual project of which he approved.

For Mead the two obvious candidates for such analysis are Charles Morris and Herbert Blumer. As chapter 5 demonstrated, Morris was the primary editor for the posthumous book by which Mead is primarily known today, *Mind, Self, and Society*. Through that editorship Morris had a hand in supplying the analyses that would become standard in Mead scholarship and first labeled Mead a "social behaviorist." The focus of the analysis of this chapter will not be on Morris's editorship but on the mobilization of Mead in his own broader life-long intellectual projects. As the introduction intimated and as chapter 7 below demonstrates in greater depth, Herbert Blumer provided a coherent label and analysis of what he called "symbolic interactionism," by which Mead continues to be known in the social sciences today. It should be noted that these two have been selected precisely because of their powerful influences on dominant understandings of Mead.

The analyses that follow do not constitute essays in intellectual biography. Instead of focusing on Morris's and Blumer's careers and ideas as such, the analysis is directed to their interactions and continued engagements with Mead during and after his life. In particular, the analyses highlight how each author understood himself in relation to Mead, along what lines each organized claims about Mead, the sources of authority each individual relied upon in making those claims, and the consequences these particular rhetorics had on understandings of Mead. Still, the chapter makes considerable appeal to Morris's and Blumer's broader intellectual careers in order to locate their handling of Mead in those enterprises. Likewise, it is important to emphasize that the following sections are not intended to catalogue all the criticisms directed at Morris and Blumer, but rather to identify how they each responded to certain criticisms in reference to their understanding of Mead. The analysis draws upon a wide variety of each author's published works, archival interviews and correspondence, and secondary material identified in the text where relevant.

MORRIS AND MEAD

Charles William Morris Jr. first attended the University of Chicago in the autumn of 1922, arriving with a bachelor of science degree from Northwestern University, where he expressed interests in psychology, biology, and engineering.[1] He later recalled that he "had gone to Chicago primarily to work with Mead" (Morris 1970, 189). Of course, living in Evanston, Illinois, as an undergraduate, he could have traveled to the University of Chicago campus in the Hyde Park neighborhood to meet Mead in person, but his acquaintance more likely came through the introduction to his ideas he would have received from instructors in the Northwestern University psychology department.[2] Although the evidence of Morris's time at Northwestern is not as complete as the records of his graduate schoolwork, it appears that by the time he arrived in Hyde Park he had already decided to focus on philosophy, with strong interests in social psychology, behaviorism, quantitative research, and psychiatry.[3] These interests, and the connections between the Northwestern and Chicago faculty members, likely helped him settle on the University of Chicago.

At Chicago from 1922 to 1925, Morris took notes in six courses with Mead: "Movements of Thought in the Nineteenth Century" and "Relativity from the Standpoint of Pragmatism" (spring 1923), "Aristotle's Metaphysics" (autumn 1923), "Advanced Social Psychology" (winter 1924), "The Problem of Consciousness" (spring 1924), and "Philosophies of Eminent Scientists" (spring 1925). He reportedly also audited the spring 1923 "Hegel's Logic" course (cf. Cook 2013, 102). This puts him in the top quarter in terms of the number of courses with Mead taken by a single student, but far from the peak (Armand J. Burke, for more on whom see chapter 4). Morris took as many or more courses with Addison W. Moore and James H. Tufts as he did with Mead, and his most frequent contacts with a faculty member were with philosopher of religion Edward S. Ames, according to his own records. Outside philosophy he had contact with Ferdinand Schevill in history, whom he credited for his understanding of Nietzsche and his quasi-Spenglerian view of the development of civilizations (Morris 1993 [1925], 4); Walter E. Clark in comparative philology, whom he thanked for "conversations on Buddhism" that influenced his thinking on "Maitreya" and human values (Morris 1942, 257); and Louis L. Thurstone in psychology, whom he called his "main statistical advisor for years."[4] Although Morris spent only three years as a graduate student at Chicago (and earned his PhD at the tender age of twenty-four) it is clear that this period was fundamental for setting the subsequent tracks of his studies, not only in semiotics but also in empirical axiology, characterology, and world religions—an "eclecticism" that characterized his work and was a central point of criticism throughout his career.

Although Morris apparently did not serve as a research or grading assistant for Mead (as did Herbert Blumer and a few others), through his courses he was exposed to a wide range of Mead's interests, and he was introduced to the necessary connections Mead saw between the various aspects of his work. Morris kept extensive handwritten notes from Mead's courses—729 pages from the six courses he took—and he referred back to them frequently throughout his career.[5] They demonstrate that by the time Morris encountered Mead's Advanced Social Psychology course, which he later helped make famous as the editor of *Mind, Self, and Society*, he was thoroughly familiar with the relations between Mead's social psychological perspective and the other aspects of his philosophy.[6] The 1924 Advanced Social Psychology course, according to Morris's notes, focused extensively on Mead's much broader view of behaviorism in relation to Watson's "radical" behaviorism and other previous methodological stances in psychology. Mead spent a considerable portion of the lectures discussing the modern history of psychological thought from Hobbes onward, echoing his thoughts in the Movements of Thought course. He discussed relativity in light of his social psychological position, and in the Advanced Social Psychology course and the Problem of Consciousness seminar Mead worked to develop a theory of the social mechanisms for the emergence of mind. It is in these courses, in particular, that Morris was exposed to a rigorous discussion of the nature of symbolism, and to Mead's view of the constitutive nature of signification to "mind."

Morris submitted a thesis in 1925 entitled "Symbolism and Reality: A Study in the Nature of Mind" with Mead as the chair of his committee. Morris called the thesis an "essay" in form, and the whole piece is organized as a set of numbered paragraph glosses. In this essay he argued that there was an "intellectual revolution" taking place regarding the nature of mind and its relation to reality, combining new insights from behaviorism, relativity theory, analytical philosophy, mathematical logic, linguistics, and philosophy of science (Morris 1993 [1925], 2–3). As he saw it, his essay posited a novel, exploratory thesis: "thought and mind are not entities, nor even processes involving a psychical substance distinguishable from the rest of reality, but are explicable as the functioning of parts of the experience of the organism as symbols to that organism of other parts of experience" (3–4). The bulk of the essay is dedicated to working out in broad strokes the prolegomenon of a behavioral analysis of semiotics, which draws from each of the above phases of the "intellectual revolution."[7] Large portions of the essay read principally as extended excurses on Mead's lectures, with added sections on formal symbolic logic and on the nature of civilization that were apparently indebted to C. I. Lewis, A. W. Moore, and Ferdinand Schevill.

The part of the essay that Morris argued was especially "heavily indebted to the ideas of Mr. Mead—ideas which as yet are not available in written form" was on the nature of the "givenness" of the world of experience. Morris argued that one can formulate an understanding of "givenness" that acknowledges the wide field of private experience that is not sharable, and at the same time one can still affirm that it does not necessitate a mental or psychical substance separate from objective reality (Morris 1993 [1925], 64ff.). That is, reference to the experience of an organism does not make something an essentially different order of reality than any other "given," and instead all existents are necessarily related to experience and hence "objectively relative" in Mead's (and A. E. Murphy's) formulation. The final section on "philosophy and civilization" argues for a cyclical theory of civilizations; it develops an analysis in which Morris purported to show that philosophical reflection is necessary in order to help guide humanity to a new age or cycle of civilization. This essay clearly set the agenda for Morris—clarifying the nature of mind as functional and semiotic, establishing a general theory of signs on the basis of biological and physical sciences, and asserting the reconstructive role of ideas in society.

Morris set about making a name for himself at the Rice Institute (now Rice University), where he was hired as an instructor. He published early essays in major philosophical journals (especially *The Monist*) in which he argued that a coherent application of what he was sometimes calling "neo-" or "critical pragmatism" gave a more adequate solution to the problems of ethics, epistemology, logic, and philosophy of mind than other extant schools of thought. In addition, he began preparing commentaries on the metaphysics and philosophies of mind of major authors, including Bertrand Russell, Alfred N. Whitehead, John Laird, A. O. Lovejoy, Charles A. Strong, G. Watts Cunningham, A. P. Brogan, C. I. Lewis, and John Dewey. In preparing these commentaries, Morris solicited responses from most, if not all, of these eminent philosophers and received significant corrections from Laird, Lovejoy, Strong, Russell, and Dewey. A few of these commentaries were published as separate essays, but they were primarily used in his public lectures on "The Nature of Mind" which constituted an early draft of parts of his first book-length published work, *Six Theories of Mind* (Morris 1932). Morris attempted, through his research and his correspondence with eminent authors, to study the major schools of thought on the nature of mind in their own terms. At the same time, he attempted to show that the "mind as function" view championed by the pragmatists was the most adequate understanding, in large part because of its "synthetic character." That is, the pragmatists' theory "is able to take into itself the positive insights of the rival theories without being forced into the predicaments met in those theories when individually taken as adequate" (329). The key to the functional view of mind, Morris proposed, was its formulation in terms of symbolic activity (328).

In his *Six Theories of Mind*, Morris also initiated one of the most distinctive aspects of his published claims about Mead: he referred to works about Mead in advance of their publication. In particular, he gave a substantial quotation from the Carus Lectures (Morris 1932, 315–16), which were still in the process of being prepared for publication as *The Philosophy of the Present* (Mead 1932), and he drew attention to the "account of the symbol in social terms" in "a volume of Mead's writings which will appear under the title, *Mind, Self, and Society*" (Morris 1932, 323). This second work was two and a half years away from publication and was being put together by Morris himself, yet he referred to it as if it already existed and had a definite "account" to give. Finally, in this work and in an earlier review of works by John F. Markey and Grace de Laguna, Morris referred to Dewey's and Mead's perspectives as "social behaviorism" for the first time in order to stress their "larger non-Watsonian sense" of behavioral study of language and symbolism (Morris 1929, 614; 1932, 320).[8]

The senior members of the Chicago philosophy department, and especially Mead, were greatly impressed with Morris's work while he was at Rice. In the late 1920s the philosophy department in Chicago began to develop specific plans for the retirement of its long-time cohort of faculty members, Mead, James H. Tufts, Addison W. Moore, and Edward S. Ames. They began an ambitious attempt to appoint young scholars of exceptional promise who could continue the distinctive work of the department, and Morris featured prominently in these discussions.[9] When the newly appointed president Robert M. Hutchins pushed to appoint three of his acquaintances (Mortimer Adler, Scott Buchanan, and Richard McKeon) to positions, Tufts proposed appointing some combination of recent Chicago PhD students "who seem to have unusual promise" as an alternative; the only former Chicago student specifically named in his report was Charles Morris.[10] The subsequent debacle in which Hutchins ignored the department's advice by appointing Adler anyway at a salary much higher than its current senior members and by stalling on other appointments—the first round in the so-called Hutchins Controversy (Cook 1993)—led Tufts to take an earlier-than-expected retirement.

Mead was appointed interim chair of the department and he argued forcefully for the appointment of Morris in his communications with the university administration:

Mr. Morris is perhaps the most brilliant of our recent Doctors, and while quite original in own position he represents the philosophical attitude which in the past has given to the "Chicago School" its national and international reputations. . . . As Mr. Morris is I think the most promising of the Chicago Doctors, it is altogether appropriate that the permanent merit of our own graduate school should be recognized by his appointment. . . . There is no available man in the country of comparable age and experience, whose work promises so much or who has already fulfilled that promise to such an extent. . . . Personally and in his contributions to philosophy Mr. Morris would fit into the plans of the Department. Both as a student and later he has held the confidence and respect of its members in every way.[11]

In another undated memorandum from this period apparently written by Mead, he identified the place of Morris in the department's plan to maintain its distinctive intellectual identity (and more practically, its course offerings) in the coming years:

The peculiar contribution which Professor Morris will make to the department in the working out of its program is indicated by the title of the treatise he is bringing out, "The Philosophy of Mind" [i.e., *Six Theories of Mind*]. Beside his interest in logic and metaphysics his field will include the work which has been carried for years in the department under "Advanced Social Psychology." His work will connect the department directly with that of Psychology and with that of Art and with the interpretation of literature.[12]

Indeed, Mead went out of his way to repeatedly advocate bringing Morris to Chicago, and specifically identified him as the most able person to take over the kind of work that he, himself, had developed in his Advanced Social Psychology courses.

The second and more consequential round of the Hutchins Controversy occurred in the 1930–31 academic year.[13] Hutchins again ignored departmental proposals to bring Morris and A. P. Brogan to Chicago for permanent appointments. He pushed instead for the appointment of Buchanan and McKeon, and he solicited secret, hand-picked outside opinions regarding the competency of the current department members (Cook 1993, 183ff.). As a result, Mead, Murphy, Burtt, and instructor Everett Hall resigned, and the controversy made the national press in early February 1931. As an apparent conciliatory move, and under the advice of Vice Pres-

ident Frederic Woodward and remaining department members Edward S.
Ames and T. V. Smith, Hutchins agreed to offer a position to Charles Morris, who was strongly ambivalent about accepting. The deciding factor for
Morris was Mead's encouragement to take the position despite his own
resignation.[14] When Morris came to Chicago as associate professor (at age
thirty) in the 1931–32 academic year, all the parties to the dispute (as well
as the larger university) understood Morris to be in some sense the successor to Mead and the tradition of the department.

MORRIS AS SYNTHESIZER

As was discussed in chapter 5, Morris was charged almost immediately
with the practical enterprise of editing some combination of materials that
would stand as a published legacy to Mead. In Morris's diary, he confided
some of his thoughts on that work as he received the final proof-sheets for
Mind, Self, and Society in October 1934:

> It is incredible how much of my time in the last three years has gone
> into this volume—and how much of myself! The passage from stu-
> dents' notes to a final and fairly satisfactory volume has been a long
> and difficult one—I have combed the material at least ten times, and
> what is printed is only the smallest portion of the thousands of pages
> of material read. What a magnificent book Mead could have made if he
> had set himself the task of systematic formulation. What I have done is
> only a shadow of that book. Nevertheless I think the basic ideas which
> I have helped to save are of tremendous fertility and suggestiveness.
> (quoted in Cook 2013, 103 n. 1)

I will not repeat the details of the creation of *Mind, Self, and Society* and
the other posthumous volumes, discussed in chapter 5, but it bears emphasis that Morris put considerable editorial effort into the volumes, and
that social pressures and expectations from Mead's former colleagues and
students, his family, and the University of Chicago Press weighed on the
editors and especially on Morris. The examination above of the circumstances of Morris's appointment further highlights these pressures. And
as a rising and ambitious young philosopher, he was also expected to do
innovative work of his own on top of his work to memorialize Mead.

   In his first years as a professor at Chicago, Morris engaged in organizing several new initiatives. In spring 1932 he proposed the creation of an
endowed "American Institute of Philosophy" at Chicago that ultimately

failed to materialize; he attempted to interest the University of Chicago Press in an edited volume on "Science and Symbolism" with proposed contributions by Herbert Blumer, Ellsworth Faris, and two dozen other prominent scholars, as a companion to his *Six Theories of Mind*; he established an interdisciplinary History of Science lecture series of Chicago faculty that by 1936 had expanded into the semi-official History of Science Committee of the university; and by 1936 Morris was an organizer of a Logic of Science discussion group which had over fifty participants at various times and provided a venue for lectures and discussions by traveling (or displaced) European scholars.[15] The work on the Mead volumes was, in this context, understood by Morris and others as a "labor of love" for which Morris received more praise than criticism, at least in private.[16]

In between his extramural endeavors, his teaching, and his editorship of the Mead volumes, Morris also became integrally involved in the so-called unity of science movement, which proved an important venue for his work on symbolism and the nature of mind. His earliest work had put him in contact with the leading philosophical innovators in the United States and Europe by 1933, including the active "logical positivist" (or logical empiricist) circles in Vienna, Berlin, and Prague. He attended the 1934 International Conference of Philosophy and the special Preliminary Conference in Prague organized by Otto Neurath explicitly to consider the "unity of science." At that meeting Morris presented "A Thesis on the Complementary Character of American Pragmatism and Logical Positivism," which gives a clear indication of the synthetic direction in which his work was moving (Stadler 2001, 360).

Mead was never far from Morris's endeavors toward a unity of science. For example, while touring European intellectual centers from May to November of 1934 in connection with the Prague conference, Morris also edited galley proofs of *Mind, Self, and Society* and apparently discussed them with his hosts.[17] When the volume appeared in press shortly after his return to the United States, he sent copies of the first printing to prominent European intellectuals he had met, including Ivan Pavlov, Karl Bühler, Rudolf Carnap, Hans Reichenbach, Louis Rougier, and Walter Dubislav. Morris subsequently became the major American partner in the various plans for an *International Encyclopedia of Unified Science* (*IEUS*), a *Journal of Unified Science* (to replace the troubled European journal *Erkenntnis*), and a "Library of Unified Science" monograph series at the University of Chicago Press; and he increasingly became a broker of relationships between displaced Europeans and American academic institutions (cf. Reisch 1995, 2005; Galison 1996; Stadler 2001). Through his work with the University of Chicago Press, the efforts to promote the unity of science movement were literally built in part on the social networks established through the Mead volumes. The press used the list of Mead's students they had generated to solicit advanced subscriptions for the posthumous Mead volumes in order to advertise for and solicit subscriptions to the *IEUS*.[18] And the press decided to include all three of its posthumous Mead volumes as well as promotional materials for them in its limited book display at the 1939 Harvard International Congress on Unified Science that Morris organized, alongside its newly published *Foundations of the Unity of Science*, volume 1.[19]

Morris saw aspects of agreement between his "critical pragmatism" and the work of the logical positivists (e.g., Morris 1933). Much of his work during the 1930s was directed toward laying out a proposed synthesis of the two intellectual traditions through the medium of his new "organon" of science, the general theory of signs, or "semiotic." His various essays along these lines were republished together as *Logical Positivism, Pragmatism, and Scientific Empiricism* (Morris 1937a), which includes his first exposition of the distinction for which he would become known in the study of signs, between "syntactics," "semantics," and "pragmatics." He argued that linguistic signs maintain three irreducible types of relations: (1) to other signs, (2) to objects signified, and (3) to persons who use them, which make up the three respective fields of semiotics. This system was further elaborated in Morris's *Foundations of the Theory of Signs* (1938) and *Signs, Language, and Behavior* (1946).

Through this schema, Morris found a solution to the synthesis of pragmatism and logical positivism, as partial perspectives primarily concerned with only one aspect of the larger philosophical task—pragmatism with pragmatics (hence the name), logical positivism with syntactics, and their common ancestor, British empiricism, with semantics (Morris 1937a, 4). Where the Europeans emphasized logical positivism derived from the physical and mathematical sciences, the American pragmatists emphasized a "bio-social positivism" derived from the biological and social sciences (Morris 1937a, 24–25). Text box 6.1 illustrates the productivity of this schema for Morris by putting in graphic form some the homologous distinctions that Morris identified in his *Scientific Empiricism*. Standing above these distinctions (and, in a sense, representing the table as a whole) is the field of semiotics and the synthetic approach of "scientific empiricism." The field of inquiry for philosophy in this conception, Morris argued, would be a "language of languages," or "meta-language," which

TEXT BOX 6.1. Homologous threefold distinctions in Morris's semiotics

	I	II	III
Relation of signs	To other signs	To objects signified	To persons who use or understand
Field of investigation	Syntactics	Semantics	Pragmatics
Attitude/emphasis of investigator	Formalism	Empiricism	Pragmatism
Aspect of scientific method	Theory	Observation	Experimentation
Associated school of thought	Logical positivism	Traditional British empiricism	Critical pragmatism
Scholastic *trivium*	Grammar	Logic	Rhetoric
Function of scientific philosophical field	Logic/clarification philosophy of meaning	Empirical cosmology	Empirical axiology

Source: Adapted from Morris 1937a.

could take up each of the component fields severally, as well as examine the conditions of their relations as a whole (Morris 1937a, 21; 1938, 42).

Morris's theory is effectively a synthesis by systematization; he identified what he thought was the appropriate location and scope of each form of philosophical inquiry as components of his larger architectonic and metadiscipline. In this way Morris was able to dismiss apparent contradictions or incompatibilities in contemporary philosophy as resulting from commitments to the immanent objects of a particular phase in the larger work of philosophy. This vision allowed him, he thought, to maintain that the unity of science was not merely something that existed or not (to be discovered by logical or conceptual analysis of the whole), but rather something that could be achieved through concerted social endeavor of scientists working on various component problems. Although the structure of the synthesis changed several times in Morris's career, the basic commitment to this strategy of argument remained throughout.

As a result of his writings on signs, especially *Signs, Language, and Behavior* (Morris 1946), in which he put forth his most comprehensive and resolute statement of his "behavioral semiotics," Morris became involved in perhaps the most elemental conflicts of his career. From his earliest work on symbolism Morris had repeatedly argued that symbols must be located in the experience of organisms, and that a behavioral focus provided an adequate basis for a comprehensive theory of signs (1993 [1925], 3–4; see also Morris 1946). He also argued that the pragmatists, and especially Dewey and Mead, had "always been behavioristic in the larger non-Watsonian sense," and that his own "behavioral" position owed much to the theories of behavior of Dewey and Mead, which he termed "social behaviorism" (Morris 1929, 614; 1932, 320; 1946, v). *Signs, Language, and Behavior* was widely discussed and criticized in the academic literature of the time. This included prominent critiques by John Dewey, Arthur F. Bentley, and others, who primarily went after the implications of his behaviorist orientation.[20] Morris decided to address their criticisms as a group in an article sarcastically titled "Signs about Signs about Signs." In addition to pointing out that his work was intended as a "prolegomenon" and not the actual accomplishment of a science of signs, the emphasis of his rebuttal was on defining and defending his "primarily methodological," not ontological, behaviorism (1948a, 115–17). He argued that his position attempted to "extend the behavioral analyses of Mead, Tolman, and Hull" and that "*Signs, Language and Behavior* is in many ways a further development of Mead's *Mind, Self, and Society*" (122, 124).[21] This behaviorism did not commit him to a "rat-level psychology," and did not require Morris to surreptitiously smuggle in "mentalistic" categories under the guise of undefined terms, as his critics charged (122–23).[22] For Morris, Mead was simultaneously located both in "pragmatics," that is, in one of the component fields, and as the person whose "social behaviorism" provided an adequate basis for the whole of semiotics by providing a firm social-objective basis for the emergence of signs.

In the 1940s Morris inaugurated a major new direction in his work with his series of studies on comparative human values, which also incorporated Mead in a distinctive way. In *Paths of Life* (1942), he proposed a tripartite division between "Dionysian," "Promethean," and "Buddhistic" personality types, which were exemplified by the philosophies of Nietzsche, Dewey, and Buddha respectively, and were considered as analogous to W. H. Sheldon's controversial "somatotypes." This book and the two that followed elaborated Morris's early interests in world religions, theories of civilization, and psychopathology, which were not previously subsumed under his formal theory of signs.

In these works, especially *The Open Self* (1948b), Morris drew from Mead and Dewey to argue that the cultivation of "new selves" is possible through social reconstruction, highlighting their analyses of the social-symbolic nature of the self. Morris argued that in order to make human personality adequate to the problems of modern society, conscious planning and effort should be directed toward the creation of open, balanced selves through open societies. His original three "paths" were expanded into a list of thirteen "ways to live" as a result of a variety of researches (73). Morris was at pains to argue both that all "ways" are valid, and that some are more adequate to the problems of modern societies than others. Thus, Morris also brought in Mead's late cosmological theory of "objective relativism" as a more satisfying alternative to existing "perspectivist" or "contextualist" pluralistic philosophies of values (130).

By his third volume in this series, *Varieties of Human Value* (1956), Morris moved away from seeing his work as a "preface to world religion," and toward explicitly identifying it as a "scientific" and empirical assessment of values. Although he admitted throughout that the results obtained from the statistical tests he developed and value surveys he administered in large numbers were at best tentative and qualified, he argued that the study had another "motivating purpose": "to develop the theory of value in such a way that it would find a place within, or make a contribution to, the general theory of behavior" (192). In this regard he explicitly compared the "categories and dimensions" of his work on values to the phases of the act as theorized by Mead and Talcott Parsons (192–94). In particular, he proposed that his own basic categories of value—detachment, dominance, and dependence—mapped onto Mead's perceptual, manipulatory, and consummatory phases, and that his "factors" somewhat coincided with Parsons' pattern variables.[23]

In perhaps Morris's final extended statement of his life's work, *Signification and Significance* (1964), he identified the place of Mead in his intellectual project:

> For several decades my work has centered around two problems: the development of a general theory of signs and the development of a general theory of values. *Signs, Language and Behavior* was the product of the first concern, and *Varieties of Human Value* was a product of the second. Both problems were approached in terms of the theory of action or behavior developed in its essentials by George H. Mead. (vii)

This echoed the many public and private acknowledgments of his debt to Mead he had made over the years.[24] Mead recurred throughout Morris's theoretical schemas both for the general orientation and in many of the particulars of his own work. In this late work, Morris attempted to bring together in a principled way his two major projects through an encompassing science of behavior, and again it was Mead that provided the framework.

Morris also wrote a final book on *The Pragmatic Movement in American Philosophy* (1970), which was part of a renewed literature on the history of pragmatism that put Mead firmly among the other classical American philosophers, Charles S. Peirce, William James, and John Dewey (e.g., Thayer 1968; Rucker 1969; Scheffler 1974).[25] Indeed, the materials that Morris prepared for the original book jackets of the posthumous Mead volumes (over thirty years previous) are, as far as I can tell, the first significant documentary source for the proposition that Mead, Peirce, James, and Dewey were to be considered the definitive set of American pragmatist philosophers.[26] Morris went out of his way to argue that Mead was not a "disciple" or "student" of the other classic authors and had no inspiring "philosopher" in the sense that James had the British Empiricists, Dewey had Hegel, or Peirce had Kant (1970, 33). Instead "Mead gave an original and independent accent to the pragmatic movement," and his most original contributions were his treatment of biological evolution, his behavioral analysis of the language symbol and its role in the development of the human self and human society, and a related pragmatist "cosmology" (8, 36, 126–28). Morris argued that overall the classical pragmatists exhibited a certain unity, not of a closed system but of a set of common themes: a behavioral semiotics, a semiotically interpreted logic, an epistemology oriented around the study of inquiry, an axiology conceived as the study of preferential behaviors, a view of experience as an integral part of the cosmos, and a semiotic theory of mind (141–42). In his final attempt to bring together the pragmatists, Morris seems to have made them into his own image, or saw himself as the expression of their essential unity—either way conflating their various projects and his.

Throughout his career Morris positioned his work as primarily synthetic in nature, but in order to accomplish his syntheses Morris distinguished different compartments or constituents governed by a more adequate whole. In each case, Mead's work both fit into one of the compartments and provided a key to the whole. His *Six Theories of Mind* distinguished six general views or metaphors for the nature of mind, with Mead in the "mind as function" view, and he argued that Mead's formulation of the mind in terms of symbolic activity allows the pragmatists' view to encompass the important aspects of the other views. In his work on symbolism Morris attempted to synthesize logical positivism and pragmatism into a "scientific empiricism" whose object of study would be sign processes in all their modes and relations. As was mentioned above, Mead was definitely located as contributor to the study of the "pragmatics," but also as the originator of the whole of behavioral semiotics. Morris's value studies brought together all of what he viewed as the ultimate, distinguishable and coherent, ways of living. In this, the pragmatists were identified with the "Promethean" path (later "Way 6"), but Mead's pluralistic philosophy and social psychology also provided the tools for the establishment of a moderated and open self appropriate to modern problems.

ACCESS AND PRIVILEGE

More than any other single individual, Morris has shaped the physical materials upon which understandings of Mead are based. As was discussed in chapter 5, he was the editor of *Mind, Self, and Society*, through which Mead's social theory is primarily known and cited today, and was also the leader of the team that put together *The Philosophy of the Act*, where he consequently had myriad influences on the resulting volume. The division created by the three posthumous works published by the University of Chicago Press—between "social psychology," "history of ideas," and "systematic pragmatism"—is in some ways part of the same kind of synthesis by systematization that segregates work into separate (arguably nonexclusive) endeavors at the same time it brings together a single, definitive body of thought. Still, as chapter 5 identified, Morris worked under difficult circumstances and based his decisions about the volumes on available materials and information and under considerable social and economic restraints, so he cannot be merely credited (or blamed) for the whole result of the project.

Morris's influence, however, did not stop with the form of the published materials that stood for Mead; he also endeavored through his published works and his actions to guide the interpretations that came from those volumes. Morris referred substantively to material by Mead not yet available in print eight times in his published work in the 1930s.[27] He even urged readers to "See Mead's *The Philosophy of the Act*" for his "conception of the act and the objective relativistic cosmology which results from its application," long before they had this privilege, and referred to that volume as "without doubt the major contribution of this wing of pragmatism to the philosophy of science" (Morris 1935, 145; 1937b, 120). In this way, Morris ensured his priority of citation to Mead and helped set the terms of debate by defining the essential propositions and contributions of these works. He also defined the works fundamentally as "Mead's," and as Mead's "writings," thereby naturalizing them as clear expressions of their attributed author's intention (and implicitly eliding their posthumous construction).

While most of the reviews of *Mind, Self, and Society* were positive, there were several notable exceptions written by influential individuals. The earliest one that came to Morris's attention was the review by Wilson D. Wallis, which was especially acute because it appeared in the *International Journal of Ethics* based out of the University of Chicago philosophy department. Among other things, Wallis (1935, 459) quipped, "One is tempted to regret this flaunting of the lecturer's implied wish that these words of his go no farther than the ears of his classroom hearers. . . . There are times when it is wise as well as appropriate to respect the wishes of the deceased." In response, there was a flurry of discussion between Morris and the editorial staff of the University of Chicago Press. Morris wanted to draft a letter to the journal's editor (his colleague T. V. Smith), but Chicago Press managing editor Donald P. Bean and general editor Gordon J. Laing convinced Morris the best course would be to include a preface in *Movements of Thought in the Nineteenth Century*, the next volume to be published in the Mead series, laying out a principled defense of the publication of such materials.[28] This "Prefatory Note," written by the volume's editor Merritt H. Moore, but based on detailed suggestions from Morris and Laing, acknowledged the difficulties of editing and publishing classroom notes while at the same time maintaining that the notes for these volumes "represent their author's mature views," that the project was begun by Mead's family (not the volume editors), and that there is "historical precedent" for publishing much less "stenographic" lecture material in the well-known works of Epictetus, Aristotle, Leibniz, Kant, Fichte, and Hegel (Moore 1936, vi–viii).

Morris also responded to F. C. S. Schiller's (1936a, 83) negative review of *Mind, Self, and Society* by locating it in a larger ongoing disagreement between himself and the British pragmatist on the social and behavioral nature of scientific knowledge and the place of pragmatism in relation to logical positivism (Morris 1936). Morris argued that "Mead's form of behaviorism," which Schiller had dismissed, provided an account of the intersubjective nature of meaning that more adequately explains the "personal" factors in scientific knowledge than did Schiller's philosophy, and that it grounds a "science of personality" as part of a self-reflexive scientific endeavor (298).[29] And Morris also responded to his sociology colleague Ellsworth Faris's (1936, 809) criticism of *Mind, Self, and Society* in the *American Journal of Sociology*, which accused Morris of having "taken the liberty to rearrange the material in a fashion that will be deprecated by many who knew Mead and thought they understood him." Morris published a letter in which he attempted to enumerate the "minor" changes he made to the order of material from the original lecture notes, asserting that while it "may not be the best order" it was nevertheless largely "Mead's order" (Morris 1937c, 561). Faris apologized in print, writing that he based his claims on his own earlier notes from Mead's classes that evinced "a very different order," but that Mead must have changed the presentation in his later teaching (Faris 1937a, 561). With each encounter Morris actively contended with critics in defining his own role as editor, the authenticity of the depiction of Mead that emerged from the posthumous volumes, and the major conceptual contributions that these volumes preserved to Mead.

Morris also remained an important gatekeeper for access to Mead's various unpublished notes and manuscripts throughout his career. Of course, Morris taught Mead in a wide variety of courses at Chicago, New School, Harvard, and Florida.[30] He apparently used manuscripts in early seminars and allowed his students access to some of the materials. He was also consulted far and wide by scholars, especially young scholars working on graduate work on Mead, for information and access to the archival materials related to Mead. Indeed, he personally supervised or provided outside advice on virtually all the dissertations on Mead in the middle decades of the twentieth century.[31] Some of these students used the manuscripts related to Mead in their own work. And Morris apparently privately circulated manuscripts by Mead to his friends and was kept informed of discoveries of other manuscript materials regarding Mead.[32]

In the ways he managed the physical manuscripts of Meads writings and students' notes, referred to Mead on the basis of materials often not generally accessible, and structured the reception of materials prior to and after their publication, Morris mobilized claims on the basis of controlled access to materials and on the privilege to interpret his former teacher on the basis of that access. In this he was bolstered by the strong, early sanction given by Mead and by the understanding that Morris was carrying the torch for the Chicago pragmatist philosophy forward into new fields of study. And this sanction likely served to make the claims about Mead and pragmatism appear legitimate to Morris himself. His authority in making these claims certainly rested on his breadth of experience in Mead's classes and especially on the breadth of materials related to Mead that he had examined.

BLUMER AND MEAD

Herbert George Blumer came to the University of Chicago first as a summer school student in 1923 while he was an instructor at the University of Missouri where he had gotten his bachelor's and master's degrees. At Missouri, Blumer had been encouraged to go to Chicago to study by Charles A. Ellwood, who was himself an early student of Dewey and Mead.[33] However, despite having worked with this pragmatist-oriented social psychologist, Blumer remembered being a committed behaviorist and follower of Max Meyer when he came to Chicago (Blumer 1977, 285).[34] Although he definitely knew of Mead before coming to Chicago, it was through his early courses with Ellsworth Faris that he recalled that he "really became familiar with the name Mead and was given some impetus to move in the direction of familiarizing myself with his work" (quoted in Smith 1977, 159). He also took courses with Robert E. Park on collective behavior and race relations, and other courses taught by Ernest Burgess, Faye Cooper Cole, and Edward Sapir in sociology and anthropology; L. L. Thurstone and Kurt Koffka (who was a visiting professor in summer 1924) in psychology; Edward S. Ames and James H. Tufts in philosophy; and Charles E. Merriam in political science.

The only formal coursework with Mead for which Blumer registered was the winter 1926 Advanced Social Psychology course, although it is quite possible that he audited additional classes.[35] He was also a registered research assistant for Mead in autumn 1926 and winter 1927, and it was in these more informal meetings that Blumer felt he got to know Mead "on a person-to-person basis" (Smith 1977, 159). This work with Mead, he thought, led him to "completely recast" his previously held "behavioristic position" into one focused on "the social act."[36] On several occasions, Blumer also emphasized the importance of the "education" the graduate students received from one another in their various formal and informal meetings, education that reportedly included discussions of Mead (Smith 1977, 161; Lofland 1980, 269).

Blumer wrote his 1928 dissertation on "Method in Social Psychology" under the supervision of Ellsworth Faris, with Mead and Park sitting on his examining committee. Most of his preparatory work was taken with Faris, including extensive work abstracting and reviewing books on topics related to social psychology and scientific method for the *American Journal of Sociology*.[37] To the extent that his dissertation had a central thesis, it was the argument that, in order to be scientific, social psychology needed to develop a method adequate to the examination of its object of study.

The primary philosophical warrant for this argument, which formed an important cornerstone throughout Blumer's career, was apparently Mead's "Scientific Method and Individual Thinker" (1917c), which Blumer referred to more than any other single work in his dissertation. The task of determining an adequate method for social psychology required "critical consideration and evaluation" both into the nature of scientific method and the nature of social psychology, but it offered no "constructive" statement of method (Blumer 1928, iii–iv).

He discussed at length the social psychological views of a long list of authors, ending with extended explications of the theories of Ellsworth Faris and George H. Mead constructed as a synthesis of their writings, lectures, and his personal acquaintance with them, not reducible to any of their individual works.[38] Indeed, in the explication of Mead's perspective, no specific quotation or citation is made to any publications, although his works are cited elsewhere in the dissertation. His examination of Mead, the most extensive of any of the authors considered, focused on his views of the nature of human interaction, the character of mental activity, and the emergence of the self and correlative organization of the individual's world. Like Morris, whose early work also methodically examined the writings of a wide variety of authors in the attempt to determine the outlines of and most satisfactory perspective in an emerging field of thought, Blumer confirmed his attachment to what he saw as the tradition of his mentors in light of a thorough examination of existing work bearing on social psychology.

Although he acknowledged that many of the writers, including Mead, did not explicitly detail the methodological approach entailed by their views of social psychology, Blumer grouped the authors into two basic approaches. The first approach viewed psychology as the objective behavioral study of the individual organism in response to stimuli, and so relied on methods of experiment and other objective assessment in which particular stimuli and responses could be separated, observed, and measured. The second group, which included Mead, Baldwin, Cooley, Faris, Dewey, Thomas, Znaniecki, and J. M. Williams, emphasized the importance of examining meaning in actual human conduct. He claimed that Cooley's "sympathetic introspection" was the exemplary method of this group, and he relied explicitly on Faris's (1937c [1926]) argument to that effect. Faris's criticisms of existing psychological methods focused on how various schools of thought relied on psychological "elements" (e.g., instincts, faculties, sensations, reflexes) as explanatory devices for human behavior instead of explaining those elements as the outcome of social action pro-

cesses. Blumer picked up the same line of criticism, in effect proposing a
firm criterion: only those theories that located explanation at the level of
the human being in social action could be adequate to a scientific social
psychology. Faris's influence on Blumer's interpretation of Mead is pervasive both in his dissertation and in his lifelong engagement with Mead's
work. The importance of Faris as a gatekeeper to Mead's ideas for Chicago
sociologists is further emphasized in chapter 7.

Blumer was immediately hired after graduation as an instructor in
the sociology department chaired by Ellsworth Faris. During this time
he taught some of the introductory courses at Chicago. In order to make
ends meet and as a venue for recreation he was also teaching at the Chicago YMCA and moonlighting as a semi-professional football player for
the Chicago Cardinals. When Mead fell ill in winter 1931 it was Blumer
who he asked to teach the Advanced Social Psychology class. It appears
that Mead likely turned first to Faris, who was teaching the prerequisite
Introduction to Social Psychology in the sociology department, and that
in light of his duties as department chair and editor of the *American Journal of Sociology* Faris proposed Blumer.[39] Writing from the hospital, Mead
confirmed to the university's administration that Blumer was "very competent to carry on the work" and encouraged them to find proper financial
compensation for him, even if that meant drawing it from Mead's own
salary.[40] During Mead's fatal illness Blumer was in contact with Charles
Morris regarding his offer to come to Chicago, and despite the latter's ar-
rival the following fall, Blumer remained the permanent instructor for the
Advanced Social Psychology course. Faris later emphasized the conceptual
importance of the fact that the social psychology course moved permanently from the philosophy to the sociology department:

> it is worth recording that, when Mead was stricken in the early part of
> his last quarter of teaching, the philosophy department approached us
> to find someone to carry on the course, a task which Professor Blumer
> of the department of sociology performed to the satisfaction of us all.
> At present the course on social psychology does not appear in the of-
> ferings of the philosophy department, and in the University of Chicago
> it is the sociologists who are trying to carry on the tradition of Mead.
> (Faris 1937b, 393)[41]

Blumer continued to teach the Advanced Social Psychology course
until he left Chicago in 1952 to take up the chairmanship of the newly
founded sociology department at the University of California–Berkeley.

And after Faris gave up many of his duties in the late 1930s Blumer added the introductory course to his offerings as well. Besides social psychology, Blumer's other major teaching commitment was to offer courses in collective behavior, in both its more organized sense of social movements and its less organized sense of fashions and folkways. Robert Park was Blumer's primary influence in these courses, but there was considerable conceptual overlap between his interests in social psychology and collective behavior.[42]

The existing materials from Blumer's courses in the 1930s indicate that he was working out his "Symbolic Interactionist" approach from his earliest teaching, although the first statement of this perspective only appeared in print at the end of the decade. In his teaching he largely followed the distinctions made in his dissertation, identifying Mead's approach as a more adequate social psychology than either the "stimulus-response" or "behaviorist" theory, or the "cultural determinist" theory of the French sociologists (with whom he had studied on a fellowship in the early 1930s), because Mead alone focused on the "self-experienced meaning of objects."[43] In his advanced courses, he gave the students an extended view of Mead's perspective, discussing the nature and development of the self, the theory of the object as self-indication, the phases of the act, and the social development of rational thought, and referring them to a variety of Mead's published writings. As early as February 1935, he had written the University of Chicago Press inquiring whether they could provide a special price for the use of the newly printed *Mind, Self, and Society* as a text in his courses.[44] In many ways he was continuing Mead's social psychology course as a formalization of his predecessor's teaching, and he was even literally using the printed version of Mead's lectures to teach Mead's lectures.[45]

The notes from Blumer's courses also indicate that, from its earliest formulations, the notion of "symbolic interaction" was contrasted with "nonsymbolic interaction," and that this clear distinction of interactional "levels" was indebted at least as much to a particular Parkian reading of Georg Simmel as it was to Mead. In teaching his introductory courses, Blumer used Park and Burgess's *Introduction to the Science of Sociology* (1924 [1921]), which contained a translation of a portion of Simmel's excursus on "the sociology of the senses." The translation makes a firm distinction between (1) "appreciation," which refers to the "affective responses" that do not "enable us to understand or to define the other person" but rather "leaves [the other's] real sense outside," and (2) "comprehension," in which "sense-impression of the other person" becomes "the medium for understanding the other" and "the bridge over which I reach his real self"

(356–57).[46] There was an analogous distinction in Mead's work, Blumer thought, between the "conversation of gestures" and the "use of significant symbols" (e.g., Blumer 1969, 8). Blumer apparently addressed Simmel's excursus in depth in his lectures and referred to it as the best discussion of the distinction of symbolic and nonsymbolic interaction.[47] Indeed, Blumer appears to have used the conceptual distinctions of the *Introduction to the Science of Sociology* extensively throughout his early courses, including his social psychology lectures. In addition to "levels" of interaction, he also distinguished "forms" or "types" of interaction including "suggestion" and "imitation," and "processes" of interaction including "competition," "conflict," "accommodation," and "assimilation," all prefigured in the Park and Burgess textbook (1924, xiii–xviii).

In his published statement that introduced the term "symbolic interactionism," Blumer (1937) made no mention of Simmel or Park, instead assigning Cooley, Mead, Dewey, Thomas, and Faris to this perspective.[48] That article is essentially a *précis* of the perspective he had been elaborating over the past decade in front of his students, in which he criticized instinct theory, cultural determinism, and stimulus-response theory from the standpoint of a more adequate conception and methodology for the study of social psychology. And that article was, in turn, taught in his social psychology classes.[49] Blumer dismissed offhand the biological determinism of the instinct theory and the cultural determinism of the French sociologists; he argued they were not appropriate for empirical study of human conduct, because they dismissed entirely either the "group setting" or the individual's "original nature," respectively (160). Thus, he was left with the fundamental distinction between the stimulus-response theory and symbolic interactionism as the "two dominant views in modern social psychology." Society, in the symbolic interactionist view, was made up of "cooperative forms of activity" guided to common understandings by the use of symbols. As in his lectures, he argued in the published article that Mead gives "the most illuminating treatment of the self" of any author, and he discussed Mead's stages of the development of the self in depth (180–85). His criticism of the "stimulus-response" approach was broadened so that it no longer referred primarily to laboratory experiments, but also to quantitative "devices" including questionnaires, schedules, and tests that were getting "a great deal of use" in "the study of attitudes" (188). Although he briefly mentioned quantitative methods of social psychology in his dissertation, his criticisms of those techniques expanded in response to developments over the following decade, especially the growth of attitude measurement surveys.[50] These devices, Blumer argued, fail to "catch the 'meanings' which mediate and determine the way in which individuals respond to objects and situations," and instead merely record "replies" to "definite stimuli" (189, 193). The symbolic interactionists, by contrast, viewed all the mediating, thinking, daydreaming, planning, and imaginative play as part of the act as a whole, because social action can have a "covert or inner career before coming to external or overt expression" (192).

BLUMER AS CRITIC

In contrast to Charles Morris, who addressed the variety of existing intellectual perspectives by finding a place for each in his synthetic approach, Blumer developed a set of criteria regarding the proper conception of the social world and the methods adequate to its study that led him primarily to criticize or dismiss approaches that could not fulfill those standards. The most explicit and extended discussion of his critical approach came in the introductory essay to his collected papers on *Symbolic Interactionism* (Blumer 1969). In that essay he argued that symbolic interactionism relied upon three "simple premises" (2), which are displayed in text box 6.2. Although these premises seem straightforward, Blumer argued that virtually all other existing social scientific approaches ignored their profound implications. Along with these premises were six "root images" that depict the nature of the social world as conceived by symbolic interactionists (6–20), also displayed in text box 6.2. In relation to these criteria, Blumer elaborated a methodological stance based on the "naturalistic" study of the social world in which the empirical social world is the final test of all concepts. He ended his essay with a "simple injunction" that echoed the thrust of his dissertation: "Respect the nature of the empirical world and organize a methodological stance to reflect that respect" (60).

In the rest of the collected essays of *Symbolic Interactionism*, which Blumer had previously published in various contexts, the reader witnesses the critical apparatus at work. Blumer viewed as inadequate any conception that constructed a view of human group life to conform to given ideas of individual psychological makeup, or that brought in schemes or concepts from other domains of study, or that used speculative reflections instead of empirical study to develop a conception of society. He argued that concepts then in wide use among sociologists, including "attitude" and "variable," abstract away from the processes of interpretation that people undertook in their actual lives and instead attributed explanation to artificial constructs. Interpretive processes, both in the ways people take account of one another in joint actions and the ways people make

---

TEXT BOX 6.2. Blumer's criteria for the study of social life

Basic Premises of Symbolic Interactionism

I.   "Human beings act toward things on the basis of the meanings that the things have for them."

II.   "The meaning of such things is derived from, or arises out of, the social interaction that one has with one's fellows."

III. "These meanings are handled in, and modified through, an interpretative process used by the person in dealing with the things he encounters."

"Root Images" of the Social World

1.   Human group life exists essentially in action.

2.   Social interaction is not merely a forum for factors that determine it, but is rather a complex formative process that occurs on both symbolic and nonsymbolic levels.

3.   An "object" is anything that can be indicated; thus, the individual's environment comprises "different worlds" through the objects recognized and known; objects are formed and learned through a social process of definition and interpretation.

4.   The human actor possesses a "self," i.e., it can make indications to itself and become an object of its own action.

5.   Because of the capacity to make indications to oneself, the human actor confronts a world that must be interpreted in order to act, allowing for dynamic formation of action rather than merely responses to stimuli.

6.   The articulation of lines of action constitutes "joint action," and hence, social organization and social collectivities; even when organization is relatively stable and recurrent, it still depends on being formed anew through ongoing action.

Source: Adapted from Blumer 1969.

---

self-indications in directing their action, were central for Blumer, and he argued that it was precisely "interpretation" that precludes the closure of concepts like attitude. In these collected essays, he criticized not only sociological approaches, but also approaches to psychology, public opinion polling, and communications research.

Even when the targets of his criticisms changed, Blumer retained a remarkably stable standpoint of critique. In his dissertation and his first reviews and articles, the targets of criticism were much the same psychological theories Faris had criticized, including behaviorism, structural psychology, and psychoanalysis. Blumer turned increasingly to a criticism of quantitative techniques, especially attitude surveys. One of his last published works was an essay on Mead for a volume on *The Future of the Sociological Classics* in which he contrasted Mead's (and implicitly his own) conceptions against others "dominant today in the social and psychological sciences." Those other perspectives viewed human society, he posited, as an organization of culture, a social structure, a social system, a process of social exchange, a conflict process, a power arrangement, a class conflict, or a "mere composite" of individuals with different psychological makeups (Blumer 1981, 153). Again, his main criticism was that in one way or another the conceptions left out the analysis of how society is constituted in joint acts through a process of symbolic interaction. Social life is not essentially conflict, cost-benefit analysis, or system maintenance, but social action and especially the interpretive process, in his view.

This 1981 essay in *The Future of the Sociological Classics* illustrates particularly well how Blumer viewed Mead's perspective as the essential standpoint for critique and for a positive conception of human action. Even at the end of his career, Blumer still thought that Mead had been "lodged at the periphery of sociological concern," subject to "stereotyped characterizations," and only finally beginning to "attract increasing interest and adherence" (Blumer 1981, 136). Yet, among the short list of precursors to his own approach, including Faris, Dewey, Thomas, and Cooley, he repeatedly singled out Mead as the individual who "above all others, laid the foundations of the symbolic interactionist approach" (Blumer 1969, 1; see also Blumer 1937, 1962). Explicating Mead and criticizing conceptions of social life were so much intertwined in Blumer's work that Tamotsu Shibutani (1973, v) could begin his account of his former teacher with the summary remark: "Among sociologists Herbert Blumer is known primarily as an expositor of George H. Mead's social psychology and as a formidable critic."

PARTICIPATION AND OPPOSITION

During his time as a faculty member at Chicago from 1928 to 1952, there is no question that Blumer was a major, insightful interpreter of Mead. As was illustrated above, he discussed Mead at length in his classes. His teaching had an impact on a large number of his students who went on to draw from Mead in their own work.[51] Students he taught, including Hubert Bonner, Tamotsu Shibutani, and Anselm Strauss, all taught Mead in their own courses at the University of Chicago.[52] Outside of this group of sociologists trained at Chicago under Blumer, however, he was not accorded the same status as the premier interpreter of Mead's work in the social sciences.

Other sociologists who had studied with Mead were publishing interpretations of him and teaching his work to their students. George A. Lundberg, one of the leading sociological positivists of the mid-twentieth century, who learned about Mead from L. L. Bernard at the University of Minnesota, argued that Mead (along with Charles Morris, Arthur Bentley, and A. P. Weiss) had established "the objective approach to language" that "definitely destroyed the necessity of a separate realm of the mental as a category in sociological explanation" (Lundberg 1939, 49). Lundberg was particularly formidable as an opponent precisely because his positivism was informed by pragmatism. He and others saw a "convergence" between his own sociological positivism, Mead's writings, and Parsons' structural functionalism (Lundberg 1954; McKinney 1954). C. Wright Mills (1939, 1940a, 1940b) was interpreting and criticizing Mead, of whom he had learned from George Gentry and David L. Miller at the University of Texas and Howard P. Becker and Kimball Young at the University of Wisconsin, as part of his sociology of knowledge. And the so-called Iowa School of symbolic interactionism had developed from 1946 under Manford H. Kuhn, who had been taught about Mead by Kimball Young at the University of Wisconsin (Kuhn 1964; Meltzer and Petras 1973), and who argued in some ways like Lundberg that Mead's concepts could be "operationalized" for empirical assessment through analyses of attitude surveys and the like (Kuhn and McPartland 1954).[53]

In contrast, Blumer had only published one chapter in an edited volume and a few reviews that discussed Mead prior to his 1952 move to Berkeley. In their mid-century overview of the discipline, Roscoe C. Hinkle and Gisela J. Hinkle (1954, 62) listed the leading social theorists as George Lundberg, Florian Znaniecki, Robert MacIver, Howard P. Becker, Talcott Parsons, and Robert K. Merton, and it is Becker whom they identify as drawing from Mead. Indeed, when the University of Chicago Press was looking for an editor for a proposed paperback reader of Mead's social psychology in 1955 they sought out not only Herbert Blumer, but also Charles Morris, Robert K. Merton, Sidney Hook, and Edward A. Shils before discovering Anselm Strauss "who perhaps is now using Mead as much in his own thinking as anyone else around."[54]

In the last decades of his career, however, Blumer published extensively on Mead. This includes his "Sociological Implications of the Thought of George Herbert Mead" (1966a) and "The Methodological Position of Symbolic Interactionism" (1969), written at the end of his active tenure at

Berkeley (reportedly at the insistence of his students), along with a variety of other essays.[55] This fact helps us treat Blumer, like Mead, as someone whose intellectual concerns have a social history. As long as he remained at Chicago his influence over the interpretation others made of Mead was primarily through his teaching, but late in his career he developed a strong program of publishing on Mead for a wider audience.

He was also increasingly active commenting on others' interpretations of Mead in his late career, in large part because those authors often attempted to contrast their interpretations of Mead with Blumer's.[56] In response to Blumer's definitive article on the "sociological implications" of Mead's thought, R. Freed Bales wrote a comment in which he argued that instead of applying Mead to empirical research Blumer had merely developed a set of abstract theoretical "antinomies" (1966). Bales was versed in Mead from his study with Lawrence S. Bee (a student of Mead's student Leonard Cottrell) at the University of Oregon and his collaboration with Charles Morris at Harvard. Blumer responded that Bales had nowhere shown that he misinterpreted Mead, and the attempt to find antinomies in Blumer's exposition showed Bales to be "ill-informed and misinformed on the nature of Mead's thought" (Blumer 1966b, 548). This set off a continued discussion in the pages of the *American Journal of Sociology* about what Mead "really meant" (Woelfel 1967; Stone and Farberman 1967; Blumer 1967). In commenting on Joseph Woelfel's response, Blumer pointed out places where he and Mead would agree with Woelfel, but when Woelfel concluded that "it makes no sense at all to discover what Mead 'really said' or 'really meant,'" Blumer declared he was "uttering nonsense":

> I am not concerned with the adjective "really"—Woelfel, not I, has introduced this word—but I am definitely concerned with what Mead *said* and *meant*. The task here is not that of trying to unearth some "intrinsic nature" or "inner essence" of Mead's scheme of thought (Mead would have shuddered at the philosophical implications of such an idea) but, instead, that of trying to determine what kind of object his scheme of thought was to Mead himself. (Blumer 1967, 411; emphasis in original)

One might note that in this endeavor Blumer was making a case for his own authority to determine the "kind of object" Mead's "scheme of thought" was to "Mead himself."

After his retirement in 1967, Blumer wrote commentaries on quite a few articles and books that questioned his views. One of the most consequential exchanges was that regarding Joan Huber's (1973) article in which she claimed that the pragmatist epistemological premises of symbolic interactionism allowed its practitioners to bias their research in directions that reflected their own preconceptions and the distribution of power in interactive settings. Blumer replied that her article misrepresents his and Mead's views in claiming that they "treat the act of scientific inquiry as beginning with a 'blank mind.'" He wrote instead that "neither Mead nor I ever advanced such an absurd position . . . both Mead and I see the act of scientific inquiry as beginning with a problem" (Blumer 1973, 797). According to virtually all the participants of a retrospective colloquium on the founding of the Society for the Study of Symbolic Interaction (SSSI), Huber's article, along with Nicholas C. Mullins's (1973) book that claimed on the basis of social network analysis that symbolic interactionism appeared to be in decline, galvanized their sentiment and were important impetuses for the foundation of the Society and its journal, *Symbolic Interaction* (Couch 1997; Denzin 1997; Farberman 1997; Lofland 1997; Maines 1997; Saxton 1997). Huber's article drew published replies not only from Blumer but also from other interested symbolic interactionists, including a group of those who helped found the SSSI (Schmitt 1974; Stone et al. 1974; Huber 1974). In the early 1970s, Blumer also wrote responses to several other essays in the same manner.[57]

Blumer's most protracted debates on Mead in print, however, were with Clark McPhail and his students from the University of Illinois. J. David Lewis (1976a), in particular, proposed that Blumer had failed to follow Mead's "social realism" and instead followed Dewey's supposed "subjective nominalism." Blumer wrote that Lewis was "dead wrong" about the intellectual history of symbolic interactionism, that his representation of Blumer's thought contained no fewer than sixteen inaccuracies, and that Mead's and his own perspectives in the realist/nominalist debate were clear and coincident. He also specifically detailed his own "direct access" to Mead while studying at Chicago:

> I was introduced to Mead's thought through my studies with Ellsworth Faris. Later I worked directly with Mead over a period of several years, serving part of this time as his research assistant. When Mead had to interrupt his teaching just prior to his death he requested me to take over his class "Advanced Social Psychology." I am sure that he would not have done this if he had any doubts that I could and would present the content of the course as he was accustomed to present it.[58]

McPhail and Rexroat (1979) followed, positing that Blumer's methodology was divergent from Mead's as a result of a basic divergence in their ontologies of the social world. Blumer (1980) attempted to combat their accusations one by one, arguing that his views were misrepresented and that Mead would not have agreed with their own conception of the scientific research appropriate to his "social behaviorism." As with previous debates, others jumped in, both in reviews and in their own journal comments (e.g., Johnson and Shifflett 1981; Fallding 1982). A third round occurred when Lewis and Richard L. Smith published the book *American Sociology and Pragmatism* (1980), and Blumer (1983) again argued that they fixated on the "recondite philosophical issue" of nominalism versus realism instead of undertaking the appropriate empirical research required to investigate such claims.[59] Blumer's review was part of a larger review symposium on the book in the pages of the journal *Symbolic Interaction*.

Throughout these debates, a clear pattern developed in the ways Blumer mobilized his claims regarding Mead. He made only infrequent references to particular passages from Mead's published writings, although he was reportedly so well versed in them as to be able to cite particular pages freely in conversation (Morrione 2004, 1). Indeed, even when his opponents in these exchanges quoted Mead to support their points, Blumer was more likely to respond by arguing that they had misinterpreted him than by quoting Mead back. As illustrated in the above-quoted remarks regarding his "direct access" to Mead, Blumer repeatedly emphasized his privileged position and the apparent approval Mead gave to his early work. Blumer used phrases including "Mead and I," or simply "we," to assert points of common affirmation; for example: "we [i.e., Blumer and Mead] recognize that the process is capable of being studied and of being analyzed into propositions" (Blumer 1975a, 61). In this line of reasoning, Blumer saw himself as participating with Mead in elaborating a larger "perspective" or "scheme." He relied on a sense of congruence between his own work and Mead's based on his understanding of how Mead worked through and presented his own thought. Without this sense of participating in a common endeavor with Mead that extended beyond his former teacher's physical existence, it would make no sense to refer to Mead in the ways Blumer seemed to do—as if the two of them had just talked and come to a common statement. And as Blumer noted, this was a sense he derived from the extended personal experience and approval he received from Mead in life.

This general pattern is prevalent in his published writings on Mead as well. His most extended statements on Mead (Blumer 1966a, 1981, 2004) make almost no specific citations, although they do freely quote phrases from Mead without attribution.[60] Some of his critics have argued that this style of presentation forced a choice between potentially inconsonant criteria in interpreting Mead: Blumer's assertions or Mead's writings; "Social Behaviorism" or "Symbolic Interactionism;" "*Ex Cathedra* Blumer or *Ex Libris* Mead" (McPhail and Rexroat 1979, 1980).

Herbert Blumer's influence on the understanding of George Herbert Mead in the social sciences is, by all accounts, pervasive. Shibutani (1973, v) proposed that "without question one of [Blumer's] major contributions to modern thought is his part in getting Mead's seminal ideas into the mainstream of social psychology." Meltzer et al. (1975, 1) noted that although "Mead's ideas have been expounded by several sociologists throughout the years," "the acquaintance of most contemporary sociologists with his work has come through the teaching and writings of his best known student, H. Blumer." And Fine (1993, 63) wrote that "while no unanimity existed as to the precise implications of the writings of George Herbert Mead . . . the primary source of the perspective of symbolic interactionism (and the meaning of Mead, for most interactionists) was the writings and teachings of Herbert Blumer. For many, Herbert Blumer *was* symbolic interactionism." While his focus on Mead could seem "obsessive" even to some of his students, the conception of social action he elaborated through his engagement with Mead was nonetheless appealing (Hochschild 1987, iii). And by the end of his career, Blumer was an imposing figure in the discipline of sociology: a founding member of the Sociological Research Association, president of the American Sociological Society for 1956 (and secretary for a period in the 1930s), one-time president of the Society for the Study of Social Problems and the Pacific Sociological Association, associate and later chief editor of the *American Journal of Sociology*, and founding chairman of the department at Berkeley.

It should be emphasized, however, that Blumer's influence in sociology was, like Mead's, a selective one. Indeed, there were effectively three generations of intellectual stewardship at the University of Chicago that occurred primarily through lectures and personal contacts: from Mead to Faris and others, from Faris and Mead to Blumer and others, and from Blumer to Chicago (and then Berkeley) sociologists of the 1930s onward. Although exposure to this tradition was not only through personal contact (as there were writings of each available in print), and not everyone who was exposed became a "convert," these links were salient in the formation of a sense of a shared, alternative perspective toward social life and social research.[61] As chapter 7 demonstrates further, an insider-outsider identity formed along the lines of personal social connections by the actions of these men, especially Faris, in defining the stakes of sociological and social psychological thought. And to the extent that Blumer was seen as the main link to this (Meadian) tradition, connection to him became a criterion for identity. He certainly helped foster this image by his appeals to his personal contact with and knowledge of Mead.

It is within this context that the battles Blumer waged over Mead's legacy are more understandable. Debates over the recovery of the "real," "realist," or "behaviorist" Mead were plausible near the end of Blumer's career precisely because Blumer had been so successful in creating the perception of an essential connection between his "symbolic interactionism" and Mead. This was a cumulative result of encounters in which he positioned himself and Mead against other (in his view, inadequate) perspectives in the social sciences.

Blumer's encounters were built in large part on the model of Faris's position through which he was introduced to Mead. Faris used virtually the same list of theorists—Dewey, Cooley, Thomas, and especially Mead—in his own critiques of instinct theory and other physiological and psychological determinisms. As chapter 7 demonstrates, through his classes by which Chicago sociology students after 1920 were introduced to Mead, Faris is the single most important influence on formulating an intellectual tradition in which Mead, Dewey, Thomas, and others were seen as a coherent alternative perspective to dominant strands in psychological research. Blumer clearly followed Faris in this regard, and more even than Faris he isolated Mead's analysis of the "social self" and of self-indication in action as his signature achievements. And, when Blumer criticized stimulus-response behaviorism, social attitude surveys, systems theory, and others for not accounting for Mead's conceptualization of the complex nature of human social action, he was also in effect deemphasizing much of Mead's own more expansive philosophical interests.

The attempts to minimize or question Mead's centrality to the Chicago School of sociology (e.g., Lewis and Smith 1980; Bulmer 1986; Harvey 1987), or to ask whether the Chicago School could even be seen as a coherent entity (Fine 1995), were plausible as a result of a perceived monopolization on the part of Blumer and the interactionists of what was (necessarily) a more multifaceted set of institutions and social actors. Again, Blumer's success in identifying his concerns with a broader tradition and positioning them in relation to other identifiable opponents promoted this understanding.

With the benefit of additional time and perspective, several recent authors have productively reexamined and further specified the conceptual relations between Blumer and Mead (Cook 2011; Silva and Vieira 2011; Puddephatt 2009). In particular Cook (2011, 33–34) argues that the impact of Blumer's infrequent references to Mead is compounded by the fact that he "often does not make it clear whether he takes himself to be merely summarizing Mead's ideas, or elucidating them, or drawing out some of their sociological implications in an original manner." He "fails to note that his own theoretical project typically begins where Mead's project ends."

CONCLUSION

There are a large number of connections between Charles Morris and Herbert Blumer, who of course knew one another quite well. Both individuals had taken coursework with Mead in the last decade of his life and had been singled out for praise by their common teacher. Both saw their encounters with Mead as transformative of their intellectual outlook and viewed themselves as, at least in part, developing the implications of Mead's perspective through their own work. Both consequently became leading figures in promoting Mead's philosophy and were forced to defend their understandings of Mead against prominent critics. We may think of Morris and Blumer as "reputational entrepreneurs" in Fine's (2001) sense, because they acted as promoters and gatekeepers of his identity for others. The reputations of academics, no less than others, are embedded in social relations and consequently influenced by the forms of communication available in those institutions. To the extent that Morris and Blumer effectively utilized and controlled the media of academic scholarship, they promoted Mead's reputation.

For all the formal similarities there were also notable differences in the ways they promoted Mead and mobilized claims. Morris edited the materials by which Mead is primarily known today, and introduced the term "social behaviorism" to describe Mead's perspective. He returned to that view repeatedly as an important tool in his attempts at synthesis. Indeed, he repeatedly adopted a rhetorical mode of argumentation in which Mead's work was both categorized or particularized and provided a key to the larger synthesis. In this, Morris's work carved up several different sets of categories by which Mead's works could be understood both in particular and in general. The pieces of Mead that Morris emphasized in this categorization were primarily those that Morris identified with his own accomplishments—especially a "behavioral" semiotics and a scientific analysis of human values. He occupied an important institutional role as gatekeeper to unpublished primary documentation about Mead, and he attempted to influence its interpretation. His claims relied heavily on the authority of his work with these documents in addition to his personal relationship with Mead.

Blumer, in contrast, appealed to what he characterized as Mead's "symbolic interactionist" perspective in his criticisms of dominant methods and theories of American social science. He utilized Mead not as a synthetic tool, but as a critical one, developing definite criteria based on his own understanding of what was most centrally important (that is, what in his view most adequately characterized the essential nature of human social life) in Mead's work. By continually posing the same basic aspects of Mead as simultaneously the most important to Mead's work and as the most important points of criticism of dominant work in the social sciences, he doubly emphasized particular concepts or propositions attributed to Mead. He publicly and repeatedly mobilized claims about Mead on the basis of his personal relationship with his former teacher and the oral tradition passed down in this way from Mead and Faris. While it risks putting the matter too strongly, one could argue that in consequence of their various endeavors, Morris provided the materials and basic categories from which to choose in understanding Mead, and Blumer's critiques picked out some of these categories and materials as those central to understanding Mead and social life.[62]

As Gross (2008) has convincingly argued, the twists and turns of intellectual careers cannot be fully understood without taking into account the definite influence of a scholar's "intellectual self concept"—his or her self-narratives of intellectual identity. I prefer to think of them as "intellectual projects" rather than merely to focus on self-narratives, because this draws attention to their sense of participating in the formation of collective intellectual endeavors, which proves key to understanding the use of Mead by both Morris and Blumer. As chapter 4 already demonstrated, the kinds of knowledge-making projects in which all intellectuals participate necessarily overlap with one another in collective endeavors, especially in the pedagogical situation. In addition, the notion of narrative "self concept" would seem to emphasize the largely *a posteriori* efforts by academics to rationalize or make coherent their intellectual trajectory, where a notion of "intellectual project" emphasizes the prospective or "anticipatory" nature of this work. While Gross stresses the importance of formative social influences on an individual's intellectual self concept, it is easy to overemphasize the self-direction of academics and to attribute their positions to a narrative of self without directing attention to the specific mechanisms or dynamics by which that sense of intellectual self is formed in common projects of action with others.

Indeed, there is a growing body of literature on the importance of personal relationships and emotional ties for the formation of novel intellectual movements (esp. Collins 1998). Farrell's (2001) notion of "collaborative circles" stresses the importance of instrumental and emotional forms of social support in fostering creativity, especially those that occur among relative status-equals who gather in centers of cultural production. And others have emphasized the importance of student-teacher mentoring ties rather than equal-status "circles" for the shape of intellectual movements and schools (e.g., Frickel and Gross 2005). The renewed focus in the sociology of ideas on the importance of personal relationships begins to explain how Morris and Blumer could both rely fundamentally on an encounter with the same individual and yet develop differently, but the notion of intellectual project helps specify this issue further. On one hand, both men appear to have found in Mead what they wanted to find for their own intellectual interests, and hence their understandings of Mead and their influences in modern academic disciplines have been noncoincident. But on the other hand, their interests were in large part shaped by Mead, and hence the noncoincidence cannot be easily explained away by some personal sense. Moreover, in their work they each attempted to claim (1) to best interpret Mead against critics, (2) that their own projects were Meadian projects, and (3) to be making unique contributions to scholarship. Rhetorically this seems to require both authors to position themselves as fellow travelers of Mead, identical with Mead, and ahead of Mead all at once, and apparently without any "bad faith" or willful deception. Only if we acknowledge that they understood themselves to be participating emphatically in a collective endeavor that encompassed themselves and their mentor in some constructive or progressive intellectual project can we explain how such formulations seemed plausible.

Morris and Blumer may well have felt a certain rivalry between them. They certainly never formed a shared, public vision of Mead, but they also appear never to have publicly clashed with one another over Mead. There are certain suggestive gaps in both of their bodies of work that may be evidence of positive avoidance. For example, Blumer seems never to have published any fleshed-out theory of "signs" beyond Mead's own distinctions (although he comes closest in his works on the nature of scientific "concepts"). Had he been concerned with conceptualizing formal systems of signs or with the variety of relations of signs to one another, he would almost necessarily have had to engage with Morris. Morris, on the other hand, seems not to have elaborated a theory of social interaction, despite his emphasis on the "social," "behavioral," and "pragmatic" formation of signs.[63] It seems likely that disciplinary structures helped prevent a face-to-face confrontation between Morris and Blumer by providing separate avenues for each of their projects and defining the problems worth exploring. This possibility seems to suggest that a necessary component of intellectual projects is a sense of their domain-specificity, but this case study cannot make a definitive conclusion on this point. The divergent structure of US academic disciplines is considered more extensively in the following chapter.

The concept of intellectual project can also direct analysis to how such a sense of collective participation is formed in an individual's self-perception. Although Farrell (2001, 151) refers to dyads of status-equals when he discusses the importance of "collaborative pairs" for an intellectual's self-perception, several of the features clearly also apply to the relationships between Mead and these two students. In particular, this chapter has highlighted the strong mutual investments or commitments that both of these pairs, Mead–Morris and Mead–Blumer, made to one another, and the ways they expressed what Farrell calls "instrumental intimacy" by exposing their hunches, plans, and draft ideas to one another. Morris formed much of his sense of the kind of intellectual endeavor in which he was engaged through his coursework and especially in his dissertation and early published studies from which he received positive public and private feedback from Mead. His project was further linked with Mead and elaborated when he was chosen as the individual appropriate to carry on Mead's legacy (and to literally write that legacy). By the time of his major formal statements of his "semiotics" in the late 1930s and 1940s, Morris saw his project as inseparable from, and essentially an extension of, Mead.

Blumer likewise had a transformative experience in his encounter with Mead, but for him it was Mead's emphasis on the importance of interpretation and meaning in the course of human action that led him to reject his earlier behaviorism. He also received positive responses from Mead and came to view himself as participating in a common intellectual project as a result of taking over for Mead in his classes. Farrell (2001, 155) argues that exchanges like these lead to intense "mirroring processes" that feed individuals' confidence, focus, and sense of cohesion in their intellectual endeavors.[64] And these relationships need not be long to have long-lasting effects; Parker and Hackett (2012), for example, find that short, emotionally and intellectually intense periods of collaboration, often in special settings, are immensely productive of creative ideas. These intellectual projects are, thus, the nexus where interpretations and claims made about Mead, the unique scholarship of Blumer and Morris, and their influence on Mead's reputation all come together in concrete social relationships. This notion, then, provides a way of specifying where to look for the production and reproduction of ideas.

A focus on the interpersonal relationships of two particular individuals is not by itself, of course, an adequate explanation of the development of a dominant understanding of Mead in modern academic disciplines. It has its strength in allowing for the in-depth examination of the way Mead's work was incorporated as an integral part of the life-work of two of his most influential former students, and in providing the occasion for an analysis of the rhetorics of authority and claims making in such cases. Already we can see the limits of an explanation that relies on idiosyncratic, individual careers but leaves unexamined academic institutions, including media of communication and structures of academic disciplines. In the following chapter, the analysis shifts to a study of how patterns of reference to Mead develop over time through these changing institutional structures. But as the analysis there attempts to show, these patterns do not develop of their own accord. Instead, building upon the analysis in this chapter, I focus on how references represent claims regarding Mead and show that an understanding of references as meaningful social practices helps explain the emergence of certain patterns.

CHAPTER SEVEN

In Reference to Mead, or How to Win Students and Influence Sociology

Earlier chapters have begun from the premise that George Herbert Mead is referred to in contemporary scholarship primarily for a book he did not write, by authors in a discipline in which he never taught. But the analyses in those chapters have not presented systematic evidence in order to examine how dominant understandings of Mead have come about, relying instead on detailed and illustrative analyses of particular moments and individuals. Those with a passing knowledge of the "founders" or "classics" in sociology already have a sense of the problematic character of understandings of Mead even if their analysis of how and why this is so ends there. A Web of Science citation analysis demonstrates that since 1955 there have been over 8,000 bibliographic citations to Mead in academic journal articles.[1] Examining this database a bit further reveals that the discipline in which the largest number of citations has occurred is sociology, especially sociologically oriented social psychology. The single journal in which the largest number of citations is recorded, with over 200, is *Symbolic Interaction,* a journal founded in 1977 primarily affiliated with the field of sociology. Since I wrote these words, no doubt, additional citations to Mead have appeared in this and many other journals, but the point is one of comparison not exhaustion. All of the ten journals that have cited Mead most often are either sociology or social psychology journals. In contrast, there are only 214 citations to Mead in all philosophy journals recorded in this dataset.

In 5 percent of citations to *Mind, Self, and Society* in this database a specific page number is recorded, giving an idea of which particular sections and concepts are found most compelling.[2] Most commonly cited is the first substantive page of "Part III: The Self" that begins "Section 18: The Self and the Organism" (Mead 1934, 135), then the first page of "Section 20:

Play, the Game, and the Generalized Other" (152), then the first page of
the whole volume that introduces "Section 1: Social Psychology and Behaviorism" (1), the first page of "Section 22: The 'I' and the 'me'" (173), and
the page that formally introduces the concept of the "generalized other"
(154). Almost all of these come from the "Self" section of the book, and it
is mere tautology to note that these pages introduce themes or concepts
central to the dominant understanding of Mead.

This chapter investigates the patterns of reference to George Herbert
Mead in published academic literature in order to explain how such a
dominant interpretation, one seemingly contradictory to Mead's own disciplinary affiliation, came about. This analysis also gives additional specificity to this dominant public image of Mead. But although this chapter
relies upon the analysis of references to Mead in published sources, such
an endeavor requires a different orientation toward patterns of published
reference than has typically been taken in "citation analysis."

The chapter engages with literature on "predecessor selection" and "legitimation" processes in the history of the social sciences as a way of answering this concern. Studies of predecessor selection serve to critique the
implicit assumption in certain forms of citation analysis that reference
to another person's work is primarily an unproblematic matter in which
cumulative bodies of knowledge are built that can then be examined separately from the particular concerns of the social actors who build them.
Camic (1992, 423) has, for example, argued that in order to understand the
selection of authorities named in later scholars' works, analysis should not
rely on a traditional "content-fit" model that views the choice of predecessor as a "fit between the arguments, concepts, themes, materials, orientations, or methods of certain earlier figures and some aspect(s) of the work
of the thinker under study." Instead he advocates a "reputational model,"
which examines the perceived reputation or standing of certain scholars
or schools of thought socially available to the author in question, through
which assessments of the scholar's or school's intellectual worth are measured. Similar works by Lamont (1987) and McLaughlin (1998) have studied the rise and fall of major scholarly reputations by focusing analysis on
the institutional contexts (both formal academic institutions and personal
networks) that structure the possibilities for the continued appropriation
and influence of an author's work. The analyst seeking to investigate the
relationship between a particular author and his or her predecessors is
thus directed toward the local institutional context in which assessments
of a theory's intellectual credibility are socially produced, not a standpoint outside of this process of social interpretation. Ben-David and Col-

lins (1966) and Danziger (1979) demonstrate through their own analyzes of psychology that the demand for this definition of professional identity (in part, through foundational figures) is itself a product of institutional shifts in academic career opportunities. Indeed, the formation of academic career tracks in certain new fields seems, in some cases, to have provided the institutional conditions for later generations to produce a body of knowledge about the field's supposed "founders."

Additional work has sought to emphasize the consequences of the iteration of these selective processes for later understandings of authors or schools of thought. Several studies have demonstrated that a particular selective understanding of a foundational figure or article can become "intertextually sedimented" through the repeated amplification of particular (often critical) assessments in a disciplinary subfield, especially when promoted by institutionally central authorities (Maines, Bridger, and Ulmer 1996; Mizruchi and Fein 1999). This iteration can produce a condition in which the accumulated weight of particular interpretations, while conventionally regarded as accurate descriptions of the original texts, produce inaccurate or "mythic facts" about an author (Maines, Bridger, and Ulmer 1996, 522).[3] The resulting analytic orientation—to examine the punctuated, sequential process of published references located within consequential but shifting institutional contexts—is central to the following study.

Expanding the scope of these studies to examine more generally the modes of reference made by one author of another allows the following analysis to address questions of broader significance about the diffusion of ideas. For example, work in the sociology of literature and elsewhere has identified the importance of what is sometimes called "disembedding" in moving a particular work or author from an initial context of production to a broader public attention (e.g., Rodden 1989). Fine (2001, 3) distinguishes between "personal," "mass-mediated," "organizational," and "historical" reputations. In his terms, we can ask how Mead's "personal" reputation formed within his intimate social circles leads to his more sedimented "historical" reputation encoded in institutionally sanctioned knowledge. Hence we can ask in what sense should we consider Mead (or certain concepts attributed to him) as a public property disembedded from Mead's life, and how is such a transition mediated by networks of personal relations, channels of communication, or organizations? In addition, the typical analyses of canonization, including that of Mead (e.g., Silva and Vieira 2011; Smith 1977; Spreitzer and Reynolds 1973), tend to treat it as a strictly retrospective process in which individuals are reaching "back" into the past to define present needs. But references to Mead and his work do not begin only after he died, and they are not unrelated to his own actions to define himself and to shape his local social environment. We can also ask how are we to understand references as symbolic social practices in the present but still acknowledge their accumulated weight over time? These concerns add further specificity to the following analysis.

In order to answer these concerns and investigate George Herbert Mead's reputation and impact in a unique way, this chapter introduces a methodological innovation. I have constructed a comprehensive database of references to Mead in academic journal articles from all available disciplines from 1894 to 1955. Instead of relying on traditional citation analysis techniques I have compiled this database from full-text searches of Mead's name in nine separate databases.[4] The dataset of 1,152 journal items constructed in this manner allows for content analysis as well as citation analysis because it is based on content searches, not merely on cited reference lists. For this same reason, it allows me to analyze all references to G. H. Mead in reviews as well as articles, even when his works are not formally cited in footnotes or bibliography. This database proves to be consequential below in explaining Mead's legacy, as it captures the large portion of references to Mead that make no formal citation to one of his works. In fact, just over one half of all references to Mead through 1955 in professional journals are such informal citations.[5] And the database constructed in this way circumvents the problem of several previous analyses of Mead's canonization in sociology—which only examined a few leading authors, articles, or monographs in sociology and so found what they were looking for relatively unproblematically (Smith 1977; Spreitzer and Reynolds 1973; Vaughan and Reynolds 1968). That is, if the question is how Mead became known and cited in sociology, an analysis that relies on the fact of those citations alone can easily answer the question descriptively, but founders on the questions of how and why such should be the case. In the following sections I trace the development of dominant patterns of published references to Mead by chronological period and identify the important transformations, both institutionally and in terms of social practices, that resulted in these patterns.

EARLY REFERENCES TO MEAD, 1894–1919

By the end of Mead's life on April 26, 1931, there were already at least 151 references to him in academic journal publications, and 72 of those are prior to 1920. The references by year are too small and fluctuate too much to demonstrate a clear linear trend, so I have resorted to comparing two periods of time; the subsequent analysis also demonstrates that this periodization is made along the lines of a salient shift in citations and institutions. Despite the considerable number of references during Mead's life, previous analyses of the development of Mead's importance in sociology have never systematically examined these early articles. Any approach that only seeks to trace Mead's rise in the canon of sociology, without considering his impact across disciplines and in this early period when he was actively working, misses the most notable aspect of this development: the transformation of the reception of Mead from a phenomenon occurring primarily in philosophy and psychology to one primarily located in sociology.

Prior to 1920 there are only nine citations to Mead in sociology journals as compared to twenty-one in philosophy journals and twenty-four in psychology journals. Even further, the boundaries between psychology and philosophy journals were not firmly drawn or stable during the early part of this period. Several authors, including John Dewey, William James, and Heath Bawden, who were institutionally affiliated with philosophy departments but whose work blended psychology and philosophy, were found referencing Mead in psychology journals. Indeed, the first recorded reference to G. H. Mead that I am able to find in an academic journal article is in Dewey's (1894) *Psychological Review* article "The Theory of Emotion."[6]

What is particularly remarkable about these early references is that twenty-five of those first seventy-two articles, including Dewey's, make absolutely no mention of Mead's published works, and so are invisible to traditional citation analysis. Instead, they refer either to ideas personally conveyed from Mead to the author, or to the content of lectures by Mead that the author attended.[7] Several of the references discuss Mead's personal suggestions to the authors on their own projects and thus indicate something of the role Mead played outside the classroom with regard to his students. For example, Jessie B. Allen (1904, 334) remarked in the published version of her dissertation that "it was suggested by Mr. G. H. Mead that the reactions of the guinea pig might be direct responses to immediate contact stimuli, and that a distant stimulus, e.g., a recollection of the path, was not responsible for the reaction." Chapter 4 makes use of materials such as these to provide a clearer understanding of Mead's day-to-day interaction with his students as constitutive of the lifelong development of his intellectual work.

The large number of articles that do not refer to specific works far outweighs references to any single published article by Mead, indicating that his contributions lay at least as much in interpersonal communication as in published material. Of those references to Mead's published works from 1894 to 1919, the most often cited is Mead's "The Definition of the Psychical" (1903a), which is referenced in fourteen instances, followed by his "Scientific Method and Individual Thinker" (1917c), and the coauthored "A Report on Vocational Training in Chicago and in Other Cities" (Mead, Wreidt, and Bogan 1912).[8] Joas (1997 [1985]) has argued that "The Definition of the Psychical" was an important foundational document in orienting the so-called Chicago School of functional psychology, along with Dewey's and James R. Angell's early work. Indeed, this article was rather widely discussed in print at the time, with references to it appearing in articles by John Dewey, William James, Mary Whiton Calkins, J. Mark Baldwin, and other major figures in early twentieth-century psychology. The other two works mentioned were referred to more often in reviews than in articles and provide indications of Mead's early reputation as a pragmatist philosopher and social reformer.

Strongly related to these informal referencing practices is the finding that fifty-three of those seventy-two references come from articles where the sole or first author was a student or colleague of G. H. Mead at the University of Chicago before or at the time when the author wrote the relevant article.[9] And, of course, this number does not include the references to those like William James, who knew Mead personally and explicitly saw him as part of the newly formed "Chicago School" of philosophy (James 1904), but who was not directly connected with the University of Chicago. This further supports the notion that Mead's impact was primarily a function of his personal and institutional importance to early Chicago psychology. That is, references to Mead, both formal and informal, were in large part signs within the relatively small psychological and philosophical community of a particular institutional and theoretical orientation.

The picture that emerges of this period from 1894 to 1919 is one in which recognition of his work was strongly tied to personal relationships with Mead and was primarily limited to fields in which Mead himself was active. Those authors referring to Mead most often knew him personally and quite frequently referred to their face-to-face experience with him, either in conversation or lectures, as being the source of their knowledge, rather than being derived from reading his published works. Discussions of Mead in print were not primarily acknowledgments of scientific priority or topical relevance but were tributes to interpersonal relations.

LOCAL REORGANIZATION OF KNOWLEDGE, 1920–1930

From 1920 to 1930 there were twenty-six additional references to Mead in sociology-affiliated publications, twenty-seven additional references in philosophy, and thirteen in psychology (including social psychology). The contrast between this array and the previous distribution of references to Mead is displayed in figure 7.1. Mead's visibility appears to have increased most precipitously in sociology while declining in psychology and remaining fairly stable in philosophy. However, the vast majority of these references still come from people personally connected to Mead. Of the seventy-nine references in this period, the authors of fifty-five of them are either students or colleagues of Mead at the University of Chicago, and forty-one references are informal mentions of his name only, an even higher proportion than before. If anything, it appears that recognition of Mead became more strongly linked to the University of Chicago. Thus, an explanation of the beginnings of this shift from psychology and philosophy to sociology cannot be found primarily in the external discovery of Mead's work but instead must be sought in the internal dynamics of the relevant disciplines at the University of Chicago. This emphasis on the local departmental emplacement of disciplinary emergence, boundaries, and transformations has been a focus of considerable literature in recent decades (esp. Camic 1995; Platt 1996; Small 1999; Abbott 1999), and the influence of the department of sociology at the University of Chicago has been a particular focus of this literature.

In this period there was a reorganization at Chicago of the relation between substantive topics and the departmental affiliation of courses, and social psychology was a focal point of this reorganization.[10] A course in social psychology had been taught by Mead beginning in 1900, and became a regularly scheduled course from 1908 onward. Mead's course was not the only one touching on social psychological issues; in particular, W. I. Thomas gave regular courses on "Social Attitudes" and "Social Origins" among others in sociology. But it is important to note that Mead's was the only regular course directly on the topic, and in any case there was no strict track of prerequisites institutionally directing students toward or away from one of these courses.

In 1904–5, after the departure of John Dewey, the psychology and philosophy departments were formally separated, although they maintained a close relation in the following period, and Mead cross-listed his social psychology course and a few others in psychology. Beginning in 1917, the

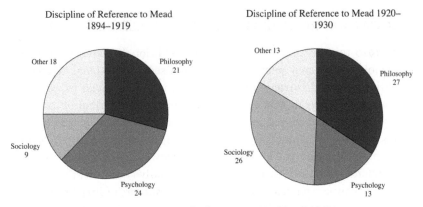

Figure 7.1. Comparison of references to Mead by discipline,
1894–1919 and 1920–1930. *Source*: Data compiled by author.

topic began to be separated into a multicourse "track" or "focus" and to
be taught in several disciplines concurrently. That year a course entitled
"Elementary Social Psychology," taught by Clarence E. Ayres, was introduced into philosophy as a prerequisite to Mead's course, which was consequently renamed "Advanced Social Psychology"—this parallels somewhat
the earlier split that saw Mead's "Comparative Psychology" course become
"Theoretical Comparative Psychology" with "Experimental Comparative
Psychology" serving as a quasi-prerequisite after 1904 in the psychology
department. In 1920 this elementary social psychology course was moved
permanently to the psychology department, and a new sociology course
entitled "Introduction to Social Psychology" was instated with Ellsworth
Faris as the instructor. Faris, a former University of Chicago psychology graduate, had been brought into sociology to replace the ousted W. I.
Thomas, whose courses he primarily took over. This is how the departmental organization of social psychology courses remained until Mead's
death: an "elementary" course in the psychology department taught by
Ayres and later by Forrest A. Kingsbury, an "introductory" course in sociology taught by Faris, and an "advanced" course in philosophy with Mead.
After 1931 the sociology department took over Mead's course and the psychology department established its own separate multicourse track in social psychology. By 1920 in Chicago, social psychology was a field institutionally claimed by three departments, and through which two separate
tracks were created—a sociological one and a psychological one.[11]

The departmental reorganization at Chicago, in effect, turned Ayres,
Kingsbury, and Faris into gatekeepers to Mead's social psychology teach-

ings for their respective departments. While all three of these men had previously taken courses from Mead as students at Chicago, neither Ayres nor Kingsbury was particularly committed to Mead's teachings and neither had taken Mead's social psychology course. They were not particularly hostile toward Mead, but they also did not go out of their way to reference his teachings.[12] In contrast, Faris was a veritable devotee of Mead.[13] Of the twenty-six sociology articles referencing Mead from 1920 to 1930, Faris alone accounts for nine.

Faris later wrote of this departmental reorganization, that in Mead's view there was a rapidly expanding literature relevant to social psychology emerging in this period, and that Mead personally asked Faris to begin offering an introductory social psychology course in the sociology department so that Mead would have the opportunity to avoid certain introductory topics in favor of "the growing body of controversial literature" (Faris 1936, 809; 1937b).[14] Of course the fact that Mead favored the sociology department rather than the psychology department as the right venue for an introductory social psychology course was also an indication, as Faris pointed out (1936, 810), that for Mead social life was the basis for psychological phenomena rather than the reverse. That is, in apparently championing Faris and a sociological view of social psychology Mead took an active part in defining the subsequent trajectory of the discipline and, as a consequence, his own posthumous reputation.

We may demonstrate the influence of these instructors who taught prerequisite courses on Mead's reception in their respective disciplines by the changing composition of students in Mead's advanced courses and especially by published references to his work. Although the evidence is a bit mixed (because of the relatively small numbers involved and the myriad factors explaining year-to-year fluctuations in student attendance), Smith (1977) reported that the average percentage of graduate students in sociology taking Mead's courses was substantially higher in the later years of Mead's courses than in earlier years and that during those same years the percentage of psychology students taking Mead's courses sharply declined. He also acknowledged the important institutional brokerage of Faris in motivating sociology students to take Mead's philosophy courses. Prior to the creation of Faris's introductory social psychology course, there was no institutionalized track whereby sociology students were directed toward Mead and there was no enthusiastic interpreter to guide them.

The evidence is even less mixed in terms of citations. Twenty-one of the twenty-six references to Mead in sociology journals come from Chi-

cago sociology students who took courses directly with Mead, and sociologists Kimball Young and Ellsworth Faris also account for four of the
thirteen citations to him in psychology journals.[15] The other psychology
references in this period include four non–Chicago trained social psychologists, two other Chicago graduate students in philosophy and anatomy,
and three articles by Chicago psychologist Curt Rosenow. This makes
Rosenow the only person trained in the Chicago psychology department to
refer to Mead during this period, and he also likely interacted with Mead
outside of class through the Institute for Juvenile Research.[16] This seems
to support the proposal that Ayres's and Kingsbury's indifference toward
Mead and Faris's enthusiasm helped shift the impact of Mead's teachings
away from psychology and toward sociology.

A final indicator of this change is in the nature of what is cited. In addition to the even stronger tendency to refer to Mead informally, the most
heavily cited works by Mead changed from his foundational psychological and pragmatic-philosophical work to his "A Behavioristic Account of
The Significant Symbol" (1922) cited eleven times, "Social Psychology as a
Counterpoint to Physiological Psychology" (1909e) cited seven times, "The
Genesis of the Self and Social Control" (1925) cited six times, and "The Social Self" (1913a) cited five times. That is, Mead's now-classic social explanation of the emergence of the self and consciousness through symbolic
social action began to emerge as his signature accomplishment.

Note that this fundamental shift in the works by Mead that are referred to cannot be fully explained by the assertion that Mead's later work
simply moved in a more sociological direction. Even if one could defend
such an argument about Mead's work—an argument that I think would
miss his early insistence upon the social nature of intelligence—that hypothesis cannot explain why this particular aspect of Mead's work should
be taken up when it was and by whom, nor does it explain why later sociological references of this kind seem to reach back to an earlier period
in Mead's work for some of their references. Smith (1977) has convincingly
demonstrated in a related analysis that there is no general correlation between when a particular work by Mead was published and when it was
first cited in sociology. If, as demonstrated above, the appearance of references to Mead in sociological journals cannot be explained primarily by
an external discovery of Mead, then it stands to reason that the institutional shift in course offerings at Chicago is related to the emergence of a
new dominant—sociological—pattern of reference to Mead. The analysis
is thus directed toward the peculiar referencing and teaching practices of
Ellsworth Faris and his students for a better understanding.

INFORMAL CITATIONS AS A BATTLEGROUND

The increasingly salient distinction between a "psychological social psychology" and a "sociological social psychology" was paralleled across American academia. As Greenwood (2004) has argued, social psychology was a dual enterprise virtually from its very institutionalization in US universities. Although there had been individual works and courses in social psychology for at least a generation—and although the notion of social influence on the individual mind had an ancient pedigree—social psychology as an institutionalized academic discipline with professional associations, journals, and departmental units emerged in the post–World War I era in the United States and it emerged more-or-less simultaneously in sociology and psychology (cf. Alvaro and Garrido 2007; White 2004; Good 2000).

Mead's name and concepts became a weapon in the conflict over the dual nature of social psychology through the efforts of Chicago sociologists. Faris introduced an important innovation in references to Mead that would be copied by several of his and Mead's prominent sociology graduate students. He was associate editor and later editor-in-chief of the *American Journal of Sociology* (hereafter *AJS*) during this period, and he repeatedly took the opportunity in reviews of other individuals' works to proselytize on behalf of Mead and his other influences. In a review of G. T. Ladd's *The Secret of Personality*, Faris remarked that "the modern social psychology as set forth by Dewey and Mead is ignored in the argument" (1918, 222). In his review of Robert H. Lowie's *Primitive Society*, he observed, "About half of the references are from American writers, but one notices some regrettable omissions. Thomas is not mentioned, nor Dewey, nor Mead, nor Herbert Spenser [*sic*]" (1921, 244). Virtually all of Faris's reviews contain some similar remarks. Indeed, these reviews constitute one of the primary reasons why the informal references to Mead in sociology expand during this period.

In his substantive articles, as well, Faris repeatedly argued against the emerging psychological social psychology, especially its theorists' notions of "imitation" and "instinct" (1937c). And Faris is without a doubt the most important early innovator of the understanding that W. I. Thomas, John Dewey, G. H. Mead, and a select few others constituted a single alternative school of thought. Witness his review of *Psychologies of 1925* in which he criticized the editors of the volume for not including work by "the school represented by Dewey, [B. H.] Bode, Mead, Thomas and others," or his review of L. L. Bernard's *Introduction to Social Psychology* in which he noted that "the distinctive aspects of Dewey, Mead, and Thomas" had not been emphasized by the author (1926a, 310; 1928, 118–19). Indeed, in Faris's review of the "Current Trends in Social Psychology" (1929, 128) he listed several "systems or 'schools'" including that of "Cooley, Dewey, Mead, Thomas, Park, and their colleagues" which in contradistinction to the other schools emphasized "the social group or matrix in which the personality takes shape" and "the social nature of individual personality." Later in that chapter he noted that "in the case of the present writer the greatest obligation is felt to Professor Mead, to whom American scholars are indebted for some invaluable and wholly unique contributions" (132).

It should be evident that this list recreates Faris's own select intellectual heritage—including those he studied under directly (Mead), those whose classes he taught (Thomas), and those about whom his teachers taught extensively (e.g., Dewey, Cooley)—and not that of social psychological thought more generally. When in 1937 Herbert Blumer coined the term "Symbolic Interactionism," he was in fact primarily giving a handle to the social psychological perspective he had been taught by Faris in the 1920s Chicago sociology department.[17] Although this grouping of predecessors to a "Symbolic Interactionist" social psychology may seem somewhat self-apparent in light of its frequent reiteration, it was not a given at this time, and the intellectual relationships between these authors were not of uniform agreement.

Camic (2008) also recently singled out what he has called "Faris's technique." Camic posits that in his work Faris condensed the history of social psychology down to certain surnames—Baldwin, McDougall, Ross—which "serve their purpose" both in communicating that social psychology possesses a "multi-threaded history" and in "emblematically allowing social psychologists to point to their historical roots without having to pause from their research to reflect on them" (Camic 2008, 329). He "effectively abbreviate[d] the already decades-long development of social psychology" and oriented contemporary work by use of such "formulaic abbreviation." Thus, by his characterization of the field in his published writings and (perhaps more important) to his students at the University of Chicago, Faris defined a distinct and, he thought, more satisfactory group of authors for a sociological social psychology, and allowed Mead and a few others to serve as shorthand symbols of this grouping.

This pattern of reference was adopted most insistently by Kimball Young and Herbert Blumer, both of whom were Chicago sociology students of Mead (Blumer was also Faris's student but Young was not).[18] From 1930 to 1955 Young wrote sixteen reviews in which he referred to G. H. Mead, and no fewer than thirteen of those mentions were attempts by Young to introduce Mead where he was not previously mentioned and to argue that a better understanding of Mead would have benefited the author of the relevant monograph.[19] These reviews appeared primarily in *AJS* and the *Annals of the American Academy of Political and Social Science*, two influential publications. Young also reprinted an excerpt from Mead's "The Behavioristic Account of the Significant Symbol" (1922) in his influential *Source Book for Social Psychology* (Young 1927).[20]

Herbert Blumer followed a similar practice in five of his reviews in the *AJS*, but even more important, Blumer championed a perspective he called "Symbolic Interactionism" (1937) that gave a name to this school. (Blumer's personal engagement with Mead and Faris is discussed at length in chapter 6.) Young and Blumer, with Faris and others, argued both against a psychological social psychology and, especially for Blumer, increasingly against one derived from a sociological-positivistic understanding of the notion of attitudes (cf. Warshay and Warshay 1986). In so doing, Blumer and Young followed Faris in arguing that Thomas, Dewey, Cooley, and Mead constituted a single alternative perspective that was neither individualistic nor simplistically sociological. Mead was the common denominator in most of these lists of forbearers and became a symbol of this alternative to both sociological attitude-measurement and psychological social psychology. Blumer (1969, 1) was most explicit in this endeavor, identifying Mead as the individual "who, above all others, laid the foundations of the symbolic interactionist approach." Thus, Mead was rhetorically positioned by a small group of his very vocal, insistent, and well-positioned sociology students as a theorist of vital relevance for a nuanced, sociological social psychology. By the early 1920s Mead had already been marginalized in the psychological literature and had begun to be appropriated in the sociological literature as a result of these advocates.

These informal references—often only referring to the name "Mead"—can be understood as "esoteric" in the sense that they would only have been meaningful to those who already had a knowledge of the referent. This is especially true of Faris's earliest reviews, which are virtually the first concerted references to Mead in the discipline of sociology and give no more hint to his identity and work than to label it "the modern social psychology of Dewey and Mead." Hence, Faris turned the name Mead into something of a shibboleth; he created a salient boundary between an "insider" and "outsider" understanding of Mead, a distinction drawn largely between those who had taken courses directly from Mead (most often through Faris's intercession) and those who had not. But at the same time these students-turned-advocates repeatedly proposed Mead, if only by name, as an important and more-thoroughly-social theorist. These supererogatory mentions thus also represented strong claims about the perceived breadth and depth of Mead's relevance for contemporary sociology. That is, Faris's references exhibit a peculiar dualism: they advocate Mead as a general theoretical resource while leaving all substantive exposition of his position to the author's own presumed knowledge of Mead.

This same proselytism through a combination of reviews and substantive articles was present to a certain extent in the philosophical literature, principally after Mead's death. Some of his later students, especially Charles W. Morris, who edited two of the posthumous publications of Mead, and his close graduate school associates Van Meter Ames and T. V. Smith, were advocates for a greater appreciation of Mead in journals like the Chicago-based *Ethics*, edited by Smith, as well as the *Journal of Philosophy* and *Philosophy East and West*. Hence, while Mead's profile was on the rise in sociology-affiliated publications and on the decline in psychology, it remained fairly visible in philosophy in the 1920s.

MEMORIALS AND POSTHUMOUS VOLUMES, 1931–1940

Mead's overall visibility in professional journals increased explosively as a result of the numerous reviews of the posthumous volumes attributed to him and the articles and books that began to appear attempting to give a synthetic overview of Mead's thought. In the years from 1931 through 1940, encompassing the period in which most of the memorial statements to Mead and reviews of the posthumous Mead volumes were published, there were at least 252 instances in which he was referenced. Mentions of Mead appeared in 96 philosophy articles, in 69 sociology articles, and in 19 psychology articles. During this period there were at least 6 reviews of *The Philosophy of the Present* (1932), 23 of *Mind, Self, and Society* (1934), 24 of *Movements of Thought in the Nineteenth Century* (1936), and 8 of *The Philosophy of the Act* (1938).

More than in previous periods, the patterns of reference to Mead began to take on endogenous characteristics whereby disciplines, and even clusters within those disciplines, exhibited similar reference patterns that were divergent from those of other disciplines. For example, almost all of the articles purporting to be syntheses of Mead's teachings appeared in philosophy journals and were written by former colleagues or students of Mead. Reviews of the posthumous volumes also appeared much more frequently in philosophy than in other disciplines. In contrast, *Mind, Self, and Society* was considerably more likely to be referenced in sociology than in other disciplines, in addition to being the most-cited single reference with fifty mentions in addition to its twenty-three reviews. Of the posthumous volumes, philosophers apparently preferred *The Philosophy of the Present* and *The Philosophy of the Act. Movements of Thought* was not at all mentioned outside of the large number of reviews it received and a couple of the reviews of the other volumes. From its first publication, *Movements of Thought* was apparently almost completely ignored outside of the initial reviews it received (perhaps the result of the more extensive promotional advertising that volume received).

There was a veritable bifurcation of interest in Mead between philosophers who referenced his cosmological writings and attempted to integrate a synthetic view of Mead and sociologists who referenced his work as foundational of a perspective in social psychology. Authors exhibited comparatively little interest in Mead's earlier essays on functional psychology or in his lectures on the history of philosophy, not to mention the various ephemeral pieces written largely in the proceedings of social work and vocational education conferences. In this sense, the sectioning off of materials attributed to Mead into different fields—a social psychology volume, a history of philosophy volume, a process philosophy volume—helped accomplish the divergence of interpretations by providing definite and circumscribed bodies of material relevant to (and seemingly intended by Mead for) particular academic disciplines and subfields.

Perhaps even more remarkable than this disciplinary split is the fact that 128 of the references to Mead, fully 50 percent, were from people not identifiable as a colleague or student of his (although several persons who referenced Mead were acquaintances of his not affiliated with the University of Chicago). Figure 7.2 displays this information graphically by year; the second graph presents the same information in logarithmic format making the relative shifts easier to identify. Forty of these references are reviews of the posthumous Mead volumes. In contrast, during the entire previous history of references to Mead while he was alive, he had been referred to only forty-two times by individuals who did not know him by personal connection in the same academic institutions, at least as far as I am able to determine (and this is likely an overestimate of the lack of direct connections of these authors to Mead). A large portion of these authors who referred to him after his death were linked indirectly to Mead, being students or colleagues of Mead's students, but this is also an indication that personal connections were beginning to take a secondary or mediated role in driving citations to Mead.

Relation of Citing Author to Mead

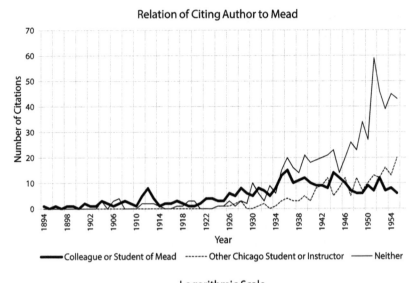

Colleague or Student of Mead ------- Other Chicago Student or Instructor ——— Neither

Logarithmic Scale

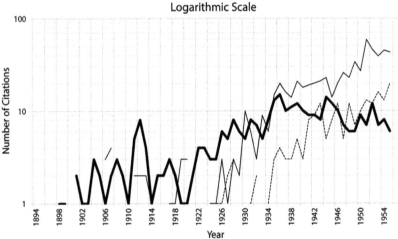

Figure 7.2. Citations by year separated by relation of author to Mead.
Source: Data compiled by author.

As in previous periods there is a large body of informal citations (107 during this decade), which make no reference to Mead's published work. Part of this group of citations comes from Blumer, Young, Morris, and the like, who promoted Mead in their reviews, but that particular strategy remained almost exclusively the practice of a small group of Mead's students. In reviews written by authors who were not his students or colleagues, Mead was mentioned almost exclusively because he was discussed already in the book under review. The books that caused individuals without a direct connection to Mead to refer to him were themselves primarily authored by Mead's former students, including Fay B. Karpf's *American Social Psychology* (1932), Charles Morris's *Six Theories of Mind* (1932), T. V. Smith's *Beyond Conscience* (1934) and Ellsworth Faris's *The Nature of Human Nature* (1937c).[21] This indicates that in addition to the proliferation of literature commenting on Mead there was an emerging body of commentary upon the commentary on Mead—an additional degree of separation of the discourse from the personal social relationships that had defined it before. However, there was not merely a "disembedding" of Mead's work from the context of his personal relations; rather a mediated relationship developed whereby his philosophy was available to the general intellectual public through the interpretation of those who knew him personally.

Mead's students and colleagues continued to occupy a particular position in this ecology of published references to him. One remarkable aspect of this is that those individuals who personally knew Mead were more likely to refer to *Mind, Self, and Society* in this period immediately after its publication than were those without direct relationship to him. This fact seems rather counterintuitive given that as former students many of them would not have had a need to rely on the volume for substantive knowledge of Mead's philosophy. But these posthumous volumes, especially *Mind, Self, and Society*, did give a definite textual warrant for their claims about Mead. Where previously Ellsworth Faris (1926b) and Charles Morris (1927) could ascribe the notion of "taking the role of the other" only to Mead as a person, for example, they and many others could later cite chapter and verse of *Mind, Self, and Society* for the concept.

The prevalence of citations to *Mind, Self, and Society* by former colleagues and students is probably driven in large part by the fact that those who had known Mead personally made up the largest single group of purchasers of the volume in its initial release, a fact verifiable in extant records. In order to ensure the financial viability of the publication of *Mind, Self, and Society* the University of Chicago Press had solicited advanced subscriptions to the book and kept complete records of all those subscriptions, a topic discussed in chapter 5.[22] Of the 243 subscriptions pledged, only 44 are not directly identifiable as a library collection (52), a bookseller (20), a colleague, close friend, or relative of Mead (13), or one of his students (111). No doubt some of these others were people who knew Mead through other avenues as well, but these connections are more difficult to trace. In other words, these 44 subscriptions represent the most generous possible number of individuals not directly connected to Mead who purchased

Mind, Self, and Society as a result of promotional mailings and advertising in the literary press prior to the book's publication. The overwhelming majority of individual purchases of the book came from those who knew the author in life and some had even attended the very lectures that made up the bulk of the text.[23] Indeed, in its first few years after publication this volume remained largely the property, both physically and symbolically, of Mead's students. After its initial spike from the advanced subscription scheme, sales of the volume plummeted to a low point of just over 100 volumes in 1939 and remained at that trough until the mid-1940s after which it rose precipitously—spurred, it would seem, by the usage the book was finding as a text in advanced courses in social psychology.

Indeed, Mead was reincorporated back into the curriculum at the University of Chicago in a peculiar way that continued to promote his relevance to the social sciences rather than philosophy. As was discussed in chapter 6, Herbert Blumer began using *Mind, Self, and Society* in his courses, and both Faris and Blumer referred extensively to Mead by name in their lectures. Mead was also definitely taught in the Chicago social psychology courses of Blumer's students Tamotsu Shibutani, Hubert Bonner, and Anselm Strauss. But from the early 1940s on Mead was also incorporated into the reformulated undergraduate social science core curriculum, and this use of Mead had little to do with what was going on in Blumer's graduate social psychology courses. Indeed, the undergraduate college at the University of Chicago developed in the 1930s as its own organizational unit with its own (sometimes co-listed) faculty and common core courses separate from the various departments.

Beginning in the early 1930s the University of Chicago was at the forefront of the "general education" movement in the development of its comprehensive undergraduate core curriculum (McNeill 1991; MacAloon 1992). In the humanities, the reorganization was directed primarily by President Robert M. Hutchins and the cohort of professors he brought in with him, especially Richard McKeon and Mortimer Adler, whose very hiring had put them in conflict with Mead and the Chicago School tradition in philosophy. In the social sciences, however, the reorganization was directed by a committee headed by Louis Wirth, and later by the school's dean Robert Redfield, both of whom had significant links to Mead. More important, however, was the group of younger instructors brought in to design and teach the new social science core classes.

The Cooperative Study in General Education (CSGE), supported by the American Council on Education and based at Chicago, was tasked with examining the existing programs in collegiate general education across the country and providing detailed recommendations for the development of core curricula (Levi 1948). Many of the employees of the CSGE who worked on the recommendations for the social sciences were hired as instructors at Chicago, where they were crucial in designing the three-year common social science core.[24] Of these instructors, Earl S. Johnson, who had taken Mead's Advanced Social Psychology course, appears to be the single most important person to advocate incorporating Mead into the curriculum.[25] In part as a result of this reformulated social science core, the University of Chicago had purchased over thirty copies of *Mind, Self, and Society* by the mid-1940s, and books of readings for several undergraduate classes reproduced portions of the volume or included it in bibliographies of recommended readings. Mead remained an important fixture of the social science curriculum through the middle decades of the twentieth century at Chicago, not only in the graduate social psychology courses but also in the undergraduate general social science core. Again, we can see a dual-movement in the reception of Mead in sociology—as an author repeatedly reinscribed in and claimed for the Chicago tradition and simultaneously as a general theoretical resource for the social sciences.

RISE OF A SOCIOLOGICAL MEAD, 1941–1955

The institutionalization of a dominant legacy of G. H. Mead in sociology occurred most strongly in the years during and immediately after World War II, and is the result of the relative success of early interpreters of Mead in relating their concerns to the trajectories of academic disciplines in the United States. Up until this point, philosophers had been leading interpreters and citers of Mead's ideas, but by the mid-1950s references were significantly declining in that discipline. This relative decline is not attributable to a loss of interest or faith on the part of his students. In fact, Charles Morris, David L. Miller, Van Meter Ames, and other former Chicago philosophy students continued to be the most frequent single individuals referring to Mead in published articles during this period. While Mead is referenced in 185 philosophy articles in this decade and a half, the number of references peaked in 1943 and declined significantly after this year. Because this decline cannot be explained by a flagging interest among this cohort of his former students, it must be the result of a lack of successful transmission of that interest. That is, philosophers were not very successful in convincing the next generation, their students, junior colleagues, and younger philosophers in general, of the continuing importance of G. H. Mead.

An attempt to seriously trace the development of American philosophy over the mid-twentieth century is beyond the scope of this analysis, but work by others has convincingly argued that the institutional structure of American philosophy was dramatically transforming in this period. In particular one may point to the rise in status of logical positivism and other forms of analytic philosophy and the corresponding decline of pragmatism in the postwar period (e.g., Gross 2002; Jewett 2011). Schorske (1997) has argued that this shift was culturally and institutional a part of a larger professionalization process occurring in American academic disciplines at mid-century that he calls the "new rigorism." Reisch (2005) has demonstrated that even among analytic philosophers there was a shift in the mid-twentieth century away from political and ethical positions to a more strictly technical, academic philosophy, motivated at least in part by fears of a hostile political atmosphere in the United States. Although analytical philosophy became dominant, Jewett (2011) identified one of the peculiar consequences of the battles between the pragmatists and analytical philosophers at Columbia University and elsewhere as the formation of a "sturdy, canonical portrait" of classical "American philosophy" in the post–World War II period. He traces in detail how the students of an earlier generation of American pragmatist philosophers helped construct this canon, stressing their tradition of commitment to public ethical issues and connections to the social sciences, in response to the rise of logical empiricism and British analytic philosophy.

As part of the larger shift, the local situation in the philosophy department at Chicago was also changing. The traditionally pragmatist-oriented department had been largely dismantled by the mid-1930s (with the exception of Charles Morris, and for a period T. V. Smith and E. S. Ames) as a result of the so-called Hutchins Controversy (Cook 1993), and had become home to a diverse group of philosophers including logical positivists, Thomists, and others (Gross 2008) who were less closely connected with the practical social sciences than the department members had been previously. As chapter 6 demonstrated, however, Morris remained committed to incorporating Mead and public ethical concerns into his philosophical writings, even though Reisch (2005) has shown how he and others moved away from the political implications of the unity of science movement.

In contrast, it is precisely in this same period when Mead's relative profile in sociology increased substantially. While there are 185 citations in philosophy, there are 278 references in sociology journals. Again, a small group of Mead's former students made up a sizeable portion of these references, but what is remarkable is that a new set of individuals began to reference Mead enthusiastically and repeatedly in sociology journals. These include students of Mead's students, especially Samuel M. Strong who worked with Herbert Blumer; C. Wright Mills who worked with George V. Gentry, David L. Miller, Kimball Young, and Howard P. Becker; Mapheus Smith who worked with Walter Reckless; and others. Frequent references to Mead also came from a group of scholars who had emigrated from Europe and elsewhere and who found intriguing ideas in Mead's work, especially J. L. Moreno, Alfred Schütz, Georges Gurvitch, Kurt H. Wolff, and Muzafer Sherif.[26] Yet, even together this group of names accounts for only a very small portion of the citations to Mead.

Instead, it appears as if Mead was becoming a general intellectual resource in sociology, and that he was increasingly understood as a social theorist who had suggestive notions relevant to a broad range of research topics, to be subjected to empirical verification. In this period the number of references that come from those not directly related to G. H. Mead skyrocketed (as figure 7.2 [above] illustrates). Content analysis of references to Mead indicates that he was frequently referred to in articles primarily concerned with communication and language, socialization and child development, small group interaction, role-taking and role-playing, personality and social attitude development, reference groups, social control, the sociology of knowledge, and in accounts of the historical development of social psychology.[27] By 1970 Robert Nisbet could, with justification, remark that it would be "hard to find anyone whose impact upon the discipline [of sociology] in the United States has been any greater" than Mead's, and that "it is fair to say that at the present time Mead's theory of symbolic interactionism is the reigning theory in sociology of the nature of the self and its relation to the social order" (1970, 38). Hence, Mead was positioned as a productive theorist, along with select others, of the dynamics of social personality and social interaction.

The same professionalization dynamics that were affecting philosophy were also affecting the other academic disciplines, including psychology and sociology. However, in sociology this "rigorism" was manifested in the development of social attitude survey and measurement techniques and new modes of coding and analyzing observed social interaction, institutionalized in major research centers like Columbia's Bureau of Applied Social Research and Harvard's Social Relations Laboratory (Platt 1996; Turner and Turner 1990; Rossi 1956). Thus, while in philosophy the professionalization dynamics led the discipline away from the pragmatism and psychological philosophy that Mead's early enthusiasts thought characterized his work, in sociology Mead was getting a strong hearing in burgeon-

ing research as an important theoretical resource now possible for empirical test.[28]

This is not to say that Mead was understood in a coherent way across
the discipline. Indeed, as chapter 6 demonstrates, Mead was positioned on
both sides of the issue, in a sense, as dramatized in the debates between
Herbert Blumer and others on the nature of "attitude" and "variable." Part
of Mead's high profile, it appears, was the result of the repeated battles
over what positions were implied in the works attributed to Mead (especially the posthumous volumes), and consequently what actually constituted Mead's "theory." This condition led Spreitzer and Reynolds (1973, 82)
to remark that by the 1970s "Mead ha[d] become all things to all sociologists." Indeed, as Vaughan and Reynolds (1968) have argued, even within
(or perhaps especially within) the perspective of Symbolic Interactionism
there has been substantial disagreement over Mead's legacy. In their study,
Vaughan and Reynolds found that one of the predominant factors that
determined one's position on Mead's work has continued to be personal
connections—almost forty years after his death (cf. Mullins 1973; Meltzer
et al. 1975; Warshay and Warshay 1986).

The patterns of citation established by the middle of the twentieth century have largely set the tracks by which Mead has been understood in the
bulk of published literature to the present day, although some new directions have also been taken in recent works. As was already mentioned,
Mead has become only more strongly associated with sociology over the
second half of the twentieth century, when measured by citation search.
At the same time, Mead's appeal has apparently diversified apace with the
emergence of newly institutionalized fields and subfields. While it would
be nearly impossible to trace out the many avenues for reception of Mead
in the later twentieth century in short order, one major development mentioned at the outset of this chapter is worth noting. With the diversification of professional journals and disciplinary subfields, Mead has found
his most substantive audience in social psychology and certain sociological journals with a focus on social interaction (especially *Symbolic Interaction*). Social psychology journals, in particular, have developed more
strongly standardized patterns of reference to Mead than other journals.
In this subfield, *Mind, Self, and Society* has become over ten times more
likely to be referenced than all of Mead's other work combined, while in all
disciplines that book makes up four out of every five citations to Mead.

With the rapidly expanding interest in Mead by the mid-twentieth century, there were repeated moves to reassess his work critically, and with
the growing dominance of *Mind, Self, and Society* and of particular in-

terpretations of his work critical responses have often taken the form of significant original research on Mead and his context, in order to move beyond narrow readings (as discussed in chapter 1). In the pages of *Symbolic Interaction*, authors asked whether there can be "a 'true' meaning of Mead" (Fine and Kleinman 1986) and sought to point out "what George Mead should have said" about the interpretation of his own work (Stewart 1981).

Finally, as Mead has become a general theoretical resource, someone to whom contemporary scholarship regularly looks for "classical" or "founding" ideas, he has also been brought into new fields or perspectives of inquiry. In this regard, one might note the use made of some of Mead's concepts in science studies or the sociology of emotion and the body. In the last few years Mead has figured in the burgeoning work on animal studies, primarily as a critical foil of contemporary works (Alger and Alger 1997; Sanders 1999; Irvine 2003), and in cognitive science (McNeill 2005; Booth 2007; Gallagher 2011), where he has even had his name attached to an explanation of the work of gesture in thought called "Mead's loop." By this eponym, applied three-quarters of a century after his death, Mead joins the company of the many scientific luminaries who have had a "law," "effect," "theorem," or "principle" named after them.

CONCLUSION

This chapter has sought to trace the dynamics by which G. H. Mead's dominant intellectual legacy and reputation came to be institutionalized. In order to explicate microlevel patterns, it has been necessary to examine the whole scope of referencing practices to Mead in journal publications from the earliest known references to the proliferation of reference at mid-century. And in order to understand these patterns in comprehensive breadth and depth this chapter has introduced the analysis of informal reference patterns based on a dataset constructed from full-text search results as a productive tool for citation analysis. Citation patterns were also utilized to give cues for where to seek more detailed explanation in local situational changes as well as in broader national professionalization dynamics.

Important turning points in the development of a dominant understanding of G. H. Mead have been identified in this analysis. In the earliest period, Mead was referred to predominately by those philosophy and psychology students and colleagues with whom he related face to face. The larger academic environment was in transition in the first decades of the

twentieth century and this played out in local concerns at the University
of Chicago to produce a reorganization whereby a conduit to Mead's teachings was opened for sociology students. They were introduced in a strongly
favorable way to his perspective through the brokerage of Ellsworth Faris
and others while the relationship between Mead and psychologists became
considerably more diffident. Through the referencing practices of Faris and
a select few others, an understanding of Mead began to form both in books
and in journal articles, which characterized him as an important resource
in a theoretically informed social psychology. A second major transformation of American academia occurred during and after World War II that
created strongly favorable conditions for the appropriation of several competing interpretations of Mead in American sociological inquiry and the
marginalization of the dominant philosophical interpretation of Mead.

There was, thus, a history of institutional transformations that occurred both at the local departmental level and at the level of national
academic disciplines to define the nature of their object of study and the
appropriate conceptual tools by which to accomplish scholarship. These
institutional shifts were not somehow made up of structures that trans-
form themselves, but are rather the compounded results of motivated social actions. Without either personal advocates or favorable disciplinary
fields, Mead lost or failed to gain a premier reputation in mid-century philosophy or psychology, but with both he gained such a reputation in sociology despite a comparatively late start to that reception. It is with this conception in mind that one can make sense of the way references to another
author's work function in the ecology of academic fields, how they develop
durable patterns, and how those patterns change.

The emphasis in the chapter is placed on the conditions under which
knowledge of a theorist is introduced and transmitted to others. Personal
relationships play an absolutely central role in generating the dynamics of
references to Mead, first primarily through those who knew him in life
and then through certain enthusiastic and privileged individual interpreters who sought to spread a knowledge of his work. The shape of these personal networks and the ability of individuals to transmit this knowledge
successfully were strongly conditioned by the structures of local academic
institutions and the broader national organization of academia, especially
at transformational junctures. Additionally, as suggested by theories of
"predecessor selection," the transmission of knowledge about a social theorist is always a selective interpretation, where the understanding of the
content of knowledge is inextricable from socially conditioned credibility
concerns. The analysis has above all attempted to demonstrate that the

dominant understanding of G. H. Mead is the integral result of this multi-level, multisite process of knowledge formation, accomplished by the referencing practices of contextually situated social actors. In this way, such work moves beyond blanket claims about the construction of classical theorists, and beyond descriptive, retrospective studies of the rise of citation patterns, to analyses of the particular social practices and actors through which that knowledge is formed.

Conclusion

George Herbert Mead has become inscribed in sociologists' perennial attempts to make sense of their discipline. He is part of the stories sociologists tell about themselves, and sociologists have often looked to the treatment of Mead to understand something about the character and history of sociology—despite, or rather because of, the problems that a case like this raises. As I have attempted to point out, the problems that academics have with Mead are at once more general and more personal than they have typically been treated. As a social actor, a speaker, a teacher, a student, a scholar, he is someone about whom knowledge is made in the course of scholarship, and those who have had a hand in producing dominant understandings of him have likewise been predominantly academics. In this sense, Mead's problems are problems of scholarship.

The following discussion brings together the reflections and lessons from this study in three parts. The first section reexamines the empirical chapters, focusing both on how the narrative of each accomplishes particular analytical tasks and on formulating lessons from the analyses of this case study. The second section offers a set of general reflections on the social processes of scholarship. In addition to drawing out the implications from the study for an understanding of knowledge as intrinsic to social action processes, I contrast the focus in the analyses with the typical focus on canonical authors and offer some heuristics for further study. In the final section, I address a few of the remaining concerns about the ways in which the study contributes to the self-reflexive study of knowledge production.

ANALYSES AND FINDINGS

By way of cues from critical literature a suitable focus was found in the social experiences of George Mead as a speaker and activist. By working to locate the development of knowledge in the experience of identifiable, historical social actors, the first chapter sets the stakes for subsequent analysis. On this basis it becomes clear that Mead participated emphatically in public issues through his acts of speech, and as a result of his action he was likely known during his lifetime first and foremost as a reformer and speaker. This public participation was constitutive of Mead's professional philosophy rather than in distinction to it. Further, Mead's public speaking was thoroughly at the core of his publications, in that many were literally published speeches, others were based on arguments that were previously given in speeches, and virtually all exhibit the rhetorics of persuasive public speech. This fact helps us to reexamine and better understand the specificity of the arguments Mead was making by seeing given manuscript or published texts as acts oriented in identifiable ways in particular social situations. Seeing them as "performative" or "illocutionary" acts (to borrow Austin's [1962] terms) is a first step toward understanding the complex social nature of Mead's written or published "works."

Mead's writings are social in several identifiable (though not empirically separate) ways. Those that were given as speeches were explicitly crafted with an audience in mind, given to an audience, and often subject to forms of response from that audience. Through his writings, which were prompted by and directed toward ongoing issues of social concern, Mead evidently sought to contribute to public discourse, and hence to participate in social dialogue in this sense that reaches beyond a given audience. Various writings make reference to abstract philosophical or scientific concepts or the opinions of other scholars, and are hence also oriented within a scholarly or intellectual dialogue (which is only partially distinguishable from the public discourse among Mead's interlocutors). And, as the analysis demonstrates, his writings were also part of what might be considered a "moral" dialogue or exchange among his close friends, in that the construction and publication of essays was inscribed in those social relationships as favors, responsibilities, or obligations. Examined in this way, these texts do not merely represent simple acts with singular intentions, but are "complex" in the sense that they participate simultaneously in multiple projects. And over the course of time, these same texts participate in new projects, becoming incorporated in new social relations, claims, and acts. Of course, none of this discussion of the sociality of

Mead's speech and writing denies the fact that Mead, as an individual, spoke and wrote certain words, phrases, or papers at certain definite times and with certain definite intentions. Such discussion is intended to push that very argument as far as possible by identifying Mead's speeches and writings as acts in connection with other acts in context, and poses the question of multiple and changing intentions.

These findings represent a first step in disentangling the production of knowledge about Mead in two ways. For one, the analysis demonstrates that an identifiable set of Mead's own practices of knowing—of producing, evaluating, and applying knowledge—were motivated by and directed toward addressing public social problems. The chapter specifies at least some of the ways in which Mead's acts were attempts to understand something about his social world in the course of changing it. One does not have to merely assert that Mead's knowledge production was social on principle, but rather, in cases identified in the chapter, the particular ways in which this is the case may be traced, the ways in which that fact shapes the form and content of knowledge can be identified, and that knowledge can be located within definite acts. Second, the analysis demonstrates that in his lifetime Mead was known by his public acts. That is, people developed understandings of Mead in large part through the social acts in which he produced knowledge. Within Mead's own lifetime, representations or accounts of him were given on the basis of these public speeches, and in this sense he participated in the production of a certain "reputation," although this, of course, does not imply that people understood him as he understood himself, or that his self-understanding was somehow static or definite.

Chapter 2 takes up the examination of Mead's own experiences of scientific research and discovery and identifies how his later work remained fundamentally dependent on these early researches. The narrative traces Mead's extensive experience in his college and graduate education with experimental methods and with scientific controversies. When Mead gained academic employment he worked in earnest on problems of psychophysical experiments, neurological specimens, and animal behavior studies. Even at the University of Chicago he continued to pursue questions of comparative and physiological psychology that were central to the way he formulated his social psychological essays and lectures.

Following on this, chapter 3 presents a very different context for Mead's ideas among the oft-romanticized Hawaiian Islands. The detailed narrative examination of Mead's engagement with Hawaii (at the expense of reviewing any of Mead's other local contexts in as much detail) not only presents us with a chance to trace the ways in which Mead's activities were related to his ideas, but also to raise questions about the presumed nature of our own understandings of him and his ideas. On the first count, the chapter shows that a more satisfactory understanding of the relation between context and ideas can be gained by examining how social actors participate in courses of experience that prompt problems and understandings by their very sequence and juxtaposition. The chapter uses this topic to examine how knowledge is emphatically addressed to the problems one finds in experience and how experience becomes problematic in different ways over the course of those experiences. The movement back and forth between Chicago and Hawaii was, for Mead, eminently generative of his ideas by putting two local sets of changing problems—problems that struck at the core of social development, democratic governance, and national identity—in dialogue over time. Moreover, one gets a thoroughly practical sense of the ways in which Mead as a social individual was dependent on unique times and places for the peculiar character of his experiences, and especially how he was essentially dependent on other people for those experiences. On the second count, the exposition raises questions about our understandings of a presumably well-known (or at least much written about) individual. Precisely because of the strong contrast they present, the emphasis on Mead's public speaking and engagement with Hawaii sets the stage for the later problems of attribution of intentions, concepts, and texts to him more strongly than they have typically been posed.

If the three chapters of part 1 demonstrated that Mead's defining acts as a public figure and scholar—his speaking, writing, and publishing—are thoroughly social, then chapter 4, in part, extends this claim to his teaching. Mead, the consummate lecturer, is shown to be someone who worked to ensure the impingement of social concerns on his teaching, especially in relation to his students. The chapter lays out an argument about how the boundaries and character of Mead's pedagogy are difficult to establish categorically. No single, firm line can be drawn between Mead's public speeches and his pedagogy when one considers the diversity of groups to which Mead spoke, including a variety of intermediate quasi-public or quasi-pedagogical settings. It is likewise clear that the fact that Mead was the instructor of a course did not mean that he was the only person lecturing, that he did not also lecture in classes and venues not officially assigned to him, or that the choice of what to present in any class was his alone. More notable still, records demonstrate that Mead taught to a wide range of differently composed audiences even in his officially assigned courses and that he repeatedly and actively sought to structure advanced work in seminars, discussion groups, and research and grading assistantships so that his students would be constitutive of his pedagogy. In one sense, by connecting the analyses of chapters 1 through 4 we also see the rhythm or punctuation of Mead's own intellectual life, moving between public speech and classroom lecture, among different audiences, and between professional duties and travels. In the course of the chapter, these analyses are first put negatively, as a problem for our presumed understanding of Mead and documents from his classes, but the later sections of the chapter recast this as a chance to consider Mead's classes as complex social environments productive of his own and his students' ideas.

Chapter 4 traces the active participation of Mead's students in his teaching. They made novel presentations, discussed controversial topics of the moment, conducted research that Mead supervised, and presented him with assignments that put on paper their understandings of his exposition. Mead was just like other teachers in this sense; his pedagogical efforts were engagements with students who made impressions on him. These students made all manner of different representations of those classes, including summaries, outlines, bibliographies, lists of definitions, quoted aphorisms, and shorthand notes. And the chapter makes the case that when understood in the context of the experiences and projects of the various students, these documents were evidence of the diversity of their concerns rather than their monomania to record Mead. Again, those students are just like other students. Even when they produced valuable records of Mead these documents were not the only ends but were part of various attempts to understand their social contexts and themselves, and the documents were reinscribed in later projects such as teaching their own classes and conducting their own research. The narrative treats a few of these cases in detail in order to trace the specific ways in which Mead and his students interacted, how they produced understandings of his lectures, and how their notes were actually used.

By tracing Mead's encounters with students such as W. I. Thomas and John B. Watson, it is possible to capture aspects of the complex back and forth flow of ideas over time and to show how these exchanges were consequential for each of the scholars involved and hence for the ideas as well, even as the ultimate source of a particular idea becomes more difficult to pin down. Put in overly simple terms, the work of these students is constitutive of Mead's own knowledge, and their work is built on his attempts to teach them. The chapter makes the case that these meaningful exchanges are clear indications of the social and processual nature of knowledge production because they demonstrate how their intellectual projects come together around particular issues and investigations of mutual interest, how over the course of interactions the scholars and ideas change, and how the exchanges had lasting consequences in each scholars' work even when they no longer work together or even agree. Perhaps most important for the analyses in subsequent chapters is the proposition that to study those who have produced knowledge about Mead and his ideas is not necessarily to leave Mead's side. In the classroom, around the discussion table, in the laboratory, and elsewhere there is a common ground where both Mead and his students and colleagues were engaged together in producing knowledge in interconnected projects.

Because *Mind, Self, and Society* is in many ways at the center of the problematic nature of knowledge about Mead, chapter 5 deals in detail with the process through which it was put together. In the chapter I stake the claim that adequately understanding *Mind, Self, and Society* as a text requires a thorough acknowledgment of the consequential process of its creation. No single individual intention, no single document, no single decision, nor even any simple agglomeration of individuals, documents, or decisions provides the unequivocal key to understanding the text, without tracing their transformation and interaction over a course of time. What one finds is that although there were desires to preserve some kind of legacy to Mead after his death, there were no clear intentions to produce anything like the books that resulted among any of the individuals or a consensus of those involved. Nor was there a given set of documents that could simply be compared or spliced together. The sequence of social actions is placed front and center here at a minute level of analysis that identifies particular meetings and decisions, readings of individual texts, and editing at the level of individual words, phrases, and lines. Each of the events, texts, and actors is relevant in identifiable ways to the process and, hence, to the final documents. This level of detail is productive because it provides the opportunity to give some clear indications of what this process looked like to the actors involved. In this way the actual accomplishment of a single body of work is shown on the basis of eminently practical actions over time.

Building on chapter 4, the analysis examines how various student and stenographic notes and manuscripts were discovered, interpreted, and manipulated within this later process, how those documents became part of different projects than they had been for the students in the classroom, and how the particular problems or forms of those documents as records of Mead were intrinsic to the course of the process itself. In this process, the series of actions appeared more or less plausible and accountable to those involved, given the kinds of practical conditions or constraints that they understood themselves to be facing. Even through the stages of composition and manufacturing for the published book, its content was not stable as negotiations took place about what could be reasonably accepted in each of the volumes, how the volumes should relate to one another, and what would have to be left out. And as examples in the chapter show, the product bears everywhere the imprint of this process of its production. By providing a single, circumscribed, and relatively systematic reference point for a field of Mead's philosophy, the publication of *Mind, Self, and Society* was key to enabling later authoritative interpretations of him.

Chapter 6 picks up on this charge from the previous analysis in that it examines how authoritative claims about Mead are mobilized, by following two cases in depth. Throughout this chapter the interpretation of one author by another is at the center of analysis. Special emphasis is placed on moments of contention in which one can identify how such claims are justified and on how the claims were understood as plausible by those making them. Charles Morris, a philosopher and the editor of *Mind, Self, and Society*, actively contended with critics in asserting that the various posthumous volumes fundamentally represented Mead's own thought, not his editorial work, and that his interpretation of Mead was based on Mead's own emphases. The chapter traces how Morris emplaced Mead in his own endeavors as someone providing definite particular insights and as providing a key to the synthetic projects he undertook. Morris retained privileged access to documents about Mead from his editorial work and he worked to bring out certain characterizations of those works even before they appeared. In this way, he continued to actively work on producing and justifying an understanding of Mead.

Herbert Blumer, a sociologist and author of *Symbolic Interactionism*, also developed a conceptual orientation in which an understanding of Mead was fundamental. He treated Mead as at the center of a countertradition in social psychology and as a crucial resource in criticizing other extant theories of human nature and social action. Certain central principles or criteria were detected in Mead's work and served over and over as an orientation in contentious literature. While Morris contended with critics of his understanding of Mead more in his early career, and especially around his editorship of *Mind, Self, and Society*, Blumer became involved in controversies more in the late years of his career, as his representations of Mead became authoritative. The chapter also identifies how both men's understandings of Mead were influenced at decisive points by their own intellectual interests.

Previous attempts to understand the work done by Blumer, Morris, and others on Mead's legacy have often ignored how these individuals understood themselves to be participating in projects with Mead. The chapter indicates how Mead singled out both Morris and Blumer as individuals who were carrying on his own work, and how both had actually accomplished graduate projects under his supervision. For Blumer especially, this proved definitive in authorizing his claims about Mead even when confronted with textual warrants for other interpretations. Their real sense of participating in broader intellectual projects with Mead allows us to bring together Morris's and Blumer's claims about how to interpret Mead, how their own projects were motivated by Mead, and how they were contributing to something beyond Mead. Indeed, this allows us to consider their career-spanning work in this regard not ultimately as some form of willful deception, but as serious attempts to pursue scholarship along lines they believed, even if other scholars do not see their understandings as true or productive.

Experience with the same individual does not mean exposure to the same emphases or concepts and does not mean the same interpretations of that experience; hence, the interpretations of Mead made by Morris and Blumer are understandable as both really related to Mead and (without contradiction) as divergent in their consequences. And this social experience leads us to a different conceptualization of how Mead was "appropriated" or "received" in particular individuals' work. It is not as though this reception begins only by those separated in time and place from Mead and on the basis of some given body of materials. Instead, as chapter 4 already showed, Mead's students were, as a matter of course, producing understandings of Mead as part of their own intellectual endeavors that implicated Mead in actual consequential interactions with them. In chapter 6 the analysis demonstrates that Morris and Blumer had particularly consequential relationships with Mead that in his own lifetime entailed his commentary and approval of the understandings they had produced about him and about the kinds of endeavors in which they were collectively involved. In this sense there is no "reception" but an active production of knowledge in which Mead participates both in person and in memory.

Chapter 7 takes the same emphasis on the active production of knowledge about Mead to a more aggregate level of patterns of reference in published literature over time, while retaining a focus on particular identifiable practices and local situational contexts. In order to gain a sense of the whole ecology or universe of references to Mead in published journal articles, techniques were developed to compile data from a variety of sources and to include a diversity of forms of reference. The chapter demonstrates on the basis of these materials that Mead was discussed and represented in published work from almost the very beginning of his career, and those references were overwhelmingly tied to social relationships in both who was citing Mead and how they were citing him. This remains true even after the references to Mead shift from psychology to sociology journals, provoking the analysis to seek the particular changes in social institutions in which Mead participated. Disciplinary reorganization at the University of Chicago (paralleled nationally in various ways) created a structure in which particular individuals became gatekeepers and interpreters for their respective disciplines through which students were introduced (or not) to Mead. Ellsworth Faris proves to be a key figure; the ways he positioned Mead and even the peculiar ways he referred to Mead were carried on by several of his students. These modes of reference were consequential in that they sought to make an argument about the need for an adequate— sociological—social psychology around a coherent tradition of authors, of whom they argued Mead was the primary exemplar. These arguments began to find purchase especially with the rapid expansion and diversification of published materials putatively by and about Mead after his death. Indeed, with the shifting institutional structure of American academia in the 1930s and 1940s, such materials provided the means for the development of divergent bodies of work on Mead in different academic disciplines and subfields.

Chapters 6 and 7 together demonstrate how Mead was successfully emplaced, not once but over and over, into particular schools and disciplines on the basis of definite and concerted claims about him. While the publication of certain texts and the transformation of local institutions provided the materials and opportunities for such moves, it required the attempts to mobilize claims about Mead's unique relevance and to have those claims taken as authoritative. In these endeavors, it was the personal relationships that structured the knowledge about Mead and that continued to mediate the published discourse about him, even as a large body of accessible literature by and about him developed. Claims had to be found authoritative (or not) and built upon (or argued against) by others for them to have a cumulative effect, and the analyses demonstrate that these patterns follow identifiable social relationships—especially among colleagues and between teachers and students. As elsewhere in the analysis, Mead is actively involved in these social relationships and the mobilization of claims about the fields in which he worked. Through the claims of his students and colleagues, direct connections to Mead remained centrally relevant to knowledge about Mead.

In attempting to capture some of the moments of this complex process chapter 7 moves back and forth between institutional structures and local social relationships and practices. It is only as a result of this successful and continued institutionalization of Mead at the level of social actions, especially in certain subfields and schools of thought in sociology, that it becomes possible to find an explanation of how certain dominant understandings of him have developed. A final indicator of this, pointed out at the end of the chapter, is that Mead's name and some of the concepts ascribed to him have been routinely deployed as relevant symbolic cues or shorthand for whole perspectives in sociology, and he is likewise deployed in negotiating the contours of new subfields or interdisciplinary fields. For Mead to be someone who is recognized and utilized in this way depends on the accomplishments of the preceding processes by which he has been claimed and placed.

KNOWLEDGE PROCESS

One of the arguments that I have sought to carry through the analyses is that Mead's knowledge-making practices are no different in principle from the practices of those who made knowledge about him. Even further, Mead the person is involved in several identifiable ways in the production of Mead the classical author, founder, or icon, although not in any way that would imply that he produced his own reputation at will. Instead, in the analyses above Mead is treated as one social actor among others, who produces understandings of himself and of others in the course of scholarship, and who participates in intellectual endeavors with others. Mead was, like those who produced knowledge about him, a practical social actor, a speaker, a teacher, a student. The study documents, further, how the people and problems of scholars' immediate social environments continually shape their decisions, how intellectual influences are multidirectional, and how subsequent interpretations of scholars shape even how we understand and formulate their own self-understandings. As a consequence, Mead's problems as an intellectual are not fundamentally unique; rather, the production of knowledge, including knowledge about other scholars, is intrinsic to the nature of scholarship as a social enterprise. Much of the account, then, is an attempt to illustrate how complex it is to get from Mead's own social experience to our understandings of him, while at the same time pointing out that such an endeavor may be accomplished by a focus on tracing the complex articulation of empirical social practices and experiences in which people engaged.

In contrast to the view presented in this study, a focus on founders, classics, and canons as a special topic in their own right invites serious problems for a satisfactory explanation. In particular, such a focus is likely to prompt a search for something specifically distinct about a particular author, text, or concept. That is, it is likely to look for the "genius" of that founder, classic, or canon in a particular characteristic of the person or work, in a particularly creative or provocative social context, or in a particular constructive mechanism such as sedimentation or disembedding. All of these various forms of explanation, when treated to the exclusion of others, serve ultimately as analytical shortcuts for complex sequences of social action. In this sense, they invite a sort of retrospective teleological account that draws descriptive lines of connection from the present back to more or less definite moments of creation in those characteristics, contexts, or mechanisms. What this study has sought to do, instead, is to sustain a prospective and analytical focus on the complex processes of knowing intrinsic to scholarship and to show on that basis the diversity of knowledge production processes in which people who were producing knowledge about Mead were involved. With this focus we can see empirically if and when particular individuals or groups had certain understandings in mind and, perhaps more important, what they did not. We can see when selections or appropriations of Mead were made and in what larger enterprises those moves were a part. And we can see what possible or incipient directions were not carried through or were lost in the course of subsequent developments. The analysis, in this way, moves beyond constructing a merely plausible account about how we got where we are and instead attempts to treat empirical problems of scholarship.

Such a focus also allows us to avoid the problematic and normative decisions about what should ultimately count as canonical. At what point is it clear that Mead was going to become, is, or had been canonical, and on what qualitative criteria can such a determination be made? What body of works or set of concepts does or should stand for him? What is most characteristic of his work, his perspective, his life? In the above analyses, much detailed, unique information regarding Mead as a person and regarding the construction of concepts and propositions (and whole documents) attributed to him is given. To ask whether we need to know some fact about Mead in order to understand some particular concept that was attributed to him, or whether it matters that some concept bears his name, is to ask a question that from the perspective outlined in this study depends entirely on the purposes to which such an analysis or concept is to be put. That is, such questions are best answered empirically rather than by *a priori* categorical argument. Moreover, such questions are addressed in the above analyses as evidence of the practical accomplishment of scholarship. In this way we find ourselves examining empirically the work of scholars who are addressing practical questions such as: What should I know about another author? Are there concepts I can use from this text? Who are other scholars referencing and how? Debates about foundational authors, classical texts, and canons become, from this perspective, evidence of how we make and use knowledge.

Knowledge progresses in a peculiar way. From the case study, we see examples of how knowledge is entailed in making claims, in drawing connections, in interpreting statements or texts, in making distinctions or priorities, in manipulating objects and ideas. Knowledge seems to follow people on their travels, to be implicated in social relationships, to be embedded in situations and institutions, and to be found in collective projects. What is common to all of these characterizations is that knowledge is necessarily a consequential move beyond itself, a part of a project or act that changes the course of that act; more simply, knowledge is found in social action and has consequences for social action. It is precisely at the points of change or consequence that knowledge is constitutive of the course of process and where analysis is directed. Indeed, one of the things the case study underscores is that the kinds of claims, interpretations, arguments, and so on, that people make have real consequences for the kinds of actions and understandings that result, not only for those immediately involved and not necessarily those that are intended.

Knowledge, in this sense, is not information; it is not the words or facts themselves, but the consequential phases of actions in which those things are placed. The practical consequences of this understanding are especially apparent in the case of George Herbert Mead. For one, there was no body of works given prior to the effort of various social actors in various settings to create, interpret, and manipulate the concepts, propositions, and texts. In addition, even when documents of various kinds exist, they do not unequivocally appear to offer the same knowledge to all those concerned, to retain the same salience or authority in different times and places, or even to be practically available to anyone who might be interested in reading them. And this phrasing does not adequately characterize the problem as examined in this study if it does not also entail questions of how such documents or interests become relevant to individuals in the first place. These are people who, the study shows, were involved first and foremost in various practical projects of action and in social relationships. One of the most recurrent and surprising findings in the analyses is that the number of people practically involved in the production of knowledge about Mead is, for most purposes, delimited and identifiable—knowledge in this case is small scale.

Summing up the above, we might say that knowledge is not self-producing or self-distributing; it is accomplished by people for purposes within their own social experience. If we are interested in understanding the production of knowledge about Mead, we must follow the social action sequences, and not any given set of documents, concepts, or individuals. And, in terms of the actual social practices of knowledge production in the human sciences, there is no "meta-" knowledge. Or put another way, all scholarship is meta-knowledge, in that academics are always making knowledge about knowledge about knowledge. Either formulation in no way changes the actual process of constructing knowledge, which always remains at the level of social practices. In this view, knowledge "moves" in a much more fundamentally social way than is typically assumed, and the examination of the production or accumulation of knowledge requires an emphatic focus on social processes of action.

There are many general models for the ways that knowledge emerges, moves, and accumulates, which attempt to capture the social process of knowledge in scholarship. No doubt the most well known of these is Kuhn's (1962) theory of "revolutions" in "paradigms" (1962), but other influential examples in the social sciences might including Peirce's community of inquiry (1877), Fleck's thought collectives (1979 [1935]), Bourdieu's intellectual fields (1969), Shils's and others' ecologies and institutions (1970), Collins's intellectual interaction ritual chains (1998), Farrell's collaborative circles (2001), and Frickel and Gross's scientific/intellectual movements (2005). Each of these authors has sought to characterize the dynamic social processes of knowledge formation and transformation, and each in one way or another treats the social action processes as the more encompassing moment in the dynamic; that is, knowledge or ideas happen in and through social action processes.

I do not aim to adjudicate between them on the basis of a single case study. Instead, I draw attention here to an orientation they have in common. This case study contributes to this literature by providing a detailed examination of the complexity of scholarship as social action and pointing out that one of the intrinsic features of scholarship is the knowledge produced about one another. The study serves as a demonstration of the ways in which an analytical focus on the various knowledges produced about a single author over a long course and through their many iterations can provide a productive frame through which to identify and examine the social action processes of knowledge production. Indeed, the study has made the case that no single set of documents, concepts, individuals, or mechanisms provides the master key to the knowledges made by and about G. H. Mead, and only a sustained focus on empirical social action processes can adequately explain these phenomena.

STUDYING SOCIAL KNOWLEDGE

The analyses of this study also offer a few heuristics for the pursuit of similar projects on the production of knowledge in scholarship. I claim no absolute novelty for the following suggestions. Instead, I hope the case study demonstrates some of the uses to which such methodological or research orientations can be put and effectively combined. First, a productive emphasis may be placed on the social experiences of scholars as social actors. In this way, one may study how and when problems are composed in their experience and the different practical ways in which scholars reflect on the nature of their experience in work. In terms of research, this focus benefits from a conscientious examination of historical documents, including both those directly related to the individuals in question and those that help specify the character of the situations in which they find themselves. In the case examined above, it has also proved useful to examine how intellectuals' activities relate to the social recognition they receive, and how the relation between those activities and forms of recognition structures the work they undertake. This study has proposed and employed the notion of "intellectual project" to help understand how individuals come together around perceived common intellectual activities, and how those endeavors generate perceptions about the scholars involved (including self-perceptions) in the course of scholarship.

In some of the analyses, this study focuses on the rhetorical strategies employed by scholars in order to examine the ways authority is mobilized, and how those claims are related to the real experiences of those individuals. This requires an attention both to the ways written or spoken texts reveal styles of argumentation and to the ways those texts serve as acts in ongoing (often contentious) dialogues among scholars or public figures. Examining these rhetorics proved important in this case study for the additional reason that they exhibit the kinds of abstractions and representations that on a very practical level inscribe particular understandings of

a scholar's work in academic discourses. That is, in scholarship the way
an individual represents or claims other peoples' work also brings those
claims or representations into effect. The work of one's scholarship demonstrates what is considered relevant, important, essential (and of course
what is irrelevant, unimportant, inessential) in another's work by the way
it is utilized. A focus on the ways in which scholars have understood themselves and each other may also serve the purpose of critically comparing
different understandings of nominally the same person, work, or concept
and of provoking a reflection on our own understandings of the same.

Research may also be directed to the examination of structures or
ecologies of social relations, especially as they change. In research for this
study, an attempt has been made to identify particular networks or patterns of relationships by significant biographical research on students and
colleagues and by extensive use of correspondence. In particular, I have
sought out moments of interrelation or articulation of social actors where
interests or projects connect. This is in contrast to a strategy that would
merely trace presumed lineages of student-teacher or other relationships
without examining the actual transformative encounters through which
these individuals come together. These networks of relationships prove
centrally important in the findings regarding the importance of "informal references" in published literature, in the personal distribution of
published works, and in the intimate nature of various publics. That is,
published references to Mead, ownership of works attributed to Mead,
and participation in public endeavors with Mead are all shown to be thoroughly related to the structures of local, social relationships. I have elsewhere traced the productivity of a research focus on the dialogic encounters of authors, especially those that bridge supposedly bounded traditions
(Huebner 2013). This focus can help us reconceptualize fields of inquiry
and schools of thought not as "grand traditions" or sets of static "camps,"
but as social dialogues with empirical continuities, connections, developments, and breaks. In terms of further research on social knowledge, such
findings should provoke us to problematize our presumed categories and
distinctions. The shape of public discourse is not everywhere the same;
journals, speeches, and classes do not unequivocally serve the same purposes; disciplinary institutions and topics change; and publication does
not imply universal distribution. The analyses above demonstrate that
identifying the actual relational patterns helps us better understand the
particular ways scholarship operates in different times and places.

As a case study, this study would benefit, above all, from comparative work. One place to look for such comparison is in additional work on

George Herbert Mead. Included in this study are appendixes that I hope will prove useful in such endeavors. The bibliography of Mead's works contains several pieces that have never previously been listed in published bibliographies, and the list of notes from Mead's classes is by far the most comprehensive list of such material prepared in print. In addition, this study draws attention to the complex projects in which various individuals were involved and in the possible understandings of Mead that have been ignored, forgotten, or marginalized, as part of the project of following the accumulating development of Mead as an icon, foundational author, or classic. I am sure that these materials would offer additional insights to other researchers and that the discoveries reported here are not the only ones to be made about Mead. In addition, other comparative cases might be found among the groups of authors listed in the introduction and others who, at least superficially, seem to exhibit many of the same problems for simple understandings of the nature of authorship, reputation, and knowledge among scholars. Comparative work might also be directed toward some of the limitations of this study. The study has had, more often than not, to presuppose the structure and boundaries of certain academic institutions and resources, although at various points the transformation of those institutions and the production of knowledge outside of strictly academic settings are also discussed. Additional work would need to be conducted in order to examine topics such as the formation of academic institutions around questions of knowledge and to interrogate the relations of academic scholarship to other forms of social knowledge.

HISTORICAL RESEARCH AND RECONSTRUCTION

Mead once asked, "How many different Caesars have crossed the Rubicon since 1800?" (1938, 95)—and we might follow in the same spirit by asking, how many different Meads have written that question? A brief review of the various knowledges that have been produced regarding Mead serves to confirm that, in a certain sense, Mead exemplifies his own remarks. Indeed, the question quoted above is from one of the many untitled manuscripts left behind after his death, which found its way into print in one of the infamous, posthumously published volumes, where it has found various uses in the work of other academics. In another of the posthumous volumes, based on lecture notes and published earlier, we might also note that Mead apparently answered his own question: "We look over histories which have dealt with Caesar, but we find a different Caesar portrayed in each one. A dozen different Caesars have crossed the Rubicon" (1936, 417).

In either case, whether positing or answering this hypothetical question, his point remained largely the same: "The history which we study is not the history of a few years ago. We cannot say that events remain the same. We are continually reconstructing the world from our present standpoint. And that reconstruction holds just as really with the so-called 'irrevocable' past as with reference to the future" (Mead 1936, 417; cf. 1938, 92–100; 1934, 256; 1932, *passim*). The ways we characterize historical persons and their actions change as a result of continual "reconstruction." In this regard, scholarship in the human sciences is no different from any other practical social activity for which its forward course changes its past.

The problem of historical knowledge is a perennial and intrinsic aspect of scholarship. We are continually presented with questions about authors, texts, and concepts—about what we know, what we can know, what we should know, and so on. In research on historical materials these problems are especially salient because every new discovery of materials not only opens the possibility of reinterpretation of existing materials on that basis, but also changes the perceptions of even further discoveries of new material that might do the same. Might there not be other lost "Hypnotism" articles, or "Comparative Psychology" notes, or exotic sojourns; might there not be keys to the understandings made of Mead to be found in other letters, manuscripts, notes, or publications? In principle there is always more to know not only about ongoing processes but also of "irrevocably past" ones.

If such an argument occasionally leads researchers into paralyzing skepticism, it has also led to the recognition of opportunity and responsibility. Our opportunity as researchers, it seems, lies in the ability to see events in new ways on the basis of the subsequent tracks these events have followed, to understand "changes, forces, and interests" (in one formulation [Mead 1934, 256]) that transcend what any of the individuals involved could see in the course of their own experience. This is the way in which the problems of historical knowledge have become the opportunities for social research time and again. Our responsibility, then, is at the very least to reflect on what it is we do as scholars and how our scholarship moves and builds. On a practical level, scholars take on some portion of this responsibility whenever they posit directions in which scholarship should move or offer guidelines to help structure later research.

A study like this begs the question of self-reflexivity with particular urgency. There are dense interconnections between the object of study and the method of study that I conscientiously attempted not to overtax in the empirical analyses. On a very concrete level, Mead was also cen-

trally focused on questions regarding the nature of knowledge and its relation to social action. In some ways, the study brings a few of Mead's own
notions to bear on a knowledge of him. In this sense, Mead both serves
as the object of study and at the same time provides some of the tools
through which to accomplish an analysis of that object. I make no special
virtue of this fact at the outset, and in the introduction I point out instead
how the practical orientation of the research does not depend ultimately
on any single author or perspective, but on a broader body of literature
in the social sciences. Nevertheless, in part 1, I point out how Mead was
self-consciously oriented to problems of the production of knowledge and
sought to ask precisely these self-reflexive questions about the grounding
of forms of thought in social practice.

More generally, as a study of knowledge production, this work also
contributes to the phenomenon it studies for better or worse. My activities
are not outside, at least in principle, of my study. However, I have made no
attempt to follow myself around taking notes about my own knowledge-
making practices. Such a task, besides the fact that it would prove practically impossible and make for tedious reading, considers the task of self-
reflexivity only in a very narrow sense. Instead, I have sought to address
this in a different way. In tracing the production of knowledge about Mead,
one begins to be able to ground alternative understandings in the various
tracks not taken or which have been eclipsed. When combined with the
discovery of new materials in the course of that research, I found what
I consider definite grounds for reevaluating Mead. In this sense, I freely
acknowledge that my work makes an explicit claim to reconstruct Mead,
and while these claims are not unimpeachable, I present a potentially
productive way forward on Mead, on similar cases, and on understanding
knowledge.

APPENDIX A

George Herbert Mead's Published Works

In preparing this list, I have attempted to note additional information where relevant about the entries, including cases in which there is good evidence to belief they are based on particular speeches, and when they are excerpted or reprinted in contemporary publications. This does not exclude the (likely) possibility that other papers are also based on public speeches. An attempt has been made, as far as practically possible, to order the publications chronologically by month as well as by year. These works are not separately entered into the general bibliography of cited references found below; instead, all citations in the text to publications by George Herbert Mead refer to the designations found here.

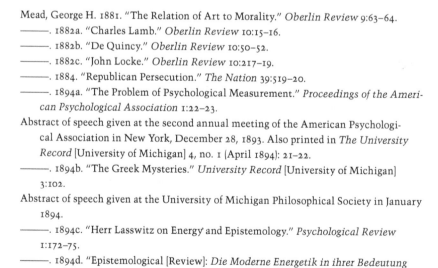

Mead, George H. 1881. "The Relation of Art to Morality." *Oberlin Review* 9:63–64.

———. 1882a. "Charles Lamb." *Oberlin Review* 10:15–16.

———. 1882b. "De Quincy." *Oberlin Review* 10:50–52.

———. 1882c. "John Locke." *Oberlin Review* 10:217–19.

———. 1884. "Republican Persecution." *The Nation* 39:519–20.

———. 1894a. "The Problem of Psychological Measurement." *Proceedings of the American Psychological Association* 1:22–23. Abstract of speech given at the second annual meeting of the American Psychological Association in New York, December 28, 1893. Also printed in *The University Record* [University of Michigan] 4, no. 1 (April 1894): 21–22.

———. 1894b. "The Greek Mysteries." *University Record* [University of Michigan] 3:102. Abstract of speech given at the University of Michigan Philosophical Society in January 1894.

———. 1894c. "Herr Lasswitz on Energy and Epistemology." *Psychological Review* 1:172–75.

———. 1894d. "Epistemological [Review]: *Die Moderne Energetik in ihrer Bedeutung für die Erkenntniskritik*. By Kurd Lasswitz." *Psychological Review* 1: 210–213.

———. 1895a. "Hypnotism." *The Dental Journal* 4 (1–2): 1–9, 33–43.
Speech given at the thirty-eighth annual meeting of the Michigan Dental Association in Ann Arbor, June 7, 1894. Digests of proceedings available in *The Dental Register* 48:380–81; and *Ohio Dental Journal* 14:408–9.

———. 1895b. "A Theory of Emotions from the Physiological Standpoint." *Psychological Review* 2:162–64.
Abstract of speech given at the third annual meeting of the American Psychological Association in Princeton, December 28, 1894. Also printed in *The American Journal of Psychology* 6:625–26.

———. 1895c. "[Review] *An Introduction to Comparative Psychology.* By C. L. Morgan." *Psychological Review* 2:399–402.

———. 1896a. "Some Aspects of Greek Philosophy." *University of Chicago Record* 1:42.
Abstract of speech given at the University of Chicago Philosophical Club, January 22, 1896.

———. 1896b. "The Relation of Play to Education." *University of Chicago Record* 1 (8): 141–45.
Speech given at Chicago Commons School of Social Economics, May 1, 1896.

———. 1897a. "[Review] Untersuchungen zur Phänomenologie und Ontologie des menschlichen Geistes. Von Dr. G. Class." *American Journal of Theology* 1:789–92.

———. 1897b. "The Child and His Environment." *Transactions of the Illinois Society for Child-Study* 3:1–11.
Speech given at the Illinois Society for Child Study in Chicago, April 30, 1897.

———. 1898. "Hawaiians are Fit. G. H. Meade Says They Have Shown Ability to Rule. Not a 'Crown Colony.' Owners of Industries are Residents and Responsible. White Labor may Succeed. Free Sugar is No Object in Seeking Annexation. Analysis of the Population." *Chicago Tribune*, January 22, 13.

———. 1899a. "The Working Hypothesis in Social Reform." *American Journal of Sociology* 5:367–71.

———. 1899b. "[Review] *The Psychology of Socialism.* By Gustave Le Bon." *American Journal of Sociology* 5:404–12.

[Mead, George H., and Helen K. Mead, eds.] 1899. *The School and Society.* By John Dewey. [Acknowledged in later editions]. Chicago: University of Chicago Press.

Mead, George H. 1900a. "Suggestions Towards a Theory of the Philosophical Disciplines." *Philosophical Review* 9:1–17.

———. 1900b. "[Review] *The Making of Hawaii: A Study in Social Evolution.* By William Fremont Blackman. *America in Hawaii: A History of the United States Influence in the Hawaiian Islands.* By Edmund Janes Carpenter. *The Real Hawaii, its History and Present Condition,* including the True Story of the Revolution. A Revised Edition of the *Boston at Hawaii.* By Lucien Young, U.S.N." *The American Historical Review* 5 (4): 786–90.

———. 1901a. "A New Criticism of Hegelianism: Is It Valid?" *American Journal of Theology* 5:87–96.

———. 1901b. "[Review] *Philosophie des Geldes.* By Georg Simmel." *Journal of Political Economy* 9:616–19.

————. 1902. "Recollections of Henry in Oberlin, and After." In *Henry Northrup Castle, Letters*, edited by Helen C. Mead and George H. Mead. London: Sands and Co. Recently republished as Henry N. Castle, *The Collected Letters of Henry Northrup Castle*, edited by George H. Mead and Helen C. Mead, with introduction by Alfred L. Castle and foreword by Martin Krislov (Athens, OH: Ohio University Press, 2013).

————. 1903a. "The Definition of the Psychical." *Decennial Publications of the University of Chicago*, 1st ser., 3:77–112.

————. 1903b. "Report of the Committee on Fellowships to the Graduate Faculty, March 19, 1898. Mr. Mead, Chairman." In *The President's Report* [University of Chicago] 1:cxvii–cxix.

————. 1904a. "The Basis for a Parents' Association." *Elementary School Teacher* 4:337–46. Speech given at the University of Chicago School of Education Parents' Association, December 17, 1903.

————. 1904b. "Image or Sensation." *Journal of Philosophy, Psychology and Scientific Method* 1:604–7. Based on a speech, "The Image," given at the Western Branch of the American Psychological Association in Chicago, November 23, 1903, and on discussion of speech "Image or Sensation?" by W. C. Gore given at the Northwestern branch of the American Psychological Association in Chicago, May 7, 1904.

————. 1904c. "The Relation of Psychology and Philology." *Psychological Bulletin* 1:375–91.

————. 1905a. "[Review] *Du Rôle de l'Individu dans le Déterminisme Social*. By D. Draghiscesco. *Le Problème du Déterminisme Social, Déterminisme biologique et déterminisme social*. By D. Draghiscesco." *Psychological Bulletin* 2:399–405.

————. 1905b. "[Review] *Études sur la Sélection chez l'Homme*. By Dr. Paul Jacoby." *Psychological Bulletin* 2:407–12.

————. 1906a. "Science in the High School." *School Review* 14:237–49. Followed by commentaries from F. R. Moulton, R. A. Millikan, and C. R. Barnes.

————. 1906b. "The Teaching of Science in College." *Science* 24:390–97. Speech given at meeting of the Sigma Chi chapter in Chicago, March 1906.

————. 1906c. "The Imagination in Wundt's Treatment of Myth and Religion." *Psychological Bulletin* 3:393–99.

————. 1907a. "Editorial Notes." *School Review* 15:160–65.

————. 1907b. "Our Public Schools." *The Public* 10 (481): 281–85. Speech originally entitled "The Chicago School Situation" given at the annual meeting of the Chicago Society for Ethical Culture, May 29, 1907.

————. 1907c. "The Educational Situation in the Chicago Public Schools." *City Club Bulletin* 1:131–38. Speech given at the City Club of Chicago, February 2, 1907.

————. 1907d. "The Relation of Imitation to the Theory of Animal Perception." *Psychological Bulletin* 4:210–11. Abstract of a speech given at the fifteenth annual meeting of the American Psychological Association in New York, December 28, 1906.

———. 1907e. "[Review] *The Newer Ideals of Peace*. By Jane Addams." *American Journal of Sociology* 13:121–28.

———. 1907f. "Concerning Animal Perception." *Psychological Review* 14:383–90. Based on speech "The Relation of Imitation to the Theory of Animal Perception" (see 1907d).

———. 1907g. "[Review] *L'Evolution créatrice*. By Henri Bergson." *Psychological Bulletin* 4:379–84.

———. 1908a. "The Social Settlement, Its Basis and Function," *University of Chicago Record* 12:108–10. Speech given on Settlement Day at the University of Chicago, October 28, 1907.

———. 1908b. "Editorial Notes." *Elementary School Teacher* 8:281–84.

———. 1908c. "Educational Aspects of Trade Schools." *Union Labor Advocate* 8:19–20. Speech given at the Women's Trade Union League in Chicago, February 9, 1908.

———. 1908d. "Editorial Notes: Industrial Education." *Elementary School Teacher* 8:402–6.

———. 1908e. "The Philosophical Basis of Ethics." *International Journal of Ethics* 18:311–23. Speech given to the Chicago Ethical Society congress, December 30, 1907.

———. 1908f. "Social Settlements and Anarchy." *The Public* 11 (524): 55–57.

———. 1908g. "Editorial Notes." *Elementary School Teacher* 9:156–57.

———. 1908h. "Editorial Notes." *Elementary School Teacher* 9:212–14. Speech given at the Woman's Trade Union League in Chicago, February 9, 1908.

———. 1908i. "McDougall's Social Psychology [Review]. *An Introduction to Social Psychology*. By William McDougall." *Psychological Bulletin* 5:385–91.

———. 1908j. "[Review] *L'Ideal moderne*. By Paul Gaultier." *Psychological Bulletin* 5:403–4.

———, Aksel G. S. Josephson, Henry W. Thurston, and John W. Stockwell. 1908. "Report on Chicago's Public Library Service by the Sub-Committee on Libraries, of the Committee of the City Club of Chicago, On Public Education." *City Club Bulletin* 2 (32): 381–88.

———. 1909a. "Editorial Notes." *Elementary School Teacher* 9:327–28.

———. 1909b. "Industrial Education, the Working-Man, and the School." *Elementary School Teacher* 9:369–83.

———. 1909c. "Editorial Notes." *Elementary School Teacher* 9:433–34.

———. 1909d. "The Adjustment of Our Industry to Surplus and Unskilled Labor." *Proceedings of the National Conference of Charities and Corrections* 34:222–25. Speech given at the National Conference on Charities and Corrections in Buffalo, New York, June 12, 1909.

———. 1909e. "Social Psychology as Counterpart to Physiological Psychology." *Psychological Bulletin* 6:401–8.

———, Harry L. Bird, and George E. Hooker. 1909. "The Civil Service Commission and the Appointment of a Librarian of the Chicago Public Library. A Joint Report of the Sub-Committee on Libraries and Museums and the Committee on the Civil Service of the City Club of Chicago." *City Club Bulletin* 2:479–85.

———. 1910a. "What Social Objects does Psychology Presuppose." *Psychological Bulletin* 7:52–53.

Abstract of speech given at the eighteenth annual meeting of the American Psychological Association in Boston, December 31, 1909.

———. 1910b. "What Social Objects Must Psychology Presuppose?" *Journal of Philosophy, Psychology and Scientific Methods* 7:174–80.

Speech described above (see 1910a).

———. 1910c. "The Psychology of Social Consciousness Implied in Instruction." *Science* 31:688–93.

Speech given to the meeting of the American Association for the Advancement of Science in Boston, December 1910. Reprinted in *Pacific Medical Journal* 53, no. 7 (July 1910): 421–26; Irving King, ed., *Social Aspects of Education: A Book of Sources and Original Discussions with Annotated Bibliographies* (New York: Macmillan, 1912); and John K. Hart, ed., *Creative Moments in Education: A Documentary Interpretation of the History of Education* (New York: Henry Holt, 1931).

———. 1910d. "Social Consciousness and the Consciousness of Meaning." *Psychological Bulletin* 7:397–405.

Probably based on a speech originally titled "Social Consciousness" given at the North Central Psychological Association in Chicago, November 28, 1908.

———, Sophonisba P. Breckinridge, and Anna E. Nicholes. 1910. "Concerning the Garment Workers' Strike. Report of the Sub-Committee to the Citizens' Committee, Nov. 5th, 1910." Chicago [Photo-reproduction: Northern Archives, 1992].

Mead, George H. 1911a. "Social Bearings of Industrial Education." *Proceedings of the Western Drawing and Manual Training Association* 18:23–34.

Speech given at the eighteenth annual meeting of the Western Drawing and Manual Training Association in Springfield, Illinois, May 2, 1911.

———. 1911b. "Fite's Individualism [Review]: *Individualism: Four Lectures on the Significance of Consciousness for Social Relations*. By Warner Fite." *Psychological Bulletin* 8:323–28.

———. 1911c. "[Review] *Social Value. A Study in Economic Theory*. (Critical and Constructive.) By B. M. Anderson Jr." *Psychological Bulletin* 8:432–36.

———. 1911d. "Report of the Committee to Make a Common Survey of the Various Agencies Involved in Educating the Eye, the Hand, and the Brain in the Interest of Successful Achievement in the Fine and Industrial Arts." *Journal of the Proceedings of the Fifty-Eight Annual Meeting of the Illinois Teachers' Association*, 43–49.

Report written by Mead with assistance from Abbie E. Lane, Eugene Davenport, Jane Addams, and read by W. B. Owen, at the fifty-eighth annual meeting of the Illinois Teachers' Association in Springfield, Illinois, December 1911.

———, Oliver C. Farrington, Henry E. Legler, and Carl O. Sauer, eds. 1911. *Educational Opportunities in Chicago: A Summary Prepared by the Council for Library and Museum Extension*. Chicago: Council for Library and Museum Extension.

———. 1912a. (Exhibit of the City Club Committee on Public Education). *City Club Bulletin* 5 (1912): 9.

Excerpt from discussions at the City Club of Chicago, 1911.

———. 1912b. "Probation and Politics: The Juvenile Court System at Chicago." *Survey* 27:2004–14.

This essay, though unsigned, has typically been attributed to Mead. For an informed discussion of the basis upon which this attribution is made, see Cook 2007, 54–55.

———. 1912c. (Remarks on Labor Night). *City Club Bulletin* 5:214–15.

Excerpt from the discussions at the City Club of Chicago, 1911.

———. 1912d. "The Mechanism of Social Consciousness." *Journal of Philosophy, Psychology and Scientific Methods* 9:355.

Abstract of speech given at the joint session of the Western Philosophical Association and Western Psychological Association in Chicago, April 6, 1912.

———. 1912e. "The Mechanism of Social Consciousness." *Journal of Philosophy, Psychology and Scientific Methods* 9:401–6.

Speech described above (see 1912d).

———. 1912f. "Gives Plan for Trade Schools—Prof. G. H. Mead Compares City Club Scheme with the Cooley Measure—Opposes Separate Board—Tells Why Vocational Training Should Be Kept Within the Public School System." *Chicago Tribune*, October 16, 4.

———, and J. Paul Goode, eds. 1912. *Educational Opportunities in Chicago: A Summary Prepared by the Council for Library and Museum Extension*, 2nd Year. Chicago: Council for Library and Museum Extension.

———, Frank M. Leavitt, and Ernest A. Wreidt. 1912. "A Report of the Public Education Committee of the City Club of Chicago upon Issues Involved in the Proposed Legislation for Vocational Education In Illinois Containing Also a Suggested Draft of a Bill and a Statement and Some Discussion of Underlying Principles." *City Club Bulletin* 5:373–83.

———, Ernest A. Wreidt, and William J. Bogan. 1912. *A Report on Vocational Training in Chicago and in Other Cities: An Analysis of the Need for Industrial and Commercial Training in Chicago, a Study of Present Provisions Therefore in Comparison with Such Provisions in Twenty-nine Other Cities, Together with Recommendations as to the Best Form in which Such Training May Be Given in the Public School System of Chicago.* Chicago: City Club of Chicago.

———. 1913a. "The Social Self." *Journal of Philosophy, Psychology and Scientific Methods* 10:324–25.

Abstract of speech given at the joint session of the Western Philosophical Association and the Western Psychological Association in Evanston, Illinois, March 22, 1913.

———. 1913b. "The Co-ordination of Social Agencies." *Institution Quarterly* 4 (2): 196–200.

Speech given at the seventh annual Illinois State Conference of Charities and the Illinois Association of County Farm Superintendents, Springfield, Illinois, October 21, 1912.

———. 1913c. "Report of Committee on Education." *City Club Bulletin* 6:206.

———. 1913d. "The Social Self." *Journal of Philosophy, Psychology and Scientific Methods* 10:374–80.

Speech described above (see 1913a).

———. 1914a. "A Heckling School Board and an Educational Stateswoman." *Survey* 31:443–44.

————. 1914b. "The Larger Educational Bearings of Vocational Guidance." *Bulletin of the Bureau of Education*, no. 14:16–26.

Speech originally titled "The Larger Social, Economic and Educational Bearings of Vocational Guidance," given to the third National Conference on Vocational Guidance in Grand Rapids, Michigan, October 21, 1913. Reprinted in Meyer Bloomfield, ed., *Readings in Vocational Guidance* (Boston: Ginn and Company, 1915).

Lovejoy, A. O., J. E. Creighton, W. E. Hocking, E. B. McGilvary, W. T. Marvin, G. H. Mead, and Howard C. Warren. 1914. "The Case of Professor Mecklin: Report of the Committee of Inquiry of the American Philosophical Association and the American Psychological Association." *Journal of Philosophy, Psychology and Scientific Methods* 11:67–81.

Mead, George H. 1915a. "Natural Rights and the Theory of the Political Institution." *Journal of Philosophy* 12:141–55.

Speech given to the American Philosophical Association, Western Philosophical Association, American Political Science Association, and Conference on Legal and Social Philosophy joint session in Chicago, December 29, 1914.

————. 1915b. "The Psychological Bases of Internationalism." *Survey* 33:604–7.

Excerpt reprinted in *Selected Articles on National Defense* 1 (White Plains, NY: H. W. Wilson Co., 1916).

————. 1915c. "Madison: The Passage of the University of Wisconsin through the State Political Agitation of 1914; the Survey by William H. Allen and His Staff and the Legislative Fight of 1915, with the Indications These Offer of the Place the State University Holds in the Community." *Survey* 35:349–51, 354–61.

Ickes, Harold L., George H. Mead, and Irwin St. James Tucker. 1915. "A Brief History of the Clothing Strike in Chicago." Publication Committee of the Citizens' Mass Meeting, Chicago.

Mead, George H. 1916a. "A Rejoinder." *Survey* 35:607, 610.

————. 1916b. "Letter to the Board of Education Relating to the Teachers' Tenure Rule." *City Club Bulletin* 9:131–32.

————. 1917a. "Professor Hoxie and the Community." *University of Chicago Magazine* 9:114–17.

Speech given at memorial for Robert F. Hoxie at the University of Chicago, December 11, 1916.

————. 1917b. "Josiah Royce—A Personal Impression." *International Journal of Ethics* 27:168–70.

Likely based on a speech given at a meeting of the University of Chicago Philosophy Department commemorating Royce in 1916.

————. 1917c. "Scientific Method and Individual Thinker." In *Creative Intelligence: Essays in the Pragmatic Attitude*, edited by John Dewey et al. New York: Henry Holt and Co.

————. 1917d. "Fitting the Educational System into the Fabric of Government." *City Club Bulletin* 10:104–8.

Speech given at the City Club of Chicago, March 3, 1917.

————. 1917e. "Education, Charities and Corrections." *Proceedings of the Illinois State Bar Association* 41:452–58.

Speech given at the forty-first annual meeting of the Illinois State Bar Association in
Danville, Illinois, June 1917.

———. 1917f. "Patriots and Pacifists in War Time." *City Club Bulletin* 10:184.

———. 1917g. "Germany's Crisis—Its Effect on Labor, Part I." *Chicago Herald*, July 26,
1917.

———. 1917h. "Germany's Crisis—Its Effects on Labor, Part II." *Chicago Herald*,
July 27, 1917.

———. 1917i. "[Review] Truancy and Non-Attendance in the Chicago Schools. By Edith
Abbott and Sophonisba P. Breckinridge." *Survey* 38:369–70.

———. 1917j. "War Issues to U.S. Forced by Kaiser." *Chicago Herald*, August 2, 1917.

———. 1917k. "America's Ideals and the War." *Chicago Herald*, August 3, 1917.

———. 1917l. "Democracy's Issues in the World War." *Chicago Herald*, August 4, 1917.

———. 1917m. "Children's War Work Peril to Nation." *City Club Bulletin* 10:268–70.

———. 1917n. "Camouflage of the Conscientious Objector." *New York Times*, December 23, 1917.

———. 1917o. "The Conscientious Objector." *National Security League, Patriotism
through Education Series*, pamphlet 33. New York.

———. 1918a. "The Psychology of Punitive Justice." *American Journal of Sociology*
23:577–602.

Based on speech originally titled "The Instinct of Hostility" given at the Western Philosophical Association in Ann Arbor, Michigan, April 6, 1917.

———. 1918b. "The Aim of Scholarship Work." *Bulletin of the Vocational Supervision
League* (March).

Likely based on speech originally titled "The Future of Scholarship Work" given at
meeting of social welfare organizations in Chicago, January 25, 1918.

———. 1918c. "Morale." *City Club Bulletin* 11:180.

Excerpt from discussions at the City Club of Chicago, 1918.

———. 1918d. "Notes from the Address of the President of the V. S. L. at the Annual
Meeting." *Bulletin of the Vocational Supervision League* (June).

Excerpt from speech given at meeting of Vocational Supervision League in Chicago,
June 1918.

———. 1918e. "[Review] *The Nature of Peace and the Terms of Its Perpetuation*. By
Thorstein Veblen." *Journal of Political Economy* 26:752–62.

———. 1918f. "The Crucial Importance of Vocational Guidance." *Bulletin of the Vocational Supervision League* (October).

———. 1918g. "The Repulsiveness of the German State." *Historical Outlook* 9 (8):
417–19.

———. 1918h. "Social Work, Standards of Living and the War." *Proceedings of the National Conference of Social Work* 45:637–44.

Speech given at the forty-fifth annual meeting of the National Conference of Social
Work (formerly the National Conference of Charities and Correction) in Kansas
City, Missouri, May.

———. 1919a. "Summary Report of War Issues Course." In *Final Report of the War
Issues of the Students' Army Training Corps*, 106–7. Washington, DC: US War
Department Committee on Education and Special Training.

———. 1919b. "Reply to Senator Medill McCormick on the League of Nations." *City Club Bulletin* 12:69–71.

Also reported in "Mead Answers McCormick as to the League of Nations." *Chicago Evening Post*, March 7.

———. 1919c. "The League and the Community." *Bulletin of the Vocational Supervision League* (April).

———. 1919d. "President Mead's Message to Members." *City Club Bulletin* 12:101–2.

———. 1919e. "A Translation of Wundt's 'Folk Psychology.'" *American Journal of Theology* 23:533–36.

———. 1919f. "The Relation of the Present Disturbed Industrial Situation to Vocational Guidance." *Bulletin of the Vocational Supervision League* (December).

———. 1920a. "An Interesting Question." *Bulletin of the Vocational Supervision League* (February).

———. 1920b. "Retiring President's Address." *City Club Bulletin* 13:94–95.

———. 1920c. "Cynthia Tufts––An Impression." In *Cynthia Whitaker Tufts* [memorial booklet]. Chicago: Privately printed by the University of Chicago Press.

———. 1920d. "The President's Report." *Bulletin of the Vocational Supervision League* (June 1920).

Speech given at a meeting of the Vocational Supervision League in Chicago, May.

———. 1921a. "Idea." In *A Dictionary of Religion and Ethics*, edited by Shailer Mathews and Gerald Birney Smith. New York: Macmillan.

———. 1921b. "Ideal." In *A Dictionary of Religion and Ethics*, edited by Shailer Mathews and Gerald Birney Smith. New York: Macmillan.

———. 1921c. "Individualism." In *A Dictionary of Religion and Ethics*, edited by Shailer Mathews and Gerald Birney Smith. New York: Macmillan.

———. 1921d. "Infinity." In *A Dictionary of Religion and Ethics*, edited by Shailer Mathews and Gerald Birney Smith. New York: Macmillan.

———. 1921e. "Law of Nature, Natural Law." In *A Dictionary of Religion and Ethics*, edited by Shailer Mathews and Gerald Birney Smith. New York: Macmillan.

———. 1922. "A Behavioristic Account of the Significant Symbol." *Journal of Philosophy* 19:157–63.

Excerpt reprinted in Kimball Young, *Source Book for Social Psychology* (New York: A. A. Knopf, 1927).

———. 1923. "Scientific Method and the Moral Sciences." *International Journal of Ethics* 33:229–47.

Speech entitled "Some Psychological and Social Conditions of the Scientific Attitude of Mind" given to the History of Science Society and American Academy for the Advancement of Science joint session in Boston, December 28, 1922.

———. 1924a. "The President's Message." *Bulletin of the Vocational Supervision League* (February).

Speech given at meeting of the Vocational Supervision League in Chicago, January 22.

———. 1924b. "Ella Adams Moore." *Bulletin of the Vocational Supervision League* (April).

———. 1924c. "The Domain of Natural Science [Review]: *The Domain of Natural Science*. The Gifford Lectures delivered at the University of Aberdeen in 1921 and 1922. By E. W. Hobson." *Journal of Religion* 4:324–27.

———. 1925. "The Genesis of the Self and Social Control." *International Journal of Ethics* 35:251–77.

———. 1926a. "The Nature of Aesthetic Experience." *International Journal of Ethics* 36:382–92.

Speech originally titled "The Character and Function of Aesthetic Experience" given at the fourth National Motion Picture Conference in Chicago, February 10.

———. 1926b. "[Solicited Response] Opinions of Non-Scholastic Philosophers on Scholasticism." In *Present-Day Thinkers and the New Scholasticism: An International Symposium*, edited and augmented by John S. Zybura, 46–47. St. Louis, MO: B. Herder Book Co.

———. 1927. "The Objective Reality of Perspectives." In *Proceedings of the Sixth International Congress of Philosophy*. New York: Longmans, Green and Co.

Speech given at the Sixth International Congress of Philosophy in Boston, September 14, 1926.

———. 1929a. "The Nature of the Past." In *Essays in Honor of John Dewey*, edited by John Coss. New York: Henry Holt and Co.

———. 1929b. "Mary McDowell." *Neighborhood: A Settlement Quarterly* 2 (2): 77–78.

———. 1929c. "National-Mindedness and International-Mindedness." *International Journal of Ethics* 39:385–407.

Speech given at the University of California Los Angeles, March 22.

———. 1929d. "Bishop Berkeley and His Message." *Journal of Philosophy* 26:421–30.

Speech originally titled "George Berkeley, Bishop of Cloyne" in honor of the two-hundredth anniversary of Berkeley's landing in North America given in Berkeley, California, January.

———. 1929e. "A Pragmatic Theory of Truth." *Studies in the Nature of Truth. University of California Publications in Philosophy* 11:65–88.

Speech given at the University of California Philosophical Union in Berkeley, California, March 8.

———. 1930a. "The Philosophies of Royce, James, and Dewey in Their American Setting." *International Journal of Ethics* 40:211–31.

Speech given at the celebration of John Dewey's seventieth birthday in New York, October 19, 1929, and at the Society for Social Research of the University of Chicago, November 7, 1929.

———. 1930b. "Cooley's Contribution to American Social Thought." *American Journal of Sociology* 35:693–706.

———. 1930c. "Philanthropy from the Point of View of Ethics." In *Intelligent Philanthropy*, edited by Ellsworth Faris, Ferris Laune, and A. J. Todd. Chicago: University of Chicago Press.

———. 1930d. "Memorial Address." In *Addison Webster Moore: A Memorial*. Chicago: privately printed.

Reprinted as George H. Mead, "Dr. A. W. Moore's Philosophy." *University of Chicago Record*, n.s. 17 (1931): 47–49.

———. 1932. *The Philosophy of the Present*. Edited by Arthur E. Murphy. Chicago: Open Court Publishing.

———. 1934. *Mind, Self, and Society: From the Perspective of a Social Behaviorist.* Edited by Charles W. Morris. Chicago: University of Chicago Press. Recently revised as George H. Mead, *Mind, Self, and Society: From the Standpoint of a Social Behaviorist,* edited by Charles W. Morris, revised edition by Daniel R. Huebner and Hans Joas (Chicago: University of Chicago Press, 2015).

———. 1935. "The Philosophy of John Dewey." *International Journal of Ethics* 46:64–81.

———. 1936. *Movements of Thought in the Nineteenth Century.* Edited by Merritt H. Moore. Chicago: University of Chicago Press.

———. 1938. *The Philosophy of the Act.* Edited by Charles W. Morris, John M. Brewster, Albert M. Dunham, and David L. Miller. Chicago: University of Chicago Press.

———. 1956. *The Social Psychology of George Herbert Mead.* Edited by Anselm Strauss. Chicago: University of Chicago Press. Revised edition published as George H. Mead, *On Social Psychology,* edited by Anselm Strauss, Heritage of Sociology series (Chicago: University of Chicago Press, 1964).

———. 1964a. "Relative Space-Time and Simultaneity." Edited by David L. Miller. *Review of Metaphysics* 17:514–35.

———. 1964b. "Metaphysics." Edited by David L. Miller. *Review of Metaphysics* 17:536–56.

———. 1964c. *Selected Writings.* Edited by Andrew J. Reck. Chicago: University of Chicago Press.

———. 1968. *G. H. Mead: Essays on His Social Philosophy.* Edited by John W. Petras. New York: Teachers College Press.

———. 1982. *The Individual and the Social Self: Unpublished Work of George Herbert Mead.* Edited with introduction by David L. Miller. Chicago: University of Chicago Press.

———. 1992. "George Herbert Mead: An Unpublished Essay on Royce and James." Edited by Gary A. Cook. *Transactions of the Charles S. Peirce Society* 28:583–92.

———. 1994. "George Herbert Mead: An Unpublished Review of Dewey's *Human Nature and Conduct.*" Edited by Gary A. Cook. *Journal of the History of the Behavioral Sciences* 30:374–79.

———. 2000. "Science in Social Practice." Edited by Harold Orbach. *Social Thought and Research* 23 (1–2): 47–63. Speech given as the annual Phi Beta Kappa address at the University of Kansas, March 3, 1911.

———. 2001. *Essays on Social Psychology.* Edited by Mary Jo Deegan. New Brunswick, NJ: Transaction Publishers.

———. 2008a. *The Philosophy of Education.* Edited by Gert Biesta and Daniel Trohler. Boulder, CO: Paradigm Publishers.

———. 2008b. "The Evolution of the Psychical Element. By George Herbert Mead (Dec. 1899–March 1900 or 1898–1899). Lecture notes by H. Heath Bawden." Edited by Kevin S. Decker. *Transactions of the Charles S. Peirce Society* 44:480–507.

———. 2011. *G. H. Mead: A Reader.* Edited by Filipe Carreira da Silva. Abingdon, Oxon: Routledge.

Extant Notes from Mead's Courses

This list contains all sets of notes of which I am aware, either from physical perusal or correspondence with librarians, located in archives and repositories, or published. I have included additional information regarding the structure or quality of the notes in some cases. The attribution of notes is made where I have encountered reasonable information to suggest an author in my research, but these attributions should be treated as tentative.

1893–1894 (Autumn–Spring): Special Topics in Psychology. 150 pages, handwritten.
    Taken by Robert Clair Campbell.
    Located in the Campbell Family Papers (Box 2, Folder 2), Bentley Historical Library, University of Michigan.
1899 (Autumn): The Theory of Ethics in Relation to Psychology. 138 pages, handwritten.
    Taken by Harriet Eva Penfield.
    Located in the Joseph Ratner Papers (Box 56, Folder 4), Morris Library Special Collections, Southern Illinois University–Carbondale.
1899–1900? (Autumn–Winter): Development of Reflective Thought? 27 pages, published.
    Taken by Henry Heath Bawden, edited by Kevin Decker.
    Published as "The Evolution of the Psychical Element" (Mead 2008b); original materials apparently in private possession.
1900 (Winter): Comparative Psychology. 43 pages, typed.
    Taken by Henry Heath Bawden, transcribed by Ralph Gregory.
    Located in the Joseph Ratner Papers (Box 42, Folder 2), Morris Library Special Collections, Southern Illinois University–Carbondale.

Records only the second half of the course.

1905 (Summer): Comparative Psychology. 4 pages, handwritten.

Taken by Walter Van Dyke Bingham.

Located in the Walter Van Dyke Bingham Papers (Reel 1, Folder 9),
Hunt Library University Archives, Carnegie Mellon University, Pittsburgh, PA.

Records only the first two lectures of the course.

1905 (Summer): Schopenhauer. 56 pages, handwritten.

Taken by Walter Van Dyke Bingham.

Located in the Walter Van Dyke Bingham Papers (Reel 1, Folder 9),
Hunt Library University Archives, Carnegie Mellon University, Pittsburgh, PA.

1906 (Winter): Hegel's Logic. 57 pages, handwritten.

Taken by Walter Van Dyke Bingham.

Located in the Walter Van Dyke Bingham Papers (Reel 1, Folder 9),
Hunt Library University Archives, Carnegie Mellon University, Pittsburgh, PA.

1908 (Autumn): Logic of the Social Sciences. Handwritten.

Taken by Luther Lee Bernard

Located in the Luther Bernard Collection (Box 16, Folders 6–9),
Historical Collections and Labor Archives, Special Collections
Library, Pennsylvania State University, University Park, PA.

1909 (Autumn): History of Greek Philosophy. 42 pages, handwritten.

Taken by Maurice Thomas Price.

Located in the Maurice T. Price Papers (Box 1, Folder "History of
Philosophy"), University of Illinois Archives, University of
Illinois–Urbana-Champaign.

1910 (Winter): Social Psychology. Handwritten.

Taken by Luther Lee Bernard

Located in the Luther Bernard Collection (Box 16, Folders 6–9),
Historical Collections and Labor Archives, Special Collections
Library, Pennsylvania State University, University Park, PA.

1910 (Summer): Social Psychology. 60 pages, typed.

Taken by Juliet Hammond.

Located in the George Herbert Mead Papers (Box 15, Folder 14),
Regenstein Library Special Collections, University of Chicago.

Reorganized as alphabetized topical entries.

1910 (Summer): Social Psychology. 229 pages, handwritten?

Taken by Wilfred Currier Keirstead.

Located in the Wilfred Currier Keirstead Fonds (Box 1, Folder 27),

Archives and Special Collections, University of New Brunswick Libraries.

1911 (Winter): Theoretical Comparative Psychology. 116 pages, typed.
Taken by Juliet Hammond.
Located in the George Herbert Mead Papers (Box 15, Folder 14),
Regenstein Library Special Collections, University of Chicago.

1911 (Spring): Logic of the Social Sciences. 94 pages, typed.
Taken by Juliet Hammond.
Located in the George Herbert Mead Papers (Box 8, Folder 8), Re-
genstein Library Special Collections, University of Chicago.
Also contains notes from a public lecture given by Mead.

1911 (Spring): Philosophy of Education. 196 pages, published.
Taken by Juliet Hammond, edited by Gert Biesta and Daniel
Trohler.
Published as *The Philosophy of Education* (Mead 2008a); original
materials located in the George Herbert Mead Papers (Box 8,
Folder 9), Regenstein Library Special Collections, University of
Chicago.
Original materials also contain a few fragmentary notes from
Mead's Autumn 1910 course "History of Ancient Science."

1911 (Autumn): Development of Thought in the Modern Period.
Handwritten.
Taken by Ellsworth Faris.
Located in the Ellsworth Faris Papers (vol. 1), Regenstein Library
Special Collections, University of Chicago.

1911 (Autumn): Philosophy of Nature. Handwritten.
Taken by Ellsworth Faris.
Located in the Ellsworth Faris Papers (vol. 1), Regenstein Library
Special Collections, University of Chicago.

1912 (Winter): Social Psychology. 87 pages, typed.
Taken by Ellsworth Faris, transcribed by John Faris (?).
Located in the Ellsworth Faris Papers (vol. 1), Regenstein Library
Special Collections, University of Chicago.
Both original handwritten notes and an edited transcription are
available in this collection.

1912? (Autumn): Social Psychology. 78 pages, published.
Possibly taken by Stuart Alfred Queen, edited by David L.
Miller.
Published as "1914 [sic] Class Lectures in Social Psychology" (in
Mead 1982), original materials located in the George Herbert

Mead Papers (Box 3, Folders 5–8; Box 15, Folders 8–10), Regenstein Library Special Collections, University of Chicago.

1913 (Spring): Movements of Thought in the Nineteenth Century.
30+ pages, handwritten.

Taken by Ethel Kitch (Yeaton).

Located in the Yeaton Family Papers (Box 11), Oberlin College
Archives, Oberlin College, Oberlin, OH.

1913 (Spring): Social Consciousness. ~30 pages, handwritten.

Taken by Ellsworth Faris.

Located in the Ellsworth Faris Papers (vol. 1), Regenstein Library
Special Collections, University of Chicago.

1915 (Winter): Social Psychology. 110 pages, handwritten.

Taken by Maurice Thomas Price.

Located in the Maurice T. Price Papers (Box 1, Folder "Course
Notes, 1915"), University of Illinois Archives, University of
Illinois–Urbana-Champaign.

Also includes notes from informal discussion group, spring 1915.

1915 (Winter): Social Psychology. 59 pages, handwritten.

Taken by Irene Tufts (Mead).

Located in the George Herbert Mead Papers (Box 14, Folder 11),
Regenstein Library Special Collections, University of Chicago.

1915 (Spring): Movements of Thought in the Nineteenth Century.
65 pages, handwritten.

Taken by Maurice Thomas Price.

Located in the Maurice T. Price Papers (Box 1, Folder "Course
Notes, 1915"), University of Illinois Archives, University of
Illinois–Urbana-Champaign.

Contains notes for only a portion of the course.

1915 (Spring): Movements of Thought in the Nineteenth Century.
69 pages, handwritten.

Taken by Irene Tufts (Mead).

Located in the George Herbert Mead Papers (Box 14, Folder 6), Regenstein Library Special Collections, University of Chicago.

1915 (Autumn): Rationalism and Empiricism. 94 pages, handwritten.

Taken by Irene Tufts (Mead).

Located in the George Herbert Mead Papers (Box 8, Folder 7), Regenstein Library Special Collections, University of Chicago.

Also contains additional typewritten notes from the course for the
period December 2–15.

1916 (Spring): Social Psychology. 26 pages, handwritten.

    Taken by Maurice Thomas Price.

    Located in the Maurice T. Price Papers (Box 1, Folder "Course Notes, 1915"), University of Illinois Archives, University of Illinois–Urbana-Champaign.

    Contains notes for only a portion of the course.

1916 (Autumn): Logic of the Social Sciences. 27 pages, typed.

    Taken by Grover Gulick Clark.

    Located in the bound collection of manuscript materials of Ezra Dwight Sanderson in general circulation at Cornell University Library (Sanderson 1916–17).

1918 (Summer): Metaphysics. 40 pages, handwritten.

    Taken by Frank Dickinson.

    Located in the Frank Dickinson Papers, Penrose Library Special Collections and Archives, University of Denver.

1920 (Autumn): Philosophy of Kant. 29 pages, handwritten.

    Taken by Van Meter Ames.

    Located in the George Herbert Mead Papers (Box 14, Folder 7), Regenstein Library Special Collections, University of Chicago.

1921 (Winter): Advanced Social Psychology. 69 pages, handwritten.

    Taken by Van Meter Ames.

    Located in the George Herbert Mead Papers (Box 14, Folder 1), Regenstein Library Special Collections, University of Chicago.

1921 (Winter): Advanced Social Psychology. 110 pages, handwritten.

    Taken by Martin Hayes Bickham.

    Located in the Martin Hayes Bickham Papers (Box 1, Folder 14), Regenstein Library Special Collections, University of Chicago.

1921 (Winter): Advanced Social Psychology. 59 pages, handwritten.

    Taken by Ernest Bouldin Harper.

    Located in the George Herbert Mead Papers (Box 15, Folder 13), Regenstein Library Special Collections, University of Chicago.

1921 (Winter): Philosophy of Kant. 29 pages, handwritten.

    Taken by Van Meter Ames.

    Located in the George Herbert Mead Papers (Box 14, Folder 8), Regenstein Library Special Collections, University of Chicago.

1921 (Spring): Hegel's Phenomenology. 21 pages, handwritten.

    Taken by Van Meter Ames.

    Located in the George Herbert Mead Papers (Box 14, Folder 4), Regenstein Library Special Collections, University of Chicago.

1922 (Spring): Hume. 36 pages, handwritten.

Taken by Van Meter Ames.

Located in the George Herbert Mead Papers (Box 7, Folder 7), Regenstein Library Special Collections, University of Chicago.

1922 (Autumn): Logic of the Sciences. 36 pages, handwritten.

Taken by Van Meter Ames.

Located in the George Herbert Mead Papers (Box 14, Folder 5), Regenstein Library Special Collections, University of Chicago.

1923 (Winter): Advanced Social Psychology. 64 pages, handwritten.

Taken by Bryan Sewall Stoffer.

Located in the Bryan S. Stoffer Papers (Box 2.25, Folder 2), Mabee
Library Archives, Washburn University, Topeka, KS.

1923 (Spring): Hegel's Logic. 50 pages, handwritten.

Taken by Van Meter Ames.

Located in the George Herbert Mead Papers (Box 14, Folder 3), Regenstein Library Special Collections, University of Chicago.

1923 (Spring): Movements of Thought in the Nineteenth Century.
46 pages, handwritten.

Taken by Charles William Morris Jr.

Located in the Charles Morris Collection (Box 20, Folder "Movements . . ."), Max Fisch Library, Institute for American
Thought, Indiana University/Purdue University–Indianapolis.

1923 (Spring): Relativity from the Standpoint of Pragmatism. 45 pages,
handwritten.

Taken by Van Meter Ames.

Located in the George Herbert Mead Papers (Box 14, Folder 10),
Regenstein Library Special Collections, University of Chicago.

1923 (Spring): Relativity from the Standpoint of Pragmatism. 46 pages,
handwritten.

Taken by Charles William Morris Jr.

Located in the Charles Morris Collection (Box 20, Folder "Relativity . . . "), Max Fisch Library, Institute for American Thought,
Indiana University/Purdue University–Indianapolis.

1923 (Autumn): Aristotle's Metaphysics. 71 pages, handwritten.

Taken by Van Meter Ames.

Located in the George Herbert Mead Papers (Box 14, Folder 2), Regenstein Library Special Collections, University of Chicago.

1923 (Autumn): Aristotle's Metaphysics. 71 pages, handwritten.

Taken by Charles William Morris Jr.

Located in the Charles Morris Collection (Box 20, Folder "Aristotle's Metaphysics"), Max Fisch Library, Institute for American
Thought, Indiana University/Purdue University–Indianapolis.

1924 (Winter): Advanced Social Psychology. 63 pages, handwritten.
Taken by Charles William Morris Jr.
Located in the Charles Morris Collection (Box 20, Folder
"Advanced Social Psychology"), Max Fisch Library, Insti-
tute for American Thought, Indiana University/Purdue
University–Indianapolis.

1924 (Spring): Problem of Consciousness. 6 pages, handwritten.
Taken by Van Meter Ames.
Located in the George Herbert Mead Papers (Box 14, Folder 9),
Regenstein Library Special Collections, University of
Chicago.
Contains only a fragment of notes for the course.

1924 (Spring): Problem of Consciousness. 86 pages, handwritten.
Taken by Charles William Morris Jr.
Located in the Charles Morris Collection (Box 20, Folder
"Problems of Consciousness"), Max Fisch Library, Insti-
tute for American Thought, Indiana University/Purdue
University–Indianapolis.

1924? (Autumn): Advanced Social Psychology? 86 pages, handwritten.
Taken by Frank Dickinson.
Located in the Frank Dickinson Papers, Penrose Library Special
Collections and Archives, University of Denver.

1925 (Winter): Aristotle's Metaphysics. 158 pages, typed.
Likely taken by George Nicholas Pappas (a.k.a., Papanicolopoulos).
Located in the George Herbert Mead Papers (Box 6, Folders 1–6),
Regenstein Library Special Collections, University of Chicago.
Contains both topical summaries and course notes.

1925 (Winter): Hume. 31 pages, typed.
Taken by George Dykhuizen.
Located in the George Herbert Mead Papers (Box 7, Folder 7), Re-
genstein Library Special Collections, University of Chicago.

1925 (Winter): Hume. 54 pages, typed
Likely taken by George Nicholas Pappas.
Located in the George Herbert Mead Papers (Box 7, Folder 10), Re-
genstein Library Special Collections, University of Chicago.
Contains notes for only a portion of the course.

1925 (Spring): Philosophies of Eminent Scientists. 50 pages, typed.
Taken by George Dykhuizen.
Located in the George Herbert Mead Papers (Box 8, Folder 3), Regenstein Library Special Collections, University of Chicago.

1925 (Spring): Philosophies of Eminent Scientists. 61 pages, handwritten.
Taken by Charles William Morris Jr.
Located in the Charles Morris Collection (Box 20, Folder "Philosophies . . . "), Max Fisch Library, Institute for American Thought, Indiana University/Purdue University–Indianapolis.

1926 (Winter): Dewey's Experience and Nature. 49 pages, typed.
Taken by George Dykhuizen.
Located in the George Herbert Mead Papers (Box 7, Folder 1), Regenstein Library Special Collections, University of Chicago.

1926 (Spring): Problem of Consciousness. 65 and 57 pages, typed.
Taken by George Enor Melvyn Shelburg.
Located in the George Herbert Mead Papers (Box 8, Folders 5–6), Regenstein Library Special Collections, University of Chicago.
Reorganized and submitted as a class paper.

1926 (Autumn): Leibniz. 123 pages, typed.
Likely taken by George Anagnos.
Located in the George Herbert Mead Papers (Box 7, Folder 16), Regenstein Library Special Collections, University of Chicago.

1926 (Autumn): Leibniz. 68 pages, typed.
Taken by George Enor Melvyn Shelburg.
Located in the George Herbert Mead Papers (Box 7, Folders 14–15), Regenstein Library Special Collections, University of Chicago.
Reorganized and submitted as a class paper.

1927 (Winter): Advanced Social Psychology. 69 pages, published.
Taken by George Enor Melvyn Shelburg.
Published as "1927 Class Notes in Social Psychology" (in Mead 1982), original materials located in the George Herbert Mead Papers (Box 3, Folder 14; Box 15, Folders 11–12), Regenstein Library Special Collections, University of Chicago.
Reorganized and submitted as a class paper.

1927 (Winter): Advanced Social Psychology. 113 pages, typed.
Unknown note-taker.
Located in the George Herbert Mead Papers (Box 3, Folder 9), Regenstein Library Special Collections, University of Chicago.

1927 (Winter): Philosophies of Eminent Scientists. 124 pages, typed.
Unknown note-taker, possibly George Anagnos.

Located in the George Herbert Mead Papers (Box 8, Folder 4), Regenstein Library Special Collections, University of Chicago.
1927 (Spring): Hume. 27 pages, typed.
Unknown note-taker, possibly Louis Bloom.
Located in the George Herbert Mead Papers (Box 7, Folder 8), Regenstein Library Special Collections, University of Chicago.
1927? (Spring): Hume. 130 pages, typed.
Unknown note-taker, possibly George Dykhuizen.
Located in the George Herbert Mead Papers (Box 7, Folder 11), Re-
 genstein Library Special Collections, University of Chicago.
1927 (Summer): Philosophy of Bergson. 51 pages, typed.
Likely taken by George Nicholas Pappas.
Located in the George Herbert Mead Papers (Box 4, Folders 2–3),
 Regenstein Library Special Collections, University of Chicago.
1927 (Autumn): Elementary Ethics. 244 pages, typed.
Unknown stenographic note-taker, possibly Walter Theodore Lillie
 or Mary Ann Lillie.
Located in the George Herbert Mead Papers (Box 7, Folders 3–4),
 Regenstein Library Special Collections, University of Chicago.
1928 (Winter): Advanced Social Psychology. 320 pages, typed.
Taken by stenographer, either Walter Theodore Lillie or Mary Ann
 Lillie.
Located in the George Herbert Mead Papers (Box 2, Folders 10–17),
 Regenstein Library Special Collections, University of Chicago.
1928 (Winter): Advanced Social Psychology. 47 pages, handwritten.
Taken by Wayne Albert Risser Leys.
Located in the Wayne A. R. Leys Papers (Box 9, Folder 3), Morris
 Library Special Collections, Southern Illinois University-
 Carbondale.
1928 (Winter): Hegel's Phenomenology. 207 pages, typed
Unknown stenographic note-taker, possibly named Stephenson.
Located in the George Herbert Mead Papers (Box 7, Folders 5–6),
 Regenstein Library Special Collections, University of Chicago.
1928 (Spring): Aristotle's Metaphysics. 50 pages, handwritten.
Taken by Wayne Albert Risser Leys.
Located in the Wayne A. R. Leys Papers (Box 9, Folder 1), Morris
 Library Special Collections, Southern Illinois University-
 Carbondale.
1928 (Spring): Aristotle's Metaphysics. 263 pages, typed.
Unknown stenographic note-taker, possibly named Stephenson.

Located in the George Herbert Mead Papers (Box 6, Folders 7–10),
Regenstein Library Special Collections, University of Chicago.

1928 (Spring): Movements of Thought in the Nineteenth Century.
100+ pages, typed.
Unknown stenographic note-taker, possibly named Stephenson.
Located in the George Herbert Mead Papers (Box 3a, Folders 1–4),
Regenstein Library Special Collections, University of Chicago.

1928 (Summer): Movements of Thought in the Nineteenth Century.
142 pages, typed.
Unknown note-taker.
Located in the George Herbert Mead Papers (Box 4, Folder 1), Regenstein Library Special Collections, University of Chicago.

1928 (Autumn): Logic. 232 pages, typed.
Unknown stenographic note-taker.
Located in the George Herbert Mead Papers (Box 8, Folders 1–2),
Regenstein Library Special Collections, University of Chicago.

1930 (Winter): Advanced Social Psychology. 31 pages, handwritten.
Likely taken by Louis Bloom.
Located in the George Herbert Mead Papers (Box 3, Folder 11), Re-
genstein Library Special Collections, University of Chicago.
Contains only fragments of notes from the course.

1930 (Winter): Advanced Social Psychology. 101 pages, handwritten.
Taken by Philip Morris Hauser.
Located in the Philip Morris Hauser Papers (Box 19, Folder 6), Re-
genstein Library Special Collections, University of Chicago.

1930 (Winter): Advanced Social Psychology. 184 pages, typed.
Taken by Robert Rand Page.
Located in the George Herbert Mead Papers (Box 3, Folders 1–2),
Regenstein Library Special Collections, University of Chicago.

1930 (Spring): Movements of Thought in the Nineteenth Century.
13 pages, handwritten.
Taken by Wayne Albert Risser Leys.
Located in the Wayne A. R. Leys Papers (Box 9, Folder 4), Morris
Library Special Collections, Southern Illinois University-
Carbondale.
Contains notes for only a portion of the course.

1930 (Spring): Philosophies of Eminent Scientists. 10 pages,
handwritten.
Taken by Wayne Albert Risser Leys.

Located in the Wayne A. R. Leys Papers (Box 9, Folder 4),
Morris Library Special Collections, Southern Illinois
University–Carbondale.

Contains notes for only a portion of the course.

1930? (Autumn): Hume. 21 pages, typed.

Unknown note-taker.

Located in the George Herbert Mead Papers (Box 7, Folder 9), Regenstein Library Special Collections, University of Chicago.

Contains notes for only a portion of the course.

1931 (Winter): Advanced Social Psychology. 40 pages, typed.

Taken by Eugene W. Sutherland.

Located in the George Herbert Mead Papers (Box 3, Folder 10), Regenstein Library Special Collections, University of Chicago.

Contains notes for only the portion of the course that Mead
taught.

NOTES

1. Productive recent elaborations of such a theory of social action and its relation to social scientific research are found in the work of Andreas Glaeser and Andrew Abbott. Glaeser (2011) proposed the notion of "process dynamics" rather than "social mechanisms" to more adequately conceptualize the dialectic between the formation of interlinkages in social action and the movement or direction they give to that social action. Glaeser's most explicit work in this regard is found in an unpublished manuscript on "process dynamics," but much of his theory is also exemplified in his recent work in *Political Epistemics*. In this latter work, Glaeser (2011) proposes a "sociology of understanding" drawing from hermeneutics, pragmatism, and other sources, which conceptualizes knowledge as consisting of multimodal (conceptual, affective, and kinesthetic) action in social processes. Hence knowledge is conceived as an aspect of the relation of embodied social actors to developing social situations over time. Abbott (2007a) contrasted the typical understanding of mechanisms with what he called a "relational position" explicitly rooted in pragmatism, which posits that the meaning of action can only be adequately understood when situated in social time and place, in relation to other actions in sequence and ensemble. Both of these authors are sensitive to the need to attend to the conduct and representation of narrative in social processes, a topic Abbott (2007b) addresses as "lyrical" sociology and Glaeser (2011, 57) calls "emplotment."

2. One of the artisans of crafting process explanations, unfortunately largely forgotten in contemporary scholarship, was Tamotsu Shibutani, whose *Derelicts of Company K* (1978) was probably the most influential single work in my own practical introduction to the structuring of processual analysis and narrative that remains at the empirical level of actual actors and situations, although my work bears little substantive resemblance to his. In his account "demoralization" is not a label to be merely applied to a group of soldiers, but rather a complex social process to be traced by following the actual social action of soldiers over time as they produce understandings of themselves and their surroundings in response to changing situational contexts.

3. Notable exceptions that attempt to connect the development of intellectual

reputations with the entrepreneurial efforts of the intellectuals in question themselves, and their supporters as structured by the shape of relevant academic institutions or fields, include Lamont's (1987) and McLaughlin's (1998) studies of the widely contrasting "legitimation" processes of Jacques Derrida and Erich Fromm. As journal article–length case studies, they necessarily leave out of account broader questions regarding the social contextual development of Derrida's or Fromm's theoretical work in their own intellectual biographies and the relationships between these prominent theorists' activities and the long-term transformations in intellectual disciplines and reputations. McLaughlin has contributed several pieces along these lines, exploring the contributions that negative cases, especially Fromm and the Frankfurt School, can make to debates about the formation and dynamics of "collaborative circles," "origin myths," and "schools of thought." Other recent sociological studies of intellectuals, including Gross's 2008 study of Richard Rorty and Scaff's 2011 study of Max Weber have offered suggestive leads in connecting a scholar with his or her intellectual reputation, but have substantively, and productively, focused on how these well-known authors produced understandings of themselves and the modern world. None of these studies provides a model for the current work, which demonstrates the advantages of a sustained, prospective focus on empirical social action processes for both Mead and those who interpret him over several different temporalities.

4. In developing his general concepts for an interpretive sociology as deployed in the introductory chapters of his posthumous *Economy and Society*, Weber (1978 [1922], 1:3) drew conscientiously from Georg Simmel's *The Problems of the Philosophy of History* (1977 [1892]) where the "problem of historical knowledge" is central to the development of sociological analysis, and where Simmel developed in detail the use of ideal types. And in Alfred Schütz's (1967 [1932]) major critical examination of Weber's sociology, he stressed how social science must be built on "social observation," rather than face-to-face interaction, in order to adequately encompass an examination of our "contemporaries" and historical "predecessors" in social analysis.

5. One may, with justification, note that these same concerns with the nature of text in social action could be ascribed to a variety of other theoretical traditions. Aspects of a similar theory could be worked out on the basis of Wittgenstein's (2001) conception of "language games," the hermeneutic "reader response" aesthetics of Iser (1978) and Jauss (1982), Latour's (1999, 2005) "actor-network theory" (especially the notion of the "trace" and "circulation of reference"), the "sociology of the text" of D. F. McKenzie (1999), and a variety of other discourses. It is unnecessary to pursue these concerns here in order to motivate the analyses that follow, especially since such a pursuit would lead into an extended set of discussions regarding the conflicting assumptions behind many of these concerns, but it is worth indicating the considerable body of diverse, theoretically sophisticated work that touches on similar issues related to social action and textual documents.

CHAPTER ONE

1. A complete listing of such work would fill many pages. A list of only the book-length studies that seek to reassess Mead's philosophy on the basis of significant origi-

nal research into sources other than *Mind, Self, and Society* and the other posthumous volumes in the past three decades would definitely include the work of Joas (1985), Baldwin (1986), Aboulafia (1991), Cook (1993), De Waal (2002), Deegan (2008), and Silva (2008), among others. A four-volume work of compiled "critical assessments" of Mead has also been published (Hamilton 1992).

2. This claim is based on reports of Mead's speeches as they appear in newspaper articles, academic journals, and other periodicals that I have been able to gather, along with occasional remarks about Mead's talks in correspondence. I have found databases of digitized print material (including JSTOR, Proquest Historical Newspapers, Library of Congress Chronicling America project, and Google Books) especially useful in this endeavor. Although these researches have been extensive they are by no means exhaustive, and I would be surprised if Mead did not give many public talks that I am unable to identify. So much appears to be hinted at by various remarks in correspondence and records of Mead and those close to him (especially in his niece Elinor Castle Nef's notes and diaries) and would seem to be implied in the kinds of positions he held in several public educational and reform organizations.

3. In the vast majority of reports of Mead's public speeches, no information, or only suggestive information, is given on the size of the audiences, but in some cases estimates are recorded. For example, Mead's 1909 talk to the Palama Settlement (discussed in chapter 3) was reportedly attended by 600 individuals; there were 400 graduates alone at his talk at the convocation exercises of Lane Technical High School in 1912 (not counting family and guests); a couple of "mass meetings" at which Mead spoke on behalf of the "Citizens' Committee" for the resolution of the 1910–11 Chicago garment workers' strike ranged well into the thousands; and "mass meetings" in 1913 and 1916 protesting the political manipulation of the Chicago Board of Education likewise reached several thousand, including a meeting in honor of his friend Ella Flagg Young, which was reported to have had at least 3,000 participants. No doubt a variety of Mead's other talks at reform meetings were similarly well attended.

4. As chapter 4 details, the claims made about Mead's students depend heavily on the archived registration records of the Examiners' and Instructors' Grade Reports collection at the University of Chicago. In opposition to a view that Mead's classes were divorced from his activism, it should be made clear that Mead's classes were also sometimes the forum for discussions on contentious social problems. For example, in the 1913 "Social Consciousness" seminar, Ellsworth Faris noted that Mead discussed the (just concluded) negotiations between striking garment workers and the company Hart, Schaffner, & Marx in light of the latest literature on "social values" (notes for January 9, 1913, Ellsworth Faris Papers [hereafter EFP], vol. 1).

5. This analysis relies on a list of newspaper reports mentioning Mead that I compiled from a variety of digitized and print sources covering the years 1890–1931. It is by no means a comprehensive analysis, but I report it because it is suggestive. It is perhaps a suitable irony that a letter received by Helen Mead from a relative in 1893 regarding the Hawaiian Revolution (discussed in chapter 3 below) was far more widely reported than any of the events mentioned above. In these reports, George Mead is identified only in relation to his wife and not for any of his own work. This letter and the subsequent interview given by Helen Mead (probably to Robert E. Park) were carried by the

Associated Press wire service and reported across the United States. Mead's coauthored "A Report on Vocational Training in Chicago and in Other Schools" was also widely discussed in the educational literature of the time.

6. One well-documented example of the reach of Mead's publications in social reform–oriented journals comes from Cook (2007). Mead (1915c, 1916a) wrote a review of a controversy surrounding the educational "survey" (a kind of early audit of the efficiency of practices and finances) of the University of Wisconsin, conducted by William H. Allen in 1914. In current scholarship this has become one of the most obscure and "puzzling" of Mead's works, but it was published in, at the time, "the leading national journal for the field of social work and the investigation of practical approaches to social problems, with a circulation of more than 20,000 copies per issue." What is more, to ensure that it was read, the president of the University of Wisconsin, C. R. van Hise, distributed as many as 500 additional offprints of Mead's article to well-placed educational professionals, likely including presidents of normal schools, college, and universities (Cook 2007, 45, 54, 64).

7. Abbott (2010) demonstrates that Henderson had the highest public profile of the early Chicago sociologists, but he also points out that each of the early faculty members had a substantially greater public visibility than the post–World War I generation of professionalized social scientists. The analysis of Henderson is instructive because it indicates that Mead's position is not unique. Indeed, Henderson's record of public appearances closely resembles Mead's (with notably more religious and perhaps fewer club talks), but apparently with higher overall visibility. Abbott also cautions that the connections between these various "islands" constituting the public sphere could be very loose, pointing in particular to the separation between the publics in which Henderson participated and the Catholic, immigrant, and ward-political publics.

8. Several commentators have noted that Mead's audiences and speeches changed after World War I (Cook 1993; Deegan 2008) as he shifted his work in part toward problems of international peace and in part toward more metaphysical or cosmological concerns of relativity, time, and sociality. This shift certainly evinces, in large part, the changes occurring in the broader arrangement of intellectual discourses, which were shifting toward more professionalized and discipline-bounded domains. But even more than it affected Mead himself, these dynamics of professionalization and disciplines became increasingly salient for the generation of Mead's later students, and hence had a major impact on the subsequent understandings of Mead's work, a topic discussed further in chapters 6 and 7.

9. "Convention of Ethical Societies," *The Public* 10, no. 508 (December 28, 1908): 921.

10. Mead gave a talk entitled "The Character and Function of Aesthetic Experience" to that audience, as acknowledged in the mimeographed and privately circulated "Proceedings of the Fourth National Motion Picture Conference" and in promotional materials and announcements for the conference (Robbins Gilman and Family Papers [hereafter RGFP], B 81). Although Mead's paper is not transcribed in the proceedings (there appears a note that reads "Professor Mead presented his paper . . ." instead of reproducing its contents), it is clear from the title and from the focus in the published paper on motion pictures, including specific remarks about Charlie Chaplin and

Douglas Fairbanks, that it is largely the same paper. Correspondence in the Gilman Papers indicates that Hilda Merriam was primarily responsible for the local conference organization.

11. "Proceedings," 106 (RGFP, B 81). Faris also reported feeling ill but thought better of leaving his colleague all alone on the panel. Faris's paper was, unlike Mead's, reproduced in the Proceedings, and there is no doubt that it represents an early draft of his "The Concept of Imitation" (Faris 1926b). This panel is likely one of the connections that led Herbert Blumer and other Chicago sociologists to participate in the later "Payne Fund Studies" examining the social influences of the movies on children (see notes to chapter 6). Blumer was a student at the time of Mead, Faris, and Thurstone, and he would later gather data for his studies through Adler's Institute. Thurstone also participated in the Payne Fund Studies, as did Chicago sociologists Robert Park, Philip Hauser, Frederic Thrasher, Paul Cressey, and Clifford Shaw. The group of Protestant ministers and social workers at the core of the film conference significantly overlapped in membership with the Motion Picture Research Council that organized the Payne Fund Studies.

12. Consider, for example, the first speaker's comments when the floor was opened: "I should like to ask, if it is appropriate to ask it here, what the right man could do to help a production, or the presentation of wholesome moving pictures, who is in a position such as Col. [Will H.] Hays [president of the Motion Picture Producers and Distributors of America] is in. I should also like to ask, if it be appropriate to ask, whether he has done that thing, according to that ideal man who might be in that position. I should like to ask, also, if it be proper, if he has not done so, what he has done. (Applause [from audience])" ("Proceedings," 106–7, RGFP, B 81). Hays, who had been charged with overseeing the self-regulation of the movies, was viewed by advocates of stringent censorship as being ineffective, and was hence called "Colonel" or "Czar" rather ironically; in that capacity he was the namesake of the Hays Code of 1930 that provided guidelines of unacceptable content for motion pictures. According to the transcript, Faris refused to answer this set of questions and chairman Smith instead sent for Hilda Merriam to field them. After a few relevant questions to Faris, the session seemingly devolved into a discussion led by Rev. William S. Chase, one of the conference's organizers, on the contents of particular legislative bills and pamphlets distributed at the conference, and a rally on the immorality of films. This discussion, including the first speaker's comments, was in part carried over from the debates of the previous morning session that opened the conference.

13. Notably these speeches include "Social Consciousness," delivered to the North Central Psychological Association in Chicago on November 28, 1908; "The Psychology of Social Consciousness Implied in Instruction," delivered to the American Association for the Advancement of Science in Boston on December 29, 1909; "What Social Objects Must Psychology Presuppose," delivered to the American Psychological Association in Boston on December 31, 1909; "The Mechanism of Social Consciousness," delivered to the Western Philosophical Association in Chicago on April 6, 1912; and "The Social Self," delivered to the Western Philosophical Association and Western Psychological Association in Evanston, Illinois, on March 22, 1913. These works have in common that they were presented at professional academic associations (but often combined

interdisciplinary ones) as opposed to more public presentations. However, these are not the only papers to be presented to those associations, making difficult any categorical distinction between these papers and some of Mead's others on the basis of the makeup of their audiences.

14. It is interesting to note in this regard that an earlier proposed volume of "published works" by Mead to have been edited by Harvey J. Locke and Ellsworth Faris in 1937 would reportedly have included many of these abstracts, editorials, City Club speeches, and other incidental pieces, apparently so as to make them more widely available (typescript "Articles for the Mead manuscript not yet typed," undated [c. August 1937], University of Chicago Press Records [hereafter UCPR], B 323, F 9).

15. This talk was published in *The Public*—"A National Journal of Fundamental Democracy and a Weekly Narrative of History in the Making"—edited by Louis F. Post, who was one of the board members dismissed by Mayor Busse.

16. This argument owes much to my reading of Bordogna's *William James at the Boundaries* (2008) in which she makes the argument that James's peculiar style of presenting ideas and cultivating social relationships across emerging intellectual boundaries represented a transformative epistemological claim through social practice. His pragmatist epistemology was on display through his social action as well as in his writings.

17. In this second case, there is a trail of correspondence indicating that Mead was asked to supply a chapter on the recommendation of John Dewey and A. W. Moore in 1913, and that the delinquency of Mead's chapter, specifically, held up the final compilation of the volume for several months (see the letters between Dewey and Horace M. Kallen from 1913 to 1917 in Dewey 1997). Mead's delay, along with remarks in Dewey's letters to Mead (e.g., "I had had enough of your experience in trying to get somewhere intellectual to sympathize with what you say. . . . The rest is largely practise in writing I think"; February 27, 1916, Dewey 1997, no. 05281) indicate that the difficulty lay in Mead's attempts to articulate his position adequately on paper. *Creative Intelligence: Essays in the Pragmatic Attitude* had its origin at least in part as a pragmatist response to the manifesto of *The New Realists* in American philosophy (Holt et al. 1912), a group competing for the claim to be the successors of Jamesian philosophy and for professional attention. One fellow traveler of the pragmatists noted in his commentary that the title was somewhat perplexing unless one knew that it was an (already dated) allusion to Bergson's 1907 *Evolution créatrice* first translated into English in 1911 (Bush 1917). Its title and tone seemed oddly out of place in the midst of world war to reviewers like F. C. S. Schiller.

18. One gets a sense of these intimate connections, in part, from authors like Bordogna (2008) and Campbell (2006) who detail the small groups that founded and socialized in the American Psychological Association, the American Philosophical Association, and like organizations. In light of the large, professional organizations of academic disciplines today I think we are likely to err on the side of assuming too few rather than too many personal connections in the early decades of these professional groups.

19. On a few documented occasions where he definitely sought publication outside these circles, especially in his early career, Mead did not find as much support. Some typescripts from Mead's early career archived in the Mead Papers bear the marks of

having been intended for publication. One in particular (George Herbert Mead Papers [hereafter GHMP], B 10, F 26) begins with a remark about an article recently published in the same journal by John Dewey on the "Superstition of Necessity," indicating that it was explicitly intended for the *Monist* about 1893. This article was not published. And again, Mead submitted his "Suggestions Toward a Theory of the Philosophical Disciplines" to the *Monist* in August 1899 only to have it rejected, and ultimately published in the *Philosophical Review* (Open Court to G. H. Mead, September 5, 1899, letterpress book index, Open Court Publishing Co. Records [hereafter OCPC], B 33, F 54; B 28). The decisions about what to publish in the *Monist* were notoriously capricious and were personally made by editor Paul Carus (cf. Henderson 1993). No doubt, some of these groups of early Chicago professors could be further examined productively as examples of "collaborative circles" in Farrell's (2001) sense, with a lack of older authorities and mentors in their immediate circles, a strong network of collaboration and support, and a fairly clear trajectory to the stages of their relationship over time. There is no doubt that Chicago was, in this period, a "magnet place," in the sense that it was a city and university rich in unique material and cultural resources that drew talented novice professionals together.

20. The first volume of the *Class Lectures of John Dewey* indicates that Dewey's students noted the frequent references Dewey made to Mead. In these published lectures from 1892 to 1903 Mead is referred to in six different classes, and Dewey discussed not only his most recent published papers ("Suggestions Toward a Theory of the Philosophical Disciplines," "The Working Hypothesis in Social Reform"), but also remarks made at Philosophical Club meetings and his general perspective and phraseology.

21. Several of these proceedings volumes are reported here for the first time; see the bibliography of Mead's works for a complete listing. The piece in the Proceedings of the Western Drawing and Manual Training Association is "Social Bearings of Industrial Education," previously only known as an unpublished, incomplete typescript in the Mead Papers (GHMP, B 9, F 24). The copy of the 1911 published proceedings now held in the University of Minnesota library was originally owned by George H. Mead. Existing copies of the Bulletin of the Vocational Supervision League are very rare. I consulted a set of these Bulletins in the Scholarship and Guidance Association Records ([hereafter SGAR], B 5, F 50–53), available in the Special Collections of the Richard J. Daley Library, University of Illinois–Chicago.

22. Mead wrote to his sister-in-law Mabel Wing Castle that he was writing "two supposedly light articles": "one written for the first time on the economic status of woman—in which I contrast the financial standard with the standard of immediate experience—with whose minutiae the woman deals so much more than man" and the other on "the 'tragic condition'—the disappearance of the same as found in Greek and Shakespe[a]rean drama. I think the raison d'etre of the tragedy is the demand for the expression of a feeling or ideal which can be only stated as negative for the time. In Greek time there was the effort to bring law to expression but it could be only done negatively in 'fate'—in Shakespeare it is the effort to express personality in the same way." He added, "However it is I presume only a personal gratification that I shall get from these things—for I don't think they will be accepted by any paying journal."

(G. H. Mead to M. W. Castle, May 27, 1901, Henry Northrup Castle Papers [hereafter HNCP], B 5, F 10). The article on the "Appearance of the Mammals" was mentioned in correspondence with John Dewey, and was apparently a topic of his early comparative psychology courses (G. H. Mead to J. and A. C. Dewey, March 24, 1895, Dewey 1997, no. 00256). Mead's many manuscript fragments, some that might be linked to these particular pieces, indicate the breadth of Mead's interests and the tenuous link between his writing and his publishing.

CHAPTER TWO

1. Mead was one of the leading figures pushing in the 1910s for the creation of a "bureau for social research" in Chicago to coordinate the many forms of data that were (and could be) collected by public and private agencies. This effort resulted in the creation of the Public Welfare Bureau and its department of social surveys by the City Council of Chicago (in an ordinance sponsored by Mead's friend and colleague Charles E. Merriam) (cf. Cook 1993, 107). Mead, with Charles R. Henderson and W. I. Thomas, advised the short-lived "Bureau of Social and Civic Information" clearinghouse in 1915 run by their student Ruth Newberry (later the wife of Thomas's son Bill), which was likely dissolved as the city's bureau began taking up such functions and perhaps also because of Henderson's death. He was also chairman of the editorial board of the Council for Library and Museum Extension in Chicago for a period in the 1910s, and was lead editor of its *Educational Opportunities in Chicago* (Mead, Farrington, Legler, and Sauer 1911; Mead and Goode 1912). This booklet series published detailed summary information on all the educational institutions of Chicago including its public schools, museums, libraries, universities, professional and technical schools, public parks, and social settlements, and the council prepared comprehensive lists of public speeches and other educational events.

2. Complementary, informative research on the exposure of Mead and Dewey to biological and evolutionary ideas in their education and the consequent impacts such exposure had on their work is being prepared in a monograph by Trevor Pearce, to be entitled *Pragmatism's Evolution: Organism and Environment in Early American Philosophy* (in preparation).

3. In the catalogue of Oberlin College for Mead's senior year one finds that many of the science courses emphasized hands-on learning: "Experimental Lectures and Demonstrations" in physics; "Practice in identifying and preserving Plants. Laboratory work in Vegetable Histology and Cryptogamic Botany" in botany; "Use of Astronomical Instruments" in astronomy; "Daily class practice in the Laboratory" in chemistry; "Study of Living and Cabinet Specimens. Laboratory work on Animal Histology and minute forms of Life" in zoology; "Adjustment and Use of Field Instruments" in engineering, "daily work in the Laboratory" in mineralogy; and "Handling and Special Study of 25 Minerals, 50 Lithological Specimens and 50 characteristic Fossils. Laboratory work in Microscopical Lithology" in geology (*Catalogue of the Officers and Students of Oberlin College* [Chicago: Blakely, Marsh and Co., 1882–83], 62–63).

4. There is at least one notable exception to this claim: student Charles M. Hall, with encouragement from Jewett, discovered the first method by which aluminum

could be successfully extracted on an industrial scale from his work in the Oberlin chemistry laboratory in 1886 (Holmes 1936).

5. H. N. Castle to J. B. Castle, February 3, 1889, HNCP, B 2, F 10. Hall was in Germany touring universities for ideas on how to structure the newly founded Clark University, the first exclusively graduate research university in the United States, of which Hall had been named president. Hall apparently recommended Morselli in the course of a "long interview" with Mead, although his reasons for this recommendation are not explicitly detailed (H. N. Castle to J. B. Castle, February 26, 1889, HNCP, B 2, F 10). Henry Castle wrote to his brother that he and Mead had already devised a plan to study Italian over the summer, and arrive in "some Italian village" a few weeks before the semester began to prepare, when their plans were suddenly changed by a letter from William James.

6. W. James to H. Ebbinghaus, April 8, 1889, Nachlass von Hermann Ebbinghaus (hereafter NHE). Mead's contact information was added to the letter, apparently in Ebbinghaus's handwriting. This letter adds a facet to our understanding of the complex relationship between James and Mead in this period, just after Mead had tutored James's son and briefly courted his sister-in-law (Cook 1993, 17–18). While Mead never took any courses with James, he spent a summer with James's family and appears to have had a number of important conversations through which James became something of a mentor to Mead.

7. In particular, the Psycho-physical (or Weber's) Law postulated a direct, measurable relationship between the magnitude of a physical stimulus (e.g., a light, sound, or weight) and the perceived intensity of a sensation (an individual's sense of "brightness," "loudness," or "heaviness"). The measurement of this relationship depended on increments of "just observable difference" in the intensity of sensations, which became the center of much study and increasing controversy. Ebbinghaus (1887) and others noted that at the extreme limits of sensation the relationship between magnitude of stimulus and intensity of sensation was far from linear. Ebbinghaus's (1889) recent studies attempted to explain the anomalies at extreme magnitudes on the basis of neurochemical mechanisms, and to James they confirmed his suspicion that *"Weber's law is probably purely physiological"* (1890, 1:548, emphasis in original). Ebbinghaus argued that, understood chemically, a sensation consisted of the dissociation of certain molecular bonds in nervous tissue—a chemical reaction. These bonds, being alike, have a certain mean point at which they tend to dissociate, around which point the tendency to dissociate was distributed more-or-less normally (i.e., formed a Gaussian distribution), a claim supported, he thought, by recent studies of equilibrium in chemical systems. This meant that incremental changes of physical stimuli at magnitudes near this mean point would cause the most regular and largest amount of dissociations, while at either extreme they would cause a disproportionately smaller amount. This understanding mapped well onto the observed logarithmic relationship between stimulus magnitude and sensation intensity, and it advanced the important proposition that perceived sensation was answerable to the laws of chemical reaction in the nervous system. A similar set of claims about how "the events in the nervous system can be explained on physical & chemical principles" was one of the ideas that fascinated James's student Charles A. Strong in his lectures with Ebbinghaus (James 1998, 298).

8. James H. Tufts recalled that Ebbinghaus subjected topics from James's *Principles of Psychology* to careful analysis in his advanced seminars (unpublished autobiography, James Hayden Tufts Papers [hereafter JHTP], B 3, F 13). Tufts took coursework at Berlin in the years immediately after Mead left to replace Tufts as instructor at the University of Michigan.

9. I am able to definitely confirm this fact for the first time on the basis of a letter dated January 23, 1890, from the participants in his laboratory—Emil Böse, Paul Cossmann, Max Dessoir, Franz Eulenburg, "Georg" (i.e., George Herbert) Mead, Carl Pappenheim, K. A. O. Relander, Charles A. Strong, and Arthur Wreschner—to Ebbinghaus congratulating him on his fortieth birthday (NHE), and from supporting correspondence between Charles Strong and William James. According to the letter to Ebbinghaus, the laboratory assistants presented him with a gift of a collection of psychology books in order to help establish a laboratory library. A similar letter the following year (dated January 27, 1891), which accompanied another gift of books, indicates that Dessoir, Eulenburg, Pappenheim, and Wreschner stayed on, and were joined by Ernst Cassirer, Broder Christiansen, W. L. (possibly Wilhelm Ludvig) Johannsen, George A. Coe, Karl Marbe, William Stern, and Edgar James Swift. It is possible that not all of these men were active laboratory assistants; Charles Strong wrote to William James that the 1890 gift was from Ebbinghaus's "pupils & admirers," but that same letter clearly indicates Mead was active in the laboratory (James 1999, 4).

Emil Böse (1868–1927) became a geologist who worked primarily in Central America. Paul Cossmann (1869–1942) was known primarily as an editor and publicist, founder of the conservative *Süddeutsche Monatshefte* in Munich. Max Dessoir (1867–1947) received both a PhD from the philosophical faculty at Berlin and a medical degree at Würzburg on the basis of his experiments at Berlin (i.e., Dessoir 1892). He is known primarily for his research on paranormal phenomena (discussed in the text), for his development of neo-Kantian aesthetics, and for works on the history of psychology. Franz Eulenburg (1867–1943) was an economist and sociologist in Germany, where he was the acquaintance of leading German social scientists. Carl Pappenheim (1865–?) was a psychologist and biologist in Germany who wrote several major studies on pedagogical psychology. K. A. O. Relander (1863–1930) was a Finnish politician and academic who authored studies of folklore. Arthur Wreschner (1866–1932) remained closest to Ebbinghaus's work, conducting experiments on memory, the association of ideas, and children's language learning. He became chair of physiological psychology at Zürich and operated the psychology laboratory there with G. F. Lipps. Charles Strong (1862–1940) was an American student from Harvard (like Mead), on his second graduate stay in Germany, after which he returned to Clark University and then the University of Chicago. Strong established the beginnings of the University of Chicago's psychological laboratory in 1893 with physiologist H. H. Donaldson; much of the original equipment was purchased from the anthropological exhibits of the World Columbian Exposition in Chicago (Angell 1899, 238). Strong was the first faculty member in the psychology department, a year before Dewey and Mead arrived. He stayed through 1896, when he moved to Columbia University and James R. Angell took over direction of the Chicago laboratory. Angell had studied at Harvard and Berlin (and previously at Michigan under Dewey). Strong and Mead thus crossed paths several times—Harvard,

Berlin, Chicago—and Ebbinghaus's laboratory likely had a notable influence on the early Chicago laboratory.

10. Berlin neurologist Albert Moll's 1892 monograph on "rapport" in hypnosis gives 166 illustrations of experiments conducted on individuals or groups in induced hypnotic states, from an indeterminate number of different individuals (they were completely anonymized), conducted by Moll, Dessoir, and a circle of Berlin political and cultural elites, with a few remarks about hypnotic influences on students. Dessoir (1947, 126–27) recalled in his memoir that by April 1888 (prior to most of the cases reported by Moll) he had personally witnessed over 200 cases of successful hypnotism in Berlin, many for research purposes. Still, Dessoir and others reportedly complained about the lack of suitable subjects for their experiments throughout this period (Sommer 2012, 17). The participation of Dessoir in Ebbinghaus's and Munk's laboratories at the university may well have influenced the research procedures of this group's experiments. Some accounts (e.g., Sommer 2012; Wolffram 2009) place emphasis on the professional pressures felt by Dessoir and others to conform to conventional psychology, but without examining where he might have learned such models of conventional psychology. And in terms of Mead's biography, it is perhaps not incidental that William James was enthusiastic about the psychical research being done in Berlin in this period, calling Moll's *Der Hypnotismus* "the best compendious work on the subject . . . extraordinarily complete and judicious" and recommending Dessoir's comprehensive bibliography on hypnotism (James 1890, 2:615–16). Sommer (2012) traces some of the ways in which James reportedly kept in contact with the work of the Gesellschaft für Experimental-Psychologie and its successor, the Gesellschaft für psychologische Forschung (Society for Psychological Research).

11. Munk was involved in several major scientific controversies over his career, including heated debates about the localization of particular mental functions (especially vision) with other leading physiologists, and on the ethics of animal vivisection. A wide variety of scientific authorities toured Munk's veterinary school, including William James and Sigmund Freud.

12. Dilthey's paper was first given in May 1890 to the Royal Prussian Academy of Sciences. The paper sounds remarkably suggestive of some of Mead's own work, including his proposed dissertation under Dilthey (cf. Joas 1997 [1985], 19). Dilthey (2010 [1890]) explained the extension of physical space and formation of objects as the result of the organism's movements and volitional impulses in the process of life (rather than being merely "given" unproblematically or being hypothetical inferences extending from mere cognition, as contemporary psychological and philosophical perspectives supposed). Judged by Mead's later work on the social self Dilthey's solution is inadequate in notable respects, but that proposition cannot dismiss the probable influence on Mead of Dilthey's argument, either through this paper or through his closely associated Ethics lectures that Mead attended. It might also be noted that Martin's *The Human Body* (1881, 463–64) makes quite similar arguments about how the action of the body as perceived by the senses causes the person to build up an understanding of an external, material world and ascribe causes to it.

13. It is likely that Henry Castle influenced Mead's decision to take so many courses with Paulsen. Castle had taken several lecture classes from him during his

previous course of study in Berlin in 1885–86, including moral philosophy, psychology, and "Exercises on Kant's *Kritik*" (see letters 1885–86, HNCP, B 2, F 1; B 2, F 4). In May 1889 Castle was reacquainted with Paulsen, receiving detailed advice on writing a German-style dissertation at one or more meetings at the professor's house (see letters from H. N. Castle to his siblings, May–June 1889, HNCP, B 3, F 1). And in December 1890 Castle and Mead were invited to the salon of the Lobedan sisters in Berlin for an evening with Paulsen, who was reportedly "very pleasant and very cordial" (H. N. Castle to S. N. and M. T. Castle, December 19, 1890, HNCP, B 3, F 3).

14. "I am still suffering more or less from my tooth. I judge from what Dr. Miller says that it would have been better if the abscess had broken on the outside, as now it has no outlet but through the tooth and does not progress to healthfulness as fast as it should. But I trust that by tomorrow it will be in a condition to be filled. I find Dr. Miller a very pleasant fellow. . . . I am doing nothing but working on German and going to the Dentist whose bill looms up before me in the nightwatches" (G. H. Mead to H. N. Castle, March 19, 1889, HNCP, B 5, F 10; see also H. N. Castle to G. H. Mead, March 20, 1889, HNCP, B 2, F 10). Miller was an American who spent his most productive years researching and practicing in Berlin, where he was one of only a few foreign-born academics to be awarded a professorship. The preface to Miller's original German version of *The Micro-Organisms of the Human Mouth* was signed March 1889.

15. G. H. Mead to S. N. and M. T. Castle, [?] June 1892, GHMP, B 1, F 4. This letter is written in large part as an apology for Mead's inability to accept the Castles' invitation to come to Hawaii that summer. Instead, Helen Mead went with John Dewey's wife, Alice Chipman Dewey. The letter is quoted at greater length, but with ellipses, in Cook 1993, 31–32.

16. J. Dewey to J. R. Angell, April 25, 1892 (Dewey 1997, no. 00466).

17. J. Dewey to J. R. Angell, May 10, 1893 (ibid., no. 00478). The letter does indicate that much of this was still in the planning state, but Dewey thought the direction Mead was taking "one of the most important working hypotheses turned up lately."

18. G. H. Mead to S. N. Castle (part of larger multiauthored letter), undated c. 1893, HNCP, B 5, F 10.

19. "Experimental Psychology," *University Record* [of the University of Michigan] 2, no. 4 (February 1893): 94–95. It is quite likely that Mead contributed significantly to this report on the psychological laboratory.

20. Mabel W. Castle wrote to her husband that "George's paper ["The Problem of Psychological Measurement"] at the [American Psychological Association] Convention in N. Y. Mr. Dewey pronounced the ablest, tho' perhaps not so recognized there" (M. W. Castle to H. N. Castle, December 31, 1893, Elinor Castle Nef Papers [hereafter ECNP], B 17, F 10).

21. H. N. Castle to M. W. Castle, December 7, 1893, ECNP, B 17, F 10. Castle wrote, "George had a sad affair at his laboratory this morning—he had left something to harden, a brain, and the flame of the light had spread and set fire to a valuable microscope with some other things which make a loss of a hundred dollars about. George felt rather badly as it is so hard to get any money for his tools from the regents, and he has not as much apparatus as he would like to have and who knows when he will ever get any more? The night-watchman on his rounds discovered the fire before it had spread,

but it was a careless thing to do, and I do not believe that he will leave any more brains to harden over night." Given the lack of much documentation regarding successful laboratory experiments leading to publications from this period of the Michigan psychology laboratory, Raphelson (1968, 9) quipped that this fire was the one "empirical" outcome of Mead's laboratory.

22. "Experimental Psychology," 95.

23. *Catalogue of the University of Michigan for 1892–93* [a.k.a. *General Register*], (Ann Arbor: University of Michigan, 1893), 67.

24. *University Record* 3, no. 2 (June 1893): 34. What animals were studied is not clear from the available announcements, but the zoology and animal morphology courses at Michigan tended to use cats for their standard classroom studies, according to course announcements. As is discussed in the text, Mead definitely referred to the behavior of cats in his courses. The close link Mead drew to the work in biology indicates that he was likely in dialogue with Jacob E. Reighard and his assistant H. S. Jennings in that department (who coauthored *Anatomy of the Cat*). The Reighards were also apparently friends of the Deweys in Ann Arbor and the families stayed in contact for many years after the Deweys and Meads left Michigan, according to John Dewey's (1997) correspondence.

25. The talk was given June 8, 1894, to the thirty-eighth annual meeting of the Michigan Dental Association, which according to the *Detroit Free Press* was attended by over 150 dentists ("Dentists in Session," June 8, 1894). The topic of the conference that year was anesthetic techniques, and other papers covered the use of cocaine, chloroform, ether, nitrous oxide, electrolysis, and methods of restoration and resuscitation (Warner 1964, 79). Mead was the only major speaker who was not also a dental practitioner. Although Mead's talk, published as a two-part article in the University of Michigan's *Dental Journal* in January and March 1895, was preceded in print by several abstracts, critical reviews, and short essays, none of these earlier pieces is longer than 1500 words, as printed.

26. The discussants were dentists Joel C. Parker of Grand Rapids, Michigan, and J. L. Sweetnam of Manistee, Michigan ("Discussion," *The Dental Register* 48:382).

27. In the article Mead identified by name over thirty different authors on hypnotism, and referred explicitly to specific works by Hippolyte Bernheim, Wilhelm Wundt, William Preyer, Albert Moll, Jonas Grossmann, Max Hirsch, Joseph-Remi-Leopold Delboeuf, and Thomas Fillebrown. Mead even noted Preyer's "lectures upon hypnotism at Berlin University" that have "done great service to the cause." It should also be noted that Mead was well familiar with James's chapter on "Hypnotism" in his *Principles of Psychology*, which makes an argument quite similar to Mead's, although it is not mentioned specifically in the article.

28. *Announcement of the Graduate School* (Ann Arbor: University of Michigan, 1893–94), 23.

29. This notebook of 150 pages, along with fifteen other notebooks from Campbell's courses at Michigan, are available in the Campbell Family Papers ([hereafter CFP], B 2, F 2, "Philosophy (Mead) 1893" notebook). After taking courses with Dewey, Mead, and others at Michigan, R. Clair Campbell became a local farmer on his family's property. Many members of his family attended the university, including his sister-in-law Mat-

tie Eudora (Ormsby) Campbell, who later recorded her thoughts on the connections between the philosophy department and other departments at the university. In particular, she noted that in her zoology course on the "Theory of Classification and Development of Species" with Joseph B. Steere (whose son later married Mattie Campbell's daughter) he "had at his tongue's end all the philosophy that I had gained from all the men in the department of philosophy" (University of Michigan Alumni Association [hereafter UMAA], 1924 Alumnae Surveys, B 110). All discussion of the specific content of Mead's "Special Topics in Psychology" course is from Campbell's notes. These notes indicate that Mead made specific reference to works by J. McKeen Catell, J. Mark Baldwin, Hermann Helmholtz, Wilhelm Wundt, Hugo Münsterberg, E. W. Scripture, William James, and G. T. Ladd. Mead referred extensively to James's *Principles of Psychology*, including the chapters on "Association," "Memory," "Stream of Consciousness," "Habit," "Attention," and "Hypnotism."

30. This particular illustration was so recurrent that at the end of his notes Campbell wrote a short poem about it: "The Post Office we bid adieu / We hope to hear of something new / We hope to get our credit too" (CFP, B 2, F 2, p. 150). Subsequent page numbers appear in the text.

31. J. Dewey to W. R. Harper, March 27, 1894 (Dewey 1997, no. 00502). Dewey wrote that Mead was "enough of an experimentalist" to offer attractive work in that "line" to students, but that after a year he would transfer to "the comparative and physiological line"—"his own specialty." In his correspondence, especially a letter to E. C. Hegeler, November 19, 1893 (Dewey 1997, no. 09328), Dewey noted that at Michigan the full development of their psychological program was hampered by the lack of funds and the heavy undergraduate teaching demands—they could make definite use, he proposed, of additional funds for graduate fellowships, laboratory assistants, the library, the laboratory, and producing their own "periodical for publishing results of research." One of the reasons the move to Chicago was so appealing to Dewey was the promise of more generous financial support for their investigations.

32. One indication of Mead's continuing interest in neurological topics is the series of lectures, accompanied by stereopticon slides that Mead gave in 1897 as part of the Hull House "Free Lecture Series" open to the public (*Hull-House Bulletin* 2, nos. 2–3). His topics were "The Story of the Brain," "The Evolution of Intelligence," and "The Present Evolution of Man" on February 26, March 7, and March 21, respectively, at Medill School (a public elementary school on Chicago's near west side). The lectures were reportedly well attended.

33. Rucker (1969, 59) is apparently one of the few to recognize the extent of this interaction; as he put it, Mead was "involved intimately in all the researches going on, a fertile source of ideas, yet publishing comparatively little."

34. The meeting of the North Central Psychological Association, November 28, 1908, is of particular interest. It was held in the new Psychological Laboratory of the University of Chicago with seventy-five participants, and it is apparently the first professional meeting at which Mead discussed his theory of "social consciousness" ("Notes and News," *Psychological Bulletin* 5, no. 12 [1908]: 406). In the following meetings of the society Mead and others debated Warner Fite's theory of "new individual-

ism," which was apparently one of the immediate provocations for Mead to write his "The Social Self."

35. Warden and Warner (1927) made a comparison of the earliest courses offered in comparative or animal psychology and the openings of comparative psychology laboratories in colleges in the United States. In their study, however, they mislabeled Mead's first class as having been given in 1899 rather than 1894. If the other dates are substantially correct Mead's was the first and only course for five years to be offered in comparative psychology in the United States.

36. Bingham's notes cover only the first two lectures of Mead's summer 1905 Comparative Psychology course. They are found archived among Bingham's professional papers ("2 Lectures, Mead," Walter Van Dyke Bingham Papers [hereafter WVDB], Rl 1, F 9). Hammond's remarkably extensive notes are preserved in the Mead Papers (GHMP, B 15, F 14). Bawden's notes are available in the Joseph Ratner Papers ([hereafter JRP], B 42, F 2). They consist of forty-three pages of notes typed by Bawden's friend, historian Ralph Gregory, from an original manuscript by Bawden (now apparently lost). They preserve only the second half of Bawden's original notes. Letters accompanying the typescript and others in the Dewey (1997) correspondence between Gregory and Joseph Ratner help identify the notes. One undated note from Gregory (page 65a in the typescript) indicates that Mead was directly in dialogue with Jacques Loeb's *Comparative Physiology of the Brain and Comparative Psychology* (1900) in the course, and that Bawden found, from his own study with Loeb, "some problems in Mead's utterance & added clarifications & comments into the *ms*. It will be difficult to isolate the Meadian parts." Loeb was on the early University of Chicago faculty until 1902, and Dewey's correspondence indicates that the Loebs and Meads were personally close. Loeb developed an essentially "mechanistic" theory of intelligence that certainly intrigued Mead. All discussion of the 1900 course in the text is by reference to this set of notes. Bawden also drew (sometimes explicitly, sometimes implicitly) from Mead's courses in several published expositions of the evolution of intelligence (Bawden 1901, 1919).

37. Much more could be said by way of tracing the specific connections between his social psychology and his comparative psychology, and particularly illustrative in this regard are notes taken in the crucial period from about 1909 to 1913 when Mead was explicitly formulating his theory of the "social self." Notes from Juliet Hammond, Ellsworth Faris, and others indicate the strong cross-fertilization of these domains in this period and how his early social psychology work was largely in (critical) dialogue with contemporary comparative, physiological, and introspective psychologists such as George Romanes, C. Lloyd Morgan, Wilhelm Wundt, E. L. Thorndike, and L. T. Hobhouse.

38. One could push this point further by noting that a major part of the shift that occurred with the reorientation of Mead's social psychology classes from 1917 to 1920, which resulted in the kind of exposition recorded in *Mind, Self, and Society* and his other late social psychology lectures, was to separate "elementary" psychological discussions from the emerging specialist literature on "social psychology" proper. That is, in order not to be prevented from teaching the latest controversial work, a division of labor was created where other courses would introduce the student to the facts of physi-

ological, comparative, and other psychological fields. Somewhat homologous shifts were made in Mead's move to Chicago where he moved out of the experimental laboratory and into serious study of comparative psychology, and in 1904–5 when experimental comparative psychology was separated from his reformulated "theoretical" comparative psychology. And again, one finds much the same in the split of the education department from philosophy which, over a course of a few years, led Mead to give up his editorial position on the *Elementary School Teacher* journal and to stop teaching explicitly in education courses. Mead repeatedly relinquished claim to fields in which he had done practical research—seemingly without serious qualms—and simultaneously embarked on an engagement with scholarship in emerging areas.

CHAPTER THREE

1. Samuel and Angeline had one child: Mary (1838–1926). Samuel and Angeline's sister Mary had ten children: Samuel (1843–43), Alfred (1844–74), Harriet (1847–1924), William (1849–1935), George (1851–1932), Tyler (1853–64), James (1855–1918), Caroline (1858–1941), Helen (1860–1929), and Henry (1862–95).

2. The Henry Northrup Castle Papers preserve an extensive collection of his correspondence and are used to support claims made throughout this section. In letters from September 1880 (B 1, F 3) Henry mentions pictures of the Hawaiian Islands sent to him by his sister Helen. And in letters to his parents in the autumn of 1882, for example, Henry proposed that they try to find George Mead a place teaching at one of the schools in Honolulu after they graduate (HNCP, B 1, F 6), a prospect he had apparently discussed with Mead.

3. G. H. Mead to H. C. Coleman, October 21, 1890, HNCP, B 5, F 10.

4. Henry Castle's letters include not only discussions of his working life but also appeals to the sensuous experience of the Islands. For example, in an early letter after college to Mead he wrote: "When my eyes are lifted from the paper, I see the Waianae mountains lifting their exquisitely twisted[?] summit, far away beyond the rich and lustrous green of the trees in our yard. They are twenty miles away, as the bird flies. The sound of church bells, which were lazily pealing a few moments since, has ceased & left an absolute silence. The silence, however is occasionally broken by the trade wind, which wakes from a moment's sleep in the quiet valleys to rush down through the town & evoke a continuous murmur in the tops of leafy algarobas & samangs. That rouses the birds too, & they twitter & call. Then I hear a whole fury of sounds, a horseman's galloping through the streets, the rattling of carriage & the intermittent crowing of a cock from some backyard. The breeze just now is rather too boisterous, thrashing my paper, but it will stop in a moment, & then will be another 'orchestral lull'" (H. N. Castle to G. H. Mead, October 7, 1883, HNCP, B 1, F 9).

5. In a long letter to Helen and George Mead, March 1, 1893, Henry Castle vehemently opposed the view of the affair trumpeted in leading American periodicals, which treated it as a revolution bought by oligarchic sugar interests. Instead, he argued, the "strength" and "warrant" of the movement came from mass meetings attended by people of every party, and by more people who had reason to distrust and hate the sugar planters than by planters themselves. After positing that the planters had too much to

lose to be motivated by self-interest to promote revolution, he wrote heatedly that the "real basis of the revolution" was to be found in the "universal feeling" that "every legitimate political & moral & social interest" in civilization was a stake (H. N. Castle to G. H. and H. K. Mead, March 1, 1893, HNCP, B 3, F 8).

6. G. H. Mead (also signed by H. K. Mead) to S. N. and M. T. Castle, April 1, 1894, GHMP, B 1, F 4. In various congressional reports of investigations into the revolution Henry Castle's *Pacific Commercial Advertiser* was often quoted at length as a primary source.

7. This discussion is based on analysis of articles in the ProQuest Historical Newspapers database and the Library of Congress' Chronicling America database. The congressional debates were extensively covered in the newspapers of the time, including long quotations and digests of congressional proceedings and speeches.

8. The Associated Press wire report was originally a special dispatch from the Detroit office, reporting the contents of a letter from an unnamed member of Helen Mead's family in Honolulu commenting on the impressions of the city made by the wife of Albert S. Willis, the newly arrived US minister to Hawaii. Willis had been appointed by President Grover Cleveland, who initially opposed the revolution and attempted to halt the annexation of Hawaii to the United States. Florence Dulaney Willis and her husband were apparently surprised to find Honolulu a city equal to any of its size in the United States in terms of culture and refinement, and the people leading the revolution in Hawaii to be men of affairs rather than "a few low-classed whites and 'beach combers,'" as was supposed on the mainland. A follow-up interview (likely conducted by Robert E. Park) of Helen Mead attempted to make plain that the revolutionists, including her family, were not in revolt against the monarchy as a system of government but against the "immorality and corruption of the court," which threatened to move the country "backward" and "undo all that the missionaries had done." She sought to emphasize that "all the better classes of the community without respect to color" were opposed to the queen's constitutional amendments that would have scaled back the power of elected officials and restrengthened the authority of the royal court (e.g., "Minister Willis Disgusted," *Milwaukee Sentinel*, December 21, 1893). Park's initial impressions of the Meads in 1893 were reported to his wife as follows: "Mr. Mead is the assistant in psychology at Ann Arbor and he has a witty and delightful wife. Her name before her marriage was Castle and she has lived all her life in Honolulu. Her brother is one of the commissioners who came over from Honolulu to ask the American government to annex Hawaii. Her father is the most important person in the Islands I guess and annexation had been his dream. She is now writing an article for the papers on the situation there and I am going up tomorrow to help her" (quoted in Raushenbush 1979, 22).

9. Addams (1930, 18). Her eulogy continued: "As I learned to know [Helen] better, affection for her seemed to include those Islands to which she was so devoted and which in later years she shared with so many of her Chicago friends. It was a great enchantment to live in those Islands even for a few weeks. Everywhere we saw evidences of her mother's wide philanthropy and the undaunted public spirit of her entire family which had gradually translated the old mission zeal into modern terms, as a primitive community had developed into a great commercial center. Yet this bustling modern

community, with ships coming and going to all the ports of the Pacific, was still unlike any other, in certain important aspects. It may have been the influence of its missionary founders; it may have been due to the gentle natives who had never been conquered and enslaved and were therefore able to stand up as Americans from the very day of annexation. Certainly some benign influence makes the race relations of Honolulu more nearly ideal than in any other part of the world. Citizens born in China, Japan, Samoa, in Fiji, mingle both politically and socially with those born on the mainland of the United States, in Australia, in various European countries" (18–19).

10. "Visiting Educationists," *Honolulu Evening Bulletin*, July 1, 1897. The claims in this section are based on a reading of the newspaper mentions of Mead in Hawaiian papers. I have found particularly useful the digitized collections of the "Chronicling America" project of the Library of Congress. Between the lists of steamship passengers, the mentions in the "variety" and "society" pages, and the reports of Mead's public speeches, a fairly detailed account of the Mead party's travels in Hawaii can be reconstructed.

11. Of particular note are the reports "Educational Revival" (*Hawaiian Gazette*, June 18, 1897) and "Visiting Educationists" (*Honolulu Evening Bulletin*, July 1, 1897). Other educators involved in the "revival" were Albert William Smith, professor of mechanical engineering, and Mary Roberts Smith (later Mary Roberts Coolidge), professor of sociology, both at Stanford; and Mary Ellis, professor of psychology and political economy, and Mary Chamberlain, professor of French and German, both at Mills College. The Smiths traveled on the same steamship from San Francisco to Honolulu as the Meads. Mills College was a women's school in California modeled after Mount Holyoke College from which it drew much of its faculty. Elmer E. Brown had previously met Mead when Brown was visiting assistant professor of "the Science and the Art of Teaching" for the 1891–92 year at the University of Michigan, where Mead was just starting out as instructor. He was later elected president of the National Education Association, then US Commissioner of Education under Theodore Roosevelt and William Howard Taft, and ended his career as president of New York University.

12. Although several announcements of the lecture appear in newspapers, my analysis is based primarily on the July 20, 1897, *Hawaiian Gazette* article, "Professor Mead Lectures before Teachers at Summer School," because it is the most detailed report. Mead had given a lecture of almost the same title the previous year to the Chicago Commons School of Social Economics (see Mead 1896b), but the two talks were apparently not identical. He also gave a talk of similar title at the April 10, 1897, "Kindergarten Conference" at the University of Chicago. The lecture in Honolulu can be seen as combining elements of the Chicago Commons lecture and his lecture on "The Child and His Environment" (Mead 1897b) at the 1897 Illinois Society for Child Study meeting.

13. "Reception at Legation," *Honolulu Evening Bulletin*, July 6, 1897.

14. Various short announcements in Hawaiian newspapers reported the doings of the Meads and their society hosts. At the Koko Head Peninsula they were entertained by Anna M. Paris, family friend of the Castles and daughter of missionary John Paris, and in Hilo the Meads stayed with Helen's half-sister Mary Tenney Hitchcock and her husband Marshal Edward G. "Holy Terror" Hitchcock ("Entertained by Miss Paris," *Ha-*

waiian Gazette, August 24, 1897; "New Water Pipes," *Hawaiian Gazette,* July 30, 1897).
The Swanzys' luau was described as follows in a newspaper report: "The feast was a
novelty to the guests of honor [the Meads], who had never seen such a sight before. The
decorations and arrangements throughout were in Hawaiian style. The luau was set under the large trees in the yard. About fifty guests attended, some coming from Honolulu
and the surrounding country districts" ("Society Notes," *Hawaiian Star,* September 1,
1897). While attempting to descend into the Haleakala crater, an unnamed member of
Mead's party stumbled and was lost for two hours before being found nearly overcome
by exposure ("An Accident," *Hawaiian Star,* September 9, 1897).

15. "Cousins' Society," *Hawaiian Gazette,* August 17, 1897. The Hawaiian Mission
Children's Society was known colloquially as the "Cousins' Society" because of the
close (often familial) ties between the early missionary settlers' families. The Castles
were integral members of the society, and George and Helen Mead were subscribing
members to the society for many years.

16. The University of Hawaii's sociology department and social laboratory were
founded by Romanzo C. Adams, a graduate of the University of Chicago's sociology
program in 1904 (who had taken Mead's Autumn 1902 Philosophy of Science class). In
the 1930s and '40s the department was host to extended visits by Robert Park, Herbert
Blumer, E. Franklin Frazier, and other prominent (often Chicago-connected) sociologists. The Pan-Pacific Union was cofounded by Alexander Hume Ford, who made Hawaii his home in part because of his interest in the Castles' experiments with labor on
their sugarcane plantations (Hooper 1972). The Union and its Research Institute were,
for many years, based out of the Castle mansion outside Honolulu (Robb and Vicars
1982; Castle 2004).

17. "Social Events of the Week," *Hawaiian Star,* August 10, 1907.

18. From newspaper reports, correspondence, and digitized passenger lists, there is
evidence that the Meads traveled to Hawaii in 1897, 1898, 1900, 1903, 1904–5 (Winter),
1907, 1909, 1911, 1913, 1920, 1921, 1922, and 1924, always in the summer, except in
1904–5. Helen Mead went to Honolulu without George in 1892 and 1917. They may have
taken additional trips but my evidence is incomplete on this point. They also apparently traveled with or sponsored the travel of several young people whom they knew,
including John U. Nef Jr., Elinor Castle, Evelyn Dewey, and Charles F. Harding Jr. That
Jane Addams accompanied the Meads is attested by her eulogy of Helen (Addams 1930).
Addams also participated with Julie Swanzy and others in the formation of the Pan-
Pacific Women's Association, which held its first meeting in Hawaii in 1928 (Paisley
2009). The Deweys made several voyages to Hawaii, which are documented in John
Dewey's correspondence (1997). Harriet Park Thomas accompanied the Meads in 1913
("Locals," *Maui News,* August 30, 1913), and later spent over two years living in Hawaii
from late 1924 to 1927 (Throop and Ward 2007b) where she lived for a period with Helen
Mead's sister Harriet Castle Coleman at the end of Coleman's life. As indicated in a
footnote of chapter 6, George and Helen's son Henry C. A. Mead sent his complimen-
tary copies of *Mind, Self, and Society* only to family and close family friends, including
Harriet.

19. Mead prepared a talk on annexation at the Sociology Club of the University of
Chicago on November 18, 1897, and also sought to arrange a talk by Lorrin A. Thurston,

a leading revolutionary against Queen Liliuokalani in Hawaii, an advocate of US annexation, and a good friend of Henry Castle (H. K. Mead to M. W. Castle, November 17, 1897, ECNP, B 18, F 11). Mead participated in public discussions of the Commercial Club of Chicago on annexation on January 29, 1898 ("Hawaii Is the Issue," *Chicago Tribune*, January 30, 1898). These discussions featured University of Chicago history professor Hermann von Holst arguing forcefully against annexation.

20. George Herbert Mead, "Hawaiians Are Fit," *Chicago Tribune*, January 22, 1898, 13. This article has apparently never been previously identified in the scholarship on Mead. Quotations in the text are from this article.

21. The Castles were also at work on experiments to introduce "white labor" to their sugarcane plantations (Hooper 1972, 47) in order to promote annexation to the United States, both because annexation would mean agreeing to severe restrictions on Chinese and Japanese immigration, and because proportionally more white laborers would strengthen American claims to possession of the Islands (over the increasing nationalistic claims of Japan and China). In his article, Mead discussed the possibilities and failures of "white labor," which he would have observed firsthand on his tour of the Castles' plantations.

22. "'Old Glory' on Diamond Head," *Hawaiian Gazette*, July 19, 1898.

23. In Parker's *Reminiscences*, she notes that among the people present when they met with the Meads on July 31, 1898, was Nathaniel B. Emerson. This may be of more than passing interest because Emerson wrote a significant monograph on the *Unwritten Literature of Hawaii* (1909) that contains a penetrating analysis of the nature of gesture in native Hawaiian communication. Frank Parker was also known for her meticulous work on the functions of gesture in the development of language, including applying the "Delsarte system of expression" to pedagogy (e.g., "Expression of Thoughts," *Honolulu Evening Bulletin*, July 15, 1898; "Gesture True to Truth," *Hawaiian Star*, July 22, 1898). There is, thus, a possible link between these authorities and Mead's work on the nature of communication. Also present at the 1898 meeting of the Parkers, Meads, and Emerson was Sanford B. Dole, formerly president of the Republic of Hawaii and current territorial governor of the US Territory of Hawaii, which was only days old at the time.

24. "University Extension," *Hawaiian Star*, December 14, 1898.

25. "The University Extension," *Hawaiian Star*, September 19, 1899; "Educators 'Slumming,'" *Hawaiian Star*, September 18, 1899. The first article notes: "Dr. Dewey has paid several visits to the local schools since they opened and expressed himself as much interested in the work here and the tasks of teachers in given instruction to classes in which the nationalities are so mixed. He said that the conditions existing made the schools of Honolulu an interesting study." The second reads in part: "Professor John Dewey and wife, of the University Extension work . . . accompanied by local friends went 'slumming' Sunday night. Deputy Marshal Chillingworth was guide of the party. The trip was made for the benefit of the Chicago educators, who desired to see all shades of Honolulu life and character before returning East. Pau Ahi street was visited and inspected from end to end. Next, the visitors were shown the confirmed opium fiends at the Tong Hing Society. From there various other slum sections were visited and the party later looked through the cells at the station house. This is the first record of 'slumming' of this order in Honolulu. In San Francisco, Chicago and the East it is

frequently done by Members of the W.C.T.U. [Woman's Christian Temperance Union] and kindred organizations, and by students of sociology."

26. Oahu College, *List of Trustees, Presidents, Instructors, Matrons, Librarians, Superintendents of Grounds, and Students, 1841–1906* (Honolulu: Hawaiian Gazette Co., 1907).

27. Although the review is not "signed" in the text as having been written by Mead, that fact is attested in the front matter and index of the volume (*American Historical Review* 5, no. 4 [1900]: inside cover, 823, 838). Mead may have been asked to write this review by Harry Pratt Judson, who was a coeditor of the journal and a friend and colleague at Chicago. This piece has not previously been listed among Mead's published works, and it is apparently his only review in this journal.

28. *Hawaiian* Gazette, February 24, 1905 (untitled brief announcement); "Local and General," *Honolulu Evening Bulletin*, March 20, 1905. Helen Mead described the engagements in a letter to her sister-in-law, Mabel Wing Castle, as follows: "You will be interested to learn that George has begun the regular professional talkee talkee, once to Punahou [a.k.a., Oahu College] (chapel ex[ercises]) once mothers & teachers, once Research Club, and I now hear his fame bruited abroad. Mr. [William Morris] Kincaid, ever on the alert, urges him to talk in Cent[ral] Union Church. I never saw your excellent brother-in-law so very nearly embarrassed as at the moment of this request, but observe, chère amie, the infinite grace of his reply. Sez he—I should be very glad to do so if I felt I had any message—Mr. K. [replied:] 'You have a message for them—I know you have.' Did you ever hear this remark that 'Blood will tell'—I cannot tell you yet whether he is really truly going to [give the talk] or not" (letter, March 3, 1905, HNCP, B 5, F 11). Kincaid was the progressive pastor of Central Union Church, the largest Christian church in Honolulu at the time, and friends not only with Mead but also with Harry Pratt Judson (possibly through Mead), who as president of the University of Chicago invited Kincaid to be "university preacher" in 1910. The title "The Relation of School to Home" leads me to believe this talk was related to the November 1905 speech on "The School and the Life of the Child" given to the Chicago Woman's Club. Based on the titles of Mead's other two named talks in Honolulu, it seems likely that they addressed some of the same issues as his later "The Philosophical Basis of Ethics" (Mead 1908e), given as a talk to the Chicago Ethical Society in December 1907 before being published, but I am unable to find further information about the content of any of these 1905 speeches.

29. "Will Build New Mill," *Hawaiian Gazette*, March 21, 1905.

30. Class, more than anything else, stratified Mead's connections on the Islands, but class also served in large part as a proxy for political influence and race, as Mead himself acknowledged. Thus, for example, he would have encountered nonwhites primarily mediated through class structures. The 1910 US Census lists a combined total of twenty-three individuals not related to the Castles living in the households of Helen's three brothers (William R., James B., and George P.). These individuals are all listed as servants or dependents of servants and all are of Chinese or Japanese descent. In addition, many of the people with whom the Meads held intimate conversations were individuals with considerable knowledge of native Hawaiian language and customs (e.g., Nathaniel Emerson, Anna Paris, Caroline [Castle] Westervelt, Julie Swanzy, William Castle), but they studied rather than lived native life. Even in his "tours" or

"walking trips," Mead's guides were invariably at the very top of Hawaiian society. But it is here, rather than in his table talk, that Mead would have at least experienced more directly the conditions of other strata. It might be added parenthetically that Mead's firsthand experience and observation of a culture of non-European origin may have been part of his appeal to some of his most devoted students who were, themselves, former missionaries—especially Ellsworth Faris and Maurice T. Price (both discussed in later chapters).

31. "Professor Mead Talks Interestingly to Research Club," *Honolulu Evening Bulletin*, September 19, 1907. The report also notes that, "Regarding immigration matters, Mr. Mead is of the opinion that America in general has lost nothing through the admission of the many thousands of coolies [i.e., Chinese and Japanese laborers]. That Americans are under the impression that the coolies are seeking this country to avoid political bondage when such is not the fact. That they are brought here by employers of labor to supply a cheap labor market." Another report from the *Hawaiian Star* of September 19, 1907 (also quoted in the text), records "We have much to learn, Prof. Mead stated, and there are some things we could learn from the immigrants as well as impart knowledge to them."

32. "Professor Mead on Municipalities. The New Honolulu Charter Criticized in Address Before Research Club," *Hawaiian Star*, September 19, 1907.

33. *Hull-House Bulletin* 3, no. 12 (1899): 1 (cf. Feffer 1993, 160). The talk was presented as a fundraiser for the "Vacation School Fund" of Hull House.

34. "The New Gymnasium," *The Friend* [Hawaii Evangelical Association Newsletter] 66, no. 10 (October 1909): 13.

35. Mead (1908a) reported having had "many conversations" with a "scientific pathologist" at work on leprosy (almost certainly Walter R. Brinckerhoff, who on the island of Molokai was making what the newspapers of the time termed the first-ever scientific study of leprosy), and Mead noted the difference between the moral tone of Father Damien's previous work with Hawaiian lepers and Brinckerhoff's intellectual ambition, which was no less capable of addressing problems with "human" as well as "scientific" interest. Brinckerhoff married James B. Castle's wife's sister in 1906, making him a sort of in-law to the Castles.

36. "Professor Mead in Address on Strikes," *Hawaiian Gazette*, September 15, 1911. According to the report, Mead "spoke from both sides of the question with a clear understanding of the difficulties attending to their solution, explaining the reasons that should compel a city to make that solution a civic matter and not an individual one between employer and employe[e]. He condemned small wages paid by great corporations who yearly turned over great profits, and dwelt briefly on the American plane of thought which is responsible for the sentiment that if 'a general increase of wages is made they might as well go out of business.'"

37. The Meads were in Hawaii for most of August and September 1909, and Evelyn Dewey (John and Alice Dewey's daughter) accompanied them. Her correspondence indicates that in addition to watching polo matches, attending society luncheons, and hiking into Haleakala crater, they also toured Ewa Plantation with Helen's brother William R. Castle, and George and Henry Mead accompanied Territorial Governor Walter F. Frear on a "walking trip" to survey agricultural conditions (E. Dewey to

J. and A. C. Dewey, August 15, 1909, Dewey 1997, no. 01974). Ewa Plantation, which was agented and part-owned by Castle & Cooke, was one of the major plantations directly affected by the strikes. The strike may have been one of the reasons why a group of public officials from the controversial US Immigration Commission (the "Dillingham Commission") toured the islands in September 1909, led by Vermont senator William P. Dillingham and former assistant secretary of the Department of Commerce and Labor William R. Wheeler. The Meads (along with all of Honolulu high society) attended a party in honor of the commission on September 16, 1909, hosted by Prince Jonah Kuhio Kalanianaole and his wife, and they traveled back to San Francisco on the same steamship as this Congressional party.

38. "Local and General," *Honolulu Star-Bulletin*, July 29, 1913.

39. "Hawaii Sends Men to Farm Congress," *Chicago Examiner*, November 11, 1909; (untitled brief announcement), *Honolulu Evening Bulletin*, October 25, 1909. Several of the reports of Mead's participation in the Congress, including this *Chicago Examiner* article, refer to him as "formerly a resident of Honolulu," apparently on the basis of his extended stays there. Walter F. Frear was a long-time acquaintance of the Castle family, and was mentioned in some of Henry N. Castle's early correspondence as a close childhood friend (HNCP, B 1, F 1). He had previously been a Supreme Court Justice in the Kingdom and Territory of Hawaii. The Meads remained good friends with Governor Frear and his wife, Mary Dillingham Frear, for many years. In 1912, for example, the Frears traveled through the United States in connection with the national election campaign, and visited the Meads in Chicago ("Meeting Old Friends," *Hawaiian Gazette*, June 21, 1912). The Frears took charge of the Meads' niece, Elinor Castle, during that visit and escorted her back to family in Hawaii by way of a stop at the Grand Canyon (G. H. Mead to M. W. Castle, June 16, 1912, ECNP, B 19, F 8).

40. "Land Congress Opens To-Day to Form New U.S. Policy," *Chicago Examiner*, November 16, 1909.

41. A summary of Mead's speech was reported in the *Chicago Examiner* for November 21, 1909, as "Hawaii Offers American Settlers Large Profits in Tropical Crops," and my research confirms that the original text of Mead's speech is almost certainly the manuscript preserved in the Mead Papers under the tentative title "On the colonization of Hawaii" (GHMP, B 13, F 12). I rely primarily upon that manuscript for the explication of the speech. The manuscript also indicates that much of the factual information for the speech came from pamphlet materials prepared by the Hawaii Promotion Committee (a collaboration of the Hawaii Chamber of Commerce and Merchants Association) for the 1909 Alaska–Yukon–Pacific (AYP) Exposition (Wilcox 1909); excerpts of these materials are pinned to pages of Mead's manuscript. The AYP Exposition in Seattle marked Hawaii's first major participation in a world's fair as a US territory, and the popularity of the territory's exhibit was closely monitored in Hawaiian newspapers.

42. "On the Colonization of Hawaii," GHMP, B 13, F 12.

43. Reports of the rescue appeared as "Chicago Professor Lost in Oahu Mountains," *Hawaiian Star*, January 12, 1905, and "Lost Man Found," *Honolulu Evening Bulletin*, January 12, 1905. I draw primarily upon the *Star* report, which offers a more detailed narrative of the events.

44. Other individuals who accompanied the Meads and Frear on this tour include

US Geological Survey geologists Marshall O. Leighton and Walter C. Mendenhall, folklorist and senator of the Territorial Legislature Eric A. Knudsen, county treasurer of Kauai Arthur H. Rice, and artist and founding leader of the Boy Scouts in Hawaii James Austin Wilder.

45. "Conservation for Hawaii," *Hawaiian Star*, July 28, 1909. W. F. Frear's promotion of the "Trail and Mountain Club" was also part of this drive for conservation; it was explicitly modeled on the Sierra Club of California.

46. Frear's (1911) account of the tour appeared in the first issue of the new *Mid-Pacific Magazine*, edited by Alexander Hume Ford. The monthly magazine of "interesting facts, fictions, poetry, and general articles concerning the lands in and bordering on the great ocean" was an important part of Ford's attempt to promote "Pan-Pacific" cooperation, with Hawaii in its center. Also of interest, the first issue of the *Mid-Pacific Magazine* included a poem written by Mary Dillingham Frear to accompany her husband's article, a photo-illustrated article on "Oriental Honolulu" documenting the Chinese and Japanese quarter of the city, and a posthumously printed article on the "Americanization of Hawaii" by Indiana congressman Abraham L. Brick also illustrated by photographs. In covering the tour, Hawaiian newspapers were particularly interested, as one might imagine, with the safety of the territorial governor, and he had to publicly downplay the danger of these hikes (e.g., "Frear Denies He Was Lost," *Hawaiian Gazette*, August 31, 1909).

47. "Governor Makes a Record Climb," *Hawaiian Gazette*, September 5, 1911; "The High Realms of Sport," *Hawaiian Star*, September 5, 1911. The *Star* article quotes from the *Gazette* report and adds additional commentary on the possible risks and adventures awaiting members of the Trail and Mountain Club on subsequent hikes. The *Gazette* reported that, as Mead attempted to descend over an arduous 150-foot portion of the trail, "the professor grappled the rope, swung out and in again and made a marvelous descent for half the distance, then clutching at a ti plant that gave way, came rolling and sliding down the narrow path between the two drop offs. There was a crash of rocks and foliage and silence. Professor Mead was lying motionless across the trail. [After being revived . . .] The professor was game, and after a drink of water, arose for the rest of the climb." The path of the climb is a bit hard to reconstruct in part because the newspaper descriptions are not precise, and in part because there was not a pre-established hiking path the party was following, but it appears the hike was at least five miles long, likely considerably longer, and ranged in elevation up to over 2,500 feet above sea level and down to below 200 feet.

48. "Personals and Social Events," *Hyde Park Herald*, September 7, 1928. George and Helen Mead were reported as having joined other "educators and professional men" in "hikes over the trails at the Randolph Mountain club," while staying at the "Ravine House" in Randolph, New Hampshire. The Meads had a long history of hiking and climbing, not only in Hawaii, but also in Europe during their long periods there studying and vacationing, and at the Grand Canyon where they had also vacationed. In college George Mead had gone on camping trips with Henry Castle in Ohio and after college he served for a period on a railroad surveying crew, which must have brought him into similar situations.

49. I have identified related illustrations in a wide variety of notes taken through-out Mead's classes. Faris's 1912 Social Psychology notes, for example, contain a set of illustrations drawn from an individual confronted by a chasm, which recur regularly throughout the course. In one lecture, the notes read: "The man must see in the chasm what he did not see at first. He must see a path, a plank, etc. He must construct an object that does not exist at the present time. His first impulse is to jump. 'Too far and I'll fall.' Then there is an impulse to climb down. 'No way.' There is an impulse to go on. 'No means.' Out of the result of all these tendencies he builds up an object. This is not the same as the immediate selection of the stimulation. The animal gives no evidence of using the result of past activity. It keeps on selecting the results from im-mediate stimulation" (typed "Social Psychology" notes, EFP, 1:32–33). These notes were from the first social psychology class Mead taught after his eventful climb the previous summer.

50. In some ways, a comparable contextualization of a classical social theorist in light of his practical engagement is the rediscovery of Max Weber's early studies of working conditions in the East Elbian region of Germany and their impact on his later work on the nature of capitalist economy and social structure. As with Mead, Weber worked through problems of agricultural production, class and race structure, and national integration early in his career in a particular local context, with definite con-sequences for his later work (cf. Scaff 1984). The rediscovery of Weber's early writings benefited substantially from the publication of the *Gesamtausgabe* (Complete Works) beginning in 1984, but several major studies of Weber already began this reevaluation, including work by Reinhard Bendix (1960) and Lawrence Scaff (1984). Recently, Scaff (2011) published a detailed examination of Weber's extended tour in the United States that adds another unique dimension to the practical contexts of his work. There may even be a more direct link between Mead's and Weber's early work as well, as Mead studied Political Economy in 1891 with Gustav Schmoller who was also the head and leading figure of the Verein für Sozialpolitik that sponsored Weber's study of East Elbian agricultural labor in 1891–93. The "agrarian question" was reportedly much debated in Schmoller's seminars and meetings of the period.

51. It might even be noted in this regard that at their home in Chicago the Meads had, for many years, a prominent reminder of Hawaii that literally served as the center of their discussions. Helen Mead wrote to their friend Ethel Sturges Dummer, "We have a new table to be used for a dining table, from Honolulu. It arrived and was set up after we came here [i.e., Miami, on vacation], but I returned to Chicago on one of our hurry up calls, stayed 3 days, and admired the table most to death. You've no idea how hospitable I felt, and how many familiar faces I seemed to see about the board, literally a board. You've no idea how pretty it is! But you will soon see it I hope" (H. K. Mead to E. S. Dummer, March 4, 1916, Ethel Sturges Dummer Papers [hereafter ESDP], B 32, F 645). Helen's remark on the word "board" seems to be a play on the fact that the word connotes both a "game board" for card-playing (the Meads often had the Dummers and many other prominent citizens over for bridge and discussion) and the physical descrip-tion of the table. On the unique range and depth of the conversations around the Mead table, as told firsthand, see Nef 1953 and Swing 1964, and for summary discussion, see

Miller 1973, xxxv–xxxvii. The Meads had several of their Hawaiian relatives stay for long periods with them in Chicago.

CHAPTER FOUR

1. Among the more prominent published remembrances of Mead in the classroom are those of Van Meter Ames (1931), Emory S. Bogardus (1962), T. V. Smith (1962), David L. Miller (1973), Leonard S. Cottrell (1980), and Kimball Young (see Lindstrom, Hardert, and Young 1988). At least two sets of systematic interviews were conducted in the 1970s with former University of Chicago sociology students, one set by James Carey in preparation for his 1975 *Sociology and Public Affairs* and the other by Richard L. Smith for his 1977 dissertation. The former set is now available at the University of Chicago library, while the latter remains in private possession. In addition, a questionnaire was sent to virtually all sociologists of note in 1928 by Luther L. Bernard (himself a former Chicagoan), and the responses he received have been archived in nonidentical collections at Pennsylvania State University and the University of Chicago. Smith (1977) used these questionnaire responses in his analysis of Mead's influence on Chicago sociology, and they have also been used by Levine, Carter, and Gorman (1976) and Baker (1973) in their work on the history of sociology. The largest cache of correspondence regarding Mead's courses is to be found in the George Herbert Mead Papers (B 2, F 3), which contains responses solicited by Charles Morris from former students regarding their classroom notes. And although most of the reviews of the posthumous volumes come from nonstudents, several were published by former students, which add some additional insights.

2. Letter from G. E. M. Shelburg to C. Morris, November 20, 1931, GHMP, B 2, F 3.

3. Throughout the chapter I utilize information from the Examiners' and Instructors' Grade Reports ([hereafter EIGR], vols. 9–156) for claims made about registrations of students in Mead's courses. Smith (1977) used portions of this collection in his analysis of Mead's influence on Chicago sociologists, but it appears that his access to the reports was severely limited to the registration of graduate students in select disciplines only. From this collection, I have documented 271 course listings and 5,360 individual registration listings of students at all levels as well as visitors, representing approximately 3,000 unique individuals who registered for courses with Mead.

4. In order to locate these disparate notes I followed out leads in correspondence and published materials wherever I suspected relevant materials. I searched online and print listings of archival materials from individual libraries and utilized electronic databases including ArchiveGrid and Archives USA to facilitate my search. In addition, I corresponded with archivists or librarians at dozens of university and historical society collections, I visited locations in person, and I solicited materials from additional repositories remotely. I have little doubt that other student notes exist, probably in private hands, because I have made almost no attempt to solicit materials not already accessible in archives.

5. Mead's courses at Michigan have been previously documented (see Throop and Ward 2007a). According to Berkeley's *Schedule of Classes and Directory* (Berkeley: University of California Press, 1928–29), 227–28, Mead taught two courses at that

school: (1) "Social Philosophy" described as "An analysis of human nature from the standpoint of social behavior," and (2) a "Seminar in Metaphysics" described as "A study of relativity as it appeared in physical theory and its relation to the relativity in experience with which philosophy has been concerned."

6. This fact is documented in the notes of Harriet E. Penfield for the course (JRP, B 51, F 2). Mead gave a lecture on the contrast between modern and ancient logic, stressing the importance of the constructive, dynamic elements in judgment as examined by modern psychologists. Tufts gave a brief general history of logic, recommending a focus on judgment as "habit, a *way* of doing something" and thereby gaining a "*dynamic theory of the concept.*" A mimeographed transcript of Dewey's course that circulated privately among the students simply omitted this first class with Mead's and Tufts' lectures. And a critical edition of this transcript recently published in *The Class Lectures of John Dewey*, vol. 1 (Dewey 2010) makes no indication of this omission. John and Alice Dewey were returning from Hawaii, where John had given lectures and toured social conditions (see chapter 3); their return steamship was delayed.

7. Mead, for example, substituted for several weeks for Edward S. Ames in his Philosophy of Religion course in 1927 when Ames fell ill, as noted by Merritt Moore (1927, 40) and Howard M. Doner (letter to C. Morris, November 9, 1931, GHMP, B 2, F 3). When Mead himself fell ill in early 1931, his courses were taken over by Arthur E. Murphy and Herbert Blumer. The claims about joint teaching of the introductory courses are based on the published *Annual Register* of courses for the University of Chicago. Ellsworth Faris's notes indicate that Mead and A. W. Moore coordinated a two-quarter sequence on "Development of Thought in the Modern Period" autumn 1911–winter 1912 (EFP, vol. 1). The Instructors' Reports also indicate that in winter and spring 1918 Mead and Moore cotaught a two-quarter seminar on "Modern Logical Theory and Hegel's Phenomenology."

8. From a letter by John Dewey to President William Rainey Harper, April 10, 1894: "It is true, as I think I mentioned the first time we talked over men, that [Mead] had difficulty at first with his teaching, being entirely new to instruction. But he has learned his trade now, and there never was any complaint about his more advanced work" (Dewey 1997, no. 00503). Dewey made much the same comment in a letter to William James, March 15, 1903: "Mead has difficulty of articulation in written discourse as you know; but I suppose he is more effective than any man in our department in giving capable advanced students independent method" (no. 00797). As their first quarter at Chicago started, Dewey and Mead worked to figure out what to do with the unexpectedly large number of students in Mead's introductory logic lectures, ultimately deciding to give Mead several smaller sections and credit him the teaching hours in exchange for a quarter of leave.

Apparently students had complaints in one of Mead's early lecture courses, as William Rainey Harper, president of the University of Chicago, noted in a letter to Mead, May 20, 1898: "I am wondering whether it would be possible for you to make your Tuesday lectures more interesting to the students. A great many complaints have come that they are so thoroughly dry that nobody has any interest in them and the attitude, I am afraid, is one of general lack of interest. This being true on the part of good students as well as poor students. Of course the statements that come to my attention may have been all one-sided, but I have thought you should know that this feeling existed" (William Rainey Harper Papers [hereafter WRHP], B 4, F 7). The course referred to is either "Movements of Thought in the Eighteenth and Nineteenth Centuries" or "Introductory Logic."

9. That Mead designed the Social Consciousness seminar to work through the implications of the social psychology lectures with advanced students is indicated in part by existing records of the 1913 seminar from Ellsworth Faris (EFP, vol. 1), and in correspondence. For example, Donald Piatt wrote to Charles Morris on December 1, 1931, that he had notes from the Social Consciousness seminar "in which Mr. Mead followed up the argument of his social psychology" (GHMP, B 2, F 3). The seminar was consistently offered in the quarter immediately following the social psychology lectures.

10. In the period from 1913 to 1917 there was a major expansion occurring at the University of Chicago overall, with almost every academic unit growing substantially. The 1913–14 *Annual Register* reports 7,301 students registered overall and the 1916–17 *Annual Register* reports 10,448, with especially large increases in the university college, followed by the graduate schools, and the college of education.

11. It appears that, at least at first, these research courses may also have functioned somewhat as seminars. The first quarter it was offered (winter 1917, concurrently with the Social Psychology lectures), for example, there were nine students registered, including two visitors. The presence of visitors doesn't make sense if the course was merely a way to assign academic credit for independent research or grading.

12. J. H. Tufts to E. D. Burton, July 5, 1921; Memorandum "On the Facilities for the Graduate Work of the Department of Philosophy—In Particular, the Library," November 13, 1922 (University of Chicago Library Office of the Director Records [hereafter LODR], B 43, F 10). Tufts wrote, in particular, that the departmental library had occupied six spaces and was in need of being moved again (which it was). The library and seminar rooms of philosophy had apparently occupied several spaces in the Anatomy Building, the Harper Memorial Library, and the Classics Building (shifting within and between the last two several times), frequently in spaces too small for all the books to be regularly shelved and available.

13. Abbott (2011) details the importance of the "scholarly habitus" structured around access to and utilization of materials in departmental libraries in the early twentieth century, and the long-term shift away from this model toward centralized facilities and technical, specialized research tools in advanced scholarship. Grafton (2011) further examines the seminar as a workshop or "atelier" for the training of advanced students in the production of scholarship (focusing on its use in the development of American historical scholarship), a model originating in nineteenth-century German research universities (at which Mead, Tufts, and others had trained).

14. "On the Facilities for the Graduate Work . . . ," November 13, 1922, LODR, B 43, F 10. According to Tufts's memorandum, T. V. Smith, who was in 1922 an instructor in the philosophy department, told him that "when he first came to the University for graduate work he read several important books just because they met his eye upon the [philosophy library] shelves. He believes that he would not have read these, had they not been visible."

15. Mary McDowell was never technically a registered visitor, but she definitely

attended some of Mead's lectures along with philanthropist Ethel Sturges Dummer in spring 1909. McDowell wrote to Dummer, May 14, 1909, "Mr. [Joseph P.] Varkala tells me that Mr. M[ead]'s lectures are so fine. Meet Thursday at 4 P.M. in the basement of the Law Bld [Stuart Hall]—at the U[niversity] of C[hicago]—he lectures on socialism— The Philosophy of Marx. I want to go & wish you could also—if you can let me know & I will ask permission." Dummer must have expressed interest because she kept some brief notes on a lecture Mead gave, apparently in his spring 1909 "Development of Thought in the Modern Period" class, which is likely the class discussing socialism and Marx referred to by Varkala. Dummer summarized, "The evolution toward human relationship, based on home environment, away from church and ecclesiasticism, toward that of a neighborly consciousness existing on the basis of human relationships developed in the home life of the community" (ESDP, B 32, F 650). Thomas D. Eliot interviewed sixty social workers in the early 1920s regarding their opinions on sociology as a "pre-vocational subject" for social work, and he quoted both Caroline Hedger and Jessie Taft regarding their experiences in Mead's classes. Hedger apparently found them uselessly abstract while Taft thought them a "most valuable background for a vital approach to society" (Eliot 1924, 731–32).

16. During the summer of 1905, William James gave a set of lectures on "Pragmatism" at the University of Chicago that comprised an early version of his world-famous 1906 Lowell Institute lectures, published as *Pragmatism: A New Name for Some Old Ways of Thinking* (James 1907). As a graduate student, Walter Van Dyke Bingham took notes on James's Chicago lectures. Bingham recorded that James gave these lectures to the "Chicago School of Tho't" in order "to strengthen their hands" ("James," June 30, 1905, WVDB, Rl 1, F 9). The following summer J. Mark Baldwin gave another set of guest lectures, on "Genetic Logic," also attended by Bingham.

17. I have run a number of analyses attempting to find correlations that explain the appearance of lecture notes, but I do not substantively report them because they are inconclusive. For example, I find no relationship between the existing notes and the size of courses or their student composition. While the existing notes overall belonged primarily to students who continued to reference Mead in their later work, the same logic does not work in reverse—it does not appear to be true that students who referenced Mead in published work kept notes that ended up in archives. I think this indicates both that what ends up in archives is somewhat capricious, and that there is no single, direct relationship between taking good notes in class and becoming a public advocate of what one was taught.

18. Ernest B. Harper's notes are located in the Mead Papers (GHMP, B 15, F 13), as are Van Meter Ames's notes (GHMP, B 14, F 1), while Martin H. Bickham's notes are located in his own papers (Martin H. Bickham Papers [hereafter MHBP], B 1, F 14).

19. Earlier in my research I conducted several more formal analyses of lecture notes but found little that could stand up to scrutiny. For example, I compared the references to authors recorded by students from Mead's lectures and compared them over time. Although the results were sometimes suggestive—for example, that some names seem to stay (e.g., Darwin, Wundt, Dewey, James) while others come and go (e.g., L. T. Hobhouse, George Romanes, G. F. Stout)—I concluded that one can say almost nothing definitive about the comparative importance of one author to another over time in this

manner. Does the absence of a particular author mean that Mead did not mention him or her, that the student didn't recognize the reference, or that the student did not think it worth recording? On the converse, does the mention of a particular author mean that a definite reference was intended by Mead or does it represent the intervention of a student's own connections? I encountered the same problems when I conducted content analysis of the prevalence of substantive words and phrases over time. A formal content analysis that traced the usage of several substantive phrases in Mead's published works is reported by Goto (1996). This analysis served as much to point out the multiplicity of meanings in Mead's works as it did to clarify a definite set of propositions and concepts.

20. For example, Stuart A. Queen recalled in his unpublished autobiography, "At first I found Mead a bit difficult to understand. Had I not been already committed to Sociology, including Social Psychology, Mead might not have appealed to me. His manner of presentation was not immediately challenging or inspiring, but bit by bit I was convinced that he had something very important to offer; it might be difficult to grasp and its usefulness might not appear until later, but it would justify the effort involved in understanding" (Stuart Alfred Queen Papers [hereafter SAQP], B 1, F 1, p. 16). William P. Carter remarked in an interview about his graduate school days, "I even had old George Mead in a Philosophy course . . . he was brilliant. But we couldn't understand half of what he was talking about" (Department of Sociology Interviews [hereafter DSI], B 1, F 5, p. 6). T. V. Smith (1962, 46–47) related an anecdote in his autobiography, "I walked away from his first lecture with another graduate student. . . . 'Did you understand him?' I asked, as we left the lecture hall. 'No, did you?' he countered. 'I didn't, but I wish I had,' I responded, yearningly. We agreed, in less laconic talk, that Mead had more symptoms of greatness than any other professor we had known." Likewise, in the University of Chicago's graduation yearbook, *Cap and Gown* (8:370) for 1916, there is a humorous sketch of Mead that reads, "his lectures may steam by fifteen feet above your head, but even though you can get only the ands and ifs, it is worth while to be in one of his classes, just to know that the human mind can reach a point of development so far above your own."

21. Martin H. Bickham Papers at the University of Illinois–Chicago ([hereafter BUIC], B 5, F 33). The classes on Mead were June 25 and July 1, 1931. That folder also contains the final exams of his students. In Bickham's papers at the University of Chicago, one also finds a set of notecards tucked in with his notes from the 1921 Advanced Social Psychology course entitled "Suggestions from rereading Meade's [sic] Lectures" dated September 1924, which parallel many of the points in his "Educational Sociology" notes (MHBP, B 1, F 14).

22. In Van Meter Ames's papers at the University of Chicago there is a manuscript on "George Herbert Mead on Relativity," and in the Archival Biographical Files for Mead there are further manuscripts from Ames entitled "The Mind of Mead," "George Herbert Mead on the Self," "Mead and Zen," "Religion and Personality," and "Chapter XIV: Mead" that draw heavily and explicitly from Ames's notes in Mead's classes. One of the manuscripts even has Ames's handwritten remark that it contains "mostly a rewrite of some student notes on Mead" (Van Meter Ames Papers [hereafter VMAP], B 1, F 3; Archival Biographical Files [hereafter ABF], "Mead, George Herbert," F 1–2). Records for Ernest B. Harper are apparently not sufficient to follow out a similar analysis.

23. On exchanging notes, for example, Ellsworth Faris borrowed Colin A. McPheeters notes for Mead's social psychology lecture on January 25, 1912, and recorded them in his own notebook for the course (EFP, vol. 1). Dwight Sanderson had a complete typed set of notes from Grover G. Clark in his own records (see Sanderson 1916–17). On different note-taking styles, Howard P. Becker recalled, "At the time I was taking the course there was a woman graduate student, doing part-time instructing in Professor Ogburn's Statistics course, who had been hired to take stenographic notes and to transcribe them" (H. P. Becker to C. Morris, December 12, 1931, GHMP, B 2, F 3).

24. Maurice Price's notes from the 1909 Greek Philosophy are, from beginning to end, organized in an outline format (Maurice T. Price Papers [hereafter MTPP], B 1, F "History of Philosophy"). L. Foster Wood told Morris that in his notes "Many of the important sentences were taken virtually as given," and Orvil F. Myers wrote that he "did not get every word that Mr. Mead said, but all the words I have are verbatim" (L. W. Wood to C. Morris, November 2, 1931, and O. F. Myers to C. Morris, November 5, 1931, GHMP, B 2, F 3). Juliet Hammond reorganized the entirety of her 1910 notes from Social Psychology into an alphabetized list of topical entries in the style of an encyclopedia (GHMP, B 15, F 14). After his 1912 Social Psychology notes, Ellsworth Faris wrote brief summaries of all forty-two lectures along with a list of major concepts and a bibliography (EFP, vol. 1).

25. G. N. Pappas to C. Morris, November 4, 1931: "In regards to this paper of Social Psychology, which was nothing else but his notes re-arranged by me and given back to him to grade them, I hold a letter from Professor Mead in which he states that 'he found my paper excellent'" (GHMP, B 2, F 3).

26. For example, "I have two sets of notes for the social psychology course. I took the second set when I was grading papers for Mr. Mead in that course. . . . I remember that the notes are good for the *Greek Philosophy*, in which I graded papers for the course. I neglected to say [previously] that I have two full sets of notes for the *19th Century Thought* course, due to the fact that I was the grader in that course" (D. A. Piatt to C. Morris, December 1, 1931, GHMP, B 2, F 3).

27. Winifred Raushenbush simplified the spelling of her father's family name from at least the time of World War I, and continued to use that spelling throughout her life. I use her elected spelling in referring to her throughout this chapter, while using the older spelling to refer to her father, Walter Rauschenbusch. An extended discussion of Raushenbush's life may be found in Neil Gross's work on her son, Richard Rorty (Gross 2008, chap. 2).

28. "A little after effect of your visit [to Oberlin]: Miss Kitch is going to give us that course in social-psy. We rustled it thru just in the nick of time, as next years courses are definitely settled by the faculty to-morrow. Its to be given as a seminar, two hours some evening, on the discussion-plan. Miss Kitch is going to give us Mead's material and work up with the small group of 4–6 the development of the concept, its seeming immutability and influence on the group, by furnishing the method and letting us furnish the material. The idea of Miss Kitch's is one that I have been keen about this spring, because to me it was the most interesting factor in sociology" (W. Raushenbush to M. T. Price, August 4, 1915, MTPP, B 1, F "Winifred Rauschenbusch, 1915").

29. W. Raushenbush to M. T. Price, October 6 and November 5, 1915 (MTPP, B 1,

F "Winifred Rauschenbusch, 1915"). She went on to remark that the participants in the seminar were going to work on "a general concept of immortality" and "the social conditions that produce the concept of reincarnation."

30. Winifred Raushenbush to Walter Rauschenbusch, April 19, 1915 (Walter Rauschenbusch Collection [hereafter WRC], B 144, F 2). The extant notes from the seminar are those of Maurice Price, which I discovered by accident among his notes from the 1915 Social Psychology lecture course (MTPP, B 1, F "Course Notes, 1915"). I suspect that other students attended the discussion group, but the only people named by Price in the notes are Mead, Faris, and Raleigh W. Stone (later a professor of industrial relations at Chicago).

31. For example: "As far as men go we [Margaret Daniels and Winifred Raush-enbush] have among our callers a trinity of virtues: Maurice for beauty, Burke for brains, and Grover Clark for original artistic ability" (Winifred Raushenbush to Walter Rauschenbusch, October [?], 1917; WRC, B 144, F 2).

32. These claims are based primarily on analysis of the Examiners' and Instruc-tors' Grade Reports. Grover Clark's typed notes for the 1916 Logic of the Social Sciences course, along with other classroom materials, are available in general circulation in the Cornell University Library bound with the graduate coursework of rural sociologist E. Dwight Sanderson (see Sanderson 1916–17), who also took some of Mead's courses.

33. Winifred Raushenbush recalled later in a letter to Herbert Blumer, "I also had the pleasure of knowing Prof. Mead a little. I took a course on Kant with him. Helen Mead befriended me and I was often in their household" (W. [Raushenbush] Rorty to H. Blumer, April 13, 1966, Robert E. Park Collection [hereafter REPC], B 18, F 6). In addition, Raushenbush, Daniels, and Burke appear in letters and diary entries of Elinor Castle (esp. John U. and Elinor Castle Nef Papers [hereafter JENF], B 3, F 3; B 4, Item "Record 1918").

34. Letter from Winifred Raushenbush to Walter Rauschenbusch undated (c. 1917) (WRC, B 144, F 2). Raushenbush's correspondence with Price, preserved in the Price Papers (MTPP), discusses controversial topics of the day at length, including pacifism, radical social movements, Nietzsche, Freud, and Chinese philosophy. It should not go without notice that several in this group—for example, Raushenbush, Price, Faris— were children of Christian religious intellectuals who pursued training in the ministry themselves and who found something fundamentally intriguing in the provocative openness and experimentalism of Mead's (and W. I. Thomas's, and others') perspective. Something of the quasi-bohemian life of graduate students at Chicago in this period is conveyed in the anonymous, thinly veiled *roman à clef* critique of the University of Chicago entitled *Grey Towers: A Campus Novel* (1923). Elinor C. Nef speculated that the character "Mr. Staunton" was based on Mead (E. C. Nef to M. W. Castle, February 1, 1924, ECNP, B 14, F 8).

35. I. T. Mead to C. Morris, August 13, 1931 (GHMP, B 2, F 3), Charles Morris un-dated notes, c. December 1931 (GHMP, B 4, F 6).

36. It was apparently common practice in this period for students to cite lectures they heard, as I found numerous other references to lectures of over a dozen other Chicago faculty members in these same theses. The dissertations that directly cite the notes that were on file at the University of Chicago library are Fay B. Karpf's 1925

"American Social Psychology and Its European Background," Eyler N. Simpson's 1926 "Wishes: A Study in Social Psychology," Lien Chao Tzu's 1926 "Morality Studied From the Standpoint of Habits," Joseph L. Duflot's 1929 "A Social Psychological Study of the Failing Student in High School and College," and Leonard Cottrell's 1933 "The Reliability and Validity of a Marriage Study Schedule."

37. Smith's (1977) interviews with Chicago sociology graduate students from the 1920s indicate that virtually all the students remember Mead being discussed in conversation with one another, more than any other source of "social recognition" of Mead at that time. "The comments of some of these former graduate students suggest that frequently this social recognition was viewed as essential if they were going to grasp the meaning of what Mead was saying in the classroom. More important, Mead and his ideas were topics of conversation for sociology graduate students after 1920" (Smith 1977, 170–71).

38. The other students registered for the autumn 1894 Comparative Psychology course were Mary R. Alling Aber, an education student and former instructor at Oswego State Normal School; John Howard Moore, a high school biology teacher and later a popular author on evolution and philosophy; and Albert Judson Steelman, a divinity student previously employed by the social welfare services of Mexico City and later chaplain of the Illinois State Penitentiary and superintendent of the Society for the Friendless in Seattle. Steelman was technically a student in the department of "ecclesiastical sociology" in the divinity school, but I can find no records of him having been an instructor in sociology, let alone for courses in "anthropology" or "social development."

39. For example, from the very beginning of Juliet Hammond's notes from the winter 1911 Comparative Psychology course, is the claim that "animal—child—pathological—folk—all these could be indicated in definition of comparative psychology" (GHMP, B 15, F 14, p. 1).

40. From the notes of Irene Tufts (GHMP, B 14, F 11, pp. 43–46).

41. The shift in Mead's engagement with Wundt is traceable in his published works. Through 1903 Mead referred to Wundt's parallelistic physiological psychology, especially his examination of the nature of mental representations ("Vorstellungen") in consciousness. Beginning in 1904, Mead referred for the first time to Wundt's folk psychology and especially to his theory of the development of language through gesture. Mead viewed the folk psychology as the product of the "later years of [Wundt's] scientific activity," after a "lifetime of arduous labors" developing a "definite and commanding" psychological standpoint (Mead 1906c, 393). He thought that Wundt's later work "subjected the concepts and categories of the Wundtian psychology" previously developed to "searching test." That is, Mead viewed the Völkerpsychologie as the outgrowth of a new phase or task of Wundt's later career, one that was as much a revelation for Wundt as for Mead. This understanding is, I think, attributable to the fact that in Mead's intellectual biography he encountered Wundt's "folk psychology" only after its systematic publication beginning in 1900, rather than seeing its longer history in Wundt's work prior to the twentieth century. It is interesting to contrast this with Thomas, who was studying in Germany during the same years as Mead, and who took an early interest in Wundt's (and Lazarus's and Steinthal's) folk psychology (Bulmer 1986, 38).

42. The building in which the Meads and Thomases lived is no longer standing. Until he left, John Dewey lived in this building, and his apartment was apparently passed to the Meads. Helen Mead wrote to her niece Elinor Castle, November 19, 1906: "I wish you would join us for Thanksgiving Dinner. We shall be eighteen at the table, because we have so many guests—but how glad we should be to be *twenty*. Mrs. [Harriet Park] Thomas, who lives on the floor above us, is going to give the dinner with me, and the Tufts are all coming" (ECNP, B 6, F 4). And although the professional relationship between G. H. Mead and W. I. Thomas is somewhat hard to document, there are clear indications that they were meeting informally and discussing social psychology, race, and other issues during this period. For example, in a letter from Mead to Robert E. Park (before he was a Chicago faculty member), July 3, 1912 is found the following: "I received a note from Mr. Thomas just before leaving asking me to send you reprints of certain articles of mine in the field of Social Psychology. . . . It has been very pleasant to hear of you and your work from Mr. Thomas, and I hope that I may have the pleasure of seeing you and talking over matters of common interest before very long" (REPC, B 14, F 3).

George Mead's son, Henry C. A. Mead, was paid for work he did for W. I. Thomas during the time the families lived in the same building. At the time, Thomas had a workshop in which he occupied himself with various avocational experiments in cabinet making and designing golf equipment. Thomas even held two patents for improvements to the golf ball (US patents 809034, 809035, filed May 8, 1905), which described how to construct more effective golfballs by winding rubber around a hard core in successively more tensioned layers in order to improve the transfer of energy from the stroke to flight distance. Henry Mead wrote to Alice C. Dewey, "Mr. Thomas is making a new kind of golf ball which is the best kind made in the United States at the very least and I think it is in the world and I am sort of stuck up at having a job in the shop of the man who makes the best golf ball in the United States—perhaps in the world. My job is to separate the gutta percha from the rubber: my wages are 12½¢ a pound of gutta percha" (H. C. A. Mead to A. C. Dewey, August 1, 1905, Dewey 1997, no. 01442).

43. Both William A. and Edward B. Thomas initially declared majors in sociology and eventually chose other paths (Throop and Ward 2007b). Bill Thomas switched to medicine and became a Chicago physician; correspondence suggests that he was a frequent medical advisor to the Meads during Helen and George's later years. Edward Thomas took Mead's winter 1915 Social Psychology course. He later entered the American diplomatic corps, a career probably related to his activism with his mother and others on behalf of peace during World War I. He was for a period attached to the State Department mission in Russia. Mead also taught Bill's wife, Ruth Newberry, who was the director of the short-lived Bureau of Social and Civic Information in Chicago, a clearinghouse of social reform data that listed Mead, W. I. Thomas, and Charles R. Henderson as constituting its advisory board.

44. Incidentally, Abbott and Egloff (2008) claim that it was W. I. Thomas rather than his son W. A. "Bill" Thomas who gave a presentation on Freud in Mead's 1913 course. The registration records show that W. A. Thomas was a regular student for this class, and I think it more plausible that he is the person who gave this talk. In either case, the overall point remains the same.

45. For the discussion of Thomas's presentation see the Faris Papers (EFP, vol. 1., notes for February 13 and March 17, 1913). In Juliet Hammond's notes for Comparative Psychology winter 1911 there is a discussion of pathological psychology in which Mead apparently argued that studies of "dissociation" were "very valuable" and "becoming more so" in that they show "the structure of consciousness." Mead appears to have referred to Morton Prince's "psychological dime novel" *The Dissociation of a Personality* (1905) in his discussion of the ethical problems of constructing a new self out of conflicting past selves, and he elaborated his concepts of "I" and "me" in the context of that discussion. Mead also apparently referred to the biblical theme of the "Old Adam" and "New Adam" from St. Paul's letters and to Robert Louis Stevenson's "Dr. Jekyll and Mr. Hyde" to help make the point (GHMP, B 15, F 14, pp. 1, 59, 85).

46. Many of the extant lecture notes from 1913 onward in Mead's social psychology courses refer to Freud. They discuss Freud's notion of the "censor" as a form of internalized social control—often compared with Mead's "me"; they also discuss Freud's notion of "complexes" as ideas or behavior that takes place without consciousness of the stimulus, and Freud's analysis of wit and humor, which Mead examined as a phenomenon in which the laughing individual fundamentally puts him- or herself in the place of another. According to his correspondence, Mead also undertook a review of Freud's work in July 1914 that was apparently never published (G. H. Mead to H. C. A. Mead, July 12, 1914, GHMP, B 1, F 7). He was apparently working with the proposal that a more adequate explanation of dream censorship could begin with a focus on the lack of contextualizing situations in dreams (perhaps a nod to Bergson's similar analysis) such that "what would be mere thought images in our waking hours become objective occurrences in our dreams, and . . . ideas which would be perfectly harmless as ideas would appear in a compromising form if the ideas were outside situations, thus there arise all sorts of more or less conscious effort to change and modify these dream images with the result of the fantasies and grotesquerie which amaze our waking hours when we remember the shadowy occurrences of the night."

47. Mead did not forget Thomas. In his "Cooley's Contribution to American Social Thought" he noted the work of Thomas, along with Park, Burgess, and Faris as constituting a more consistently "behavioristic" sociology than Cooley's (Mead 1930b, 704–5). Note also the remarkably broad and action-theoretic connotation this gives to the term "behaviorism" in Mead's thought. Mead also assigned Kimball Young's *Source Book for Social Psychology* (1927; modeled after Thomas's *Source Book for Social Origins*) in his late Advanced Social Psychology classes, a text that included several important selections from Thomas's writings. And Thomas did not forget Mead. In the *Proceedings of the Second Colloquium on Personality Investigation* it was Thomas, not Herbert Blumer, Harry Stack Sullivan, Harold Lasswell, or any other notables present who had taken courses with or had extend acquaintance with Mead, who contributed items by Mead to the general bibliography for the conference (*Proceedings* 1929, 198). The works Thomas recommended were "The Behavioristic Account of the Significant Symbol" and "The Genesis of the Self and Social Control," both works written after he left Chicago, indicating that he continued to follow Mead's work.

48. Mead was familiar not only with Watson's experiments, but also with the work of several other experimental psychology students at Chicago during this period. Jessie

Blount Allen, for example, wrote in her 1904 dissertation on *The Associative Processes of the Guinea Pig* that "it was suggested by Mr. G. H. Mead that the reactions of the guinea pig might be direct responses to immediate contact stimuli, and that a distant stimulus, e.g., a recollection of the path, was not responsible for the reaction" (334). And in his social psychology lectures for 1912, Mead mentioned Wallace Craig's 1909 dissertation on *The Expressions of Emotion in the Pigeons* (Mead 1982, 54). Craig, in turn, acknowledged his indebtedness to Mead and W. I. Thomas for reading and critiquing an accompanying article on "The Voices of Pigeons Regarded as a Means of Social Control" (Craig 1908, 86). Watson was also involved in experiments on language and imitation in monkeys (see Watson 1908), which must have intrigued Mead, as was apparently implied in Watson's autobiographical statement.

49. The earliest surviving notes from Mead's Comparative Psychology course that I am able to find are from the winter 1900 course, taken by H. Heath Bawden. In those notes we find the following statement: "If intelligence is to be cut off at the point where we can find consciousness of the type of our own [i.e., human intelligence] any attempt to make a study of comparative psychology might as well be given up at the start. If we regard our own activity then as simply the expression of an intellectual faculty which is without any connection with the environment, except that it happens to be there, then we have practically cut ourselves off from the lower forms. We can state this intelligence of ours in its objective phase, however, so that it can be compared with the lower. We can state it in terms of control. In the lower form this control must be one over the food environment, over the vegetable environment. This is not a statement which is at all alien to that of human intelligence" (JRP, B 42, F 2, p. 72).

50. From Juliet Hammond's notes for the winter 1911 Comparative Psychology course: "Animal imagery = kinaesthetic. This much proved here [Chicago] by Prof. Watson and Prof. Carr. We depend largely on kinaesthetic imagery to get skill" (GHMP, B 15, F 14, p. 15).

51. Mead's paper was originally entitled "The Relation of Imitation to the Theory of Animal Perception" and was given December 28, 1906, along with Watson's "Kinaesthetic Sensations: Their Rôle in the Reactions of the White Rat to the Hampton Court Maze" at Columbia University. Mead's paper was significantly revised and published as "Concerning Animal Perception" in 1907; the original paper was itself published much later (see Mead 2001). At the same 1906 APA meeting William James gave his famous "The Energies of Men" address and James R. Angell defined "The Province of Functional Psychology."

52. All existing sets of notes from 1915 and later that I have been able to examine from Mead's social psychology courses have references to works by Watson, and those that contain bibliographic lists indicate that Mead consistently assigned portions of either his 1914 *Behavior* or his 1919 *Psychology*.

53. All three sets of student notes from the winter 1921 Advanced Social Psychology course attest to Mead's favorable references to behaviorism (GHMP, B 14, F 1, and B 15, F 13; MHBP, B 1, F 14). Mead's later position is well known through the medium of *Mind, Self, and Society*; the introductory section of that work that discuss Mead's relation to Watson comes primarily from a stenographic transcript made in Mead's winter 1928 Advanced Social Psychology course.

54. Much of the appeal, as well as the danger, of behaviorism to people like Mead and Dewey was its promise of conceptual clarity. Dewey wrote that "the notion of behavior is already having a simplifying and reducing effect upon epistemology," but that in its rush to deny the "subjective and private metaphysics" of previous psychological concepts, it was in danger of "oversimplifying," "omitting and virtually denying obvious facts"—the one "marked exception" Dewey found to this oversimplification was in Mead's work (Dewey 1922, 7). For his part, Mead found the "value and advantage of the behavioristic account of mind" to be found in its identification of communication as the essential feature of the "mind," but cautioned that behaviorists like Watson did not take into account how vocal stimuli were "essential elements in elaborate social processes and carry with them the value of those social processes" (Mead 1934, 50, 69).

55. From Charles Morris's notes in Mead's winter 1924 Advanced Social Psychology course (Charles Morris Collection [hereafter CMC], B 20, F 4, p. 1).

56. Both Moore and Ames took courses with Mead in 1895 (including the same Methodology of Psychology course that Thomas took). As mentioned earlier in the chapter, Moore and Mead later traded off teaching courses in the history of philosophy over the years and even taught consecutive seminar sequences designed to build on one another. Moore's wife, Ella Adams Moore, was a compatriot of Mead's in his work at the Vocational Supervision League. And Mead later taught the history of philosophy to their daughter, Catherine Moore. Mead taught all of the Ames children—Van Meter, Damaris, Adelaide, and Polly—over the years. And as mentioned above, he also took over lectures in Ames's course on the Philosophy of Religion at least once. That the work of their children sometimes had an impact on the understandings these professors had of one another is demonstrated in the following anecdote collected by Elinor Castle Nef: "Jimmie [Angell, son of Chicago psychology professor James R. Angell] told me that he and Donald Jordan [Henry Donaldson Jordan, son of Chicago biology professor E. O. Jordan] when they were taking graduate work here [at Chicago] decided to elect a course with Uncle George [Mead]. They found, as they sat in class listening to him lecture, that they could not make head or tail of what he was saying. It was almost meaningless and incomprehensible. They consulted together as to what they had better do about it and decided to stick to the course and simply religiously make notes of all he said. They did this until the end of the term when the course was completed and then met together in long sessions with their note books to summarize, reinterpret, outline, and translate into English what they had taken down from his flow of talk. I do not know philosophy, and I cannot remember exactly what they found, but it turned out to be something not uninteresting and not altogether unoriginal according to Jimmie's story, which they termed a form of behaviorism, applied to social psychology. Jimmie told his Father and reported him as saying—'Oh, is that what George Mead professes, in all these years I have never known what he was trying to get at'" (ECNP, B 26, F 4).

57. That there was real and continued effort in Mead's attempts to create productive classroom environments is also evidenced in part by the evident difficulties he had teaching early in his career, as letters from John Dewey and William Rainey Harper quoted above indicate. These difficulties go back at least to his jobs teaching and tutoring after college (Cook 1993, 6–10). But as Dewey noted, he worked progressively to get his pedagogical "bearings." Floyd Allport (1924, 404), an early social psychologist

sympathetic to many of Mead's concerns, seemed also to note the connection between Mead's theoretical work on the social nature of pedagogy and the practical structuring of classrooms when he wrote that "teachers are becoming more and more impressed by the possibilities of face-to-face relations. Recitation now involves more discussion and interchange of ideas than formerly. Classes are sometimes subdivided into small discussion groups. In some colleges the inauguration of a tutorial system serves the same purpose. The modern teacher is more than a mere monitor for keeping the student fixed upon the right course; she serves as an interlocutor by whose aid the student acquires a deeper understanding of the lesson (Mead). The chief benefits to be derived from this method are increased incentive for thought, heightened interested, development of self-expressive personality traits, discovery of facts and viewpoints through discussion, and training in social values and desirable forms of behavior."

CHAPTER FIVE

1. A revised edition of *Mind, Self, and Society* is currently being prepared by the University of Chicago Press, which includes a new preface by Hans Joas and an appendix by the present author. The appendix compares the published text of the book with the source materials paragraph by paragraph, identifying many of the most substantial differences between the texts (Huebner 2015).

2. ISI Web of Science citation searches I conducted in the winter of 2009 and 2010 indicated that four-fifths of all article citations to G. H. Mead in social scientific journals since 1956 are citations to *Mind, Self, and Society*. In social psychology journals nine out of every ten citations recorded have been to that work. Although the exact figures are not definitive because this database is not exhaustive, such a measure does indicate the strong reliance upon *Mind, Self, and Society* among a large number of published articles since 1956 in major academic journals. These analyses are more fully discussed in chapter 7.

3. To acknowledge a few of the most negative early reviews, Wilson Wallis remarked, "One is tempted to regret this flaunting of the lecturer's implied wish that these words of his go no farther than the ears of his classroom hearers. . . . There are times when it is wise as well as appropriate to respect the wishes of the deceased" (1935, 459). Eduard C. Lindeman (1935, 280) wrote that while the "editor has made a valiant attempt to perform this service [of systematizing Mead's thought] in the present volume through the use of lecture notes," he "regret[ted] the obligation to say that it seems to me that the effort has not been successful. Dr. Morris has performed an excellent logical feat in arranging Mead's material under meaningful categories but the material itself lacks flow and form." F. C. S. Schiller wrote, "The edited . . . 'Mead' therefore read[s] like mediumistic messages from the departed rather than the living [man], and raise[s] the old ethical issue how far discipular piety should turn into books lectures not intended for publication. . . . In this case I should judge that the basic text was too conscientious: it omitted all the jokes and illustrations which must have enlivened the original lectures, but retained too many of the repetitions of the central ideas which are demanded by the lecture form" (1936a, 83). Mead's long-time colleague Ellsworth Faris (1936, 809) was perhaps the first and most direct in charging that "the editor has, un-

fortunately, seen fit to give [the social psychology lectures] another title and has taken the liberty to rearrange the material in a fashion that will be deprecated by many who knew Mead and thought they understood him."

4. This second Festschrift was intended at least in part as a response to the so-called Hutchins Controversy during which Robert Maynard Hutchins, the newly appointed president of the University of Chicago, attempted to reshape the character of the philosophy department through appointments by executive fiat and spoke disparagingly about the accomplishments of the current philosophy faculty members. As a result, Tufts resigned from the department in protest, followed by Mead a year later, along with their junior colleagues Arthur E. Murphy, E. A. Burtt, and Everett Hall (Cook 1993, 183ff.). Correspondence in the Charles Morris Collection (B 1, F 1931a–c) indicates that considerable initial impetus for the second Festschrift had come from Mead's long-time colleagues, John Dewey and Edward S. Ames.

5. The Paul A. Carus Lectures are a series of three lectures given in conjunction with the American Philosophical Association meetings awarded to eminent philosophers in exchange for granting publication rights to the Open Court Publishing Company, for which Paul Carus had been founding editor. John Dewey and A. O. Lovejoy had given Carus Lecture series prior to Mead's lectures in Berkeley, California, in late December 1930.

6. Murphy was chosen in part no doubt because the topic of the lectures was close to his own interest in the metaphysics of process philosophy. And despite not being a former student of Mead, himself, he demonstrated a strong loyalty to Mead and the tradition of the Chicago philosophy department when he resigned alongside Mead in the Hutchins Controversy. Murphy was among the audience to Mead's Carus lecture series.

7. J. Dewey to C. Morris, May 5, 1931; E. S. Ames to C. Morris, May 6, 1931 (CMC, B 1, F 1931c). See also Murphy's (1932) introduction to *The Philosophy of the Present*.

8. E. S. Ames to C. Morris, May 6, 1931; E. S. Ames to C. Morris, May 28, 1931 (CMC, B 1, F 1931c).

9. E. S. Ames to C. Morris, May 6, 1931; C. Morris to E. S. Ames, May 11, 1931 (CMC, B 1, F 1931c). After the resignations of Mead, Murphy, Burtt, and Hall, Charles Morris was invited to return to Chicago to take up an associate professorship in philosophy, an invitation about which he was strongly conflicted. Arthur Murphy notified Morris of the resignations saying, "I think the president [Hutchins] will find it difficult to get self-respecting men to join the department under existing conditions" (A. E. Murphy to C. Morris, February 18, 1931, CMC, B 1, F 1931a). Because of Murphy's letter Morris worried that "some people here [at Chicago] and elsewhere might resent my coming" or see it as "immoral double-crossing of those who felt it necessary to resign" (telegram from C. Morris to G. E. Morris, March 27, 1931; circular letter from Morris [unaddressed], March 31, 1931, CMC, B 1, F 1931a). He discussed the decision with a number of close friends at Chicago, and he was reportedly encouraged to take the position by Mead himself in the weeks before he died, which was an influential factor in Morris's decision (C. Morris to G. H. Mead, April 10, 1931, CMC, B 1, F 1931b).

Morris's acceptance of this offer, far from being interpreted as "double-crossing," was widely seen as an important step in preserving the pragmatist character of the philosophy department. For example, former Chicago graduate student C. F. Arrowood wrote that his appointment showed that "the work of Mr. Dewey, Mr. Moore, Mr. Tufts, and Mr. Mead will be carried forward from the point at which they laid it down there" (C. F. Arrowood to C. Morris, April 12, 1931, CMC, B 1, F 1931b). Morris quite literally took over Mead's place in that he moved into Mead's former office, a gesture which must also have made it easier to coordinate Mead's manuscripts and effects (E. S. Ames to C. Morris, May 15, 1931, CMC, B 1, F 1931c).

10. E. S. Ames to C. Morris, May 15, 1931 (CMC, B 1, F 1931c).

11. C. Morris to E. S. Ames, May 10, 1931; E. S. Ames to C. Morris, May 28, 1931 (CMC, B 1, F 1931c).

12. E. S. Ames to C. Morris, May 28, 1931 (CMC, B 1, F 1931c). Irene Tufts Mead's father, James H. Tufts, had apparently been pursuing the question of whether Mead's earlier contract with Henry Holt for a book of essays (in 1910–11, which remained unpublished until 2001 [cf. Mead 2001; Orbach 1998]) could be made the basis for an agreement.

13. Unlike Arthur Murphy and Charles Morris, who were both rising stars in tenure-track positions when they were asked to work on their respective projects, Merritt H. Moore was still an instructor at Chicago, who had taken courses with Mead but who did not consider himself "as great an admirer of Mr. Mead as were some others of his students and colleagues" (Moore 1936, ix). In addition to being recommended by Murphy, he had a strong interest in the history of philosophy (especially French philosophy) and was apparently working out of Ames's office at the time, helping to explain his selection. Moore went on to a long-term tenured position in philosophy at Knox College, a position he first accepted while still editing the transcript of notes that was subsequently published as *Movements of Thought in the Nineteenth Century* (Mead 1936).

14. Laing memo, August 8, 1933; C. Morris to H. C. A. Mead, April 5, 1934 (UCPR, B 323, F 8).

15. Neither the claim that these are the notes prepared by Stuart A. Queen, a former sociology graduate student at Chicago nor that they are from the autumn 1912 course is indisputable. Both claims are supported by Cook (1993, 195–96) and Lewis and Smith (1980, 276) from their respective readings of Charles Morris's notes to himself (GHMP, B 4, F 6). At the top of a sheet in Morris's handwriting that quotes passages from this manuscript for possible inclusion in *Mind, Self, and Society*, Morris appears to have written "Queen 1912," but the note may have been merely Morris's hunch about its possible author and date (and it may also be read "Quinn"). For purposes of referring to these notes in the following analysis I have provisionally accepted the interpretation of Cook, Lewis, and Smith in order to distinguish them from other sets of notes. According to correspondence, G. H. Mead had seen these notes and thought highly of them, although Morris was ambivalent about their quality (C. Morris to I. T. Mead, August 21, 1931, GHMP, B 2, F 3). The manuscript was subsequently published in an edited version by David L. Miller as part of *The Individual and the Social Self* (Mead 1982), although it was labeled there as coming from 1914 and without attribution to a note-taker. No indication is given in that volume concerning how Miller came to this conclusion. For his part, Stuart Queen later recalled, "I took very full notes which I read and re-read,

annotated, and summarized. (Unhappily they have long since disappeared.) To me it was a new universe of discourse and I had to 'learn the language'" (SAQP, B 1, pp. 16–17).

16. C. Morris to I. T. Mead, July 29, 1931 (GHMP, B 2, F 3).

17. I. T. Mead to C. Morris, August 13, 1931 (GHMP, B 2, F 3). Irene Mead also remarked in this letter that the "printing of things that were not intended for print is sometimes a doubtful business."

18. C. Morris to I. T. Mead, August 21, 1931 (GHMP, B 2, F 3). For a rising young professional the task of editing these materials must have been exceedingly tedious. Indeed, Morris begged to point out to the University of Chicago Committee on Humanistic Research that "the work he is doing is not merely editorial, and that the production of the volumes has necessitated a great deal of real research work" (memo from G. J. Laing to Olmstead, August 28, 1933, University of Chicago Division of the Humanities Research Grants Records [hereafter HRGR], B 3, F 17). And when the volume was close to publication he wrote to John Dewey that "the key volume based on the social psychology material has taken much spare time for two years, but is now coming out very nicely" (C. Morris to J. Dewey, June 19, 1933, CMC, B 1, F 1931c).

19. Indeed, in his response to Morris, Martin H. Bickham explicitly noted that Smith's article "seems to precipitate the plans" for the publication of posthumous volumes, coming as it did on the heels of Morris's own circular letter (M. H. Bickham to C. Morris, November 12, 1931, GHMP, B 2, F 3). Note that Smith's memorial article mentions "forthcoming" posthumous volumes three years before even the first of the volumes was actually forthcoming. By October 1931 Smith (1931, 371) had also examined the manuscript notes for "Movements of Thought in the Nineteenth Century," which he was "drawing loosely here upon" to help substantiate his analysis of Mead's "social psychology."

20. There is considerable evidence from matched quotations from a few of these theses to suggest that the notes from Mead's social psychology course once on file at the University of Chicago library are the same as those attributed to Stuart A. Queen from 1912 that Morris had in his possession, although as I indicate in chapter 4 there was also speculation that this set could have been authored by Margaret Daniels.

21. The most well known of these attempts was that of George Anagnos and Alwin Carus, discussed further in the text, but correspondence indicates that there were several other students who explicitly considered publishing their own notes. Particularly determined in this respect was George N. Pappas, who wrote to Morris, "Last July I conceived the idea to publish the lectures of Mr. Mead myself. . . . Last month I made an agreement with the Athens Publishing Co., to publish in a pamphlet form, the notes on Social Psychology. . . . I took them down for the sake of publishing them, and I made a point not to use my own words" (G. N. Pappas to C. Morris, November 4, 1931, GHMP, B 2, F 3). Pappas' notes were not subsequently published, but were used in part by Morris in the preparation for his Mead volumes.

22. A. Meyer to G. H. Mead, January 26, 1926 (Adolf Meyer Collection [hereafter AMC], Unit I/2636, F 1). Meyer wrote, "I wish I could do my share to induce you, by the way, to think favorably of the suggestion that Miss [Ethel] Kawin's notes of your [social psychology] lectures might become more widely accessible and that more of

your courses might be treated that way. So many of us would derive a great advantage through this, and your more favored neighbors and hearers [in Chicago] would get such a fine basis for discussions!" Irene Mead and Charles Morris speculated about what had become of this set of notes in their own discussions.

23. Morris's notes to himself (GHMP, B 4, F 6) indicate that he paid Louis Bloom and Eugene W. Sutherland to transcribe their shorthand notes. Bloom, who had worked for Alwin Carus transcribing Mead's lectures earlier, was apparently part of an informal pool of former Chicago students willing to take up temporary clerical positions with Chicago-based projects or organizations through the University of Chicago Office of Employment at this time. Morris's correspondence with Robert R. Page indicates that Page was asked to write up his notes in order to fill them out. Page described the process of rewriting his notes as follows: "They're quite rough, and in typing them I have made only such revisions or alterations as were necessary to put them into grammatical English. To what extent they are 'straight Mead,' and to what extent they are my own expression and interpretation of Mead's thought, I'm quite unable to tell" (R. R. Page to C. Morris, October 14, [1932?], GHMP, B 3, F 2). George E. M. Shelburg's notes, as Morris received them, had been submitted as term papers and graded by Mead in their respective courses. As Shelburg indicates in the preface to one of the sets: "The present aim [in writing up the notes] is to offer, so far as possible, a faithful interpretation of the matter *as presented*, so that only to minor degree has there been alteration and thus, generally, by way of further illustrative material, or re-arrangement" (GHMP, B 8, F 5; emphasis in original). All four of these reconstructed note sets—from Bloom, Sutherland, Page, and Shelburg—ultimately contributed content to the published *Mind, Self, and Society*.

24. The fact that, in most cases, Morris preserved both the original notes and his notes on them provides a wealth of data about the material construction of the published volume. He appears to have returned some to their original owners, as in the case of Clifford P. Osborne's 1930 Social Psychology notes, which are not located in the George Herbert Mead Papers. He also kept his own notes from his courses with Mead among his own papers, deposited near the end of his life at the Institute for American Thought in Indianapolis. The records of the construction of the later two volumes, *Movements of Thought in the Nineteenth Century* and *The Philosophy of the Act*, are not nearly as complete, because the original manuscript materials upon which they are based have not been as faithfully preserved.

25. For example, Juliet Hammond, a master's degree student in 1910–11, prepared uniquely full notes for four of Mead's courses. These notes have since been deposited in the George Herbert Mead Papers (GHMP, B 8, F 8–9; B 15, F 14), and an edited version of one of the sets has been published as *The Philosophy of Education* (Mead 2008a). Notes from an unidentified early course of Mead's taken down by H. Heath Bawden have also recently come to light and been published (Mead 2008b). A listing of the existing sets of notes forms an appendix to this study.

26. This topic was discussed in some detail in chapter 3. In the classrooms where these notes originated, they were essential to students' practical attempts to understand the implications of the perspective developed by Mead, and were thus deeply contextual documents. In his courses, Mead lectured without written notes. Thus, their

notes evidence students' attempts to engage with a dynamic perspective that emerged through the lectures, some of whom reworked their notes to make them more orderly or understandable. However, in bringing notes from various courses authored by different students all under one rubric of comparison, they were treated as a medium for the more or less correct recording and relaying of a delimited body of what could count as Mead's theory.

27. Alwin C. Carus was an executive at the Carus Chemical Corporation run by his family and at various times worked in his family's Open Court Publishing Company. He had been a University of Chicago student, but had never registered for a course with Mead. The Carus family was also known for its interest in philosophy; indeed, his father was Paul A. Carus, after whom the eponymous lectures are named. George Anagnos was a former student of Mead who went on to become a local historian and librarian in the Works Progress Administration after a period working temporary jobs with railroad construction gangs.

28. C. Morris to H. C. A. and I. T. Mead, June 3, 1932 (GHMP, B 2, F 3). Henry Mead asked the University of Chicago Press for its legal opinion on the claims of ownership of the Carus collection. Mead's attorney had thought the University likely owned the rights to them, but the editor of the press informed Mead that the University would not pursue any claim to ownership, and he proposed that Henry, as representative of G. H. Mead's estate, was the legitimate owner of the rights to the materials. Alwin Carus was entitled to compensation for his work preparing the manuscripts, according to this interpretation, but he did not own publication rights (D. P. Bean to G. J. Laing, September 29, 1931; G. J. Laing to H. C. A. Mead, September 29, 1931; G. J. Laing to D. P. Bean, November 11, 1931; UCPR, B 323, F 8).

29. Morris had apparently examined the transcript Carus had prepared for the 1928 Advanced Social Psychology course as early as February 1932 and had compared in carefully against other manuscripts by April 1932, but he did not have free use of it until the notes were purchased from Carus (see C. Morris to A. Carus, February 15, 1932; C. Morris to A. Carus, April 18, 1932, Alwin C. Carus Papers [hereafter ACCP], Box 3, Folder 4).

30. In Morris's preface to the volume he mistakenly identifies this set as coming from 1927. Substantial correspondence and supporting notes taken by Morris himself indicates that it is from 1928. Additionally, each lecture recorded in the transcript begins with a notation of the complete date, including 1928 as the year. He apparently made a simple typographical error in dating them that has remained through all the reprints of the volume and much of the secondary literature.

Although the stenographer who took the notes is not identified anywhere in *Mind, Self, and Society*, or in anything written by Charles Morris, a note at the end of the original transcript provides the name W. T. Lillie and a Chicago address (GHMP, B 2, F 17). Further genealogical research in the 1930 US Census enumerator's schedules, local Sanborn maps, and other sources indicates that this is almost certainly a reference to Walter Theodore Lillie, a former University of Chicago business undergraduate student who became an accountant for Walgreen's Drug Company. This research also suggests that it may actually have been his wife, Mary Ann Lillie (née Hatch), who took down and transcribed the notes, since she was explicitly identified in the 1930 Census as a "stenographer" by profession. It would not be surprising to find that, given the structure of gender relations at the time, she asked for correspondence to be addressed with her husband's name. As far as I know, this is the first research that has been able to suggest an identity for the stenographer of this important document beyond what is available from the transcript itself.

31. Omission was Morris's solution, for example, to the 1928 stenographer's attempt to transliterate the German term *"Vorstellung"* as "(porstellmundt)" and the Latin *"hostis"* as "(hastis?)" (GHMP, B 2, F 10–17, pp. 49, 163). In the first case Mead discussed the term, it appears, as part of his attempt to explain the problems of Wundt's "parallelistic" psychology that his own theory would overcome: Wundt had to assume psychical ideas—*Vorstellungen*—as somehow connected to physiological conditions or acts without being able to explain how those ideas emerge in gestural communication. In the second, Mead was making a point about the ambiguity of the encounter with a stranger by recourse to amateur etymology—*hostis* is related both to "hostile," as in an enemy relation, and to "host," as in an amicable relation to a guest.

32. Indeed, a JSTOR search conducted in winter 2011 indicates that the first mention of the phrase "universal discourse" in any journal indexed by that resource was in a 1936 article quoting from *Mind, Self, and Society* (i.e., Brewster 1936, 545).

A set of notes for the 1928 course taken by student Wayne A. R. Leys does not include the phrase "universal discourse" but does include the phrase "universe of discourse" twice, including at least once in a context parallel to one in which the stenographer's transcript reports the phrase "universal of discourse" (Wayne A. R. Leys Papers [hereafter WARL], B 9, F 3, p. 19, 39). Leys' notes also seem to suggest that the hired stenographer may have missed references Mead made to works by Wolfgang Köhler, Alexander Bain, C. S. Sherrington, and C. H. Cooley (all of whom are discussed in Kimball Young's *Source Book for Social Psychology* [1927] that Mead assigned in 1928), although it is of course possible that Leys editorialized these references from his own concerns and previous coursework.

33. In preparing an appendix to the new revised edition of *Mind, Self, and Society* (Huebner 2015), I came across a variety of other words that Morris apparently substituted for what he took to be errors in transcription by the stenographer: including substituting "innervation" for "enervation" in the transcript, "actor" for "act," "James's" for "Daine's," "common whole" for "common fold," "chasm" for "cavern," "inorganic" or "own organic," and "differentiated selves" for "differentiated cells."

34. J. G. Randall's (1937, 535) review explicitly notes this problem of transcription errors from impromptu speech to abbreviated notation and then to a typed transcript: "the reviewer [i.e., Randall] offers a guess with regard to a passage in the first chapter [of *Movements of Thought*]. The intellectual or scientific world of the Middle Ages, so the passage reads, was 'all shot through with magic and historiology' (p. 4). In his skepticism concerning any meaning for 'historiology' in this connection the undersigned begs to suggest that the word spoken was 'astrology,' and it may be added that, if 'historiology' is an error, it is precisely the type of error that would arise in transmuting stenographic symbols into words." There were many reviews of *Movements of Thought* (more than the other volumes, see chapter 7), and they varied widely in tone. Certainly one of the most negative was Charles F. Mullett (1937, 115–16), who wrote in the *Psychological*

Bulletin: "Those persons who share in the responsibility for the publication of *Movements of Thought in the Nineteenth Century* can rest assured that they have done the late George Mead a great and, what under the circumstances is worse, an unnecessary disservice. . . . By reducing the jejune obviousness and verbosity, the short-cut generalizations, the dubious assumptions, the loaded words—in short, the paraphernalia of the classroom—an *editor* could have produced a volume that would stimulate the specialist and inform the general reader. If perchance this could not be done, why disinter the corpse?" (emphasis in original).

35. GHMP (B 2, F 10–17, 1928 transcript, pp. 167–69).

36. R. D. Hemens to D. P. Bean, June 16, 1933 (UCPR, B 323, F 8).

37. That the exposition of this early set of notes follows the pattern "mind"–"self"–"society" was acknowledged unintentionally by David L. Miller when he published an edited version of the notes in 1982 along with a set from winter 1927 rewritten and submitted by George Shelburg as a class paper later that year (Mead 1982). From his memory and incomplete records of fifty years previous, Miller claimed that the notes were from 1914 and implicitly that they had not been used in the composition of *Mind, Self, and Society*. But, on the basis of the notes he was publishing, he argued, "I believe that *Mind, Self, and Society*, as published, presents Mead's thinking in the order he presented it to his classes" (Miller 1982, 1, 2–3).

38. The quotations in the text come from 1928 stenographic transcript, p. 300 (GHMP, B 2, F 17).

39. Several reviewers noted that the published topical organization of material actually reversed the logical development of concepts in Mead's theory; instead of mind and self developing from society, society appears—at least in the exposition—after mind and self (Faris 1936; Schiller 1936). The reorganization and composition of *Mind, Self, and Society* is traced in detail in my appendix to the revised edition of that text (Huebner 2015).

40. D. P. Bean to R. D. Hemens, July 9, 1933 (UCPR, B 323, F 8). Morris had first used the phrase "social behaviorist" in a review of works by John F. Markey and Grace de Laguna, linking their works with those of Dewey and Mead (Morris 1929). Markey, who had studied with Mead's students Ellsworth Faris and L. L. Bernard, was the first to use the the term to describe his own perspective (Markey 1928); see chapter 6.

41. Memo of meeting between C. Morris and G. J. Laing, July 26, 1933 (UCPR, B 323, F 8). Indeed, one could even speculate that Morris patterned the main title of the work on C. Lloyd Morgan's 1926 *Life, Mind, and Spirit*, which he explicitly contrasted with Mead's view of symbolization in an early article (Morris 1927, 289). As chapter 6 indicates, Morris more than once used allusions to other works in titles and typically analyzed intellectual structures into trichotomies, perhaps on the basis of his reading of fundamental threes in the works of Mead and Peirce.

42. R. R. Page to C. Morris, November 22, [1931?] to July 30, [1933?] (GHMP, B 2, F 3; B 3, F 1; B 3, F 2). As mentioned in a footnote above, Page rewrote the material in a way that caused him to be unable to distinguish how much they were "straight Mead" and how much his own "interpretation." After his graduate work at Cambridge, Page went on to become a long-time professor of philosophy at the University of Illinois–Chicago.

43. It is clear from correspondence that Morris was well acquainted with the Pages,

who were prominent Chicago citizens. According to a letter from Morris to Benjamin E. Page, Robert's father (and secretary of Frank Lloyd Wright's corporation), May 11, 1931, he even borrowed money from the Pages (CMC, B 1, F 1931c). Eight other letters from Bob Page to Morris are scattered in the George Herbert Mead Papers (B 2, F 3; B 3, F 1–2) and the Charles Morris Collection (B 8, F 1933–1937). These letters together evince a strongly familiar tone as, for example, Page repeatedly discussed family news with Morris.

44. It appears that Page, in rewriting his notes, relied on stock phrases or formulations like "social process of experience" or "social process of behavior" (these two phrases appear a combined sixty-five times in Page's rewritten notes) where other sets use simply "social process." The same holds for "conversation of significant gestures," which was clearly meant to emphasize the difference between "significant" communication and the "conversation of gestures"; the latter phrase is found in many sets of notes. The specific outline of a three-part process of meaning (which appears seven times in the published *Mind, Self, and Society*) comes exclusively from the Page notes. Other works from 1929–30 indicate Mead was explicitly interested in "triadic" relations (Mead 1929d, 429; 1929e, 84), so it seems likely that this was not merely invented by Page. The word "social" is perhaps the most significant single outlier, appearing over eight times as frequently per word in the Page notes as in the 1928 stenographic transcript; it is the sixth most common word in the Page notes—more common even than "is." It seems likely that in rewriting his notes Page sought to add his own emphasis or clarification to the materials by the use of such words and phrases.

45. I have been able to match Morris's annotated notes with the corresponding quotations as they appear in the footnotes of the published volume and can indicate definitively that the following sets of notes contributed supplemental content to *Mind, Self, and Society*: 1912 [?] "Social Psychology" notes of Stuart A. Queen [?]; 1924 "Advanced Social Psychology" notes of Charles W. Morris; 1924 "Problem of Consciousness" notes of Charles W. Morris; 1925 "Philosophies of Eminent Scientists" notes of Charles W. Morris; 1926 "Problem of Consciousness" notes of George E. M. Shelburg; 1927 "Advanced Social Psychology" notes of George E. M. Shelburg; 1928 "Movements of Thought in the Nineteenth Century" stenographic transcript; 1930 "Advanced Social Psychology" notes of Clifford P. Osborne; 1930 "Advanced Social Psychology" notes of Louis Bloom; and 1931 "Advanced Social Psychology" notes of Eugene W. Sutherland. These are in addition to the 1928 "Advanced Social Psychology" stenographic transcript and Robert R. Page's 1930 "Advanced Social Psychology" notes that make up the bulk of the volume's text.

46. It seems quite unlikely that Morris did not discuss the editing of *Mind, Self, and Society* with other relevant authorities on scholarly editing at the time. He was a colleague and friend of Charles Hartshorne, who was coeditor of the *Collected Papers of Charles S. Peirce* that were currently appearing in press. Morris owned and annotated a copy of these *Collected Papers*. He was also a correspondent of Hartshorne's coeditor Paul Weiss and a correspondent and friend of Horace Kallen, who had recently published *The Philosophy of William James: Drawn from His Own Works*. In published statements Morris explicitly drew attention to the parallels between his editions of Mead texts and those of Peirce and James (e.g., Morris 1934a, 9). There is no evidence, how-

ever, that these editors discussed criteria of proper scholarly editing with one another. Indeed, in each of the cases, the editor was also engaged full-time in his own research and teaching and was not trained in professional editorial techniques and principles (which existed, for example, in the philological scholarship occurring in several University of Chicago departments at the time). Other models of conscientiously produced posthumous editions had been completed for zoologist Charles Otis Whitman and political economist Robert Franklin Hoxie (both colleagues of Mead at the University of Chicago), but again Morris appears not to have consulted the relevant editors, several of whom were still living in Chicago in the early 1930s.

47. In a report of the University of Chicago business manager to the faculty's Committee on Press and Extension on April 7, 1932, William B. Harrell reported that the revenue for the University of Chicago Press in the 1931–32 fiscal year fell by 13 percent over the previous year and could be expected to fall, conservatively, at least another 8 percent, due primarily to the drastically reduced purchasing power of educational institutions. As it turned out, Harrell's figure of an 8 percent decline drastically underestimated the collapse in sales, which amounted to a 27.6 percent decrease in 1932–33 over the previous year, and to further declines through the next two fiscal years. At its lowest point, in the 1934–35 fiscal year, the book sales of the University of Chicago Press were only 53 percent of the volume of 1930–31 sales (Shugg 1966).

48. D. P. Bean to C. Morris, June 12, 1933 (UCPR, B 323, F 8).

49. See, for example, C. Morris to D. L. Miller, August 6, 1936 (GHMP, B 4, F 5).

50. D. P. Bean to C. Morris, June 12, 1933 (UCPR, B 323, F 8). There is direct evidence that the price still proved too high for at least some individuals whose incomes had been disturbed. In a letter to the press, April 4, 1934, a former student admitted, "Professor Mead was one of the faculty in the Department of Philosophy with whom I took several courses, and I am indebted to him for an insight into methods and movements which have been of greatest value. I am, however, humiliated by the consciousness that I am unable at this time to subscribe to the volumes. So many demands have recently been made on a very slender income that I must deny myself the privilege of ordering these books" (UCPR, B 323, F 9).

51. R. D. Hemens to C. Morris, March 16, 1934 (UCPR, B 323, F 8).

52. Adjusted for inflation, this total project would have been worth approximately $124,000 in 2011 dollars as measured on a GDP deflation scale measure. As it turned out, the actual total expense for Henry and Irene Mead, as far as I have been able to confirm it, was $1808.23, or approximately $29,000 adjusted. It was justifiably remarked in the correspondence that "it appeared difficult for [Henry] Mead to raise the necessary funds" (memo from R. D. Hemens to M. D. Alexander, August 21, 1934; UCPR, B 323, F 8). It seems quite plausible, although there is no direct evidence of this preserved in the correspondence I have found, that Henry Mead appealed to his mother's wealthy and philanthropic family, the Castles of Honolulu, for money.

53. D. P. Bean to H. C. A. Mead, May 29, 1934; D. P. Bean to R. D. Hemens, June 18, 1935 (UCPR, B 323, F 8).

54. In the preface to The Philosophy of the Act Morris, Brewster, Dunham, and Miller (1938, v–vi) noted that "except for a large body of student notes, which contain much of interest on Mr. Mead's interpretation of the history of ideas, the present mate-

rial exhausts all the known literary remains deemed worthy of publication. . . . It is hoped later to publish in one volume all of Mr. Mead's writings which were published during his lifetime." The "published works" volume was seriously considered for several years, according to correspondence I have discovered. It was to have been edited by Harvey J. Locke with an introduction by Ellsworth Faris (both sociologists, unlike all the other former students involved) and would have included some two dozen of Mead's articles and other published pieces ("Request for Estimate," July 30, 1937, UCPR, B 323, F 8). This volume was approved by the Board of University Publications if 500 advanced subscriptions could be secured before its manufacture (D. P. Bean to H. J. Locke, January 11, 1938, UCPR, B 323, F 8)—a benchmark that apparently was never reached. In 1932, the Vanguard Press considered publishing a selection of Mead's works with an introduction by Morris R. Cohen, but this project never materialized (J. Henle to M. R. Cohen, April 1, 1932, Morris Raphael Cohen Papers [hereafter MRCP], B 6, F 14).

At least two other serious proposals to republish articles by G. H. Mead were made between the 1930s and the 1950s before the 1964 *Selected Writings* edited by Andrew Reck finally appeared in print. One was to have been edited by Milton B. Singer under the title "George Herbert Mead: Selected Readings from His Works, with an Introduction to His Sociological and Philosophical Writings" and published in Karl Mannheim's International Library of Sociology and Social Reconstruction series, according to the backmatter of volumes in that series published in the late 1940s. The other was to have been titled "Science, Society, and Education" edited by Harold L. Sheppard and David W. McKinney and published by the University of Chicago Press (Board of University Publication minutes, April 24, 1955, UCPR, B23, vol. 1). It is unclear what halted the first of these publications, but the second was likely halted by the imminent publication of Chicago's *The Social Psychology of George Herbert Mead* edited by Anselm Strauss. The "history of thought" volume was championed for many years as an independent project by Charles Morris (G. J. Laing memo, August 9, 1933, UCPR, B 323, F 8) because of the large collection of notes Morris had been able to gather on Mead's courses on Aristotle, the Development of Thought in the Modern Period, Hegel, Bergson, Hume, Dewey, Leibniz, Philosophies of Eminent Scientists, Kant, and Rationalism and Empiricism. This volume has never subsequently appeared because the series would have been "harder to sell," according to Laing.

55. M. Tyler to D. P. Bean, January 13, 1934 (UCPR, B 323, F 8).

56. D. P. Bean to H. C. A. Mead, July 8, 1935 (UCPR, B 323, F 8). As a result of the changes in the contract after each publication, the three volumes were classified into three different "financing group" categories in the records of the University of Chicago Press (Office Managers Reports, 1935/36–1938/39, UCPR, B 9, F 5).

57. D. P. Bean to H. C. A. Mead, November 13, 1935 (UCPR, B 323, F 8).

58. Memo from D. P. Bean to M. D. Alexander, June 9, 1933 (UCPR, B 323, F 8).

59. "Estimate to Publication Department," August 14, 1934 (UCPR, B 323, F 8).

60. M. H. Moore to D. P. Bean, May 28, 1935 (UCPR, B 323, F 8).

61. This cut was one of the more irreparable. While the original manuscripts for most of the other materials edited out from the volumes still exist in the Mead Papers, Moore appears to have edited to pieces and then thrown out the only existing manuscript from this course, making the published, edited version apparently the only

existing record of the course. Moore described his procedure as follows: "The original manuscript with which I had to work, was of course, completely beyond recall before I got through with it. As I found repetitious material I would cut sections and paste them together, getting the basis for the chapter and subject matter rather than for the lecture division. When the mechanics of rearrangement were completed, that copy was so mutilated that it would have been of no use to anyone. Besides, I believe there were duplicate copies, at least one carbon I am sure, of that original stuff. . . . I was not concerned over the loss of the other portions of my manuscript when I discovered their destruction, for I thought once the book was published they would be of no value" (M. H. Moore to C. Morris, June 15, 1936, GHMP, B 2, F 3).

62. D. P. Bean to C. Morris, undated [June 1937?] (UCPR, B 323, F 8).

63. C. Morris to D. L. Miller, August 6, 1936 (GHMP, B 4, F 5).

64. F. Wieck to M. H. Moore, June 8, 1950 (UCPR, B 323, F 8).

65. Especially before the development of a significant body of critical work on Mead's intellectual biography, authors like Maurice Natanson (1956) and Grace Lee (1945) relied heavily on the posthumous volumes in making claims about Mead's intellectual development, the connections among his domains of study, and an apparent detachment from practical problems of biology and civic life. Natanson even treated the order of the volumes as a key to understanding the genesis of the categories of Mead's thought. Stevens (1967) criticized these authors on this point explicitly, and he was an early advocate of returning to the manuscript lecture notes and to Mead's published works in reassessing his philosophical significance.

CHAPTER SIX

1. Fuller biographical information regarding Morris's life is available in several secondary accounts (see Petrilli 2001; Sebeok 1981; Rossi-Landi 1953).

2. There are many likely candidates for instructors at Northwestern at the time with connections to Mead and Chicago pragmatist philosophy, including Robert H. Gault, L. W. Webb, and Delton T. Howard in psychology; Arthur J. Todd in sociology; and E. L. Schaub in philosophy. I think Howard is the most likely to have introduced Mead to Morris. Howard was teaching the social psychology classes at Northwestern at the time, wrote extensively on pragmatism, and is mentioned in some of Morris's correspondence as the person who introduced him to William James. However, Webb had taken Mead's 1914 Social Psychology course while a student at Chicago; Gault was in dialogue with many of the same people in social psychology and participated in several of the same social betterment causes in Chicago as Mead; Todd later published a book with Faris in which Mead wrote an article; and Schaub was a philosopher well connected with the other leading philosophers of the time who edited the "Living Philosophers" series of monographs, including one on Dewey. In general, there appear to have been long-standing close ties between Northwestern University and the Chicago philosophers.

3. On the last account, in particular, there is informative correspondence with psychiatrist Adolf Meyer, in which Morris reported that as he contemplated graduate school, he had considered "very seriously" pursuing work with Meyer in "psychopathol-

ogy" instead of going into the "no man's land of philosophy," but that he increasingly found his interest "becoming more theoretical" (C. Morris to A. Meyer, December 3, 1932, CMC, B 1, F "1932"). The correspondence of Meyer and Morris is interesting also in that it discusses Meyer's perception of the relationship of his work to Mead's. For example, "I am quite sure that my development was quite independent and have the impression that the perfectly clear formulation [in "Misconceptions at the Bottom of 'Hopelessness in all Psychology,'" *Psychological Bulletin*] of 1907 may have been known to Dr. [*sic*] Mead at least—at any rate it was accessible" (A. Meyer to C. Morris, December 14, 1932, CMC, B 1, F "1932").

4. C. Morris to W. H. Cowley, September 9, 1970 (CMC, B 16, F "1970–1"). The instructors in philosophy were also close with these professors in other departments. Thurstone had even taken Mead's 1915 Social Psychology as a student. When Clark was being considered for a position at Harvard (which he took), Mead and Tufts wrote to President Max Mason drawing his attention to the importance of Clark to the Chicago philosophy department, where he had advised students and was "one of the few competent students of Indian Philosophy in this country," a fact that was becoming more salient as Eastern philosophers were being rediscovered in their original languages (J. H. Tufts and G. H. Mead to M. Mason, June 6, 1927, Office of the President, Mason Administration Records [hereafter OPMA], B 17, F 3). Schevill was one of the earliest faculty members along with Tufts and Mead, and he participated in a variety of common pursuits with the philosophers over their long careers together.

5. Morris's notes from Mead's courses are preserved in the Morris Collection (CMC, B 20), as are notes from courses with Moore and Tufts. Throughout his notes are Morris's annotations often accompanied with dates indicating that they were from later rereadings of the material.

6. In his "Movements of Thought in the Nineteenth Century" and his other historical courses such as "Philosophies of Eminent Scientists," Mead endeavored to examine scientific and philosophical advance as the result of the attempts to solve practical problems that emerged in social life. Thus, in the lectures Morris heard (according to his notes) Mead argued that the psychological theories of modern philosophers including Hobbes and the Utilitarians were attempts to conceptualize human motivation and action in the service of an adequate social control. In the Relativity seminar he heard Mead working through the implications of his theory of "role taking" and the co-constitution of organism and environment for the fundamental nature of existence, arguments expanded in the last years of Mead's life in his Carus Lectures and in his theory of "objective relativism." And in the course on Aristotle's metaphysics, Mead sustained a comparison between contemporary metaphysics, psychology, and logic and their counterparts in Aristotle. This included the first reference in any surviving materials from Mead's courses to C. K. Ogden and I. A. Richards's *The Meaning of Meaning* (1923), which was one of the earliest works in the revival of interest in the study of semantics and one of the early avenues for the popularization of Peirce's foundational work on semiotics, accompanied the same year by Morris R. Cohen's collection of Peirce's work entitled *Chance, Love and Logic* (cf. De Waal 2002). Notable also is what Mead did not mention in his lectures. The Advanced Social Psychology lectures do not proceed along lines that could easily be understood to be "mind," "self," and "society" and the notes

make almost no mention of the nature of social reconstruction and fundamental social attitudes that make up such a large portion of the "Society" section of the published *Mind, Self, and Society.*

7. Because of his own published statements (e.g., Morris 1937b) and especially his work on semiotics, Morris is often remembered as an important (and controversial) interpreter of Peirce. For his part, Morris sometimes disclaimed any expert knowledge of Peirce, and noted that his semiotics owed first and foremost to Mead. In a letter to Max H. Fisch he wrote, "During my three years as a graduate student at Chicago (1922–1925) there was no reference to (let alone a study of) Peirce in any of the courses I took. I had of course read Ogden and Richards *The Meaning of Meaning* [in courses with Mead, according to his notes], which had some pages on Peirce, but I cannot recall that they made any impression on me. My Ph.D. Dissertation in 1925 (*Symbolism and Reality*) made no use of Peirce. My own approach to signs was originally an outgrowth of the work of George H. Mead (who directed my dissertation). In my book *Six Theories of Mind* (1932) I do have a few pages on Peirce and considerably more on him in *Signs, Language, and Behavior* (1946). I appropriated some parts of Peirce's terminology and framework, and my own 'behavioral' orientation to semiotic might be regarded as continuing the late Peircean analysis of 'interpretant' in terms of 'habit.' But my work was not *historically* dependent upon Peirce for its foundation or direction" (C. Morris to M. H. Fisch, May 23, 1968, Max H. Fisch Collection [hereafter MHFC], Bank A10–Drawer 3, "Morris, Charles" folder). He made almost identical remarks in letters to Fisch dated June 23, 1959, and February 11, 1969.

8. John F. Markey, in his work *The Symbolic Process and Its Integration in Children* (1928) reviewed by Morris, is apparently the first person to use the phrase "social behaviourist" to describe his own work (although the possibility of a "social behaviorist" sociology had been criticized a decade earlier by A. A. Goldenweiser [1918]). It is interesting to note also that Markey acknowledged his indebtedness to Ellsworth Faris and L. L. Bernard, both former students of Mead, in the preface to his 1928 work.

9. The other young scholars discussed included Arthur E. Murphy, Charles Hartshorne, Sidney Hook, Edwin A. Burtt, and Donald A. Piatt. The department had success in appointing several of the non–Chicago trained men (Murphy, Hartshorne, and Burtt) to positions and developed a specific proposal to bring a couple of their former students (Piatt and Morris) to fill temporary positions in the 1928–29 academic year when A. W. Moore had taken a reduced teaching schedule and Mead was away as visiting Mills Professor at Berkeley.

10. J. H. Tufts to R. M. Hutchins, October 28, 1929 (Office of the Hutchins Administration Records [hereafter OPHA], B 163, F 12).

11. G. H. Mead to F. Woodward (vice president of the university), November 1, 1930 (OPHA, B 163, F 12). I have quoted only a portion of the much longer, glowing assessment of Morris's work and his ability to carry on the distinctive Chicago School tradition found in this letter.

12. Untitled five-page memorandum (c. November 1930) apparently written on behalf of the department, likely by Mead as interim chair and senior representative (OPHA, B 163, F 12).

13. For collections of primary documents on the Hutchins Controversy see the

archived papers of Edward S. Ames ([hereafter ESAP], B 1), Charles Morris (CMC, B 1, F 1931a–c), Robert M. Hutchins (OPHA, B 163, 294), and Elinor Castle Nef (ECNP, B 26).

14. Mead apparently gave word to Morris through his daughter-in-law, Irene Tufts Mead, and through Edward S. Ames that he thought Morris should take the position (see C. Morris to H. Blumer March 30, 1931, and C. Morris to H. Schultz and to F. Schevill, April 1, 1931, CMC, B 1, F "1931a," "1931b"). In a letter to Mead April 10, 1931, he wrote, "I am happy to think of directing my work into the great university tradition which you have so splendidly helped to create. I appreciate very much your kindly attitude to me expressed through Mrs. Mead and Mr. Ames—it was a generous act. Had I thought that my acceptance would in any sense be discourteous to you, nothing could have induced me to accept" (CMC, B 1, F "1931b").

15. The proposed institute was, for Morris, a "chance to rethink from the very foundation what a philosophy department might be in a great university and what part it might play in the modern world" (CMC, B 33, F "Institute of Philosophy"). Neither the institute nor the proposed "Science and Symbolism" volume could secure sufficient financial resources in the early Great Depression (CMC, B 33, F "Science & Symbolism—'a proposed book,'" UCPR, B 345, F 8). The complete list of proposed contributors for the proposed book (who had not yet been approached) is as follows: Herbert Blumer, Ernst Cassirer, L. E. Dickson, Ralph M. Eaton, Franklin Edgerton, Ellsworth Faris, A. Eustace Haydon, Henry Head, C. J. Herrick, H. L. Hollingworth, Walter S. Hunter, Ernest Jones, Charles H. Judd, Wolfgang Köhler, Karl S. Lashley, Victor F. Lenzen, C. I. Lewis, D. A. MacKenzie, Bronislaw Malinowski, John F. Markey, C. K. Ogden, Jean Piaget, Robert Redfield, I. A. Richards, Edward Sapir, L. L. Thurstone, and Paul Weiss. On the "History of Science Committee," see the Louis Wirth Papers ([hereafter LWP], B 8, F 9). This committee appears to have largely disbanded with the university reorganization in World War II. Lists of participants for the "Logic of Science" group may be found in Morris's papers (CMC, B 6, F "1941–42") and UCPR, B 345, F 8).

16. "The amount of labor necessary to carry through the task [of editing Mind, Self, and Society] must have been enormous. You deserve not only congratulations on a fine piece of editing but the warm thanks of all who knew Mead. It is a labor of love carried through most carefully and beautifully" (E. A. Burtt to C. Morris, August 2, 1935, CMC, B 1, F "1935"). Portions of this letter from Burtt were privately circulated by Morris to members of the University of Chicago Press in response to a negative review of the volume written by W. D. Wallis, discussed below. Letters of praise from John Dewey, James H. Tufts, Theodore T. Lafferty, Robert R. Page, and Van Meter Ames were also retained by Morris throughout his career.

17. Morris kept the University of Chicago Press updated on his latest travels so as to ensure that the proofs would reach him (correspondence between Morris, Mary D. Alexander, and Marjorie Tyler, May 6–November 6, 1934, UCPR, B 323, F 8). The initial list of names to receive free copies of Mind, Self, and Society prepared by Charles Morris may be found in the UCPR on two sheets dated February 13, 1935. Henry Mead prepared his own list dated December 13, 1934, which consists entirely of relatives and family friends including Harriet Park Thomas (UCPR, B 323, F 8). In a later letter to Henry Mead, Morris wrote: "In my opinion the point of view represented by your father is best going to be influential and to survive by being caught up within this larger [unity of sci-

ence] movement. It was to members of this group that I am sending the extra copies of the Mead volumes which you made available to me. I know that some of the contributors think well of Mr. Mead's general position, and that it will be considered in their monographs" (April 24, 1938, UCPR, B 348, F 3).

18. A circular letter dated October 22, 1937, promoting the *IEUS* was marked by the press "Sent to Mead's" and the corresponding envelop is marked as sent to "Mead's for[mer] Stud[ents]" list. The letter begins, "As a former student of philosophy at the University of Chicago you will be interested to hear more about the Unity of Science movement which has the active endorsement of many members of the Chicago faculty as well as that of philosophers and scientists throughout the world" (UCPR B 347, F 3). In addition, Morris and Donald P. Bean, manager of the University of Chicago Press, personally asked Henry Mead to help support the journal *Erkenntnis*, the early home journal for advocates of the "unity of science."

19. See the letter from R. D. Hemens to C. Morris, March 18, 1939, in which he says, "In our discussion a few days ago we considered including in the exhibit to be handled by the Press the titles we publish in cooperation with your Committee, but we did not mention exhibiting books such as the Mead volumes which might be of interest to this same group. Don't you think we should expand our display to include such volumes?" A list prepared on March 29, 1939, notes that all three of the posthumous Mead volumes published by the University of Chicago Press were included in their final display. After the Congress, Abraham Kaplan prepared a "Report to the University of Chicago Press on Exhibit at Fifth International Congress for the Unity of Science, Harvard, Sept. 3–9, 1939" in which he noted that none of the Mead books had sold a single copy at the conference (UCPR, B 346, F 2).

20. Besides Dewey and Bentley, other critics that Morris responded to included Virgil C. Aldrich, Max Black, Daniel J. Bronstein, George Gentry, Elaine Graham, L. O. Kattsoff, Philip Blair Rice, David Rynin, Thomas Storer, John Wild, and W. K. Wimsatt. Wild and Gentry had both been students at the University of Chicago and took courses with Mead.

21. Note that here Morris seemingly acknowledged his use of parallelism in the formation of titles: *Signs, Language, and Behavior* and *Mind, Self, and Society*. The title of his 1956 *Varieties of Human Values*, discussed below, was also constructed on analogy with W. H. Sheldon's *Varieties of Human Physique*.

22. The conflict between Dewey and Morris went back at least to 1939 when Dewey was writing "Theory of Valuation" and reading Morris's "Foundations of the Theory of Signs," both pieces that appeared in the Foundations of the Unity of Science series. Dewey saw "a pretty basic difference" between his own philosophy and that of the logical positivists, which he characterized as "a blind alley" (J. Dewey to C. Morris, May 25, 1939, CMC, B 1, F "1939"). As their disagreement grew Dewey wrote, "I confess I do not understand how you can write as you seem to do at times as if there was any similarity between my position and yours. In general I get the feeling that in your broad eclecticism you are trying to bring together a variety of views that are mutually inconsistent with one another" (J. Dewey to C. Morris, July 30, 1946, CMC, B 2, F "1946b"). In letters to others Dewey characterized Morris's semiotics as "distributive pigeon-holing" of his various interests that resulted in a merely "mechanical union of Mead & Carnap"

(Dewey 1997, nos. 08614, 09308). Morris objected to Dewey's view and wrote, "I take the synthetic task of philosophy very seriously, and I have attempted a synthesis of the various views of meaning on the basis of a simple behavioral orientation" (Morris to Dewey, September 23, 1946, CMC, B 2, F "1946b"). Arthur F. Bentley's letters to Dewey, with whom he collaborated, include very harsh words regarding Morris's philosophical acuity and his editing of the Mead volumes.

23. Morris collaborated with Parsons, R. Freed Bales, and others in the Harvard Social Relations department in the early 1950s, where he was a visiting professor. He is explicitly acknowledged in *The Working Papers in the Theory of Action* for his "important leads" in the "theory of symbolism" in relation to values and culture in action (Parsons, Bales, and Shils 1953, 10, 31–33, 69). From 1947 until 1958 he held a research lectureship, instead of a regular professorship, at Chicago, which allowed him to spend considerable amounts of time at Harvard and New School participating in interdisciplinary seminars and research projects. At New School he interacted with Alfred Schütz, Albert Salomon, and Ernst Kris, with all of whom he discussed Mead (C. Morris to L. Wirth, April 7, 1946, LWP, B 8, F 9).

24. "Following Mead and Dewey, my views are biologically oriented"; "My work in semiotic may be regarded from one point of view as a continuation of Mead's work. In technical philosophy I feel closer to Mead than to anyone else"; "My own approach to signs was originally an outgrowth of the work of George H. Mead" (C. Morris to E. B. Holt, January 17, 1931, CMC, B 1, F "1931a"; C. Morris to F. Rossi-Landi, May [?], 1950, CMC, B 26, F "Charles Morris Rossi-Landi Letters"; C. Morris to M. H. Fisch, May 23, 1968, MHFC, "Morris, Charles" file). "With Mead's general position we are in essential agreement and it is in large part due to his influence that the present position was developed"; "The approach is, in a wide sense, of the term, behavioral, and owes much to the theories of behavior developed by George H. Mead, John Dewey, Edward C. Tolman, and Clark L. Hull" (Morris 1927, 290; 1946, v).

25. Morris had proposed a book project on the "pragmatic movement" from as early as 1933 and expressed a desire to write such a work several times across his career (see C. Morris to J. Dewey, June 19, 1933, CMC, B 1, F "1933"; C. Morris to D. W. Prall, December 1, 1938, CMC, B 1, F "1938"; C. Morris to C. Kluckhohn, April 17, 1949; CMC, B 3, F "1949b").

26. The book jacket for the first edition of *The Philosophy of the Act* (Mead 1938) contains a summary description of that work prepared by the University of Chicago Press's editorial staff on the basis of materials written by Charles Morris. It notes, "The three-volume series reveals Mead as a thinker of the magnitude and importance of Peirce, James, and Dewey" (UCPR, B 324, F 1). This remark was brought into reviews of the posthumous volumes by Harold A. Larrabee, L. M. Pape, and Paul A. Schilpp.

27. Morris referred repeatedly to the content of "a number of volumes of Mead's writings and lectures ready for press," including discussing (and quoting without attribution from) *The Philosophy of the Act* over four years before it was published (Morris 1934a, 9; 1934c, 553, 560, 561). This even includes referring in the footnotes of *Mind, Self, and Society* (Mead 1934, 247, 198, 330) to specific topics such as "the relation of the world of common experience and of science" to be found in particular sections of *The Philosophy of the Act*, again, four years prior to its publication. It is also note-

worthy that the students who worked with Morris on the posthumous Mead volumes sometimes referred to their content in print prior to their publication, as in Albert M. Dunham's (1933, 7) dissertation that cites "unpublished manuscripts which will form part of a forthcoming volume edited by Prof. Chas. Morris"; and that Morris referred to the volumes in public lectures and classes as well, as in his mimeographed handouts for a lecture on the Nature of Mind in 1933 which included the recommended reading: "Mead *Mind, Self, and Society* (to appear next Fall)" (Unity of Science Movement Records [hereafter USMR], B 2, F 16).

28. This analysis is based on extensive correspondence regarding what to do about the Wallis review found in the University of Chicago Press Records from July to December 1935 (UCPR, B 323, F 8).

29. Schiller's (1936b) response to Morris's remarks was published immediately following, and Morris rebutted this response in his subsequent statement on "Peirce, Mead, and Pragmatism" (Morris 1937b). Morris and Schiller also sparred privately in letters to one another (see F. C. S. Schiller to C. Morris, December 3, 1935, CMC, B 1, F "1935").

30. Morris's records contain various course bibliographies indicating that he taught Mead in courses including "Contemporary Pragmatism," "Symbols and Values," "Symbolism," and "Mead" at Chicago; "Meaning and Communication" and "The Human Frontier" at the New School; "General Theory of Signs" and "Value and Science" at Harvard; and "The Pragmatic Movement" and "Mead" at the University of Florida.

31. Morris's correspondence indicates he participated in one way or another in the graduate research on Mead of Fred Brown, William H. Desmonde, Tom Clifton Keen, Grace Chin Lee, David Miller, Maurice Natanson, Raymond Nelson, Darnell Rucker, Surindar Suri, David Wallace, John Wilkinson, and others. He worked with students John M. Brewster, Albert M. Dunham, and David Miller to prepare the materials for *The Philosophy of the Act*. He facilitated access to the archived Mead materials—for example, "Please send me the letter for the Chicago University library for access to the Mead manuscript in the archives at your convenience" (S. Suri to C. Morris, January 9, 1952, CMC, B 9, F "1952"). When Morris's student Lyle K. Eddy quoted unpublished notes from Mead's 1926 seminar on Dewey in a class paper it caused a minor commotion; Morris disagreed with his interpretation of the materials and Eddy, in protest, appealed to Dewey. Ultimately Eddy left Chicago and continued graduate work at Columbia (see letters between Eddy, Morris, Dewey, and Joseph Ratner in summer 1948 in the Dewey correspondence [1997]).

32. For example, Van Meter Ames apparently borrowed manuscript materials—"the Mead stuff"—from Morris at various times (V. M. Ames to C. Morris, May 21, 1955, CMC, B 11, F "1955"). Grace C. Lee (1945, vii), in her early published study of Mead, acknowledged Morris "for placing at my disposal Mead's unpublished manuscripts," one of which she directly quoted (50). Ames, David Miller, Charner Perry, and Robert Rosenthal all kept Morris informed of discoveries they heard about regarding Mead, according to Morris's correspondence.

33. A detailed 1972 interview in which Blumer recalled the circumstances of his graduate schooling is available in the Department of Sociology Interviews (B 1, F2). I utilize this document for several of the claims in this section. Much of the detailed

information about Blumer's graduate education and early career comes from this and other late interviews and autobiographical statements. Blumer reportedly destroyed virtually all of his accumulated files in his move from Chicago to Berkeley in 1952, reputedly done because he did not want what had been done with Mead's manuscripts after his death to be repeated with his own manuscripts (Abbott 1999). This fact makes it particularly difficult to pose correspondence and manuscripts as sources of confirmation or contradiction with regard to Blumer's career, or to trace in sharp precision Blumer's intellectual development. For published discussions of aspects of Blumer's life, see Shibutani 1973, 1988; Hochschild 1987; and Morrione 2004.

34. Blumer had studied with Max Meyer at the University of Missouri, and in his 1928 dissertation he discussed Meyer's views in detail, labeling him in various places as the earliest, most thorough, and most scholarly behaviorist. Although he did not use that term in this work, Meyer's 1911 *The Fundamental Laws of Human Behavior* predates the earliest published pronouncements of Watson's "behaviorism." Blumer claimed in interviews that Mead respected Meyer's work.

35. Blumer wrote a paper on "The Development of the Self" for the winter 1926 course that reportedly impressed Mead, and he retained the copy of the paper on which Mead had commented throughout his career, even when he threw out other materials (Morrione 2004, 1). The original paper is apparently located in the collection of Herbert Blumer's materials at Colby College.

36. DSI, B 1, F 2, pp. 2-8.

37. Prior to the appearance of his first published article in 1931 Blumer had already contributed two dozen reviews of such material, and over his career he would go on to be a remarkably prolific reviewer, with at least 114 reviews listed in bibliographies of his work, all but a few of them appearing in the *American Journal of Sociology*. Almost all of these reviews were written prior to his 1952 move to Berkeley.

38. "The writer, in presenting Faris's views, will have to resort to material gathered through lectures and personal conversations"; "We confine our brief presentation to those perspectives which are of marked significance for social psychology. These perspectives must be pieced together from Mead's scattered writings" (Blumer 1928, 180, 202-3). The authors considered at length in Blumer's dissertation, a list that does not include the much longer catalogue of authors mentioned, includes Floyd Allport, J. Mark Baldwin, Luther Lee Bernard, Charles H. Cooley, John Dewey, Knight Dunlap, Charles A. Ellwood, Ellsworth Faris, J. R. Kantor, Alfred Kroeber, William McDougall, George H. Mead, Max Meyer, E. A. Ross, W. I. Thomas, Wilson D. Wallis, John B. Watson, A. P. Weiss, James Mickel Williams, Kimball Young, and Florian Znaniecki.

39. Smith (1977, 160) quoted Blumer in an interview as saying "it is possible that Mead may have asked Faris first to take over the course; I have a faint recollection that Faris said something to this effect to me."

40. G. H. Mead to F. Woodward, February 6, 1931 (OPHA, B 294, F 5).

41. This paper by Faris was originally read at a session of the American Sociological Society meeting in 1937, which Faris chaired. It was the first session by that body to focus its topic explicitly on Mead. The other participants were J. O. Hertzler of the University of Nebraska and Walter B. Bodenhafer of the University of Washington. The

paper likely also would have served as a draft of the introduction Faris was to have written for an edited volume of Mead's published essays (see notes of chapter 5).

42. I make no attempt to survey Blumer's complete body of work. He was, for example, a contributor to the sociology of industrial and labor relations and of race and ethnic relations, which some commentators have indicated are Blumer's unique contributions to democratic political philosophy (Lyman and Vidich 1988). Prominent commentators have noted, however, that Blumer's analysis of particular social phenomena relies on his larger "ontology" of social life which was most heavily indebted to Mead (e.g., Maines and Morrione 1990, xi, xiv). Robert Park, whom Blumer followed in other respects, was a friend of Mead's and referred approvingly to his work, once even remarking that Mead "has made a more penetrating analysis of the relations we describe as social than anyone else I happen to know" (Park 1942, 218).

43. The primary materials from this period are the Edward Jackson Baur Papers (hereafter EJBP). Mead is discussed in the lecture notes from Blumer's winter 1933 "Contemporary Social Psychology," winter 1934 "Introduction to Sociology," winter 1935 "Introduction to Sociology," spring 1935 "Advanced Social Psychology," and spring 1938 "Methods of Social Research" (B 2, F 2). Mead is also referred to in notes from courses given by Ellsworth Faris and Louis Wirth in this collection. The quotation in the text is from the winter 1933 Contemporary Social Psychology notes, p. 3. Philip M. Hauser also retained notes from his courses at Chicago during the early 1930s, including his 1930 Advanced Social Psychology course with Mead, and others taught by Blumer, Faris, and Park that refer to Mead (see Philip M. Hauser Papers [hereafter PMHP], B 23). He also apparently kept notes from special public lectures by Faris and Charles Morris that discuss Mead. These notes are probably the most promising primary sources of materials from which to reconstruct Blumer's early intellectual career apart from his published essays and reviews.

44. Memos from D. P. Bean to R. D. Hemens, February 28, 1935; R. D. Hemens to H. Blumer, March 15, 1935 (UCPR, B 323, F 8). The University of Chicago Press was prevented from selling Mind, Self, and Society below retail price, even for use as a textbook, because of a provision of the newly instated Graphic Arts Code as part of the National Industrial Recovery Act of 1933. Blumer had commented on at least a portion of the manuscript for Mind, Self, and Society before it was published (Morris 1934b, vii), and he apparently continued to use the book regularly in his courses. Note however, as is discussed further in this chapter and in chapter 7, Blumer's claims about Mead both in his classes and in published literature predate Mind, Self, and Society and thus do not depend either for their genesis or their ultimate authority on that volume. The Society for Social Research, an important graduate student and faculty institution in the Department of Sociology at the University of Chicago, purchased a copy of Mind, Self, and Society in August 1935, apparently for the use of the society's members (J. N. Symons to Publication Department, August 1, 1935, Society for Social Research Records [hereafter SSRR], B 2, F 4).

45. Blumer even reportedly imitated Mead's teaching style in these lectures. In an interview with Ernest and Harriet Mowrer, James Carey (the interviewer) followed a discussion by the Mowrers of Mead's teaching style with the remark: "I took my social

psychology and advanced social psychology from Herbert Blumer and he uses the same procedure. I see now where it came from. You could ask him questions but he would do the same thing, a recap of the previous lecture which would take about fifteen minutes and . . . go in . . . to the new material" (DSI, B 1, F 16, p. 10, ellipses in original).

46. Park and Burgess's excerpt is originally from Simmel's 1908 *Soziologie* and includes only a portion of the larger "Excursus on the Sociology of the Senses." Contemporary translations of the excursus (Simmel 1997, 2009) tend to emphasize a less stark distinction of levels than Park and Burgess's earlier interpretation.

47. For example, from Baur's winter 1934 "Introduction to Sociology" typed notes: "TWO LEVELS OF INTERACTION (SIMMEL): Unconscious, non-symbolic, response of attraction or repulsion as reaction to voice, appearance, etc. Conscious, symbolic, comprehension as reaction to meaning of words or attitudes" (EJBP, B 2, F 2).

48. Blumer had used the term "symbolic interaction" in one previous publication: his 1936 "Social Attitudes and Nonsymbolic Interaction," although this piece is not often acknowledged in secondary literature. That article is rather peculiar; it argues that it is precisely "symbolic interaction" that had been thoroughly examined in previous studies of social attitudes, and that such analyses typically ignored the "nonsymbolic" or affective level despite its essential importance in the formation of social attitudes. The focus on the nonsymbolic level and on the concept of social "attitudes" may explain Blumer's later neglect of the article. It also seems clear that, located as it was in the *Journal of Educational Sociology*, where there had been ongoing debates regarding the methods and findings of the so-called Payne Fund Studies (see Jowett, Jarvie, and Fuller 1996), the article's implicit target was survey or questionnaire methods that presumed their linguistically formulated (and, thus, "symbolic" in that sense) data were related to equivalent affective motivations in the experiences of their individual respondents to behave in certain ways consonant with their symbolic responses—that what respondents reported in surveys was a valid measure of how they felt.

49. Many of the extant volumes of *Man and Society*, in which the article appeared, in the Regenstein library at the University of Chicago are marked "Soc. 220" in the prefatory materials, indicating that they were used as reserve or rental copies for Blumer's "Introduction to Social Psychology" course. Blumer was also the series editor for the Prentice-Hall sociological series in which the volume appeared.

50. Blumer's developing criticisms of survey techniques may be traced through his frequent reviews of monographs on sociological methods in the early 1930s; especially relevant is his review of George A. Lundberg's 1929 *Social Research*. Beginning in fall 1928 Blumer was engaged in a major empirical research project examining the social influence of motion pictures on adolescents' conduct and delinquency, for which he apparently led a research team that collected and analyzed a total of over 2,000 autobiographical "life-history" statements, 3,000 responses to questionnaires, almost 200 transcribed interviews, and accounts of conversations and direct observations of motion-picture attendance from high school and college students as well as juvenile and adult criminals (Blumer 1933; Blumer and Hauser 1933; Hauser 1933). In this project he came into close contact with L. L. Thurstone, with whom he had also previously studied and whose methods he later explicitly criticized in his "Social Psychology" article (Blumer 1937, 189), along with a variety of other cutting-edge methodologists. Blumer's

methods were debated both publicly and privately among this group (e.g., Hauser 1932; Jowett, Jarvie, and Fuller 1996). He also taught a regular course on "Methods of Social Research" (a course previously taught by Robert Park) in which he knowledgeably discussed the various ways of conducting social inquiry, including life histories, case methods, interviews, questionnaires, schedules, tests, direct observations, personal documents (e.g., letters), studies of conversation, and collective documents (e.g., newspapers, literature, art). His criticisms of sociological methods were based on fairly thorough acquaintance, and his infamous criticisms of Thomas and Znaniecki's "life-history" methods (Blumer 1939) can, thus, also be viewed in part as self-criticisms of his own tribulations with those methods.

51. This list of students might include, among others, Howard S. Becker, Hubert Bonner, Fred Davis, Hugh Dalziel Duncan, Joseph B. Gittler, Joseph R. Gusfield, Alfred R. Lindesmith, Bernard N. Meltzer, Frank Miyamoto, Virginia Olesen, Arnold M. Rose, Tamotsu Shibutani, Gregory P. Stone, Anselm Strauss, Samuel M. Strong, Guy E. Swanson, Ralph H. Turner, and S. Kirson Weinberg.

52. Bonner cotaught "Introduction to Social Psychology" with Blumer in the mid-1940s and included *Mind, Self, and Society* as a recommended reading in his other courses (memo from "LBS" to "DF," December 1, 1945, UCPR, B 323, F 10). Shibutani taught Introduction to Social Psychology in 1949 with the course description "An introduction to the social psychology of George H. Mead, with an elaboration and critical evaluation of his theories in the light of contemporary research" (*Announcements: Graduate Programs in the Divisions* [Chicago: University of Chicago Press, 1949], 90). According to my personal communication with Donald N. Levine, Shibutani continued to teach the introductory course as an introduction to Mead and to assign *Mind, Self, and Society* in years other than 1949 as well. Strauss used offprints of sections of his edited volume on Mead in courses (Strauss 1965).

53. Manford Kuhn (1964, 63) himself remarked as late as the mid-1960s that "Blumer, the young and promising heir apparent [of Symbolic Interactionism], has published relatively little and has nowhere gathered together a rounded version of his point of view." Instead, Kuhn drew attention to the influence of textbooks in social psychology written by other authors oriented toward Symbolic Interactionism, including Alfred Lindesmith and Anselm Strauss's 1949 *Social Psychology*, R. E. L. Faris's 1953 *Social Psychology*, Tamotsu Shibutani's 1961 *Society and Personality*, and (in part) Theodore Newcomb's 1950 *Social Psychology*.

54. The University of Chicago Press asked Blumer first, who wrote that he could not take on the task but recommended Tamotsu Shibutani, Samuel Strong, or G. E. Swanson; Morris recommended Milton Singer; Merton recommended Blumer (who "has long considered himself almost a disciple of Mead") or Shils; and Shils recommended Blumer, Shibutani, William Kornhauser, or Hugh Dalziel Duncan (UCPR, B 323, F 7; CMC, B 11, F "1955"). The quote in the text is from a letter from A. J. Morin, editor of the University of Chicago Press, to E. A. Shils, July 21, 1955. Several of these individuals did agree to be readers of the manuscript, which was published as *The Social Psychology of George Herbert Mead*, and later reprinted with emendations under the modified title *On Social Psychology* in the "Heritage of Sociology" series.

55. Other prominent essays that discuss Mead after his 1952 move to Berkeley are

"Psychological Import of the Human Group" (1953) where he discusses Mead's theory of "self-interaction"; "Attitudes and the Social Act" (1955) in which he criticizes the concept of "attitude" from the "line of thought of George H. Mead"; "Society as Symbolic Interaction" (1962) intended as a summary statement for a collection on that perspective; and the above-mentioned chapter on "George Herbert Mead" (1981).

56. The analyses that follow focus primarily on Blumer's methodological controversies with others in regard to Mead. This focus should not lead us to forget that Blumer was also criticized at various times for other aspects of his understanding of Mead, especially by those who charged in one way or another that he neglected Mead's examinations of instrumental action, corporeality, the physical object, or social structure (not to mention Mead's many other disparate intellectual interests outside of social psychology, strictly defined). Recall that I proposed in the introduction to the chapter that, in terms of the analysis, the key is not to encompass all the major criticisms made of Blumer but rather to examine the major ways in which he responded to criticism of his interpretation of Mead—not the fact of criticism but Blumer's typical modes of response. Especially because unpublished materials from Blumer are so incomplete, I focus on his published battles in his various "comments" and "replies" to other authors made in professional journals. In this regard, it is interesting to note that the criticisms to which Blumer chose to respond and the kinds of responses he made to critics tended to focus on methodological issues, perhaps indicating something of Blumer's views on the most salient or controversial aspects of his interpretation of Mead.

57. For example, he wrote a comment on Irwin Deutscher's (1970) paper criticizing social psychological explanations. Blumer (1970) pointed out that Mead, among others, had "sketched a broad outline" of an analysis of the "formation of conduct" through "defining the situation" that could contribute to the discussion. Jonathan H. Turner's (1974) proposal that there was a theoretical convergence between Parsons and symbolic interactionism was the occasion for Blumer (1975a) to argue that Parsons's schema of "pattern variables" were "preposterous misrepresentation of human experience"; that Parsons's "social system" was fundamentally incongruent with Mead's view of social organization; that Mead's view of personality was distinguishable from Parsons's in its conception of role-taking, the nature of "self," motivation, and the human act; and that the deductive research approach of Parsons was not amenable to the same forms of study as symbolic interactionism. Blumer even wrote a second reply to Parsons's (1975) own response in which he asserted that not only Turner but Parsons too, had "an erroneous understanding of the symbolic interactionist point of view that stems from George Herbert Mead," primarily because he did not adequately grasp the nature of the self as a social process of self-indication (Blumer 1975b).

58. Blumer 1977, 286. Blumer made a similar claim in his posthumously published essay on Mead in order to justify his "elaboration" of Mead's views without citation: "The writer studied under Mead, wrote his doctoral dissertation under Mead's guidance, performed research under his direction, assisted him in some of his work, and at his request took over the instruction of his classes in social psychology during the period of illness that preceded his death" (Blumer 2004, 15). His privileged position has been questioned by at least one former student of the same period, Kimball Young, who

remarked: "Blumer may have taken courses with Mead, but I doubt he was any closer to him than may others including Harold Lasswell, Louis Wirth . . . , and the present speaker [i.e., Young]. Blumer liked to give the impression that the mantle of Mead had fallen on his shoulders. . . . I doubt if Blumer knew Mead as well as some of us such as Harold and myself. We used to go visit Mead and have long conversations with him on all kinds [of] topics. I don't know how close Blumer ever got to him" (quoted in Lindstrom, Hardert, and Young 1988, 304).

59. Lewis and Smith's (1980) book is based on a combination of the two authors' individual dissertations (Lewis 1976b; Smith 1977). Lewis's part restates in depth much of the argument he made in his published article (1976a), while Smith's portion gives a detailed empirical examination of the influence of Mead on Chicago School sociology. Although Smith's work is framed in such a way that it claims to dispel the myth of Mead's influence (and was relied upon heavily by Harvey [1987] to make that argument), his empirical research gives a much more nuanced account of the particular or selective influences Mead had. This book was reviewed widely at the time, and some even pointed out that the approaches of the two essays—one in which philosophical positions are judged on theoretical grounds alone and the other in which personal social contacts are the crucial determinant of the transmission of ideas—are at cross-purposes (e.g., Kuklick 1984).

60. Blumer's most extended remarks on this mode of argument occur in his long posthumous essay *George Herbert Mead and Human Conduct*: "In the interest of clarity and brevity, I will present Mead's views without resorting to the use of quotations from his published works, with possibly one or two exceptions. Much of Mead's own exposition, particularly his central exposition, is unfortunately not easy to understand. Further, it is frequently presented in skeletal and unfinished form and, in addition, oriented to philosophical problems in such a way that their import for social and psychological science is obscured. For these various reasons, I am led to present in my own expository form his views as they relate to our matters of concern. In doing so, there are occasions where I have to go beyond what Mead has written, beyond what he has said as recorded in the notes of his students, and indeed beyond what he had occasion to say in my many intimate conversations with him. I have tried to clarify much that he did not make clear and to fill out important areas that were implicit in his scheme of thought but that he had no occasion to develop orally or in writing. There are, accordingly, parts of the exposition in this essay that are my own elaboration, but they have been made faithfully inside of the scheme of his thought and are congruent with it" (Blumer 2004, 14). One might even note that Blumer's conversations, themselves, sometimes became authoritative sources on Mead for others, as well. For example, Lewis Coser's (1977) influential *The Masters of Sociological Thought* includes an extended portrait of Mead's social psychology, life, and context that draws heavily (and explicitly) from one or more conversations with Blumer for much of its characterization of Mead. This is apparently also true for Robert Nisbet's (1970) discussions of Mead in his popular introductory book, *The Social Bond*.

61. For example, Maines (1997, 141) recalled that at the first symposium for the foundation of the Society for the Study of Symbolic Interaction (SSSI), "it seemed that

Blumer had fathered us all, since there were direct student-teacher relationships that formed a lineage from the oldest to the youngest of us." And Saxton (1997, 210) wrote that "as a student at the University of Minnesota, one had a strong sense of being part of a long-established symbolic interactionist tradition in sociology—a tradition that began with George Herbert Mead at Chicago, passed on to his student, Herbert Blumer, and then continued with Blumer's student, Greg Stone, who transmitted that tradition to us." Compare, also, Warshay and Warshay's (1986) analysis in which they indicate that the "individualistic" and "subjectivistic" aspects of Blumer's interpretation of Mead were taken up by his students. Rock's (1979) *The Making of Symbolic Interactionism* was particularly explicit about the essential importance of informal, orally transmitted tradition to the identity of symbolic interactionists. This view contrasts with Kuhn's (1964, 62) proposal that the publication in the 1930s of the posthumous volumes attributed to Mead effectively "ended what must be termed the long era of the 'oral tradition,' the era in which most of the germinating ideas had been passed about by word of mouth."

62. This latter point is emphasized by Silva and Vieira (2011, 367), when they argue that "the biographical circumstance that [Blumer] saw himself as Mead's 'appointed successor' had an important consequence for his reading of *Mind, Self, and Society.* The fact that this book had been assembled from notes from the very same course which made him Mead's intellectual heir helps explain why Blumer never seriously addressed any of the many editorial issues that plague the book. He was more interested in controlling its interpretation, with a view to also governing a certain tradition of scientific inquiry, than in questioning what interpretation it was of. In what surely is one of sociology's greatest ironies, Blumer, the creator of one of sociology's earlier and most accomplished social constructionist approaches, failed to adequately address the constructed nature of his view of the discipline's past."

63. The relationship between Morris and Blumer is quite difficult to trace. Very early in their careers they exchanged letters and appear to have had conversations with one another. At the University of Chicago they were sometimes involved in the same faculty endeavors, including the reorganization of the social science and humanities core in the 1930s-40s. Near the end of their careers, they remained cordial. For example, they exchanged professional courtesies such as negotiating research privileges for one another's students (e.g., H. Blumer to C. Morris, September 15, 1954, CMC, B 10, F "1954"). However, I am unable to find primary documentation on how they felt about one another privately.

64. Farrell (2001, 153) makes explicit reference to Mead's theory of socialization and self-development, along with Heinz Kohut's interpersonal psychoanalysis, in making his argument about the mirroring processes of interaction and their internalization. Mead's work on the social nature of personality influenced the development of social psychiatry, especially through Harry Stack Sullivan (1953, 16–19; cf. Lindstrom, Hardert, and Young 1988; Cottrell 1978; Burke 1959). Randall Collins's (1998) *The Sociology of Philosophies* develops a similar theory regarding the importance of emotional feedback processes of social encounters between intellectuals, on the basis of his "interaction ritual chains" concept.

CHAPTER SEVEN

1. These figures and all the following ones that make claims about the period after 1955 are from a citation search I conducted in winter 2010–11 in the ISI Web of Science "Cited Reference Search" database. This analysis includes all citations recorded from 1956 to 2008 in the Social Science Citation Index (SSCI), the Arts and Humanities Citation Index, and the Science Citation Index Expanded. The starting year was chosen because 1956 is the year for which the SSCI began recording a large amount of citations, and because preliminary analysis has made clear that by this period certain dominant patterns to Mead were firmly in place. Indications that Mead was firmly established by the mid-1950s abound, including the publication within a two-year period of the following major studies of Mead: Paul E. Pfuetze's *The Social Self* (1954), Maurice Natanson's *The Social Dynamics of George H. Mead* (1956), and *The Social Psychology of George Herbert Mead* edited by Anselm Strauss (1956) and later included under an edited title (and contents) as one of the original books in the University of Chicago Press's Heritage of Sociology series. The exact figures given in the chapter should not be treated as definitive, because this database is not exhaustive, but these do each represent unique articles (unlike search results in a database like Google Scholar where there are many repetitions). I have also manually cleaned the data of a few duplicate entries. I use the numbers here as a convenient and powerful way to index the relative visibility of Mead over time in academic disciplines. This analysis suggests that, as compared to citations in the second half of the twentieth century to other "masters of sociological thought" (Coser 1977), Mead has had a profile higher than Auguste Comte, W. I. Thomas, C. H. Cooley, and Robert Park, but well below that of Karl Marx, Max Weber, and Emile Durkheim. The claims made regarding the relative prevalence of citations to Mead in different disciplines are based on an analysis of the primary subject classifications reported in the Web of Science database for each journal. This classification is somewhat problematic, as journals often cut across disciplinary boundaries. This difficulty is most acute with regard to journals classified as falling into psychology subdisciplines. Given the interdisciplinary and somewhat contested nature of the field of social psychology during the study period, I have chosen to analyze journals classified under that subject separately from other psychology subfields at certain points. This separation is important to the analytical clarity of the analysis.

2. These are the results of a supplemental analysis utilizing data from a Web of Science cited reference search. In only 360 cases is a specific page recorded, but the five most frequently cited pages account for 25 percent of all references to specific pages, and the most common accounts for 10 percent by itself. I treat the most commonly cited single pages as a suggestive indicator of interest in particular concepts or sections, although I acknowledge that this small subsection cannot be said definitely to represent the larger body of citations.

3. A much larger literature on "origin myths" in schools of thought and academic disciplines exists, but I focus primarily on those that offer clear suggestions for mechanisms or orientations to the data that prove useful in the present study. For older reviews of this literature, see Platt (1996, chap. 7) and Baehr (2002). Much of this literature

primarily serves the purpose of criticizing or disputing "mythical" accounts of school
or disciplinary foundation, but only relatively few works go beyond this to trace the
process by which actual historical events led ultimately to mythical accounts.

4. This dataset is compiled from full text search results from six general purpose
periodical databases (Web of Science, JSTOR, PsychNET, ProQuest Periodicals Archive
Online, Science Direct, and Philosophy Documentation Center) as well as from three
sources specific to George Herbert Mead: the appendixes of Richard L. Smith's 1977 dissertation, the "Mead Project" bibliography (Throop and Ward 2007c), and the University
of Chicago Press Records (B 324, F 1–3) for the works of George H. Mead. The procedure
was as follows. First I searched for all mentions of the term "Mead" over the specified period, as this is the minimal identifiable reference in common. I supplemented
this with searches of several common misspellings and character-recognition errors
of Mead's name. Then, I examined each of the search results manually, ensuring that
it is definitely a reference to George Herbert Mead and eliminating references which
occur in front or back matter of journals, books received lists, and reports of conferences, because these do not represent substantive engagement by another scholar with
Mead's work. I also supplemented this with physical perusal of volumes for select
journals not included in any of these databases. This procedure returned results from
220 academic journals with a wide range of scope and topic. The average number of
articles or reviews per journal mentioning Mead was 5.2, but the modal response was
1 indicating a strong skew in the distribution. The single largest number of articles
or reviews referencing Mead came from the *American Journal of Sociology* with 126.
Although the dataset constructed in this way cannot claim to be a final census, it is
certainly by far the most comprehensive compilation of early references to Mead of
which I am aware. Two significant limitations of this database should be noted. First,
this database does not contain a systematic analysis of monographs, primarily because
a comprehensive examination of possible books that reference Mead is beyond the practical limits of my research. I have, however, analyzed a subset of books which Smith
(1977) compiled, supplemented by ones I have come upon in the course of my research,
and find suggestive support for the general arguments of this chapter. These results are
discussed below. Book-length works are also discussed as they impact the patterns of
journal citations through the reviews of those works. Second, because the sources used
to compile this database are primarily oriented to English-language journals, this work
cannot claim to adequately represent Mead's influence in non-English scholarship,
although I have made a concerted effort to physically peruse volumes in several other
languages and have discovered a number of relevant cases, especially in the latter part
of the period under consideration. The ending year for the dataset, 1955, was chosen to
pair it with the Web of Science search, which begins in 1956, and because of the analysis
presented above that indicates the dominant understandings of Mead were in place by
the mid-twentieth century.

5. This finding regarding the importance of "informal citations" is echoed in
other recent work in bibliometrics. In particular, Marx and Cardona (2009) find that
the impact of seminal publications in chemistry and physics is only very imperfectly
captured in formal citation patterns, and that informal citation practices, in which
only the name or initials of the author are mentioned, often substitute for rather than

supplement formal citations. On the basis of such findings they have argued that the impact of pioneering articles cannot be fully and accurately determined by formal citation measures alone. Unfortunately, Marx and Cardona utilize a sample based not on full-text searches but on databases of chemistry and physics article abstracts, which no doubt causes their analysis still to underestimate the importance of informal citation patterns. My findings are even starker in emphasizing the importance of informal citations, especially in review articles, which make up fully 52 percent of the informal citations to Mead through 1955 in professional journals.

6. Dewey noted in this article, "Being unable to do anything with these cases, I called them to the notice of my friend and colleague, Mr. G. H. Mead. The explanation given, which seems to me indubitable, is his. The relation between the vegetative and the motor functions, given above in discussion of pathological emotion and to be used again below, I also owe to him. While I have employed the point only incidentally, Mr. Mead rightly makes it essential to the explanation of emotion and its attitudes, as distinct from the identification and description which alone I have attempted. I hope, therefore, that his whole theory may soon appear in print" (Dewey 1894, 568). Note that this reference does not include a formal bibliographical entry, or even a reference to a published work by Mead. Thus, it is, by my method of analysis, an "informal" reference.

7. These citations are particularly important to an assessment of Mead and his influence, because they substantially supplement the views otherwise available. The large number of works citing Mead's lectures gives an outstanding and heretofore-unutilized source on Mead's early theoretical development. For example, Heath Bawden wrote, "We have not the facts to enable us to sketch in detail the stages in the evolution of animal consciousness. An instructive outline of the probable steps, however, forms the substance of a course of lectures on comparative psychology by Professor George H. Mead of the University of Chicago, which have not as yet been published. I will give in my own words the drift of that part of his argument which is relevant here as I recall it from his lectures to which it was once my privilege to listen" (1901, 272). A *précis* of Mead's early comparative psychology lectures follows. The importance of Bawden's records of Mead's early classes has just recently begun to be recognized (Decker 2008), and there is surely more to be learned from sources like these. Similar examples are also given in previous chapters.

8. Further support for the drastic sea change in how Mead is referenced comes from the subsequent trajectory of citations to these early articles. While the three articles mentioned above were the most commonly cited works in this early period they were quickly forgotten. From 1956 to 2008 those three articles were cited a combined 42 times, according to a Web of Science citation search, in comparison to *Mind, Self, and Society*, which was cited 6,200 times.

9. A full listing of every student who registered for a course taught by G. H. Mead at the University of Chicago, available in EIGR, vols. 9–156, was utilized in coding the authors as students. The authors were also cross-referenced against the lists of faculty at the University of Chicago available in the *Annual Register* (1894/5–1929/30, Chicago: University of Chicago Press) and *University of Chicago Magazine* (1908/9–1954/5, Chicago: University of Chicago Press) in order to determine if they had been faculty colleagues of Mead, and other Chicago connections were determined by reference to

the World Biographical Information System electronic database. Not incidentally, all of the earliest references to Mead in sociology journals prior to 1920 come from his former students or colleagues: L. L. Bernard, J. F. Bobbitt, Walter B. Bodenhafer, Charles A. Ellwood, Ellsworth Faris, Frank M. Leavitt, Edwin H. Lewis, and Frank L. Tolman.

10. The following analysis of the disciplinary structure at the University of Chicago is based on an examination of course listings in the *Annual Register* from 1900 to 1931 (Chicago: University of Chicago Press), supplemented by narrative evidence available from the archived DSI and correspondence from various archival sources, cited where relevant.

11. Additional social psychology courses were taught intermittently in the psychology department by Charles H. Judd and G. M. Stratton after 1920. In 1930 Herbert Blumer took over Faris's "Introduction" course once. As discussed in chapter 6, when Mead was hospitalized in February 1931 Blumer took over his Advanced Social Psychology course and philosophy instructor Arthur Murphy took over his Problems of Philosophy course. After Mead's subsequent death Blumer took over the advanced course permanently and Murphy took over the courses Mead intended to teach on the History of Philosophy.

12. In retrospect, Ayres remembered the break with Mead's social psychology as a definitive one. He wrote in a letter to John Dewey, January 10, 1927, "When they first set me teaching elementary social psychology at Chicago, in 1917, I broke out in wild rebellion against [William] McDougall. (It took some temerity to do it, since Mead was quite the monopolist of social psychology at Chicago then, and he was still aboard McDougall. Them days is gone forever!)" (Dewey 1997, no. 05444). This account of Mead's reliance on McDougall is clearly mistaken based on the existing lecture notes from later courses (though Mead did assign portions of McDougall's *Introduction to Social Psychology* as a starting point for discussion and criticism in some courses), but Ayres's statement does indicate that this shift was salient and somewhat contentious. Ayres went on to be primarily remembered as an important Institutional Economist and, in sociology, an influence on the early Talcott Parsons and C. Wright Mills. The only published reference I can find among Ayres's works to G. H. Mead is in his 1944 *The Theory of Economic Progress* where he merely refers to Mead's notion of the "role." Kingsbury, a longtime psychology professor at Chicago, referred to Mead only in passing in a history of the psychology department at Chicago. It appears that neither Ayres nor Kingsbury made any substantial engagement with Mead's philosophy in their writings.

13. On G. H. Mead's death, Faris wrote to Mead's son and daughter-in-law, "There is no one to whom I owe more—no one in all the world. . . . I have for years regarded it as one of my chief aims to interpret and, if possible, extend the ideas which his great mind originated. Many others have written you. None have more cause than I to love him, thank him, honor him. For in an academic sense I call myself his son" (GHMP, B 11, F 8). Faris also dedicated the definitive collection of his own essays, *The Nature of Human Nature* (Faris 1937c), to Mead. The records from Faris's coursework at the University of Chicago indicate that he took four of Mead's courses (Development of Thought in the Modern Period [1911], Philosophy of Nature [1911], Social Psychology [1912], and Seminar: Social Consciousness [1913]) but none of Thomas's courses. Indeed, the only sociology course he took was apparently from Charles R. Henderson on the Social Treatment of Crime.

14. Mead was explicit in his later social psychology lectures about aligning his course with the introductory course in sociology. According to the transcript for the 1928 Advanced Social Psychology course, Mead remarked to the students in his first lecture that the course presupposes "the point of view that has already been given in elementary social psychology as given in the Department of Sociology." He also assigned as the primary course text that year the *Source Book for Social Psychology* by Kimball Young, his former student in sociology (GHMP, B 2, F 10, 1928 transcript, p. 1).

15. Smith (1977) provides an analysis of books that supports this conclusion. He prepared a list of 182 book-length works in sociology or social psychology from 1905 to 1935 and found references to Mead in 47 of those. His analysis underestimates the number of those who were connected to Chicago, because of incomplete information. My own analysis finds that 33 of the authors (or 70%) who cited him were directly connected to Mead as his students or as affiliated faculty, and I find that there were no references to Mead from those not directly connected to him prior to 1920. In addition, if one considers the major influential sociology works on the list that did not refer to Mead (e.g., Dealey and Ward's 1907 *A Textbook in Sociology*, Ross's 1915 *Social Psychology*, Dunlap's 1925 *Social Psychology*, Cooley's 1930 *Sociological Theory and Social Research*) one gets further confirmation of the relative neglect of Mead in sociology in this period, with only a few Chicago-based exceptions. One final note: this argument is further strengthened if we consider some major works left off of Smith's original list that refer to Mead, including Bernard's 1926 *An Introduction to Social Psychology* or L. L. Thurstone's 1927 *The Nature of Intelligence*, as these authors are both former Mead students.

16. Rosenow was a "biometrist" at the Institute for Juvenile Research, an organization Mead had helped to found as the "Juvenile Psychopathic Institute" in 1909. That Rosenow definitely connected his work at the Institute with Mead was noted by his colleague David M. Levy (1962b, 295): "I learned of this [i.e., the act as "an operational concept in psychodynamic thinking"] when I attended Mead's course of lectures on the 'Philosophy of Behaviorism' [i.e., Advanced Social Psychology] in 1920. I was then a psychiatrist on the staff of the Illinois Institute for Juvenile Research, and it was the strong persuasion of the psychologist, Curt Rosenow, which overcame my reluctance to take the time away from the clinic." Levy's article, which was also apparently the basis for a radio lecture and a previous talk he gave (Levy 1962a), provides an example of how influence can be retained without being explicitly acknowledged in print for a long time. Levy did not refer to Mead in other published works, as far as I am able to determine, but at the end of his long career he published a theory of the "act as a unit" for behavioral psychiatric study that drew very heavily from his own experience forty-two years previous in Mead's class. Mead had strong connections with the institute, not only by helping to choose its founding director, William Healy, but also through quite a few students who became institute staff members (e.g., Ethel Kawin, Clifford Shaw, Curt Rosenow). Adolf Meyer's proposal, quoted in the notes of chapter 5 above, that Mead should allow Kawin's notes from his courses to be published seems to imply that Mead's ideas were in general discussion at the institute, and that the institute's focus on "behavioral" study may have had a Meadian inflection, especially when read in the context of Levy's account.

17. Faris's students explicitly recall that he was responsible not only for tracking them to Mead's social psychology course but also for creating a unified alternative perspective in social psychology. In a set of interviews in the early 1970s Walter C. Reckless remarked, "Now Faris was a social psychologist and was very much influenced by Cooley, Dewey and by Mead, don't you see? So you got a very good insight into an integration of Dewey, Mead and Cooley, don't you see, through Faris . . . we liked his interpretation of Mead and Cooley and Dewey and the social psychological approach which was very much done by him" (DSI, B 1, F 21, p. 3, 10). Samuel Kincheloe likewise remembered that "Faris was a great interpreter of George Herbert Mead and that led back to Cooley and all the way back to the pragmatists," and Ernest Mowrer noted that he "got into the courses under Faris who also was very much influenced by Mead. By the time I got into Mead's course there wasn't very much left over. It wasn't very new . . . basically I already knew it" (DSI, B 1, F 13, p. 1; B 1 F 16, p. 10). Herbert Blumer recalled that his initial coursework at Chicago was with Faris before "spread[ing] out" to his work with Mead, and that "Faris' course was to a large extent . . . based on Mead's point of view" (DSI, B 1, F 2, p. 1, 4). In another interview he remarked that in Faris's course he "really became familiar with the name Mead and was given some impetus to move in the direction of familiarizing myself with his work" and that Faris "was very influential in taking his own students . . . and directing them toward Mead's [Advanced Social Psychology] course" (quoted in Smith 1977, 159, 162–63). See chapter 6 for a further discussion of Blumer's relationships to Mead and Faris.

The impact of Faris's reviews on his students was emphasized in a memorial statement written by Harvey J. Locke. Before discussing any of Faris's substantive work, Locke (1954, 226) highlighted how "his criticalness was particularly revealed in his book reviews, which were always impersonal, always coldly analytical, and always enjoyable, even when on one's own work. He assumed that 'you can tell your friends by those who say unpleasant things about you.'" The specific reference seemingly implied but left unsaid in this memorial statement is Faris's review shortly before he died of Talcott Parsons's *The Social System*. Faris strongly criticized Parsons's neglect of the long "roster of gifted men" in the United States who had worked on relevant questions, a list which included Mead and many other familiar names (Faris 1953).

18. Young reported being highly influenced by Mead, although records indicate that he only registered for one course with him—the winter 1917 Social Psychology course, for which he was a registered visitor. He later recalled that he and Harold Lasswell would "go visit Mead and have long conversations with him on all kinds of topics" (Young 1988, 304). However, Lasswell did not enter the University of Chicago until after Young had taken his master's degree in 1917 and left for Stanford. This would seem to indicate that some of Young's later returns to Chicago were occasions for further development of his interest in and understanding of Mead (perhaps when teaching a few courses there in the late 1920s while he was a professor at the University of Wisconsin, and while Lasswell was a new professor of political science at Chicago).

19. Kimball Young's most extended comment along these lines comes in a review of a work that actually does refer to Mead, Sherif and Cantril's *The Psychology of Ego-Involvements*, but apparently not with sufficient comprehension. Young (1948, 85) remarked: "To this reviewer the most serious omission of Sherif and Cantril—in

common with the writings of the Allports, the Murphys, and most other social psychologists whose training and background is that of the laboratory and the statistical measurement—is their failure to grasp and use the mechanisms of interpersonal interaction long ago explored by C. H. Cooley, John Dewey, and George H. Mead. These contemporary writers, like most of their followers, are consciously or unconsciously still oriented to traditional *individual* psychology, not *social* psychology in its basic meaning. It is interesting to note that year after year the significant theoretical formulations of George H. Mead, in particular, continue to be ignored or neglected by most workers in social psychology. True, the present authors take two minor quotations from Mead, but nowhere do they state, accept, reject, or analyze his profound analysis of the rise and function of the social self. Yet this is, in essence, the heart of their own concern. While one hardly expects every piece of research in the field of personality to pay attention to Mead's views, surely a serious systematic treatise of this kind should do so."

20. Young's *Source Book* was definitely the source for some individuals' information about Mead (e.g., House 1928) and was singled out by Manford Kuhn (1964) as one of the earliest attempts by Mead's students to promote his ideas in published works. Young's *Source Book*, explicitly modeled on W. I. Thomas's *Source Book for Social Origins* (1909), was an attempt to "present pertinent materials in the field of social psychology which are not easily available either for the student or for the general reader" (Young 1927, v). Faris and Young had this desire in common, as Faris also sought to publish some of Mead's less accessible writings in a more accessible form (for more on which see the notes to chapter 5).

21. Karpf's history of American social psychology was particularly influential in terms of the number of references and reviews it received. The study was a rewrite of her 1925 sociology dissertation supervised by Ellsworth Faris. A comparison of the dissertation and the published book indicates that they are couched in significantly different narratives. In the dissertation Karpf outlined the work of individual scholars from different European traditions of thought in order to specify the emergence of a differentiated and scientifically more adequate social psychology in the United States as identified by the accomplishments of individual American authors. In the published work, which had been twice revised with Faris's "intimate" involvement (Karpf 1932, viii), the social psychologists in the United States are identified not only for individual achievements but more importantly as belonging to identifiable "schools" of thought—Mead, Dewey, Thomas, and Cooley make up the "environmentalist" school. An added "Foreword" by Faris (1932, xvi) makes the claim explicit: "Social Psychology as a definite discipline known by distinctive terms is relatively young, but it is old enough already to have many 'schools.' We have our partisans, our sectarian champions, our orthodoxies, and our heresies . . . even in this little arena the student can witness wars of words, the annihilating phrases, and the savage battle cries which show how human scholars are. Here the alliances are across jurisdictional boundaries, and behaviorism, instinctivism, Gestaltism, and the rest seek their allies in any camp. What these schools are, what their claims are, and what shibboleths are required to membership within the company are matters not hard to learn, but their real significance requires most careful interpretation and insight." Faris (1937c, vii) said of his own volume of collected essays,

The Nature of Human Nature, that "much of it is polemic, which will surprise no one who is familiar with the history of social psychology in this generation."

22. Extensive records of correspondence and memoranda regarding the University of Chicago Press's role in publishing the posthumous volumes attributed to G. H. Mead are archived in the University of Chicago Press Records (B 323, F 8–10; B 324, F 1–3) in the Regenstein Library Special Collections at the University of Chicago. I have examined the complete list of advanced subscribers to the series of volumes from this collection for their relations to Mead using course registration data, alumni lists, and biographical databases. This analysis probably underestimates the number of subscriptions coming from former students of Mead. It has been impossible to definitely identify each person from the incomplete information available in the records, and this is especially true of those married women listed as subscribing to the volumes under their husband's surname or initials.

23. Of course, one should not deny the importance of the ability to discover this work without the introduction of someone who knew Mead personally, although accounts of this occurring without such intercession are very rare. One exception comes from the autobiography of Grace Lee Boggs who in 1945, under her maiden name Grace Chin Lee, published the first monograph-length treatment of Mead's philosophy, *George Herbert Mead: Philosopher of the Social Individual* (*pace* V. E. Helleberg's [1941] self-published *The Social Self* and a couple of dissertations on Mead in limited circulation). As she recounted, "one day in 1939, browsing in the [Bryn Mawr] philosophy library, my eye was caught by four bright-blue volumes with gold lettering. They turned out to be the posthumously published works of George Herbert Mead. . . . It was one of those happy accidents that, in retrospect, seemed necessary if I was to continue to develop. Until that moment I had never heard of Mead" (Boggs 1998, 32). By virtue of being on library shelves, *Mind, Self, and Society* was garnering some readers, even in places with little direct connection to Mead. Still, in the finished study Lee (1945, vii) also acknowledged her debt to Paul Weiss and Charles Morris; even in this case of accidental discovery the participation and help of Mead scholars was influential in the result. Another example is found in a study of book circulation at Osterhout Free Library, in Wilkes-Barre, Pennsylvania, where C. P. Eaton (1936, 655) found that *Mind, Self, and Society* circulated ten times between June and December 1935 to two social workers, one physician, one housewife, one "buyer," and one clerk.

24. Those who were both employees of the Cooperative Study in General Education and social science instructors at Chicago included Earl S. Johnson, Joseph D. Lohman, Maynard C. Krueger, Leland C. DeVinney, and Albert W. Levi. These men were also all graduate students at Chicago, although not all got degrees from the school. Several of these men, including Johnson, Lohman, and DeVinney, were officers in the University of Chicago's Society for Social Research graduate organization, which was an important venue for communication among graduate students (cf. Bulmer 1986). There was not a significant overlap between the humanities instructors and the CSGE employees, and indeed several people who had studied humanities at Chicago, including Albert Levi and Milton Singer, became instructors in the social sciences. There was, instead, a considerable tension between Hutchins' view for the college and the recommendations of the CSGE. For example, Krueger (1941, 34) remarked in a CSGE workshop, "We

are not discussing Mr. Hutchins' idea of the ideal college. In my general statement of objectives of the college faculty here [in Chicago] at the university there are some fairly square conflicts with Mr. Hutchins' educational philosophy. That statement makes one point clearly antithetical to Mr. Hutchins' ideas—we are concerned with the student not only as a *knower* but as an *appreciator* and as a *doer*: the notion of educating the whole man rather than only the intellect." The real irony is that Hutchins's advocacy of a fundamental transformation in undergraduate education, coupled with his apparent animosity toward the Chicago pragmatists, seems to have opened an enduring place for them in the university outside the humanities and provided some of their former students with academic positions in the reformulated social science core. That is, he helped place them conceptually and institutionally in the social sciences in the course of displacing them from his reformulated humanities.

25. Johnson had been a sociology graduate student at Chicago where he worked primarily with Robert Park, but he had also taken Mead's winter 1926 Advanced Social Psychology (the same quarter Blumer took the course), and had worked as an editorial assistant at the *American Journal of Sociology* under Faris and Ernest W. Burgess. While working at the CSGE as lead researcher for the social sciences, where he helped develop the suggestions for general education in the social sciences (including the suggestion to include *Mind, Self, and Society* as a recommended reading in the undergraduate core [Levi 1948, 247]), he was instructor in sociology and the college. The syllabi and readers he helped prepare for the social science curriculum included several items by Mead (e.g., Johnson 1942; *Social Sciences 2: Syllabus and Selected Readings. A Second Year Course in a Three-Year Sequence in the Social Sciences*, 1949, Chicago: University of Chicago Press, 6). Johnson's published writings also include discussions of Mead's ideas (e.g., Johnson 1945, 276; 1963, 394). A former student recalled later that Johnson referred to Mead in his seminars and draft papers as one of those individuals who "spoke with intelligent eloquence about the democratic pathos and the common man" (Rosengren 1985, 559).

26. A particularly remarkable aspect of the references to Mead coming from European scholars was that after World War II several prominent scholars took Mead back with them, so to speak, as an intellectual resource in the rebuilding of European social science. As early as mid-1943 Alfred Schütz posited in a departmental memorandum that "it may reasonably be expected that the present war will end in the not too distant future with the complete victory of the Allies and the total collapse of Germany," which will leave the German people "in a state of utter confusion, not only politically and economically, but also in the field of culture and science and especially of education." In this environment, he proposed, a "special task will arise" to "make German teachers and students familiar with the Anglo-American contributions to these [social] sciences" as an "excellent way to spread democratic ideas." He singled out "philosophers like John Dewey, Peirce, G. H. Mead, [and] Royce" as important theorists "practically unknown in Germany." In order to remedy this he proposed that the graduate faculty at the New School for Social Research embark on a series of German-language introductions to Anglo-American contributions in various fields (memorandum, August 18, 1943, Albert Salomon Collection [hereafter ASC], B 1, F 2). Although this particular memorandum was apparently not implemented, references to Mead (followed

by translations of his work) began to appear in France by Georges Gurvitch, David Victoroff, and others, and in Germany by Howard P. Becker, Arnold Gehlen, and others, as Gurvitch, Becker, and others taught in Europe after the war. This appropriation of Mead and American pragmatism into the continental debates on social philosophy had a major impact on subsequent American interpretations especially through the work of Jürgen Habermas, Karl Otto Apel, Hans Joas, and Axel Honneth (cf., Joas 1997 [1985]; Silva and Vieira 2011, 368–70). Schütz also had an impact through the work of his various students in the United States: for example, Maurice Natanson (1956) wrote one of the early book-length studies of Mead, and the treatises on "social construction" or "reality construction" by Peter Berger and Thomas Luckmann (1966) and Burkart Holzner (1968) both contain informed discussions of Mead.

27. In contrast, Max Weber's work was becoming "standard fare" during this same period in "the sociology of religion, political sociology, studies of bureaucracy and organization, investigations of inequality and social stratification, the comparative historical analysis of social institutions, and the discussion of modernization" (Scaff 2011, 244). And although there was some overlap both with Weber and Mead in regard to how Durkheim was referred to, interpreters of the French sociologist primarily emphasized symbolic systems, shared societal norms and mores, and institutions instead of the dynamics of social action or modern social structures (e.g., Alpert 1939). While Weber served, in this reading, as an overarching theoretical resource for macrohistorical social science, and Durkheim as the arch resource for the formation of societal norms and values, the work of Mead (and others, including Cooley) served increasingly as an important resource in the study of observable human behavior and personality formation.

28. Merton specifically identified this "rediscovery" of older theory as a common phenomenon resulting from scientific progress, itself. He remarked that "rediscoveries commonly occur precisely in this form: a cumulation of scientific knowledge results in making clearly relevant ideas and observations long existing in the public print. . . . In this reasonably strict sense, these ideas are 'before their time'" (Merton 1968, 413).

BIBLIOGRAPHY

MANUSCRIPT COLLECTIONS

Note: Each manuscript collection is given an acronym for ease of reference in the text. Only those collections that were directly utilized in the preparation of the text are listed here, although several others were consulted in the course of research.

ABF   University of Chicago Archival Biographical Files. Special Collections Research Center, Joseph P. Regenstein Library, University of Chicago. Files: "Mead, George Herbert, I–II."

ACCP   Alwin C. Carus Papers, 1900–2004. Special Collections Research Center, Delyte W. Morris Library, Southern Illinois University–Carbondale.

AMC   Adolf Meyer Collection. Alan Mason Chesney Medical Archives, Johns Hopkins Medical Institutions, Baltimore, MD.

ASC   Albert Salomon Collection, 1926–59. Leo Baeck Institute Archives, available online at http://www.archive.org/details/albertsalomon.

BUIC   Martin Hayes Bickham Papers, 1903–72. Special Collections, Richard J. Daley Library, University of Illinois–Chicago.

CFP   Campbell Family Papers, 1860–65, 1879–1949. Bentley Historical Library, University of Michigan–Ann Arbor.

CMC   Charles Morris Collection. Max Fisch Library, Institute for American Thought, Indiana University/Purdue University–Indianapolis.

DSI   University of Chicago Department of Sociology Interviews, 1972. Special Collections Research Center, Joseph P. Regenstein Library, University of Chicago.

ECNP   Elinor Castle Nef Papers, 1894–1953. Special Collections Research Center, Joseph P. Regenstein Library, University of Chicago.

EFP   Ellsworth Faris Papers. Special Collections Research Center, Joseph P. Regenstein Library, University of Chicago. Vols. 1–6.

EIGR   Examiners' and Instructors' Grade Reports, 1892–1982. Special Collections Research Center, Joseph P. Regenstein Library, University of Chicago. Vols. 9–156.

EJBP   Edward Jackson Baur Papers, 1933–1952. Special Collections Research Center, Joseph P. Regenstein Library, University of Chicago.

ESAP   Edward Scribner Ames Papers, 1893–1958. Special Collections Research Center, Joseph P. Regenstein Library, University of Chicago.

ESDP   Ethel Sturges Dummer Papers, 1866–1954. Arthur and Elizabeth Schlesinger Library on the History of Women in America, Radcliffe College, Cambridge, MA.

GHMP   George Herbert Mead Papers, 1883–1964. Special Collections Research Center, Joseph P. Regenstein Library, University of Chicago.

HNCP   Henry Northrup Castle Papers, 1872–95. Special Collections Research Center, Joseph P. Regenstein Library, University of Chicago.

HRGR   University of Chicago Division of the Humanities Research Grants Records, 1926–44. Special Collections Research Center, Joseph P. Regenstein Library, University of Chicago.

JENF   John U. and Elinor Castle Nef Papers, 1916–21. Special Collections Research Center, Joseph P. Regenstein Library, University of Chicago.

JHTP   James Hayden Tufts Papers, 1908–42. Special Collections Research Center, Joseph P. Regenstein Library, University of Chicago.

JRP   Joseph Ratner Papers, 1862–1978. Special Collections Research Center, Delyte W. Morris Library, Southern Illinois University–Carbondale.

LODR   University of Chicago Library Office of the Director, Ernest DeWitt Burton and J. C. M. Hanson Records, 1910–28. Special Collections Research Center, Joseph P. Regenstein Library, University of Chicago.

LWP   Louis Wirth Papers, 1918–52. Special Collections Research Center, Joseph P. Regenstein Library, University of Chicago.

MHBP   Martin Hayes Bickham Papers, 1911–65. Special Collections Research Center, Joseph P. Regenstein Library, University of Chicago.

MHFC   Max H. Fisch Collection. Max H. Fisch Library, Institute for American Thought, Indiana University/Purdue University–Indianapolis.

MRCP   Morris Raphael Cohen Papers, 1898–1981. Special Collections Research Center, Joseph P. Regenstein Library, University of Chicago.

MTPP   Maurice Thomas Price Papers, 1909–34, 1937–40, 1945–48. University of Illinois Archives. University of Illinois–Urbana.

NHE   Nachlass von Hermann Ebbinghaus, 1844–1920. Adolf-Würth-Zentrum für Geschichte der Psychologie, University of Würzburg.

OCPC   Open Court Publishing Co. Records, 1886–1998. Special Collections Research Center, Delyte W. Morris Library, Southern Illinois University–Carbondale.

OPHA   University of Chicago Office of the President, Hutchins Administration Records, 1892–1951. Special Collections Research Center, Joseph P. Regenstein Library, University of Chicago.

OPMA   University of Chicago Office of the President, Mason Administration Records, 1910–29. Special Collections Research Center, Joseph P. Regenstein Library, University of Chicago.

PMHP   Philip Morris Hauser Papers, 1925–77. Special Collections Research Center, Joseph P. Regenstein Library, University of Chicago.

REPC   Robert Ezra Park Collection, 1882–1979. Special Collections Research Center,
        Joseph P. Regenstein Library, University of Chicago.
RGFP   Robbins Gilman and Family Papers, 1699–1997. Minnesota Historical Society
        Library, Minnesota History Center, St. Paul, MN.
SAQP   Stuart Alfred Queen Papers, n.d. Special Collections Research Center, Joseph
        P. Regenstein Library, University of Chicago.
SGAR   Scholarship and Guidance Association Records, 1916–1963. Special Collec-
        tions, Richard J. Daley Library, University of Illinois–Chicago.
SSRR   Society for Social Research Records, 1923–56. Special Collections Research
        Center, Joseph P. Regenstein Library, University of Chicago.
UCPR   University of Chicago Press Records, 1892–1965. Special Collections Research
        Center, Joseph P. Regenstein Library, University of Chicago.
UMAA   University of Michigan Alumni Association, 1924 Alumnae Surveys. Bentley
        Historical Library, University of Michigan–Ann Arbor.
USMR   Unity of Science Movement Records, 1934–68. Special Collections Research
        Center, Joseph P. Regenstein Library, University of Chicago.
VMAP   Van Meter Ames Papers, 1931–85. Special Collections Research Center, Joseph
        P. Regenstein Library, University of Chicago.
WARL   Wayne A. R. Leys Papers. Special Collections Research Center, Delyte W.
        Morris Library, Southern Illinois University–Carbondale.
WRC   Walter Rauschenbusch Collection, 1861–1918. American Baptist Historical
        Society Library, Mercer University, Atlanta, GA.
WRHP   William Rainey Harper Papers, 1872–1938. Special Collections Research Cen-
        ter, Joseph P. Regenstein Library, University of Chicago.
WVDB   Walter Van Dyke Bingham Papers, 1852–1965. Hunt Library University Ar-
        chives, Carnegie Mellon University, Pittsburgh, PA.

PUBLISHED MATERIALS AND SINGLE VOLUMES

Abbott, Andrew D. 1999. *Department and Discipline: Chicago Sociology at One Hun-
    dred*. Chicago: University of Chicago Press.
———. 2007a. "Mechanisms and Relations." *Sociologica* 2/2007 (online journal).
———. 2007b. "Against Narrative: A Preface to Lyrical Sociology." *Sociological Theory*
    25 (1): 67–99.
———. 2010. "Pragmatic Sociology and the Public Sphere: The Case of Charles Rich-
    mond Henderson." *Social Science History* 34 (3): 337–71.
———. 2011. "Library Research Infrastructure for Humanistic and Social Scientific
    Scholarship in America in the Twentieth Century." In *Social Knowledge in the
    Making*, edited by Charles Camic, Neil Gross, and Michèle Lamont, 43–87. Chi-
    cago: University of Chicago Press.
Abbott, Andrew D., and Rainer Egloff. 2008. "The Polish Peasant in Oberlin and
    Chicago: The Intellectual Trajectory of W. I. Thomas." *American Sociologist*
    39:217–58.
Aboulafia, Mitchell. 1991. *Philosophy, Social Theory, and the Thought of George Her-
    bert Mead*. Albany: State University of New York Press.

————. 2010. *Transcendence: On Self-Determination and Cosmopolitanism*. Stanford, CA: Stanford University Press.

Adams, Romanzo C. 1924. "Hawaii a Sociological Laboratory." *The Friend* 94 (12): 289–90.

Addams, Jane. 1930. "Helen Castle Mead." In *Helen Castle Mead* [memorial booklet]. Chicago: Privately printed.

Alger, Janet M., and Steven F. Alger. 1997. "Beyond Mead: Symbolic Interaction between Humans and Felines." *Society and Animals* 5 (1): 65–81.

Allen, Jessie B. 1904. "The Associative Processes of the Guinea Pig: A Study of the Psychical Development of an Animal with a Nervous System Well Medullated at Birth." *Journal of Comparative Neurology and Psychology* 14 (4): 293–359.

Allport, Floyd. 1924. *Social Psychology*. Boston: Houghton Mifflin.

Alpert, Harry. 1939. *Emile Durkheim and His Sociology*. New York: Columbia University Press.

Alvaro-Estramiana, José Luis, and Alicia Garrido-Luque. 2007. "Orígenes sociológicos de la psicología social (The Sociological Origins of Social Psychology)." *REIS: Revista Española de Investigaciones Sociológicas* 118:11–26.

Ames, Edward S. 1931. "George Herbert Mead." In *George Herbert Mead* [memorial booklet]. Chicago: Privately printed.

Ames, Van Meter. 1931. "George Herbert Mead: An Appreciation." *University of Chicago Magazine* (June): 370–72.

Angell, James R. 1899. "The Psychological Laboratory." In *The President's Report. July, 1897–July, 1898*. Chicago: University of Chicago Press.

————. 1913. "Behavior as a Category of Psychology." *Psychological Review* 20:255–70.

Austin, J. L. 1962. *How to Do Things with Words*. Cambridge, MA: Harvard University Press.

Baehr, Peter. 2002. *Founders, Classics, and Canons: Modern Disputes over Sociology's Heritage*. New Brunswick, NJ: Transaction Publishers.

Baker, Paul J. 1973. "The Life Histories of W. I. Thomas and Robert E. Park." *American Journal of Sociology* 79 (2): 243–60.

Bakhtin, M. M. 1981. "Discourse in the Novel." In *The Dialogic Imagination: Four Essays*, edited by Michael Holquist, translated by Caryl Emerson and Michael Holquist, 259–422. Austin: University of Texas Press.

Baldwin, John D. 1986. *George Herbert Mead: A Unifying Theory for Sociology*. Newbury Park, CA: Sage Publications.

Bales, Robert F. 1966. "Comment on Herbert Blumer's Paper." *American Journal of Sociology* 71 (5): 545–47.

Barry, Robert M. 1968. "A Man and a City: George Herbert Mead in Chicago." In *American Philosophy and the Future*, edited by Michael Novak, 173–92. New York: Charles Scribner's Sons.

Bawden, H. Heath. 1901. "The Psychological Theory of Organic Evolution." *Journal of Comparative Neurology* 11 (3): 251–76.

————. 1919. "The Evolution of Behavior." *Psychological Review* 26 (4): 247–76.

Ben-David, Joseph, and Randall Collins. 1966. "Social Factors in the Origins of a New Science: The Case of Psychology." *American Sociological Review* 31 (4): 451–65.

Bendix, Reinhard. 1960. *Max Weber: An Intellectual Portrait.* New York: Doubleday.

Berger, Peter, and Thomas Luckmann. 1966. *The Social Construction of Reality: A Treatise in the Sociology of Knowledge.* Garden City, NY: Doubleday.

Biesta, Gert, and Daniel Tröhler. 2008. "Introduction: George Herbert Mead and the Development of a Social Conception of Education." In George H. Mead, *The Philosophy of Education,* 1–16. Boulder: Paradigm Publishers.

Blumer, Herbert. 1928. "Method in Social Psychology." PhD dissertation. University of Chicago.

———. 1933. *Movies and Conduct.* New York: Macmillan.

———. 1937. "Social Psychology." In *Man and Society: A Substantive Introduction to the Social Sciences,* edited by Emerson P. Schmidt, 148–98. New York: Prentice-Hall.

———. 1939. *An Appraisal of Thomas and Znaniecki's* The Polish Peasant in Europe and America. Critiques of Research in the Social Sciences 1. New York: Social Sciences Research Council.

———. 1953. "Psychological Import of the Human Group." In *Group Relations at the Crossroads,* edited by Muzafer Sherif and M. O. Wilson, 185–202. New York: Harper and Row.

———. 1955. "Attitudes and the Social Act." *Social Problems* 3 (2): 59–65.

———. 1962. "Society as Symbolic Interaction." In *Human Behavior and Social Processes: An Interactionist Approach,* edited by Arnold M. Rose, 179–92. Boston: Houghton Mifflin.

———. 1966a. "Sociological Implications of the Thought of George Herbert Mead." *American Journal of Sociology* 71 (5): 535–44.

———. 1966b. "Reply." *American Journal of Sociology* 71 (5): 547–48.

———. 1967. "Reply to Woelfel, Stone, and Farberman." *American Journal of Sociology* 72 (4): 411–12.

———. 1969. *Symbolic Interactionism: Perspective and Method.* Englewood Cliffs, NJ: Prentice-Hall.

———. 1970. "Comment on Deutscher's Paper." *Sociological Quarterly*: 11 (4): 541–43.

———. 1973. "A Note on Symbolic Interactionism." *American Sociological Review* 38 (6): 797–98.

———. 1975a. "Comments by Herbert Blumer." *Sociological Inquiry* 45 (1): 59–62.

———. 1975b. "Reply to Parsons' Comments." *Sociological Inquiry* 45 (1): 68.

———. 1977. "Comment on Lewis' 'Classical American Pragmatists as Forerunners to Symbolic Interactionism.'" *Sociological Quarterly* 18 (2): 285–89.

———. 1980. "Mead and Blumer: The Convergent Methodological Perspectives of Social Behaviorism and Symbolic Interactionism." *American Sociological Review* 45 (3): 409–19.

———. 1981. "George Herbert Mead." In *The Future of the Sociological Classics,* edited by Buford Rhea, 136–69. London: Allen and Unwin.

———. 1983. "Going Astray with a Logical Scheme." *Symbolic Interaction* 6 (1): 127–37.

———. 2004. *George Herbert Mead and Human Conduct.* Edited by Thomas J. Morrione. Walnut Creek, CA: AltaMira Press.

Blumer, Herbert, and Philip M. Hauser. 1933. *Movies, Delinquency, and Crime.* New York: Macmillan.

Bogardus, Emory S. 1959. "W. I. Thomas and Social Origins." *Sociology and Social Research* 43:365–69.

———. 1962. *Much Have I Learned.* Los Angeles: University of Southern California Press.

Boggs, Grace Lee. 1998. *Living for Change: An Autobiography.* Minneapolis: University of Minnesota Press.

Booth, Kelvin J. 2007. "Animal Mind, Human Mind: George H. Mead, Animality and the Evolution of Embodied Cognition." PhD dissertation. Southern Illinois University–Carbondale.

Bordogna, Francesca. 2008. *William James at the Boundaries: Philosophy, Science, and the Geography of Knowledge.* Chicago: University of Chicago Press.

Boring, Edwin G. 1950. *A History of Experimental Psychology.* 2nd ed. New York: Appleton-Century-Crofts.

Bourdieu, Pierre. 1969. "Intellectual Field and Creative Project." Translated by Sian France. *Social Science Information* 8 (2): 89–119.

Brewster, John M. 1936. "A Behaviorist Account of the Logical Function of Universals, II." *Journal of Philosophy* 33 (20): 533–47.

Bulmer, Martin. 1986. *The Chicago School of Sociology: Institutionalization, Diversity, and the Rise of Sociological Research.* Chicago: University of Chicago Press.

Burke, Armand J. 1923. "The Significance of Adjustment in Aesthetics." PhD dissertation. University of Chicago.

Burke, Richard John. 1959. "George Herbert Mead and Harry Stack Sullivan: A Study in the Relations between Philosophy and Psychology." PhD dissertation. University of Chicago.

Bush, Wendell T. 1917. "Constructive Intelligence." *Journal of Philosophy, Psychology, and Scientific Methods* 14 (19): 505–20.

Camic, Charles. 1992. "Reputation and Predecessor Selection: Parsons and the Institutionalists." *American Sociological Review* 57 (4): 421–45.

———. 1995. "Three Departments in Search of a Discipline: Localism and Interdisciplinary Interaction in American Sociology, 1890–1940." *Social Research* 62: 1003–33.

———. 2008. "Classics in What Sense?" *Social Psychology Quarterly* 71 (4): 324–30.

Camic, Charles, and Neil Gross. 2001. "The New Sociology of Ideas." In *Blackwell Companion to Sociology,* edited by Judith R. Blau, 236–49. Malden, MA: Blackwell.

Camic, Charles, Neil Gross, and Michèle Lamont. 2011. "Introduction: The Study of Social Knowledge Making." In *Social Knowledge in the Making,* edited by Charles Camic, Neil Gross, and Michèle Lamont, 1–40. Chicago: University of Chicago Press.

Campbell, James. 1992. *The Community Reconstructs: The Meaning of Pragmatic Social Thought.* Urbana: University of Illinois Press.

———. 2006. *A Thoughtful Profession: The Early Years of the American Philosophical Association.* Chicago: Open Court Publishing.

Canales, Jimena. 2009. *A Tenth of a Second: A History*. Chicago: University of Chicago Press.

Castle, Alfred L. 1989. "Harriet Castle and the Beginnings of Progressive Kindergarten Education in Hawai'i, 1894–1900." *Hawaiian Journal of History* 23:119–36.

———. 2004. *A Century of Philanthropy: A History of the Samuel N. and Mary Castle Foundation*. Rev. ed. Honolulu: University of Hawaii Press.

Clark, Grover G. 1918. "The Stages of the Social Self Compared with Those of the Hegelian Dialectic." Master's thesis. University of Chicago.

Collins, Harry M. 1983. "The Sociology of Scientific Knowledge: Studies of Contemporary Science." *Annual Review of Sociology* 9:265–85.

Collins, Randall. 1998. *The Sociology of Philosophies: A Global Theory of Intellectual Change*. Cambridge, MA: Belknap Press of Harvard University Press.

Cook, Gary A. 1993. *George Herbert Mead: The Making of a Social Pragmatist*. Urbana: University of Illinois Press.

———. 2007. "George Herbert Mead and the Allen Controversy at the University of Wisconsin." *Journal of the History of the Behavioral Sciences* 43 (1): 45–67.

———. 2011. "Revisiting the Mead–Blumer Controversy." *Studies in Symbolic Interaction* 36:17–38.

———. 2013. "Resolving Two Key Problems in Mead's *Mind, Self, and Society*." In *George Herbert Mead in the Twenty-first Century*, edited by F. Thomas Burke and Krzysztof Piotr Skowronski, 95–105. Lanham, MD: Lexington Books.

Cooley, Charles H. 1927. *Life and the Student: Roadside Notes on Human Nature, Society, and Letters*. New York: A. A. Knopf.

Coser, Lewis. 1977. *Masters of Sociological Thought: Ideas in History and Social Context*. New York: Harcourt Brace.

Cottrell, Leonard S., Jr. 1978. "George Herbert Mead and Harry Stack Sullivan: An Unfinished Synthesis." *Psychiatry* 41 (2): 151–62.

———. 1980. "George Herbert Mead: The Legacy of Social Behaviorism." In *Sociological Traditions from Generation to Generation: Glimpses of the American Experience*, edited by Robert K. Merton and Matilda White Riley, 45–65. Norwood, NJ: Ablex Publishing.

Couch, Carl. 1997. "Forming the Unformable." *Symbolic Interaction* 20:101–6.

Coughlan, Neil. 1975. *Young John Dewey: An Essay in American Intellectual History*. Chicago: University of Chicago Press.

Craig, Wallace. 1908. "The Voices of Pigeons Regarded as a Means of Social Control." *American Journal of Sociology* 14 (1): 86–100.

Danziger, Kurt. 1979. "The Social Origins of Modern Psychology: Positivist Sociology and the Sociology of Knowledge." In *The Social Context of Psychological Theory: Towards a Sociology of Psychological Knowledge*, edited by A. R. Buss, 27–45. New York: Irvington.

Daston, Lorraine, and Peter Galison. 2007. *Objectivity*. New York: Zone Books.

De Waal, Cornelis. 2002. *On Mead*. Belmont, CA: Wadsworth/Thomson Learning.

Decker, Kevin S. 2008. "The Evolution of the Psychical Element. George Herbert Mead at the University of Chicago. Lecture notes by H. Heath Bawden 1898–1900. Introduction." *Transactions of the Charles S. Peirce Society* 44 (3): 469–79.

Deegan, Mary Jo. 1988. *Jane Addams and the Men of the Chicago School, 1892–1918.* New Brunswick, NJ: Transaction Publishers.

———. 2008. *Self, War, and Society: George Herbert Mead's Macrosociology.* New Brunswick, NJ: Transaction Publishers.

Deegan, Mary Jo, and John Burger. 1978. "George Herbert Mead and Social Reform: His Work and Writings." *Journal of the History of the Behavioral Sciences* 14 (4): 362–72.

Denzin, Norman. 1997. "Contingency, Biography, and Structure: On the History of the Society for the Study of Symbolic Interaction." *Symbolic Interaction* 20:107–13.

Dessoir, Max. 1890. *Das Doppel-Ich.* Leipzig: Ernst Günthers Verlag.

———. 1892. *Über den Hautsinn. Separat-Abzug aus Archiv für Anatomie und Physiologie* (3–4:177–339.

———. 1947. *Buch der Erinnerung.* Stuttgart: F. Enke.

Deutscher, Irwin. 1970. "Buchenwald, Mai Lai, and Charles Van Doren: Social Psychology as Explanation." *Sociological Quarterly* 11 (4): 533–40.

Dewey, John. 1894. "The Theory of Emotion I: Emotional Attitudes." *Psychological Review* 1 (6): 553–69.

———. 1897. *The Significance of the Problem of Knowledge.* University of Chicago Contributions to Philosophy 1, no. 3. Chicago: University of Chicago Press.

———. 1922. "Knowledge and Speech Reaction." *Journal of Philosophy* 19 (21): 561–70.

———. 1927. *The Public and Its Problems.* New York: Henry Holt and Co.

———. 1930. "How Much Freedom in New Schools?" *New Republic* 63 (July 9): 204–6.

———. 1931. "George Herbert Mead." *Journal of Philosophy* 28 (12): 309–14.

———. 1932. "Prefatory Remarks." In George H. Mead, *The Philosophy of the Present,* edited and with an introduction by Arthur E. Murphy. Chicago: Open Court Publishing.

———. 1997. *The Correspondence of John Dewey,* 3 vols. Charlottesville, VA: InteLex Past Masters (electronic resource).

———. 2010. *The Class Lectures of John Dewey,* vol. 1. Charlottesville, VA: InteLex Past Masters (electronic resource).

Dewey, John, Addison W. Moore, Harold C. Brown, George H. Mead, Boyd H. Bode, Henry W. Stuart, James H. Tufts, and Horace M. Kallen. 1917. *Creative Intelligence: Essays in the Pragmatic Attitude.* New York: Henry Holt.

Dilthey, Wilhelm. 2010 [1890]. "The Origin of Our Belief in the Reality of the External World and Its Justification (1890)." In *Selected Works,* vol. 2, *Understanding and the Human World,* translated by Maximilian Aue, edited with an introduction by Rudolf A. Makkreel and Frithjof Rodi, 8–57. Princeton, NJ: Princeton University Press.

Diner, Stephen. 1972. "A City and Its University: Chicago Professors and Elite Reform, 1892–1919." PhD dissertation. University of Chicago.

Dunham, Albert M., Jr. 1933. "The Concept of Tension in Philosophy." PhD dissertation. University of Chicago.

Dykhuizen, George. 1973. *The Life and Mind of John Dewey.* Edited by Jo Ann Boydston. Carbondale: Southern Illinois University Press.

Eaton, Casindania P. 1936. "'Now Give Me a Book to Read': The Public Library Reports on Book Reports." *English Journal* 25 (8): 653–58.

Ebbinghaus, Hermann. 1887. "Die Gesetzmässigkeit des Helligkeitskontrastes." *Sitzungsberichte der Königlich preussischen Akademie der Wissenschaften zu Berlin* 49:995–1009.

———. 1889. "Über den Grund der Abweichungen von dem Weber'schen Gesetz bei Lichtempfindungen." *Pflüger's Archiv für die gesamte Psychologie* 45:113–33.

———. 1890. "Über Nachbilder in binocularen Sehen und die binocularen Farbenerscheinungen überhaupt." *Pflüger's Archiv für die gesamte Psychologie* 46:498–508.

———. 1893. "Theorie des Farbensehens." *Zeitschrift für Psychologie und Physiologie der Sinnesorgane* 5:145–238.

———. 1913 [1885]. *Memory: A Contribution to Experimental Psychology.* Translated by Henry A. Ruger and Clara E. Bussenius. New York: Teachers College Educational Reprints, Columbia University.

Eliot, Thomas D. 1924. "Sociology as a Pre-Vocational Subject: The Verdict of Sixty Social Workers." *American Journal of Sociology* 29 (6): 726–46.

Ellwood, Charles A. 1909. "The Origin of Society." *American Journal of Sociology* 15 (3): 394–404.

———. 1912. *Sociology in its Psychological Aspects.* New York: D. Appleton.

Emerson, Nathaniel B. 1909. *Unwritten Literature of Hawaii: The Sacred Songs of the Hula, Collected and Translated with Notes and an Account of the Hula. Bulletin of the Bureau of American Ethnology* 38. Washington, DC: Government Printing Office.

Fallding, Harold. 1982. "G. H. Mead's Orthodoxy." *Social Forces* 60 (3): 723–37.

Farberman, Harvey A. 1997. "Founding the Society for the Study of Symbolic Interaction: Some Observations from the Co-Chairman of the Steering Committtee, 1974–1975." *Symbolic Interaction* 20:115–29.

Faris, Ellsworth. 1918. "[Review] *The Secret of Personality* by George Trumbull Ladd." *American Journal of Sociology* 24 (2): 221–22.

———. 1921. "[Review] *Primitive Society* by Robert H. Lowie." *American Journal of Sociology* 27 (2): 243–44.

———. 1926a. "[Review] *Psychologies of 1925. Powell Lectures in Psychological Theory.*" *American Journal of Sociology* 32 (2): 309–11.

———. 1926b. "The Concept of Imitation." *American Journal of Sociology* 32 (3): 367–78.

———. 1928. "[Review] *Introduction to Social Psychology* by L. L. Bernard." *Psychological Bulletin* 25 (2): 118–20.

———. 1929. "Current Trends in Social Psychology." In *Essays in Philosophy by Seventeen Doctors of Philosophy of the University of Chicago,* edited by T. V. Smith and William Kelley Wright, 119–33. Chicago: Open Court Publishing.

———. 1932. "Foreword." In Fay Berger Karpf, *American Social Psychology: Its Origins, Development, and European Background,* xiii–xvii. New York: McGraw-Hill.

———. 1936. "[Review] *Mind, Self, and, Society* by George H. Mead, edited and with introduction by Charles W. Morris." *American Journal of Sociology* 41 (6): 809–13.

———. 1937a. [Untitled letter]. *American Journal of Sociology* 42 (4): 561.

———. 1937b. "The Social Psychology of George Mead." *American Journal of Sociology* 43 (3): 391–403.

———. 1937c. *The Nature of Human Nature: And Other Essays in Social Psychology.* New York: McGraw-Hill.

———. 1953. "[Review] *The Social System* by Talcott Parsons." *American Sociological Review* 18 (1): 103–6.

Farrell, Michael. 2001. *Collaborative Circles: Friendship Dynamics and Creative Work.* Chicago: University of Chicago Press.

Feffer, Andrew. 1993. *The Chicago Pragmatists and American Progressivism.* Ithaca, NY: Cornell University Press.

Fine, Gary A. 1993. "The Sad Demise, Mysterious Disappearance, and Glorious Triumph of Symbolic Interactionism." *Annual Review of Sociology* 19:16–87.

———, ed. 1995. *A Second Chicago School?: The Development of a Postwar American Sociology.* Chicago: University of Chicago Press.

———. 2001. *Difficult Reputations: Collective Memories of the Evil, Inept, and Controversial.* Chicago: University of Chicago Press.

Fine, Gary A., and Sherryl Kleinman. 1986. "Interpreting the Sociological Classics: Can There Be a 'True' Meaning of Mead?" *Symbolic Interaction* 9:129–46.

Fleck, Ludwik. 1979 [1935]. *The Genesis and Development of a Scientific Fact.* Edited by Thaddeus J. Trenn and Robert K. Merton. Chicago: University of Chicago Press.

Frear, Walter F. 1911. "Napali." *Mid-Pacific Magazine* 1 (1): 18–27.

Frickel, Scott, and Neil Gross. 2005. "A General Theory of Scientific/Intellectual Movements." *American Sociological Review* 70 (2): 204–32.

Galison, Peter. 1996. "Constructing Modernism: The Cultural Location of *Aufbau*." In *Origins of Logical Empiricism*, edited by Ronald N. Giere and Alan W. Richardson, 17–44. Minneapolis: University of Minnesota Press.

Gallagher, Timothy J. 2011. "G. H. Mead's Understanding of the Nature of Speech in the Light of Contemporary Research." *Journal of the Theory of Social Behavior* 41 (1): 40–62.

Glaeser, Andreas. 2011. *Political Epistemics: The Secret Police, the Opposition, and the End of East German Socialism.* Chicago: University of Chicago Press.

Goldenweiser, A. A. 1918. "History, Psychology and Culture: A Set of Categories for an Introduction to Social Science." *Journal of Philosophy, Psychology and Scientific Methods* 15 (21): 561–71.

Good, James M. M. 2000. "Disciplining Social Psychology: A Case Study of Boundary Relations in the History of the Human Sciences." *Journal of the History of the Behavioral Sciences* 36 (4): 383–400.

Goto, Masayuki. 1996. "George Herbert Mead: A Text Database Analysis of His Writings." PhD dissertation. University of California–Santa Barbara.

Grafton, Anthony T. 2011. "In Clio's American Atelier." In *Social Knowledge in the Making*, edited by Charles Camic, Neil Gross, and Michèle Lamont, 89–117. Chicago: University of Chicago Press.

Greenwood, John D. 2004. *The Disappearance of the Social in American Social Psychology.* Cambridge: Cambridge University Press.

Grey Towers: A Campus Novel. 1923. Chicago: Covici-McGee Co.

Gross, Neil. 2002. "Becoming a Pragmatist Philosopher: Status, Self-Concept, and Intellectual Choice." *American Sociological Review* 67 (1): 52–76.

———. 2008. *Richard Rorty: The Making of an American Philosopher*. Chicago: University of Chicago Press.

———. 2009. "A Pragmatist Theory of Social Mechanisms." *American Sociological Review* 74 (3): 358–79.

Hamilton, Peter, ed. 1992. *George Herbert Mead: Critical Assessments*, 4 vols. London: Routledge.

Harvey, Lee. 1987. *Myths of the Chicago School of Sociology*. Aldershot: Avebury.

Hauser, Philip M. 1932. "How Do Motion Pictures Affect the Conduct of Children?: Methods Employed in 'Movies and Conduct' and 'Movies, Delinquency, and Crime.'" *Journal of Educational Sociology* 6 (4): 231–37.

———. 1933. "Motion Pictures in Penal and Correctional Institutions: A Study of the Reactions of Prisoners to Movies." PhD dissertation. University of Chicago.

Helleberg, Victor E. 1941. *The Social Self: The Star in the Human Comedy: An Evolutionary Social Psychology Sketch*. Lawrence, KS: privately printed.

Henderson, Harold. 1993. *Catalyst for Controversy: Paul Carus of Open Court*. Carbondale, IL: Open Court Publishing.

Hinkle, Roscoe C., Jr., and Gisela J. Hinkle. 1954. *The Development of Modern Sociology: Its Nature and Growth in the United States*. New York: Random House.

Hochschild, Arlie R. 1987. "Memorium for Herbert Blumer." *Berkeley Journal of Sociology* 32:i–iii.

Holmes, Harry N. 1936. "A Great Pupil and a Great Discovery—Both Supported by a Great Teacher." *Science* 83 (2147): 175–77.

Holt, Edwin B., Walter T. Marvin, W. P. Montague, Ralph B. Perry, Walter B. Pitkin, and E. G. Spaulding. 1912. *The New Realism: Cooperative Studies in Philosophy*. New York: Macmillan.

Holzner, Burkart. 1968. *Reality Construction in Society*. Cambridge, MA: Schenkman Publishing.

Hooper, Paul Franklin. 1972. "A History of Internationalism in Hawaii between 1900 and 1940." PhD dissertation. University of Hawaii.

House, Floyd N. 1928. "Development in the Theory of the Social Personality." *Social Forces* 6 (3): 357–67.

Huber, Joan. 1973. "Symbolic Interaction as a Pragmatic Perspective: The Bias of Emergent Theory." *American Sociological Review* 38 (2): 274–84.

———. 1974. "The Emergency of Emergent Theory." *American Sociological Review* 39 (3): 463–67.

Huebner, Daniel R. 2013. "Wilhelm Jerusalem's Sociology of Knowledge in the Dialogue of Ideas." *Journal of Classical Sociology* 13 (4): 430–59.

———. 2015. "Appendix: The Sources of *Mind, Self, and Society*." In George H. Mead, *Mind, Self, and Society: From the Standpoint of a Social Behaviorist*, edited by Charles W. Morris, revised edition edited by Daniel R. Huebner and Hans Joas. Chicago: University of Chicago Press.

Irvine, Leslie. 2003. "George's Bulldog: What Mead's Canine Companion Could Have Told Him about the Self." *Sociological Origins* 3 (1): 46–49.

Iser, Wolfgang. 1978. *The Act of Reading: A Theory of Aesthetic Response.* Baltimore: Johns Hopkins University Press.

James, William. 1885. "Experiments in Memory." *Science* 6:198–99.

———. 1890. *The Principles of Psychology.* 2 vols. New York: Henry Holt.

———. 1904. "The Chicago School." *Psychological Bulletin* 1 (1): 1–5.

———. 1907. *Pragmatism: A New Name for Some Old Ways of Thinking.* New York: Longmans, Green.

———. 1998. *The Correspondence of William James,* vol. 6: *1885–1889.* Edited by Ignas K. Skrupskelis and Elizabeth M. Berkeley, with the assistance of Bernice Grohskopf and Wilma Bradbeer. Charlottesville: University of Virginia Press.

———. 1999. *The Correspondence of William James,* vol. 7: *1890–1894.* Edited by Ignas K. Skrupskelis and Elizabeth M. Berkeley, with the assistance of Bernice Grohskopf and Wilma Bradbeer. Charlottesville: University of Virginia Press.

———. 2003. *The Correspondence of William James,* vol. 11: *April 1905–March 1908.* Edited by Ignas K. Skrupskelis and Elizabeth M. Berkeley, with the assistance of Bernice Grohskopf and Wilma Bradbeer. Charlottesville: University of Virginia Press.

Jauss, Hans Robert. 1982. *Aesthetic Experience and Literary Hermeneutics.* Translated by Michael Shaw. Minneapolis: University of Minnesota Press.

Jewett, Andrew. 2011. "Canonizing Dewey: Naturalism, Logical Empiricism, and the Idea of American Philosophy." *Modern Intellectual History* 8 (1): 91–125.

Jewett, F. F., and Frances Gulick Jewett. 1922. "The Chemical Department of Oberlin College from 1833 to 1912." Oberlin College Laboratory Bulletin 22 [Chemistry Supplement]. *Oberlin College Magazine* 18 (10): 2–15.

Joas, Hans. 1996. *The Creativity of Action.* Translated by Jeremy Gaines and Paul Keast. Chicago: University of Chicago Press.

———. 1997 [1985]. *G. H. Mead: A Contemporary Re-Examination of His Thought,* Revised Edition. Translated by Raymond Meyer. Cambridge, MA: MIT Press.

———. 2003. *War and Modernity.* Translated by Rodney Livingstone. Malden, MA: Blackwell.

Johnson, Earl S., ed. 1942. *Readings in Society and Education.* Chicago: University of Chicago Bookstore.

———. 1945. "The Need for a Philosophy of Adult Education." *Journal of Negro Education* 14 (3): 272–82.

———. 1963. "The Social Studies versus the Social Sciences." *School Review* 71 (4): 389–403.

Johnson, G. David, and Peggy A. Shifflett. 1981. "George Herbert Who?: A Critique of the Objectivist Reading of Mead." *Symbolic Interaction* 4 (2): 143–55.

Jowett, Garth S., Ian C. Jarvie, and Kathryn H. Fuller, eds. 1996. *Children and the Movies: Media Influences and the Payne Fund Controversy.* New York: Cambridge University Press.

Karpf, Fay Berger. 1932. *American Social Psychology: Its Origins, Development, and European Background.* New York: McGraw-Hill.

Kotani, Roland. 1985. *The Japanese in Hawaii: A Century of Struggle.* Honolulu: Hawaii Hochi.

Krohn, William O. 1892. "Facilities in Experimental Psychology at the Various German Universities." *American Journal of Psychology* 4 (4): 585–94.

Krueger, Maynard C. 1941. "The Study of Contemporary Society (A Report on the Introductory General Course in the College at the University of Chicago)." *Proceedings of the Workshop in General Education. University of Chicago, 1940*, vol. 5: *Social Sciences*. Chicago: Cooperative Study in General Education.

Kuhn, Manford H. 1964. "Major Trends in Symbolic Interaction Theory in the Past Twenty-Five Years." *Sociological Quarterly* 5 (1): 61–84.

Kuhn, Manford H., and Thomas S. McPartland. 1954. "An Empirical Assessment of Self-Attitudes." *American Sociological Review* 19 (1): 68–76.

Kuhn, Thomas S. 1962. *The Structure of Scientific Revolutions*. Foundations of the Unity of Science 3, no. 2. Chicago: University of Chicago Press.

Kuklick, Henrika. 1984. "The Ecology of Sociology." *American Journal of Sociology* 89 (6): 1433–40.

Lamont, Michèle. 1987. "How to Become a Dominant French Philosopher: The Case of Jacques Derrida." *American Journal of Sociology* 93 (3): 583–622.

Latour, Bruno. 1999. *Pandora's Hope: Essays on the Reality of Science Studies*. Cambridge, MA: Harvard University Press.

———. 2005. *Reassembling the Social: An Introduction to Actor-Network Theory*. Oxford: Oxford University Press.

Lee, Grace Chin. 1945. *George Herbert Mead: Philosopher of the Social Individual*. New York: Kings Crown Press.

Levi, Albert William. 1948. *General Education in the Social Studies*. Washington, DC: American Council on Education.

Levine, Donald N., Ellwood B. Carter, and Eleanor Miller Gorman. 1976. "Simmel's Influence on American Sociology, I." *American Journal of Sociology* 81 (4): 813–45.

Levy, David M. 1962a. "The 'Act' as an Operational Concept in Psychodynamics." *Psychosomatic Medicine* 24 (1): 49–57.

———. 1962b. "The Act as a Unit." *Psychiatry* 25 (4): 295–314.

Lewis, J. David. 1976a. "The Classic American Pragmatists as Forerunners to Symbolic Interactionism." *Sociological Quarterly* 17 (3): 346–59.

———. 1976b. "The Pragmatic Foundation of Symbolic Interactionism." PhD dissertation. University of Illinois Urbana–Champaign.

Lewis, J. David, and Richard L. Smith. 1980. *American Sociology and Pragmatism: Mead, Chicago Sociology, and Symbolic Interaction*. Chicago: University of Chicago Press.

Lindeman, Eduard C. 1935. "[Review] *Mind, Self, and Society from the Standpoint of a Social Behaviorist*, by the late George H. Mead; edited by Charles W. Morris." *Survey* 71 (September): 280–81.

Lindstrom, Fred B., Ronald A. Hardert, and Kimball Young. 1988. "Kimball Young on the Chicago School: Later Contacts." *Sociological Perspectives* 31 (3): 298–314.

Locke, Harvey J. 1954. "Ellsworth Faris, 1874–1953." *American Sociological Review* 19 (2): 226.

Loeb, Jacques. 1900. *Comparative Physiology of the Brain and Comparative Psychology*. New York: G. P. Putnam's Sons.

Lofland, Lyn H., ed. 1980. "Reminiscences of Classic Chicago: 'The Blumer-Hughes Talk.'" *Urban Life* 9 (3): 251–81.

———. 1997. "From 'Our Gang' to 'Society For': Reminiscences of an Organization in Transition." *Symbolic Interaction* 20:135–40.

Lundberg, George A. 1939. "Contemporary Positivism in Sociology." *American Sociological Review* 4 (1): 42–55.

———. 1954. "Methodological Convergence of Mead, Lundberg, and Parsons." *American Journal of Sociology* 60 (2): 182–84.

Lyman, Stanford M., and Arthur J. Vidich. 1988. *Social Order and Public Philosophy: An Analysis and Interpretation of the Work of Herbert Blumer.* Fayetteville: University of Arkansas Press.

MacAloon, John J. 1992. *General Education in the Social Sciences: Centennial Reflections on the College of the University of Chicago.* Chicago: University of Chicago Press.

Maines, David R. 1997. "Talking Interactionism: The Intellectual Exchanges at the First SSSI Symposium." *Symbolic Interaction* 20:141–67.

Maines, David R., Jeffrey C. Bridger, and Jeffrey T. Ulmer. 1996. "Mythic Facts and Park's Pragmatism: On Predecessor-Selection and Theorizing in Human Ecology." *Sociological Quarterly* 37 (3): 521–49.

Maines, David R., and Thomas J. Morrione. 1990. "On the Breadth and Relevance of Blumer's Perspective: Introduction to His Analysis of Industrialization." In Herbert Blumer, *Industrialization as an Agent of Social Change: A Critical Analysis*, xi–xxiv. New York: Aldine de Gruyter.

Markey, John F. 1928. *The Symbolic Process and Its Integration in Children.* New York: Harcourt, Brace.

Martin, Henry Newell. 1881. *The Human Body: An Account of Its Structure and Activities and the Conditions of Its Healthy Working.* New York: Henry Holt.

Marx, Werner, and Manuel Cardona. 2009. "The Citation Impact Outside References—Formal versus Informal Citations." *Scientometrics* 80 (1): 1–21.

McCarthy, E. Doyle. 1996. *Knowledge as Culture: The New Sociology of Knowledge.* London: Routledge.

McKenzie, D. F. 1999. *Bibliography and the Sociology of Texts.* Cambridge: Cambridge University Press.

McKinney, John C. 1954. "Methodological Convergence of Mead, Lundberg, and Parsons." *American Journal of Sociology* 59 (6): 565–74.

McLaughlin, Neil. 1998. "How to Become a Forgotten Intellectual: Intellectual Movements and the Rise and Fall of Erich Fromm." *Sociological Forum* 13 (2): 215–46.

McNeill, David. 2005. *Gesture and Thought.* Chicago: University of Chicago Press.

McNeill, William H. 1991. *Hutchins' University: A Memoir of the University of Chicago, 1929–1950.* Chicago: University of Chicago Press.

McPhail, Clark, and Cynthia Rexroat. 1979. "Mead vs. Blumer: The Divergent Perspectives of Social Behaviorism and Symbolic Interactionism." *American Sociological Review* 44 (3): 449–67.

———. 1980. "Ex Cathedra Blumer or Ex Libris Mead?" *American Sociological Review* 45 (3): 420–30.

Meltzer, Bernard N., and John W. Petras. 1973. "The Chicago and Iowa Schools of Symbolic Interactionism." In *Human Nature and Collective Behavior: Papers in Honor of Herbert Blumer*, edited by Tamotsu Shibutani, 3–17. New Brunswick, NJ: Transaction Books.

Meltzer, Bernard N., John W. Petras, and Larry T. Reynolds. 1975. *Symbolic Interactionism: Genesis, Varieties, and Criticism*. London: Routledge and Kegan Paul.

Merton, Robert K. 1968. *Social Theory and Social Structure*. Revised edition. New York: Simon and Schuster.

———. 1973. *The Sociology of Science: Theoretical and Empirical Investigations*. Chicago: University of Chicago Press.

Miller, David L. 1973. *George Herbert Mead: Self, Language, and the World*. Austin: University of Texas Press.

———, ed. 1982. "Introduction." In George H. Mead, *The Individual and the Social Self: Unpublished Work of George Herbert Mead*. Chicago: University of Chicago Press.

Miller, Willoughby D. 1890. *Micro-Organisms of the Human Mouth: The Local and General Diseases Which Are Caused by Them*. Philadelphia: S. S. White Dental Mfg. Co.

———. 1891. "The Human Mouth as a Focus of Infection." *Dental Cosmos* 33 (9–11): 689–713, 789–804, 913–19.

Mills, C. Wright. 1939. "Language, Logic, and Culture." *American Sociological Review* 4 (5): 670–80.

———. 1940a. "Methodological Consequences of the Sociology of Knowledge." *American Sociological Review* 46 (3): 316–30.

———. 1940b. "Situated Actions and Vocabularies of Motive." *American Sociological Review* 5 (6): 904–13.

Mizruchi, Mark S., and Lisa C. Fein. 1999. "The Social Construction of Organizational Knowledge: A Study of the Uses of Coercive, Mimetic, and Normative Isomorphism." *Administratie Science Quarterly* 44 (4): 653–83.

Moll, Albert. 1892. *Der Rapport in der Hypnose: Untersuchungen über den thierischen Magnetismus*. Schriften der Gesellschaft für psychologische Forschung 3–4. Leipzig: von Ambr. Abel.

Moore, Merritt H. 1927. "Certain Distinctions between Morality and Religion." Master's thesis. University of Chicago.

———, ed. 1936. "Preface" and "Introduction." In George H. Mead, *Movements of Thought in the Nineteenth Century*. Chicago: University of Chicago Press.

Morrione, Thomas J., ed. 2004. "Preface," "Editor's Introduction," and "Appendix III. Herbert Blumer: A Biography." In Herbert Blumer, *George Herbert Mead and Human Conduct*. Walnut Creek, CA: AltaMira Press.

Morris, Charles W. 1927. "The Concept of the Symbol, II." *Journal of Philosophy* 24 (11): 281–91.

———. 1929. "[Review] *Speech: Its Function and Development* by Grace Andrus de Laguna and *The Symbolic Process and Its Integration in Children* by John F. Markey." *Philosophical Review* 38 (6): 612–15.

———. 1932. *Six Theories of Mind*. Chicago: University of Chicago Press.

———. 1933. "[Review] *Vers de Concret: Études d'Histoire de la Philosophie Contemporaine* by Jean Wahl." *Journal of Philosophy* 30 (26): 714–16.

———. 1934a. *Pragmatism and the Crisis of Democracy.* Edited by Harry S. Gideonse. Public Policy Pamphlet 12. Chicago: University of Chicago Press.

———, ed. 1934b. "Preface" and "Introduction." In George H. Mead, *Mind, Self, and Society: From the Standpoint of a Social Behaviorist.* Chicago: University of Chicago Press.

———. 1934c. "Pragmatism and Metaphysics." *Philosophical Review* 43 (6): 549–64.

———. 1935. "Some Aspects of Recent American Scientific Philosophy." *Erkenntnis* 5:142–51.

———. 1936. "Professor Schiller and Pragmatism." *Personalist: A Quarterly Journal of Philosophy, Religion and Literature* 17 (3): 294–300.

———. 1937a. *Logical Positivism, Pragmatism, and Scientific Empiricism.* Actualités scientifiques et industrielles 449. Paris: Hermann et cie.

———. 1937b. "Peirce, Mead, and Pragmatism." *Philosophical Review* 47 (2): 109–27.

———. 1937c. "*Mind, Self, and Society* [Rejoinder]." *American Journal of Sociology* 42 (4): 560–61.

———. 1938. *Foundations of the Theory of Signs.* International Encyclopedia of Unified Science 1, no. 2. Chicago: University of Chicago Press.

———. 1942. *Paths of Life: Preface to a World Religion.* New York: Harper and Brothers.

———. 1946. *Signs, Language, and Behavior.* New York: Prentice-Hall.

———. 1948a. "Signs about Signs about Signs." *Philosophy and Phenomenological Research* 9 (1): 115–33.

———. 1948b. *The Open Self.* New York: Prentice-Hall.

———. 1956. *The Varieties of Human Value.* Chicago: University of Chicago Press.

———. 1964. *Signification and Significance: A Study of the Relations of Signs and Values.* Cambridge, MA: MIT Press.

———. 1970. *The Pragmatic Movement in American Philosophy.* New York: G. Braziller.

———. 1993 [1925]. *Symbolism and Reality: A Study in the Nature of Mind.* Amsterdam: J. Benjamin's Publishing Co.

Morris, Charles W., John M. Brewster, Albert M. Dunham, and David L. Miller, eds. 1938. "Preface" and "Introduction." In George H. Mead, *The Philosophy of the Act.* Chicago: University of Chicago Press.

Mullett, Charles F. 1937. "[Review] George H. Mead, *Movements of Thought in the Nineteenth Century.*" *Psychological Bulletin* 34 (2): 115–17.

Mullins, Nicholas C. 1973. *Theories and Theory Groups in Contemporary American Sociology.* With the assistance of Carolyn J. Mullins. New York: Harper and Row.

Munk, Hermann. 1890. *Über die Funktionen der Grosshirnrinde: Gesammelte Mittheilungen mit Anmerkungen.* Berlin: Verlag von August Hirschwald.

Murphy, Arthur E, ed. 1932. "Preface." In George H. Mead, *The Philosophy of the Present.* Chicago: Open Court Publishing.

Natanson, Maurice. 1956. *The Social Dynamics of George H. Mead.* Washington, DC: Public Affairs Press.

Nef, Elinor Castle. 1953. *Letters and Notes.* Los Angeles: Ward Ritchie Press.

Nisbet, Robert A. 1970. *The Social Bond: An Introduction to the Study of Society.* New York: Knopf.

Ogden, C. K., and I. A. Richards. 1923. *The Meaning of Meaning: A Study of the Influence of Language upon Thought and of the Science of Symbolism.* New York: Harcourt, Brace.

Orbach, Harold. 1998. "Mead's *Essays on Psychology*: The History of an Unpublished Book." Paper presented at the meeting of the Society for the Advancement of American Philosophy, Milwaukee, WI, March 5–7.

Paisley, Fiona. 2009. *Glamour in the Pacific: Cultural Internationalism and Race Politics in the Women's Pan-Pacific.* Honolulu: University of Hawaii Press.

Park, Robert E. 1942. "Modern Society." In *Biological Symposia*, vol. 8: *Levels of Integration in Biological and Social Systems*, edited by Robert Redfield, 217–40. Lancaster, PA: The Jaques Cattell Press.

Park, Robert E., and Ernest W. Burgess. 1924 [1921]. *Introduction to the Science of Sociology.* Chicago: University of Chicago Press.

Parker, Frances Stuart. 1909. *Reminiscences and Letters.* Chicago: Privately printed.

Parker, John N., and Edward J. Hackett. 2012. "Hot Spots and Hot Moments in Scientific Collaborations and Social Movements." *American Sociological Review* 77 (1): 21–44.

Parsons, Talcott. 1975. "Comments by Talcott Parsons." *Sociological Inquiry* 45 (1): 62–65.

Parsons, Talcott, Robert F. Bales, and Edward A. Shils. 1953. *Working Papers in the Theory of Action.* Glencoe, IL: Free Press.

Peirce, Charles S. 1877. "The Fixation of Belief." *Popular Science Monthly* 12 (November): 1–15.

Petrilli, Susan. 2001. "In the Sign of Charles Morris." *Recherches sémiotiques/Semiotic Inquiry* 21:163–87.

Pfuetze, Paul E. 1954. *The Social Self.* New York: Bookman Associates.

Platt, Jennifer. 1996. *A History of Sociological Research Methods in America, 1920–1960.* Cambridge: Cambridge University Press.

Price, Maurice T. 1924 [1922]. "The Analysis of Christian Propaganda in Race Contact." PhD dissertation. University of Chicago.

Prince, Morton. 1905. *The Dissociation of a Personality: A Biographical Study in Abnormal Psychology.* New York: Longmans, Green.

Proceedings of the Second Colloquium on Personality Investigation, Held under the Joint Auspices of the American Psychiatric Association Committee on the Relations of Psychiatry and the Social Sciences, and of the Social Science Research Council, November 29–30, 1929, New York City. 1930. Baltimore: Johns Hopkins University Press.

Puddephatt, Antony. 2009. "The Search for Meaning: Revisiting Herbert Blumer's Interpretation of G. H. Mead." *American Sociologist* 40 (1): 89–105.

Randall, J. G. 1937. "[Review] George H. Mead, *Movements of Thought in the Nineteenth Century.*" *American Historical Review* 42 (3): 535–37.

Raphelson, Alfred C. 1968. "Psychology at the University of Michigan, 1852–1950, vol. 1: The History of the Department of Psychology." Prepared for the University of

Michigan Department of Psychology. Available online at http://www.lsa.umich .edu/UMICH/psych/Home/About/Volume1%202MBPDF.pdf.

Raushenbush [Rorty], Winifred. 1979. *Robert E. Park: Biography of a Sociologist.* Durham, NC: Duke University Press.

Reisch, George A. 1995. "A History of the International Encyclopedia of Unified Science." PhD dissertation. University of Chicago.

———. 2005. *How the Cold War Transformed Philosophy of Science: To the Icy Slopes of Logic.* Cambridge: Cambridge University Press.

Robb, Peggy, and Louise Vicars. 1982. "Manoa's 'Puuhonua': The Castle Home, 1900–1941." *Hawaiian Journal of History* 16:171–83.

Rock, Paul E. 1979. *The Making of Symbolic Interactionism.* Totowa, NJ: Rowman and Littlefield.

Rodden, John. 1989. *The Politics of Literary Reputation: The Making and Claiming of "St. George" Orwell.* New York: Oxford University Press.

Rosengren, William R. 1985. "[Review] Earl. S. Johnson, *The Humanistic Teachings of Earl S. Johnson,* edited by John D. Haas." *American Journal of Education* 93 (4): 557–60.

Rossi, Peter H. 1956. "Methods of Social Research, 1945–55." In *Sociology in the United States of America: A Trend Report,* edited by Hans L. Zetterberg, 21–34. Paris: UNESCO.

Rossi-Landi, Ferruccio. 1953. *Charles Morris.* Rome: Bocca.

Rucker, Darnell. 1969. *The Chicago Pragmatists.* Minneapolis: University of Minnesota Press.

Sanders, Clinton. 1999. *Understanding Dogs: Living and Working with Canine Companions.* Philadelphia: Temple University Press.

Sanderson, E. Dwight. 1916–17. "Social Psychology and Mead's Logic of the Social Sciences." Unpublished, available from Cornell University Library.

Saxton, Stanley L. 1997. "SSSI: Outsiders Become Established." *Symbolic Interaction* 20:169–76.

Scaff, Lawrence A. 1984. "Weber before Weberian Sociology." *British Journal of Sociology* 35 (2): 190–215.

———. 2011. *Max Weber in America.* Princeton, NJ: Princeton University Press.

Scheffler, Israel. 1974. *Four Pragmatists: A Critical Introduction to Peirce, James, Mead, and Dewey.* London: Routledge and Kegan Paul.

Schiller, F. C. S. 1936a. "Social Behaviorism [Review]: Mind, Self, and Society, From the Standpoint of a Social Behaviorist. By George H. Mead. Edited with Introduction by Charles W. Morris." *The Personalist: A Quarterly Journal of Philosophy, Religion and Literature* 17 (1): 82–84.

———. 1936b. "Comments by F. C. S. Schiller." *Personalist: A Quarterly Journal of Philosophy, Religion and Literature* 17 (3): 300–306.

Schmitt, Raymond. 1974. "SI and Emergent Theory: A Reexamination." *American Sociological Review* 39 (3): 453–56.

Schorske, Carl. 1997. "The New Rigorism in the Human Sciences, 1940–1960." *Daedalus* 126 (1): 289–309.

Schütz, Alfred. 1967 [1932]. *The Phenomenology of the Social World*. Translated by George Walsh and Frederick Lehnert. Evanston, IL: Northwestern University Press.

Sebeok, Thomas A. 1981. "The Image of Charles Morris." In *Zeichen über Zeichen über Zeichen: 15 Studien über Charles W. Morris*, edited by Achim Eschbach, 267–84. Tübingen: Narr.

Shalin, Dmitri N. 1988. "G. H. Mead, Socialism, and the Progressive Agenda." *American Journal of Sociology* 93 (4): 913–51.

———. 2011a. "George Herbert Mead." In *The Wiley-Blackwell Companion to Major Social Theorists*, edited by George Ritzer and Jeffrey Stepnisky, 373–425. Malden, MA: Wiley-Blackwell.

———. 2011b. *Pragmatism and Democracy: Studies in History, Social Theory, and Progressive Politics*. New Brunswick, NJ: Transaction Publishers.

Shibutani, Tamotsu. 1973. "Foreword." In *Human Nature and Collective Behavior: Papers in Honor of Herbert Blumer*, edited by Tamotsu Shibutani, v–viii. New Brunswick, NJ: Transaction Books.

———. 1978. *The Derelicts of Company K: A Sociological Study of Demoralization*. Berkeley: University of California Press.

———. 1988. "Herbert Blumer's Contributions to Twentieth-century Sociology." *Symbolic Interaction* 11 (1): 23–31.

Shils, Edward A. 1970. "Tradition, Ecology, and Institution in the History of Sociology." *Daedalus* 99 (4): 760–825.

Shugg, Roger W. 1966. *The University of Chicago Press*. Chicago: University of Chicago Press.

Silva, Filipe Carreira da. 2003. "In Dialogue with Modern Times: The Social and Political Thought of G. H. Mead." PhD dissertation. University of Cambridge.

———. 2006. "G. H. Mead in the History of Sociological Ideas." *Journal of the History of the Behavioral Sciences* 42 (1): 19–39.

———. 2007. *G. H. Mead: A Critical Introduction*. Malden, MA: Polity Press.

———. 2008. *Mead and Modernity: Science, Selfhood, and Democratic Politics*. Lanham, MD: Lexington Books.

Silva, Filipe Carreira da, and Monica Brito Vieira. 2011. "Books and Canon Building in Sociology: The Case of Mind, Self, and Society." *Journal of Classical Sociology* 11 (4): 356–77.

Simmel, Georg. 1977 [1892]. *The Problems of the Philosophy of History: An Epistemological Essay*. Edited by Guy Oakes. New York: Free Press.

———. 1997. *Simmel on Culture: Selected Writings*. Edited by David Frisby and Mike Featherstone. Thousand Oaks, CA: Sage Publications.

———. 2009. *Sociology: Inquiries into the Construction of Social Forms*. Translated and edited by Anthony J. Blasi, Anton K. Jacobs, and Mathew Kanjirathinkal. Leiden: Brill.

Small, Mario L. 1999. "Departmental Conditions and the Emergence of New Disciplines: Two Cases in the Legitimation of African-American Studies." *Theory and Society* 28 (5): 659–707.

Smith, Dorothy E. 2006. "Incorporating Texts into Ethnographic Practice." In *Institu-*

tional Ethnography as Practice, edited by Dorothy E. Smith, 65–88. Lanham, MD: Rowman and Littlefield.

Smith, Richard L. 1977. "George Herbert Mead and Sociology: The Chicago Years." PhD dissertation. University of Illinois at Urbana-Champaign.

Smith, T. V. 1931. "The Social Psychology of George Herbert Mead." *American Journal of Sociology* 37 (3): 368–85.

———. 1932. "The Religious Bearings of a Secular Mind: George Herbert Mead." *Journal of Religion* 12 (2): 200–213.

———. 1934. *Beyond Conscience*. New York: McGraw-Hill.

———. 1962. *A Non-Existent Man: An Autobiography*. Austin: University of Texas Press.

Smith, T. V., and William Kelley Wright, eds. 1929. *Essays in Philosophy: By Seventeen Doctors of Philosophy of the University of Chicago*. Chicago: University of Chicago Press.

Sommer, Andreas. 2012. "Normalizing the Supernormal: The Formation of the 'Gesellschaft für Psychologische Forschung' ('Society for Psychological Research'), C.1886–1890." *Journal of the History of the Behavioral Sciences* 49 (1): 1–27.

Spreitzer, Elmer, and Larry T. Reynolds. 1973. "Patterning in Citations: An Analysis of References to George Herbert Mead." *Sociological Focus* 6 (1): 71–82.

Stadler, Friedrich. 2001. *The Vienna Circle: Studies in the Origins, Development, and Influence of Logical Empiricism*. Translated by C. Nielson, J. Golb, and S. Schmidt. New York: Springer.

Stevens, Edward. 1967. "Bibliographical Note: G. H. Mead." *American Journal of Sociology* 75 (5): 551–57.

Stewart, Robert L. 1981. "What George Mead Should Have Said: Exploration of a Problem of Interpretation." *Symbolic Interaction* 4: 157–66.

Stone, Gregory P., and Harvey A. Farberman. 1967. "Further Comment on the Blumer-Bales Dialogue concerning the Implications of the Thought of George Herbert Mead." *American Journal of Sociology* 72 (4): 409–10.

Stone, Gregory P., David R. Maines, Harvey A. Farberman, Gladys I. Stone, and Norman K. Denzin. 1974. "On Methodology and Craftsmanship in the Criticism of Sociological Perspectives." *American Sociological Review* 39 (3): 456–63.

Strauss, Anselm, ed. 1965. *The Social Psychology of George Herbert Mead. Part Six: Self* [Syllabus for Social Sciences 121–23]. Chicago: Syllabus Division of the University of Chicago Press.

Sullivan, Harry Stack. 1953. *The Interpersonal Theory of Psychiatry*. Edited by Helen Swick Perry and Mary Ladd Gawel. New York: Norton.

Swidler, Ann, and Jorge Arditi. 1994. "The New Sociology of Knowledge." *Annual Review of Sociology* 20:305–29.

Swing, Raymond. 1964. *"Good Evening!": A Professional Memoir*. New York: Harcourt, Brace and World.

Taylor, Edward Wyllys. 1893. "The Study of the Anatomy of the Central Nervous System." *Boston Medical and Surgical Journal* 129:322–24.

Thayer, H. S. 1968. *Meaning and Action: A Critical History of Pragmatism*. Indianapolis, IN: Bobbs-Merrill.

Thomas, William I. 1909. *Source Book for Social Origins: Ethnological Materials, Psychological Standpoint, Classified and Annotated Bibliographies for the Interpretation of Savage Society.* Chicago: University of Chicago Press.

———. 1917. "The Persistence of Primary-Group Norms in Present-Day Society and Their Influence in Our Educational System." In *Suggestions of Modern Science Concerning Education,* ed. Herbert S. Jennings, John B. Watson, Adolf Meyer, and William I. Thomas, 158–97. New York: Macmillan.

———. 1966. *W. I. Thomas on Social Organization and Social Personality: Selected Papers.* Edited by Morris Janowitz. Chicago: University of Chicago Press.

Thomas, William I., and Florian Znaniecki. 1918–20. *The Polish Peasant in Europe and America: Monograph of an Immigrant Group.* 5 vols. Boston: Richard G. Badger.

Throop, Robert, and Lloyd Gordon Ward. 2007a. "Courses Taught by Mead at University of Michigan." Toronto: The Mead Project, http://www.brocku.ca/MeadProject/ Timeline/MICHIGAN.HTML.

———. 2007b. "A Beautiful and Impressive Southern Woman of Decidedly Individualistic Outlook: Notes on the Life of Harriet Park Thomas." Toronto ON: The Mead Project, http://www.brocku.ca/MeadProject/Scrapbooks/Holding/Harriet_Thomas2 .html.

———. 2007c. "A Bibliography of Commentaries on Mead and His Ideas." Toronto: The Mead Project, http://www.brocku.ca/MeadProject/Mead/commentaries4.html.

Towse, Ed. 1900. "The Changed Homestead." In *Hawaiian Almanac and Annual for 1900: A Handbook of Information and Statistics Relating to the Hawaiian Islands, of Value to Merchants, Tourists and Others.* Compiled by Thomas G. Thrum. Honolulu: Hawaiian Gazette Co.

Tsanoff, Radislav A. 1937. "[Review] George H. Mead, *Movements of Thought in the Nineteenth Century.*" *Philosophical Review* 46 (4): 434–36.

Tufts, James H. 1931. "George Herbert Mead." In *George Herbert Mead* [memorial booklet]. Chicago: Privately printed.

Turner, Frederick Jackson. 1911. "Social Forces in American History." *American Historical Review* 16 (2): 217–33.

Turner, Jonathan H. 1974. "Parsons as a Symbolic Interactionist: A Comparison of Action and Interaction Theory." *Sociological Inquiry* 44 (4): 283–93.

Turner, Stephen P., and Jonathan H. Turner. 1990. *The Impossible Science: An Institutional Analysis of American Sociology.* Newbury Park, CA: Sage Publications.

Vaughan, Ted R., and Larry T. Reynolds. 1968. "The Sociology of Symbolic Interactionism." *American Sociologist* 3: 208–14.

Waldeyer, Wilhelm. 1891. "Ueber einige neuere Forschungen im Gebiete der Anatomie des Centralnervensystems." *Deutsche medizinische Wochenschrift* 17 (44–47, 49–50): 1213–18, 1244–46, 1267–72, 1287–89, 1331–32, 1350–56.

Wallis, Wilson D. 1935. "[Review] George H. Mead, *Mind, Self, and Society from the Standpoint of a Social Behaviorist.*" *International Journal of Ethics* 45 (4): 456–59.

Warden, C. J., and L. H. Warner. 1927. "The Development of Animal Psychology in the United States during the Past Three Decades." *Psychological Review* 34 (3): 196–205.

Warner, Robert M. 1964. *Profile of a Profession: A History of the Michigan State Dental Association*. Detroit, MI: Wayne State University Press.

Warshay, Leon H., and Diana W. Warshay. 1986. "The Individualizing and Subjectivizing of George Herbert Mead: A Sociology of Knowledge Interpretation." *Sociological Focus* 19 (2): 177–88.

Watson, John B. 1907. *Kinaesthetic and Organic Sensations: Their Role in the Reactions of the White Rat to the Maze*. Monograph supplement *to Psychological Review* 8, no. 2.

———. 1908. "Imitation in Monkeys." *Psychological Bulletin* 5 (6): 169–78.

———. 1913. "Psychology as the Behaviorist Views It." *Psychological Review* 20:158–77.

———. 1914. *Behavior: An Introduction to Comparative Psychology*. New York: Henry Holt.

———. 1919. *Psychology: From the Standpoint of a Behaviorist*. Philadelphia: J. B. Lippincott.

———. 1936. "John Broadus Watson." In *A History of Psychology in Autobiography*, vol. 3, edited by Carl Murchison, 271–81. Worcester, MA: Clark University Press.

Weber, Max. 1978 [1922]. *Economy and Society*. 2 vols. Edited by Guenther Roth and Claus Wittich. Berkeley: University of California Press.

———. 2001 [1904–5]. *The Protestant Ethic and the Spirit of Capitalism*. Translated by Talcott Parsons. London: Routledge.

Wellman, Rowena. 1937. "An Examination of Certain Factors Involved in the Reporting and Transcribing of Stenographic Materials." PhD dissertation. Columbia University.

White, Sheldon H. 2004. "The Contemporary Reconstruction of Developmental Psychology." In *The Life Cycle of Psychological Ideas: Understanding the Prominence and the Dynamics of Intellectual Change*, edited by Thomas C. Dalton and Rand B. Evans, 281–97. New York: Kluwer Academic/Plenum Publishers.

Wilcox, Earley V. 1909. *Hawaii: Its Agricultural Possibilities*. Issued by the Board of Commissioners for the Territory of Hawaii of the Alaska–Yukon–Pacific Exposition. Honolulu: Bulletin Press.

Wittgenstein, Ludwig. 2001 [1953]. *Philosophical Investigations: The German Text, with a Revised English Translation*. Translated by G. E. M. Anscombe. Oxford: Blackwell.

Woelfel, Joseph. 1967. "Comment on the Blumer-Bales Dialogue Concerning the Interpretation of Mead's Thought." *American Journal of Sociology* 72 (4): 409.

Wolffram, Heather. 2009. *The Stepchildren of Science: Psychical Research and Parapsychology in Germany, c. 1870–1939*. Amsterdam: Rodopi BV Editions.

Wreschner, Arthur. 1898. *Methodologische Beiträge zu psychologischen Messungen (Auf experimenteller Grundlage)*. Leipzig: Verlag von Johann Ambrosius Barth.

Young, Kimball. 1927. *Source Book for Social Psychology*. New York: Alfred A. Knopf.

———. 1948. "[Review] Muzafer Sherif and Hadley Cantril, *The Psychology of Ego-Involvements*." *American Journal of Sociology* 54 (1): 85.

The letter *t* following a page number denotes a table, and the letter *f* following a page number denotes a figure.

(1) A theory of Action

(2) Max Weber

— Interpretive
social thought

Lightning Source UK Ltd.
Milton Keynes UK
UKHW02f0146100318

319140UK00008B/324/P